The Big Book of
Designer
House Plans

500+ Homes in Full Color
1,200 to 6,000 Square Feet

The Big Book of
Designer
House Plans

hanley▲wood

Published by Hanley Wood
One Thomas Circle, NW, Suite 600
Washington, DC 20005

DISTRIBUTION CENTER
PBD
Hanley Wood Consumer Group
3280 Summit Ridge Parkway
Duluth, Georgia 30096

Vice President, Home Plans, Andrew Schultz
Associate Publisher, Development, Jennifer Pearce
Director, Plans Marketing, Mark Wilkin
Editor, Simon Hyoun
Assistant Editor, Kimberly Johnson
Publications Manager, Brian Haefs
Production Manager, Amy Dean
Senior Plan Merchandiser, Nicole Phipps
Plan Merchandiser, Hillary Huff
Graphic Artist, Joong Min
Plan Data Team Leader, Susan Jasmin
Marketing Director, Holly Miller
Marketing Manager, Brett Bryant

Most Hanley Wood titles are available at quantity discounts with bulk purchases for educational, business, or sales promotional use. For information, please contact Andrew Schultz at aschultz@hanleywood.com.

BIG DESIGNS, INC.
PRESIDENT, CREATIVE DIRECTOR Anthony D'Elia
VICE PRESIDENT, BUSINESS MANAGER Megan D'Elia
VICE PRESIDENT, DESIGN DIRECTOR Chris Bonavita
EDITORIAL DIRECTOR John Roach
ASSISTANT EDITOR Carrie Atkinson
SENIOR ART DIRECTOR Stephen Reinfurt
PRODUCTION DIRECTOR David Barbella
PRODUCTION MANAGER Rich Fuentes
PHOTO EDITOR Christine DiVuolo
ART DIRECTOR Frank Augugliaro
GRAPHIC DESIGNER Billy Doremus

PHOTO CREDITS
Front Cover, Main: Design HPK2900503 on page 169, photo by Scott Moore. Front Cover, Inset (left to right): Design HPK2900213 on page 188, photo by Donald A. Gardner, Inc.; Design HPK2900198 on page 174, photo by Donald A. Gardner Architects, Inc.; Design HPK2900001 on page 6, photo by William E. Poole Designs, Inc.; Design HWEPL12559 on eplans.com, photo by Kim Sargent. Back Cover: Design HPK2900072 on page 68, photo by Scott Moore.
10 9 8 7 6 5 4 3 2 1

Printed in the United States of America

Library of Congress Control Number: 2006925916

ISBN-13: 978-1-931131-68-1
ISBN-10: 1-931131-68-6

378

The Big Book of *Designer* House Plans

ONLINE EXTRA!

Hanley Wood Passageway

The Hanley Wood Passageway is an online search tool for your home plan needs! Discover even more useful information about building your new home, search additional new home plans, access online ordering, and more at www.hanleywoodbooks.com/bigbookofdesigner

hanley▲wood

Hand Crafted

What makes a house a designer home? *The Big Book of Designer House Plans* is a compilation of such homes, and offers the quality and assurance you would receive from your own personal architect. A designer home is created by an individual, either a residential designer or an architect, and is planned with the same consideration as it would be if it were being drawn for a specific customer. In fact, many pre-designed house plans begin as custom homes, and the acclaim and praise they receive encourage the designer to share them with the public. In *The Big Book of Designer House Plans*, we bring you hand-picked selections from the industry's most acclaimed, most praised, and award-winning designers that you won't find through any other publisher.

The book is organized by style, but each section contains plans from the nation's top design professionals exclusively published by Hanley Wood, including Donald Gardner, William Poole, Frank Betz, Dan Sater, Stephen Fuller, and Frank Snodgrass. Gardner fashions homes with families in mind that have global appeal, with open floor plans and abundant amenities. Poole's Southern upbringing is seen in classic-styled plans that often recall the antebellum era.

Sater, a member of the American Institute of Building Design, creates flowing interiors and expansive outdoor spaces informed by a coastal and Mediterranean sensibility. If you prefer a more traditional style, Fuller brings the best of American neighborhoods to each of his modernly laid out plans. Betz's high standards assure excellent quality and exquisite taste. The designs by Snodgrass, a registered architect and a builder, are elegant and highly functional. And

these are just six of the many designers and architects whose best homes are collected here.

The difference between a designer house plan and an ordinary plan is the care and forethought put into the design. Each and every plan offered in this book was created with you, the homeowner, in mind. You can have a designer, custom-style home without the custom price. From Colonial and Country to Craftsman and New American to European Cottages and Manors, plus a wide range of square footages, we have a plan for you. We even offer expertly coordinated landscape plans, to put that finishing touch on your home and truly give it that custom impression. So look no further for the home you've been dreaming of. Nowhere else will you find the integrity of designers plus the variety and quality of homes that are showcased in *The Big Book of Designer House Plans.*

Past and Present

The homes in this section combine the historical characteristics of Colonial style with the functionality of a modern layout. Designer William Poole achieves this with the Longview, a grand Federal-Adams home of symmetrical windows and columns on the outside, and an interior that includes everything today's family could need.

A grand foyer with a flanking formal dining room is a staple of Colonial design. While this entry style can be easily found in this section, as shown by the Longview, many designers have fused the old format with a more current, open combination of rooms. In this case, an open layout comprising a keeping room, nook, and kitchen lies right of the central living room.

The new look of the Colonial home excels at blending historical charm with up-to-date amenities. Kitchens are designed for families on-the-go, with island snack bars for quick meals, as well as the family chef who enjoys entertaining, with gourmet stainless-steel appliances. Details such as wood-beamed ceilings or distressed-finish cabinetry contribute to the historical ambiance.

This Colonial home, like many others, also recognizes the importance of privacy for family members. The Longview's master suite is secluded on the first floor, away from the upstairs bedrooms. The three second-floor bedrooms are actually private suites, each with its own full bath and walk-in closet. A rec room is also on this floor, with a built-in wet bar and room for a pool table or theater set-up, for modern-day entertainment.

LEFT: The soft-toned facade of this Federal-Adams home is a customization that strays from the red-brick conformity of most Colonial homes. ABOVE: A spindle staircase through the foyer helps to frame the fanlit front entrance.

ABOVE: A masterful living room greets guests at the foyer with comfortable seating near the fireplace. TOP: A decorative ceiling treatment centers the crystal chandelier over an elegant dining table for six. ABOVE RIGHT: The master library has access from both the main hall and the master suite. Seclusion from the casual living areas makes it a quiet retreat.

FIRST FLOOR

SECOND FLOOR

plan (#) HPK2900002

SQUARE FOOTAGE: 1,670
BEDROOMS: 3
BATHROOMS: 2
WIDTH: 70' - 0"
DEPTH: 46' - 0"
FOUNDATION: CRAWLSPACE,
SLAB, UNFINISHED
BASEMENT

ORDER ONLINE @ EPLANS.COM

The clean lines of this modified Cape Cod enhance single-level living. The kitchen is positioned at the front and opens to the spacious great room and large, open dining area. Enjoy a warm fire—from any of these rooms—and built-ins in the great room. The laundry room is outfitted with extensive shelving for storage. The left wing of the home is dedicated to private quarters. The master suite enjoys its own sumptuous bath and walk-in closets. Two family bedrooms flank a full hall bath.

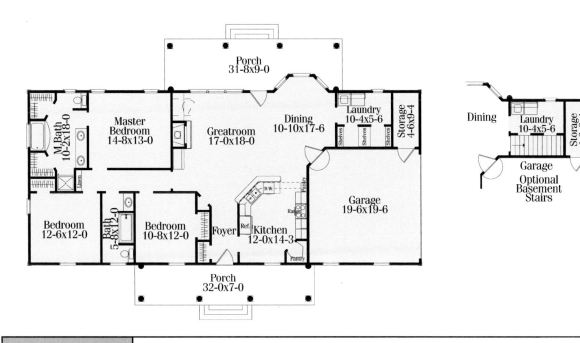

HELPFUL HINT: Modify your plan with our easy-to-use customization service.

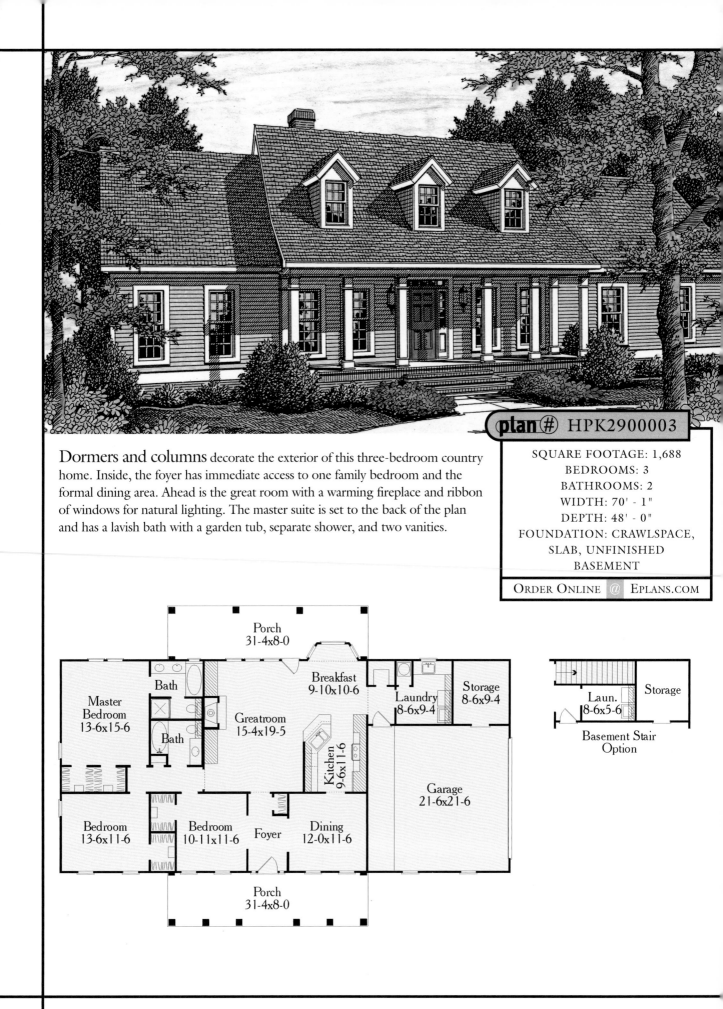

plan # HPK2900003

SQUARE FOOTAGE: 1,688
BEDROOMS: 3
BATHROOMS: 2
WIDTH: 70' - 1"
DEPTH: 48' - 0"
FOUNDATION: CRAWLSPACE,
SLAB, UNFINISHED
BASEMENT

ORDER ONLINE @ Eplans.com

Dormers and columns decorate the exterior of this three-bedroom country home. Inside, the foyer has immediate access to one family bedroom and the formal dining area. Ahead is the great room with a warming fireplace and ribbon of windows for natural lighting. The master suite is set to the back of the plan and has a lavish bath with a garden tub, separate shower, and two vanities.

Porch
31-4x8-0

Bath

Master
Bedroom
13-6x15-6

Bath

Greatroom
15-4x19-5

Breakfast
9-10x10-6

Kitchen
9-6x11-6

Laundry
8-6x9-4

Storage
8-6x9-4

Garage
21-6x21-6

Bedroom
13-6x11-6

Bedroom
10-11x11-6

Foyer

Dining
12-0x11-6

Porch
31-4x8-0

Laun.
8-6x5-6

Storage

Basement Stair
Option

plan# HPK2900004

FIRST FLOOR: 876 SQ. FT.
SECOND FLOOR: 834 SQ. FT.
TOTAL: 1,710 SQ. FT.
BEDROOMS: 3
BATHROOMS: 2½
WIDTH: 35' - 0"
DEPTH: 39' - 8"
FOUNDATION: SLAB

ORDER ONLINE @ EPLANS.COM

When you enter this congenial two-story home, you immediately step into the spacious great room with a charming corner fireplace. From here a wide door opens to the dining and kitchen area, marked by its open and flexible layout. Especially appealing on this floor is the back-corner home office with a close-by half-bath. An extraordinary master suite and two family bedrooms are upstairs. Highlights of the private master bath are twin vanities, an oversize tub, and a separate shower. The other bedrooms share a bath with hall access. Extra room is available on the second level for storage.

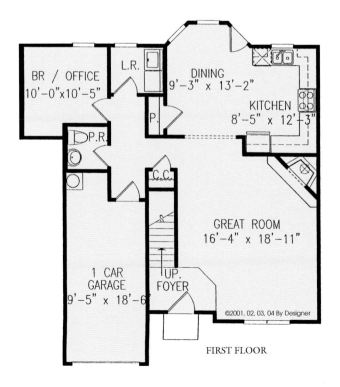

FIRST FLOOR

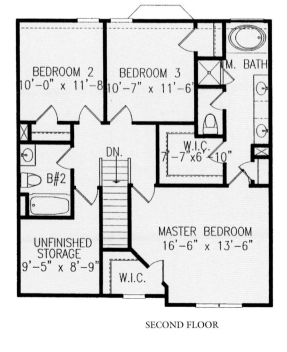

SECOND FLOOR

© 2003 Donald A. Gardner, Inc.

plan# HPK2900005

SQUARE FOOTAGE: 1,727
BONUS SPACE: 346 SQ. FT.
BEDROOMS: 3
BATHROOMS: 2
WIDTH: 46' - 0"
DEPTH: 66' - 4"

ORDER ONLINE @ EPLANS.COM

Signature Designer

This home exhibits the hallmarks of a Don Gardner design: a flexible, open floor plan with thoughtful details. The Jarrel provides excellent livability in just over 1,700 square feet of efficiently-planned space. Plentiful windows invite light inside, and front and screened porches extend living space outdoors. Tray ceilings and built-in cabinetry add beauty and function. The Jarrel is a modest but elegant home, perfect for first-time builders as well as empty-nesters.

SCREEN PORCH
17-8 x 10-0

DINING
11-0 x 12-4

MASTER BED RM.
16-4 x 14-8

linen

walk-in closet

cl

fireplace

KIT.
11-0 x 12-4
(cathedral ceiling)

master bath

bath

seat

GREAT RM.
17-2 x 19-4
(cathedral ceiling)

cabinets

coats

FOYER
7-4 x 6-8

cl

up

BED RM.
11-0 x 12-4

BEDROOM/ STUDY
11-0 x 12-4

UTIL.

w
d

PORCH

GARAGE
21-0 x 22-0

down

attic storage

attic storage

BONUS RM.
13-4 x 22-0

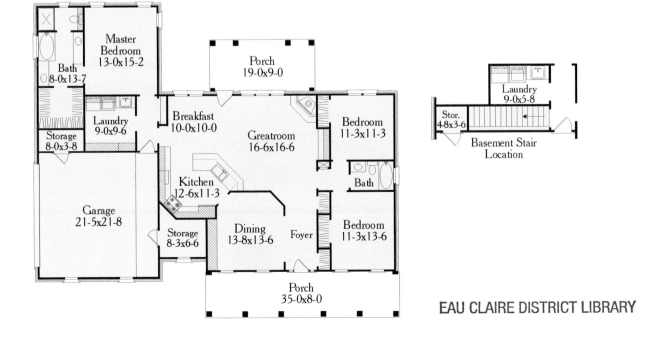

plan # HPK2900006

SQUARE FOOTAGE: 1,836
BEDROOMS: 3
BATHROOMS: 2
WIDTH: 65' - 8"
DEPTH: 55' - 0"
FOUNDATION: CRAWLSPACE,
SLAB, UNFINISHED
BASEMENT

ORDER ONLINE @ EPLANS.COM

Pillars, beautiful transoms, and sidelights set off the entry door and draw attention to this comfortable home. The foyer leads to a formal dining room and a great room with a ribbon of windows pouring in light. To the left of the kitchen is a roomy laundry area, with lots of storage space for those extra household supplies. Privacy is assured with a master suite; a large walk-in closet and full bath with separate shower and large tub add to the pleasure of this wing. Two family bedrooms occupy the right side of the design and share a full bath.

Master Bedroom 13-0x15-2
Bath 8-0x13-7
Storage 8-0x3-8
Laundry 9-0x9-6
Garage 21-5x21-8
Breakfast 10-0x10-0
Kitchen 12-6x11-3
Storage 8-3x6-6
Porch 19-0x9-0
Greatroom 16-6x16-6
Dining 13-8x13-6
Foyer
Bedroom 11-3x11-3
Bath
Bedroom 11-3x13-6
Porch 35-0x8-0

Laundry 9-0x5-8
Stor. 4-8x3-6
Basement Stair Location

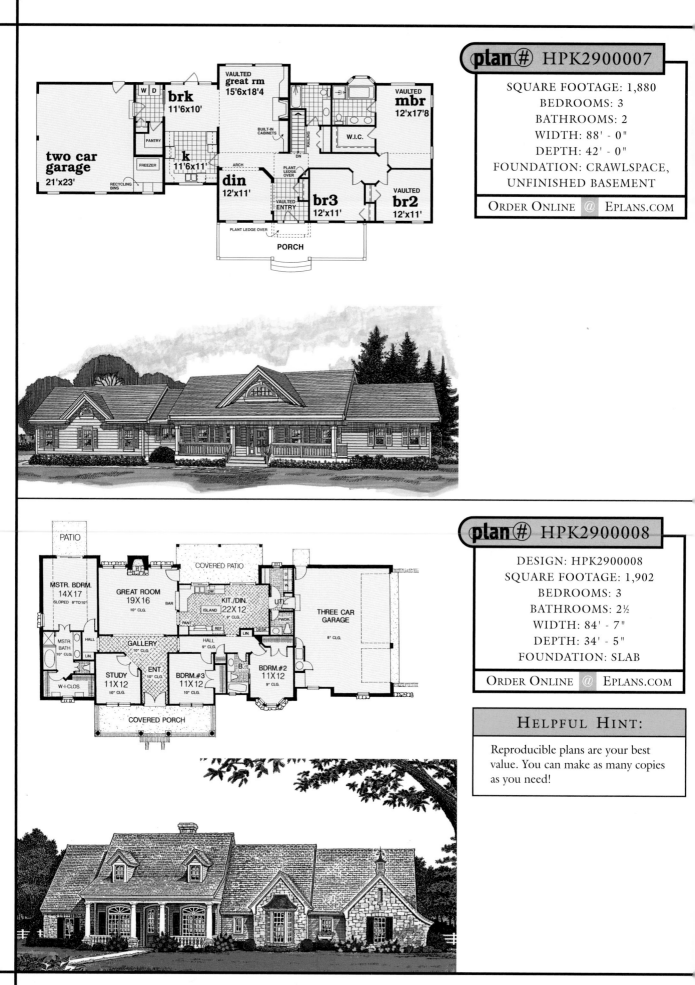

plan # HPK2900007

SQUARE FOOTAGE: 1,880
BEDROOMS: 3
BATHROOMS: 2
WIDTH: 88' - 0"
DEPTH: 42' - 0"
FOUNDATION: CRAWLSPACE,
UNFINISHED BASEMENT

ORDER ONLINE @ EPLANS.COM

Floor plan labels (HPK2900007):
- two car garage 21'x23'
- RECYCLING BINS
- FREEZER
- PANTRY
- W | D
- brk 11'6x10'
- k 11'6x11'
- ARCH
- din 12'x11'
- VAULTED great rm 15'6x18'4
- BUILT-IN CABINETS
- PLANT LEDGE OVER
- VAULTED ENTRY
- PLANT LEDGE OVER
- DN
- RAILING
- W.I.C.
- VAULTED mbr 12'x17'8
- br3 12'x11'
- VAULTED br2 12'x11'
- PORCH

plan # HPK2900008

DESIGN: HPK2900008
SQUARE FOOTAGE: 1,902
BEDROOMS: 3
BATHROOMS: 2½
WIDTH: 84' - 7"
DEPTH: 34' - 5"
FOUNDATION: SLAB

ORDER ONLINE @ EPLANS.COM

HELPFUL HINT:

Reproducible plans are your best value. You can make as many copies as you need!

Floor plan labels (HPK2900008):
- PATIO
- MSTR. BDRM. 14X17 SLOPED 8'TO10'
- MSTR. BATH 10' CLG.
- W-I-CLOS.
- HALL
- LIN.
- GREAT ROOM 19X16 10' CLG.
- BAR
- GALLERY 10' CLG.
- STUDY 11X12 10' CLG.
- ENT. 10' CLG.
- COVERED PATIO
- KIT./DIN. 22X12 9' CLG.
- DW
- ISLAND
- PANT.
- REF
- UTL.
- PWDR.
- HALL 9' CLG.
- LIN.
- BDRM.#3 11X12 10' CLG.
- B.
- BDRM.#2 11X12 9' CLG.
- THREE CAR GARAGE 8' CLG.
- COVERED PORCH

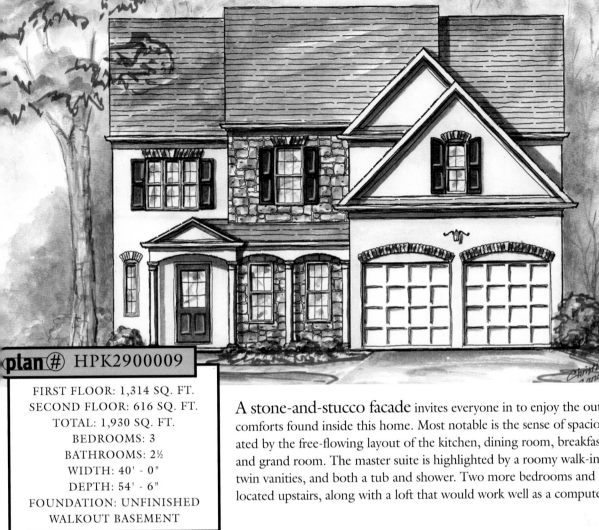

plan # HPK2900009

FIRST FLOOR: 1,314 SQ. FT.
SECOND FLOOR: 616 SQ. FT.
TOTAL: 1,930 SQ. FT.
BEDROOMS: 3
BATHROOMS: 2½
WIDTH: 40' - 0"
DEPTH: 54' - 6"
FOUNDATION: UNFINISHED
WALKOUT BASEMENT

ORDER ONLINE @ EPLANS.COM

A stone-and-stucco facade invites everyone in to enjoy the outstanding comforts found inside this home. Most notable is the sense of spaciousness created by the free-flowing layout of the kitchen, dining room, breakfast nook, and grand room. The master suite is highlighted by a roomy walk-in wardrobe, twin vanities, and both a tub and shower. Two more bedrooms and a bath are located upstairs, along with a loft that would work well as a computer room.

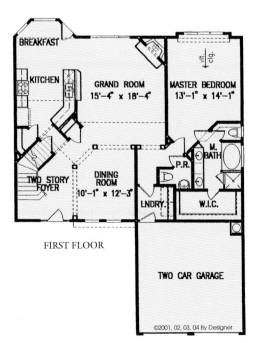

FIRST FLOOR

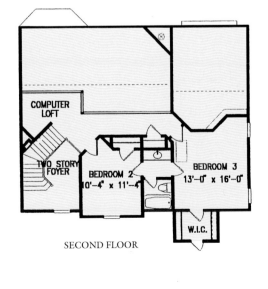

SECOND FLOOR

Reminiscent of the popular townhouses of the past, this fine clapboard home is perfect for urban or riverfront living. Two balconies grace the second floor—one at the front and one on the side. A two-way fireplace between the formal living and dining rooms provides visual impact. Built-in bookcases flank an arched opening between these rooms. A pass-through from the kitchen to the dining room simplifies serving, and a walk-in pantry provides storage. On the second floor, the master bedroom opens to a large balcony, and the relaxing master bath is designed with a separate shower and an angled whirlpool tub. Two secondary bedrooms and a full bath are located at the rear of the plan.

plan# HPK2900010

FIRST FLOOR: 904 SQ. FT.
SECOND FLOOR: 1,058 SQ. FT.
TOTAL: 1,962 SQ. FT.
BEDROOMS: 3
BATHROOMS: 2½
WIDTH: 22' - 0"
DEPTH: 74' - 0"
FOUNDATION: CRAWLSPACE, SLAB

ORDER ONLINE @ EPLANS.COM

FIRST FLOOR

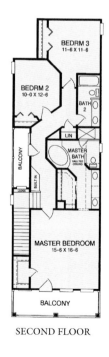

SECOND FLOOR

plan # HPK2900011

FIRST FLOOR: 1,383 SQ. FT.
SECOND FLOOR: 595 SQ. FT.
TOTAL: 1,978 SQ. FT.
BONUS SPACE: 617 SQ. FT.
BEDROOMS: 3
BATHROOMS: 2
WIDTH: 48' - 0"
DEPTH: 42' - 0"
FOUNDATION: ISLAND
BASEMENT

ORDER ONLINE @ EPLANS.COM

This fabulous Key West home blends interior space with the great outdoors. Designed for a balmy climate, the home boasts expansive porches and decks—with outside access from every area of the home. A sun-dappled foyer leads via a stately mid-level staircase to a splendid great room, which features a warming fireplace tucked in beside beautiful built-in cabinetry. Highlighted by a wall of glass that opens to the rear porch, this two-story living space opens to the formal dining room and a well-appointed kitchen. Spacious secondary bedrooms on the main level open to outside spaces and share a full bath. Upstairs, a 10-foot tray ceiling highlights a private master suite, which provides French doors to an upper-level porch.

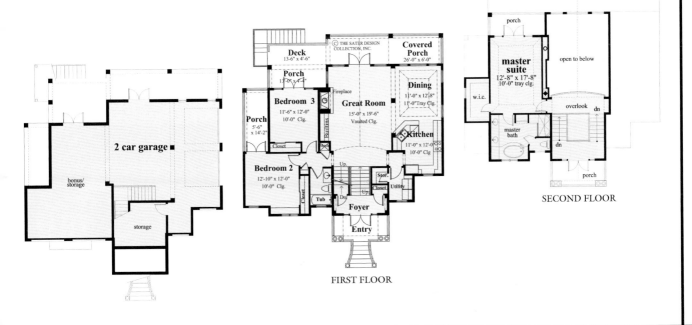

FIRST FLOOR

SECOND FLOOR

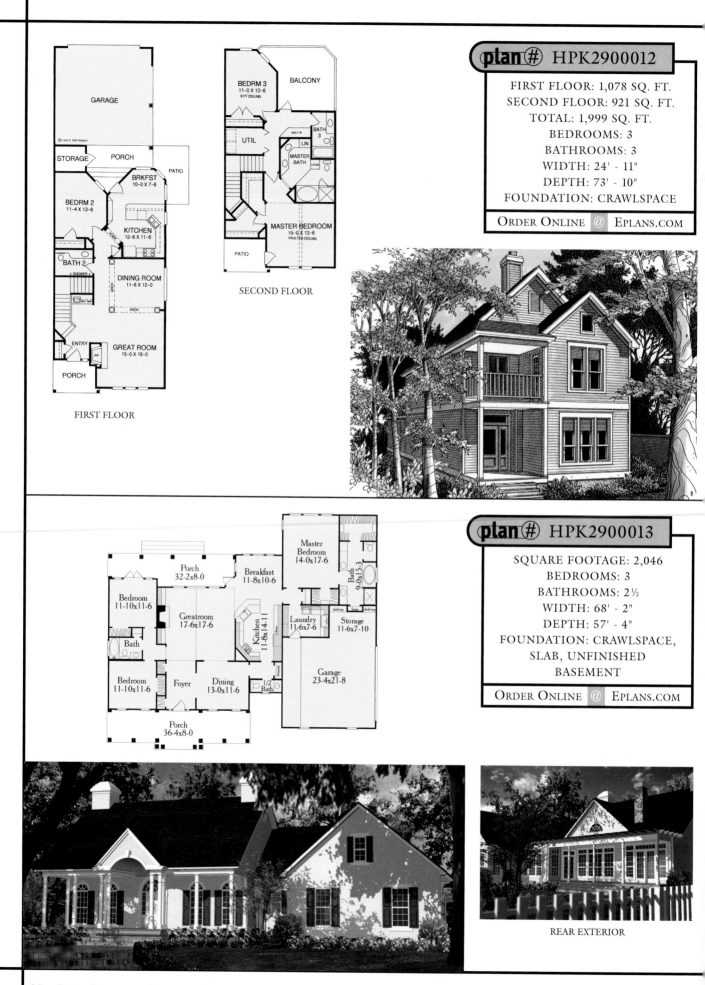

GARAGE

© Larry E. Belk Designs

STORAGE   PORCH

BRKFST
10-0 X 7-6

PATIO

BEDRM 2
11-4 X 13-6

KITCHEN
12-6 X 11-6

BATH 2

SHOWER

DINING ROOM
11-6 X 12-0

ARCH

ENTRY

GREAT ROOM
15-0 X 16-0

FP

PORCH

FIRST FLOOR

BEDRM 3
11-0 X 13-6
9 FT CEILING

BALCONY

BUILT IN

BATH
3

UTIL   LIN

MASTER
BATH

LEDGE

MASTER BEDROOM
15-0 X 13-6
VAULTED CEILING

PATIO

SECOND FLOOR

plan # HPK2900012

FIRST FLOOR: 1,078 SQ. FT.
SECOND FLOOR: 921 SQ. FT.
TOTAL: 1,999 SQ. FT.
BEDROOMS: 3
BATHROOMS: 3
WIDTH: 24' - 11"
DEPTH: 73' - 10"
FOUNDATION: CRAWLSPACE

ORDER ONLINE @ EPLANS.COM

Porch
32-2x8-0

Breakfast
11-8x10-6

Master
Bedroom
14-0x17-6

Bath
9-0x15-3

Bedroom
11-10x11-6

Greatroom
17-6x17-6

Kitchen
11-8x14-11

Laundry
11-6x7-6

Storage
11-6x7-10

Bath

Bedroom
11-10x11-6

Foyer

Dining
13-0x11-6

1/2
Bath

Garage
23-4x21-8

Porch
36-4x8-0

plan # HPK2900013

SQUARE FOOTAGE: 2,046
BEDROOMS: 3
BATHROOMS: 2 ½
WIDTH: 68' - 2"
DEPTH: 57' - 4"
FOUNDATION: CRAWLSPACE,
SLAB, UNFINISHED
BASEMENT

ORDER ONLINE @ EPLANS.COM

REAR EXTERIOR

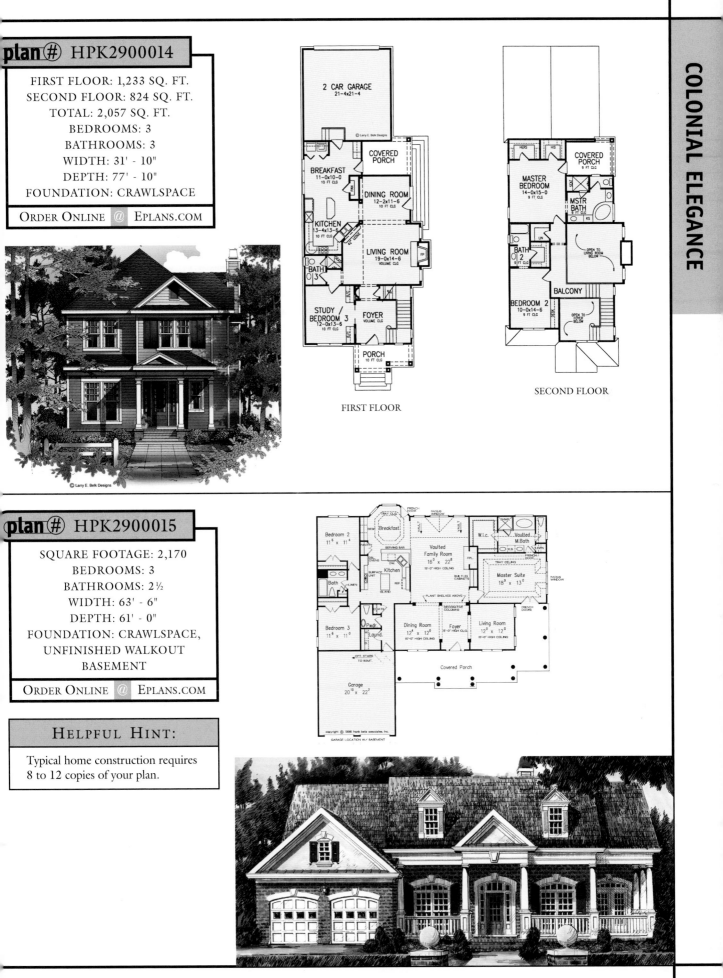

plan# HPK2900014

FIRST FLOOR: 1,233 SQ. FT.
SECOND FLOOR: 824 SQ. FT.
TOTAL: 2,057 SQ. FT.
BEDROOMS: 3
BATHROOMS: 3
WIDTH: 31' - 10"
DEPTH: 77' - 10"
FOUNDATION: CRAWLSPACE

ORDER ONLINE @ EPLANS.COM

FIRST FLOOR

SECOND FLOOR

plan# HPK2900015

SQUARE FOOTAGE: 2,170
BEDROOMS: 3
BATHROOMS: 2½
WIDTH: 63' - 6"
DEPTH: 61' - 0"
FOUNDATION: CRAWLSPACE,
UNFINISHED WALKOUT
BASEMENT

ORDER ONLINE @ EPLANS.COM

HELPFUL HINT:

Typical home construction requires
8 to 12 copies of your plan.

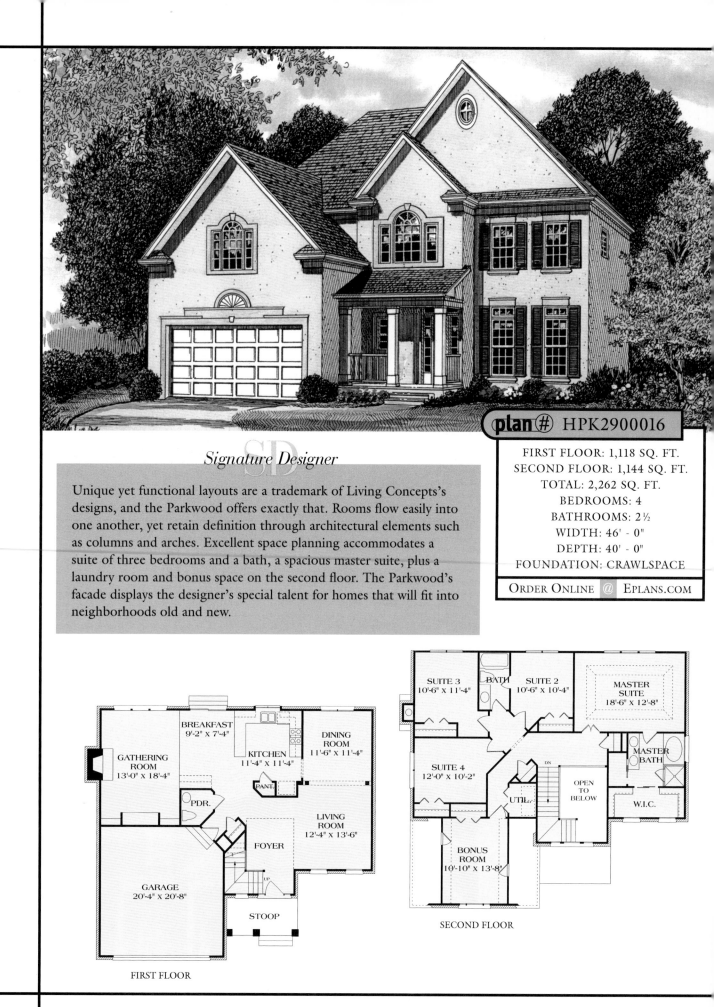

Signature Designer

Unique yet functional layouts are a trademark of Living Concepts's designs, and the Parkwood offers exactly that. Rooms flow easily into one another, yet retain definition through architectural elements such as columns and arches. Excellent space planning accommodates a suite of three bedrooms and a bath, a spacious master suite, plus a laundry room and bonus space on the second floor. The Parkwood's facade displays the designer's special talent for homes that will fit into neighborhoods old and new.

plan(#) HPK2900016

FIRST FLOOR: 1,118 SQ. FT.
SECOND FLOOR: 1,144 SQ. FT.
TOTAL: 2,262 SQ. FT.
BEDROOMS: 4
BATHROOMS: 2 ½
WIDTH: 46' - 0"
DEPTH: 40' - 0"
FOUNDATION: CRAWLSPACE

ORDER ONLINE @ EPLANS.COM

FIRST FLOOR

- GATHERING ROOM 13'-0" x 18'-4"
- BREAKFAST 9'-2" x 7'-4"
- KITCHEN 11'-4" x 11'-4"
- DINING ROOM 11'-6" x 11'-4"
- PDR.
- PANT.
- LIVING ROOM 12'-4" x 13'-6"
- FOYER
- GARAGE 20'-4" x 20'-8"
- STOOP

SECOND FLOOR

- SUITE 3 10'-6" x 11'-4"
- BATH
- SUITE 2 10'-6" x 10'-4"
- MASTER SUITE 18'-6" x 12'-8"
- SUITE 4 12'-0" x 10'-2"
- UTIL.
- DN
- OPEN TO BELOW
- MASTER BATH
- W.I.C.
- BONUS ROOM 10'-10" x 13'-8"

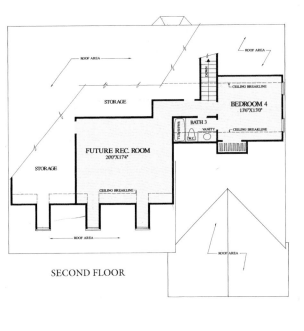

plan # HPK2900017

FIRST FLOOR: 1,981 SQ. FT.
SECOND FLOOR: 291 SQ. FT.
TOTAL: 2,272 SQ. FT.
BONUS SPACE: 412 SQ. FT.
BEDROOMS: 4
BATHROOMS: 3½
WIDTH: 58' - 0"
DEPTH: 53' - 0"
FOUNDATION: CRAWLSPACE

ORDER ONLINE @ EPLANS.COM

With three dormers and a welcoming front door accented by side-lights and a sunburst, this country cottage is sure to please. The dining room, immediately to the right from the foyer, is defined by decorative columns. In the great room, a volume ceiling heightens the space and showcases a fireplace and built-in bookshelves. The kitchen has plenty of work space and flows into the bayed breakfast nook. A considerate split-bedroom design places the plush master suite to the far left and two family bedrooms to the far right. A fourth bedroom and future space upstairs allow room to grow.

FIRST FLOOR

SECOND FLOOR

plan # HPK2900018

If you are looking for a home that grows with your family, this is it! Six columns grace the front porch and lend a Colonial feel to this great home plan. Inside, the foyer opens to the formal dining space, which is only a few steps from the kitchen. A walk-in pantry, spacious counters and cabinets, snack bar, adjoining breakfast area, and planning desk make this kitchen efficient and gourmet. A private master suite features a sitting bay, twin walk-in closets, and an amenity-filled bath. Two oversized secondary bedrooms have walk-in closets and share a corner bath. The entire second level is future space that will become exactly what you need. Plenty of storage can be found in the garage.

SQUARE FOOTAGE: 2,379
BONUS SPACE: 367 SQ. FT.
BEDROOMS: 3
BATHROOMS: 2½
WIDTH: 61' - 0"
DEPTH: 81' - 9"
FOUNDATION: CRAWLSPACE, SLAB, UNFINISHED BASEMENT

ORDER ONLINE @ EPLANS.COM

plan # HPK2900019

SQUARE FOOTAGE: 2,387
BONUS SPACE: 377 SQ. FT.
BEDROOMS: 3
BATHROOMS: 2½
WIDTH: 69' - 6"
DEPTH: 68' - 11"
FOUNDATION: CRAWLSPACE,
SLAB

ORDER ONLINE @ EPLANS.com

This three-bedroom home brings the past to life with columns, dormers, and fanlight windows. The entrance is flanked by the dining room and study. The great room boasts cathedral ceilings and a fireplace, with an open design that connects to the kitchen area. The spacious kitchen adjoins a breakfast nook and accesses the rear covered veranda. The master bedroom includes a sitting area, access to the veranda, and a spacious bathroom. This home is complete with two family bedrooms.

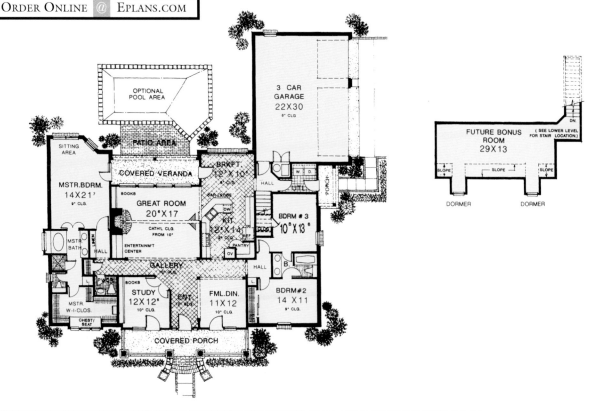

An attention-grabbing exterior and a versatile layout inside highlight this two-story country home. The kitchen, with an island counter and a serving bar, fits well with the sunny breakfast bay and the hearth-warmed family room. The master suite, embracing the entire left wing, contains a well-lit sitting area and a lavish bath with twin vanities, a shower with a seat, and a huge tub. Upstairs, two bedrooms share a bath and an overlook into the family room. Access to the attic can be made from this floor, and additional space is available for expansion.

FIRST FLOOR: 1,805 SQ. FT.
SECOND FLOOR: 593 SQ. FT.
TOTAL: 2,398 SQ. FT.
BONUS SPACE: 255 SQ. FT.
BEDROOMS: 4
BATHROOMS: 3
WIDTH: 55' - 0"
DEPTH: 48' - 0"
FOUNDATION: CRAWLSPACE, SLAB, UNFINISHED WALKOUT BASEMENT

ORDER ONLINE @ EPLANS.COM

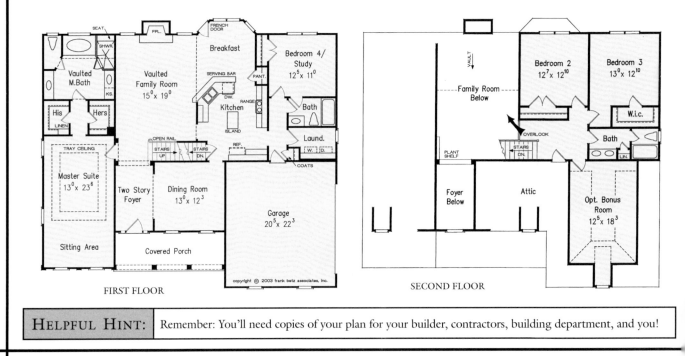

FIRST FLOOR

SECOND FLOOR

HELPFUL HINT: Remember: You'll need copies of your plan for your builder, contractors, building department, and you!

plan # HPK2900021

SQUARE FOOTAGE: 2,400
BONUS SPACE: 595 SQ. FT.
BEDROOMS: 4
BATHROOMS: 2
WIDTH: 61' - 10"
DEPTH: 66' - 5"
FOUNDATION: CRAWLSPACE,
SLAB

ORDER ONLINE @ EPLANS.COM

This home blends a traditional brick-and-stucco exterior with a contemporary interior. Inside, the foyer introduces a formal dining room featuring sunburst windows and easy access to the breakfast nook and kitchen. Built-in bookcases, a corner fireplace, and French doors to the rear covered porch and patio highlight the living room. Raised ceilings add volume and a dramatic touch to the luxurious master suite—with private patio access—and to the kitchen with a U-shaped counter. A side-entry garage adds to the appeal. Three family bedrooms and a second full bath complete the plan.

plan # HPK2900022

SQUARE FOOTAGE: 2,409
BONUS SPACE: 709 SQ. FT.
BEDROOMS: 3
BATHROOMS: 2½
WIDTH: 85' - 8"
DEPTH: 68' - 4"
FOUNDATION: CRAWLSPACE,
SLAB, UNFINISHED
BASEMENT

ORDER ONLINE @ EPLANS.COM

The great room of this home provides a large masonry fireplace. Built-ins are included on one wall for entertainment equipment and books. The master suite is located to the rear of the house and has a luxury bath that includes large walk-in closets. The kitchen, equipped with a snack bar, walk-in pantry, and desk, is well designed for the busy cook. From the kitchen area, the staircase rises to an expandable second floor. With a future bedroom, game room, and bath upstairs, this home will fit the needs of a growing family.

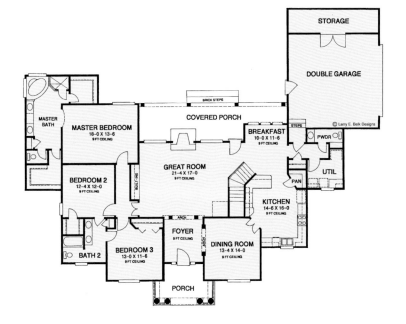

plan # HPK2900023

SQUARE FOOTAGE: 2,424
BEDROOMS: 3
BATHROOMS: 2½
WIDTH: 68' - 2"
DEPTH: 67' - 6"
FOUNDATION: CRAWLSPACE,
SLAB, UNFINISHED
BASEMENT

ORDER ONLINE @ EPLANS.COM

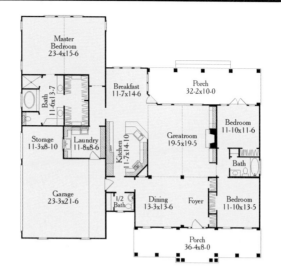

plan # HPK2900024

FIRST FLOOR: 1,327 SQ. FT.
SECOND FLOOR: 1,099 SQ. FT.
TOTAL: 2,426 SQ. FT.
BONUS SPACE: 290 SQ. FT.
BEDROOMS: 4
BATHROOMS: 3
WIDTH: 54' - 4"
DEPTH: 42' - 10"
FOUNDATION: CRAWLSPACE,
UNFINISHED WALKOUT
BASEMENT

ORDER ONLINE @ EPLANS.COM

FIRST FLOOR

SECOND FLOOR

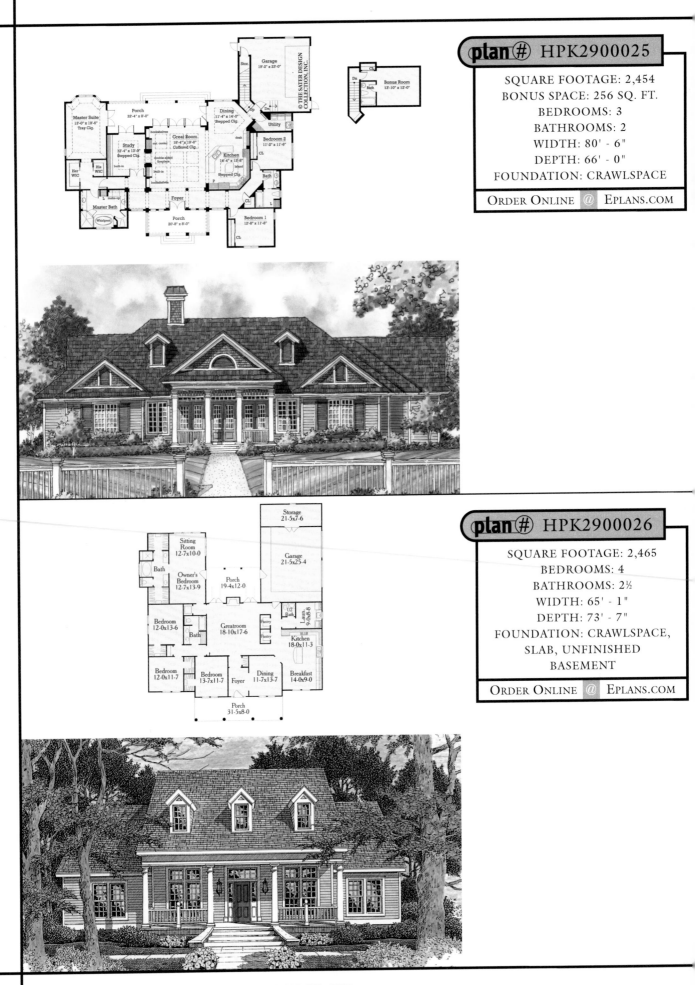

plan# HPK2900025

SQUARE FOOTAGE: 2,454
BONUS SPACE: 256 SQ. FT.
BEDROOMS: 3
BATHROOMS: 2
WIDTH: 80' - 6"
DEPTH: 66' - 0"
FOUNDATION: CRAWLSPACE

ORDER ONLINE @ EPLANS.COM

plan# HPK2900026

SQUARE FOOTAGE: 2,465
BEDROOMS: 4
BATHROOMS: 2½
WIDTH: 65' - 1"
DEPTH: 73' - 7"
FOUNDATION: CRAWLSPACE,
SLAB, UNFINISHED
BASEMENT

ORDER ONLINE @ EPLANS.COM

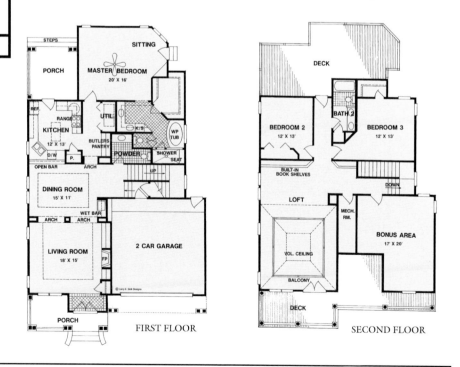

plan # HPK2900027

FIRST FLOOR: 1,530 SQ. FT.
SECOND FLOOR: 968 SQ. FT.
TOTAL: 2,498 SQ. FT.
BONUS SPACE: 326 SQ. FT.
BEDROOMS: 3
BATHROOMS: 2½
WIDTH: 40' - 0"
DEPTH: 66' - 4"
FOUNDATION: CRAWLSPACE,
SLAB, UNFINISHED
BASEMENT

ORDER ONLINE @ EPLANS.COM

The timeless influence of the French Quarter is exemplified in this home designed for riverfront living. The double French-door entry opens into a large living room/dining room area separated by a double archway. A railed balcony with a loft on the second floor overlooks the living room. A pass-through between the kitchen and dining room also provides seating at a bar for informal dining. The spacious master bedroom at the rear includes a sitting area and a roomy bath with a large walk-in closet. Two additional bedrooms, a bath, and a bonus area for an office or game room are located upstairs.

FIRST FLOOR

SECOND FLOOR

HELPFUL HINT: Want an upgrade? Exchange your first purchase for a credit on a higher-priced plan within 90 days of ordering.

plan # HPK2900028

Shutters and multipane windows dress up the exterior of this lovely stucco home. Formal and informal areas flow easily, beginning with the dining room sized to accommodate large parties and function with the adjacent living room. A gourmet kitchen is complete with a walk-in pantry and a cozy breakfast nook. Double doors lead to the spacious master suite. The lavish master bath features His and Hers walk-in closets, a tub framed by a columned archway, and an oversized shower. Off the angular hallway, two bedrooms share a Pullman-style bath and a study desk. A bonus room over the garage provides additional space.

SQUARE FOOTAGE: 2,551
BONUS SPACE: 287 SQ. FT.
BEDROOMS: 4
BATHROOMS: 3
WIDTH: 69' - 8"
DEPTH: 71' - 4"
FOUNDATION: SLAB

ORDER ONLINE @ EPLANS.COM

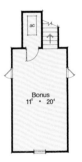

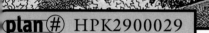

plan # HPK2900029

SQUARE FOOTAGE: 2,561
BONUS SPACE: 1,494 SQ. FT.
BEDROOMS: 3
BATHROOMS: 2½
WIDTH: 76' - 8"
DEPTH: 62' - 0"
FOUNDATION: CRAWLSPACE,
SLAB, UNFINISHED
BASEMENT

ORDER ONLINE @ EPLANS.COM

Three dormers sit atop a wide, friendly porch that welcomes visitors to this attractive stucco-and-brick home. Inside, well-defined spaces use half-walls and columns to keep the layout open. A lovely dining room sits off the open island kitchen. A halfwall accented with columns creates a transition to the great room. A beautiful fireplace and flanking built-ins complete the space. Two family bedrooms offer plenty of closet space and share a full bath. The master suite enjoys nine-foot ceilings, a massive walk-in closet, and a super bath made for two. The second level is a great space for storage, a media room, or future expansion space.

REAR EXTERIOR

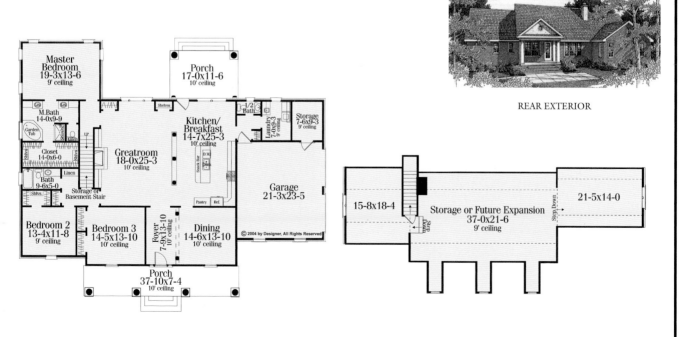

© William E. Poole Designs, Inc.

Signature Designer

William Poole's Back Bay Cottage is a fine example of what makes his designs so compelling: simple Southern charm on the outside, livable layouts on the inside. The full-facade columned porch offers a warm welcome and a fine vantage point from which to enjoy the neighborhood. Like many of Poole's designs, this one-and-a-half story home features a first-floor master suite, making it an ideal choice for both empty-nesters and growing families alike. Spacious bedrooms for guests or children are located on the second floor, along with a common lounge area and expandable space.

FIRST FLOOR

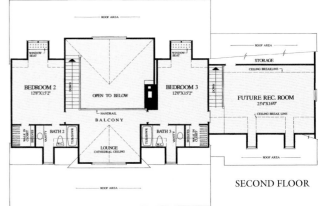

SECOND FLOOR

plan# HPK2900031

FIRST FLOOR: 1,809 SQ. FT.
SECOND FLOOR: 785 SQ. FT.
TOTAL: 2,594 SQ. FT.
BONUS SPACE: 353 SQ. FT.
BEDROOMS: 5
BATHROOMS: 4
WIDTH: 72' - 7"
DEPTH: 51' - 5"
FOUNDATION: CRAWLSPACE,
SLAB, UNFINISHED WALKOUT
BASEMENT

ORDER ONLINE @ EPLANS.COM

With elements of country style, this unique Colonial-inspired home presents a rustic attitude blended with the delicate features that make this design one of a kind. Upon entry, a second-story arched window lights the foyer. Straight ahead, the family room soars with a two-story vault balanced by a cozy fireplace. A pass-through from the island kitchen keeps conversation going as the family chef whips up delectable feasts for the formal dining room or bayed breakfast nook. A bedroom at the rear provides plenty of privacy for guests, or as a home office. The master suite takes up the entire right wing, hosting a bayed sitting area and marvelous vaulted bath. Upstairs, three bedrooms access a versatile bonus room, limited only by your imagination.

FIRST FLOOR

SECOND FLOOR

ORDER BLUEPRINTS ANYTIME AT EPLANS.COM OR 1-800-521-6797   33

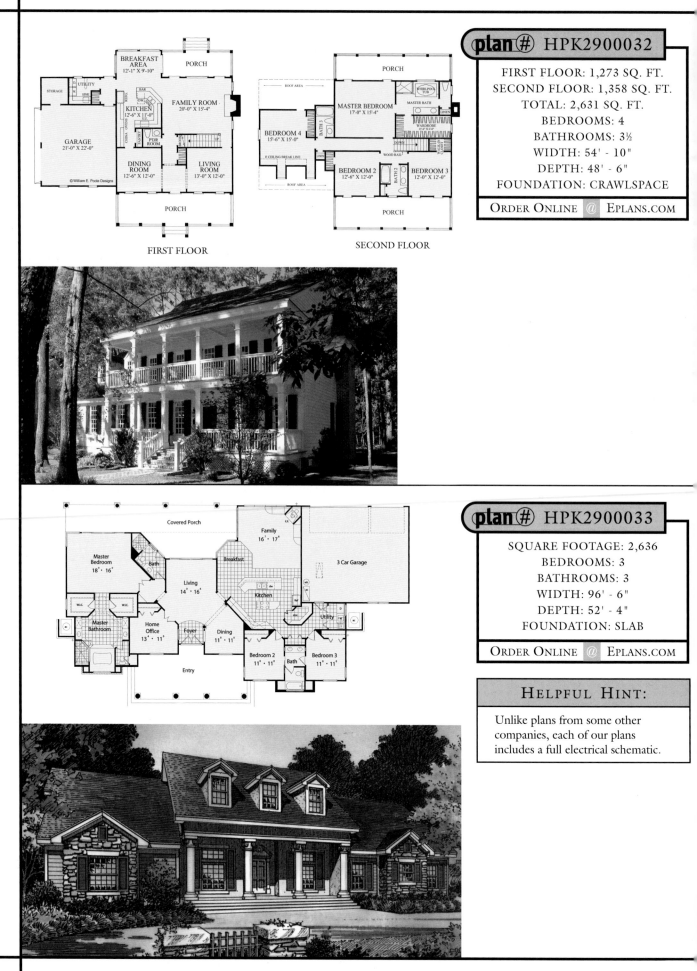

FIRST FLOOR

SECOND FLOOR

plan # HPK2900034

SQUARE FOOTAGE: 2,648
BONUS SPACE: 266 SQ. FT.
BEDROOMS: 4
BATHROOMS: 2
WIDTH: 68' - 10"
DEPTH: 77' - 10"
FOUNDATION: CRAWLSPACE,
SLAB, UNFINISHED
BASEMENT

ORDER ONLINE @ EPLANS.COM

This charming Colonial Revival home with side-loading garage is perfect for a corner lot. The inviting porch opens to the foyer that is flanked by the formal dining room on the right and a flex room on the left. Twin arches announce the great room where the warming fireplace is framed by windows. The generous island kitchen is certain to please the gourmet of the family and the sunny breakfast nook offers a casual alternative to the formal dining room. The family bedrooms are situated on the left sharing a Jack-and-Jill bath. And on the far right, the master suite offers a pampering private bath that includes His and Hers walk-in closets and a delightful garden tub.

Four graceful columns support a long covered porch topped by three attractive dormers. The two-story foyer is flanked by a formal dining room and a cozy study—or make it a guest suite with the full bath nearby. The island kitchen is sure to please with a walk-in pantry and easy access to the breakfast area. A spacious great room has a balcony overlook from the second floor and a fireplace. The master suite boasts two walk-in closets, a whirlpool tub, and a separate shower. Upstairs, three bedrooms—all with window seats—share a full hall bath.

plan# HPK2900035

FIRST FLOOR: 1,813 SQ. FT.
SECOND FLOOR: 885 SQ. FT.
TOTAL: 2,698 SQ. FT.
BEDROOMS: 5
BATHROOMS: 3
WIDTH: 70' - 2"
DEPTH: 51' - 4"
FOUNDATION: CRAWLSPACE, SLAB, UNFINISHED BASEMENT

ORDER ONLINE @ EPLANS.COM

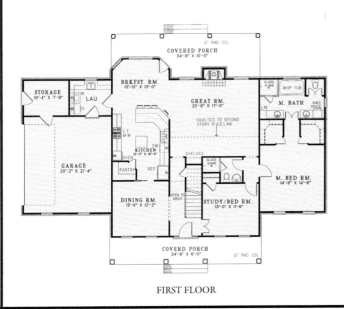

FIRST FLOOR

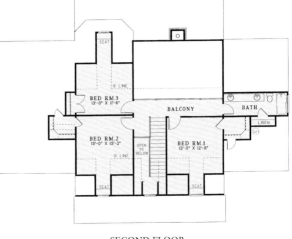

SECOND FLOOR

plan # HPK2900036

FIRST FLOOR: 1,855 SQ. FT.
SECOND FLOOR: 901 SQ. FT.
TOTAL: 2,756 SQ. FT.
BEDROOMS: 3
BATHROOMS: 3½
WIDTH: 66' - 0"
DEPTH: 50' - 0"
FOUNDATION: ISLAND
BASEMENT

ORDER ONLINE @ EPLANS.COM

This southern tidewater cottage is the perfect vacation hideaway. An octagonal great room with a multifaceted vaulted ceiling illuminates the interior. The island kitchen is brightened by a bumped-out window and a pass-through to the lanai. Two walk-in closets and a whirlpool bath await to indulge the homeowner in the master suite. A set of double doors opens to the vaulted master lanai for quiet comfort. The U-shaped staircase leads to a loft, which overlooks the great room and the foyer. Two additional family bedrooms offer private baths. A computer center and a morning kitchen complete the upper level.

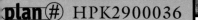

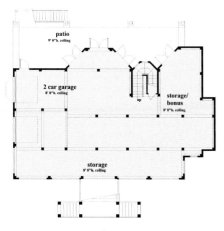

FIRST FLOOR

SECOND FLOOR

plan# HPK2900037

FIRST FLOOR: 1,874 SQ. FT.
SECOND FLOOR: 901 SQ. FT.
TOTAL: 2,775 SQ. FT.
BONUS SPACE: 382 SQ. FT.
BEDROOMS: 3
BATHROOMS: 3½
WIDTH: 90' - 0"
DEPTH: 58' - 6"
FOUNDATION: CRAWLSPACE

ORDER ONLINE @ EPLANS.COM

From the wraparound porch to the gabled dormer windows, this sweet cottage is pure country. Inside, an open floor plan lends a spacious appeal. The formal dining room is defined by a pentagonal stepped ceiling. To the right, the study has unique angles and a sophisticated coffered ceiling. The two-story vaulted octagonal great room is brimming with architectural interest. Three sets of French doors extend to the rear porch; a lateral fireplace can be viewed from the gourmet kitchen with a cooktop island. An outdoor grill invites dining alfresco. The master suite is designed to pamper, with French doors and a plush bath. Two bedroom suites and bonus space reside on the second level and enjoy upper-deck access.

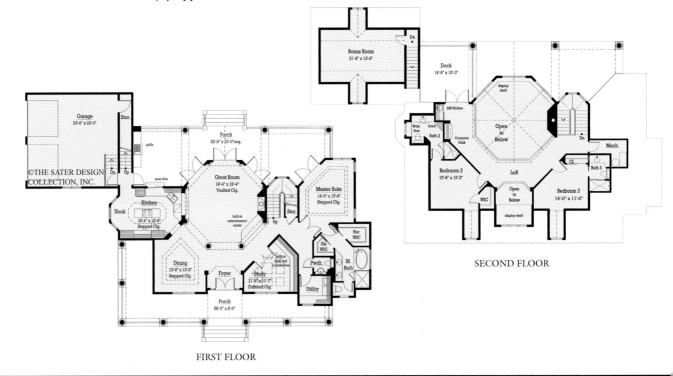

FIRST FLOOR

SECOND FLOOR

© WILLIAM E POOLE DESIGNS, INC.

plan # HPK2900038

SQUARE FOOTAGE: 2,777
BONUS SPACE: 424 SQ. FT.
BEDROOMS: 3
BATHROOMS: 2½
WIDTH: 75' - 6"
DEPTH: 60' - 2"
FOUNDATION: CRAWLSPACE,
UNFINISHED BASEMENT

ORDER ONLINE @ EPLANS.COM

This home is an absolute dream when it comes to living space! Whether formal or casual, there's a room for every occasion. The foyer opens to the formal dining room on the left; straight ahead lies the magnificent hearth-warmed living room. The island kitchen opens not only to a breakfast nook, but to a huge family/sunroom surrounded by two walls of windows. The right wing of the plan holds the sleeping quarters: two family bedrooms sharing a bath, and a majestic master suite. The second floor holds an abundance of expandable space.

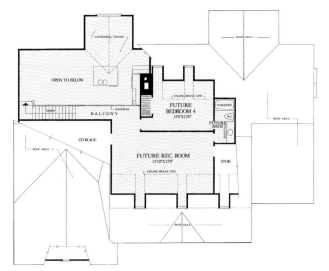

HELPFUL HINT: Our custom modification service can add a walk-out basement to any plan—great for hillside lots!

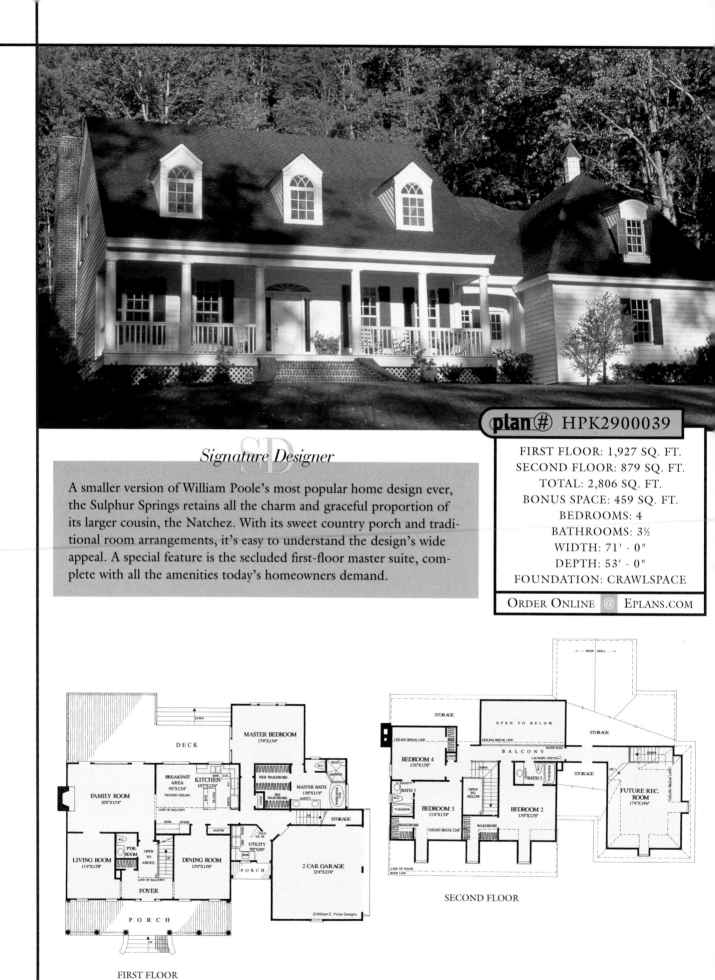

plan # HPK2900039

FIRST FLOOR: 1,927 SQ. FT.
SECOND FLOOR: 879 SQ. FT.
TOTAL: 2,806 SQ. FT.
BONUS SPACE: 459 SQ. FT.
BEDROOMS: 4
BATHROOMS: 3½
WIDTH: 71' - 0"
DEPTH: 53' - 0"
FOUNDATION: CRAWLSPACE

ORDER ONLINE @ EPLANS.COM

Signature Designer

A smaller version of William Poole's most popular home design ever, the Sulphur Springs retains all the charm and graceful proportion of its larger cousin, the Natchez. With its sweet country porch and traditional room arrangements, it's easy to understand the design's wide appeal. A special feature is the secluded first-floor master suite, complete with all the amenities today's homeowners demand.

FIRST FLOOR

SECOND FLOOR

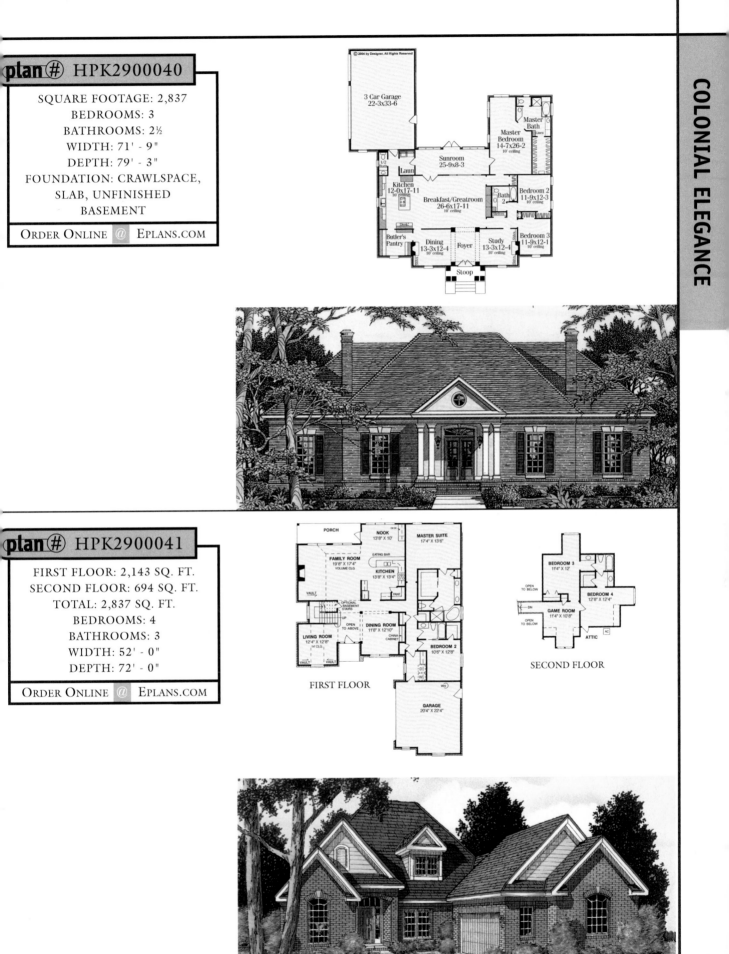

plan # HPK2900040

SQUARE FOOTAGE: 2,837
BEDROOMS: 3
BATHROOMS: 2½
WIDTH: 71' - 9"
DEPTH: 79' - 3"
FOUNDATION: CRAWLSPACE,
SLAB, UNFINISHED
BASEMENT

ORDER ONLINE @ EPLANS.COM

plan # HPK2900041

FIRST FLOOR: 2,143 SQ. FT.
SECOND FLOOR: 694 SQ. FT.
TOTAL: 2,837 SQ. FT.
BEDROOMS: 4
BATHROOMS: 3
WIDTH: 52' - 0"
DEPTH: 72' - 0"

ORDER ONLINE @ EPLANS.COM

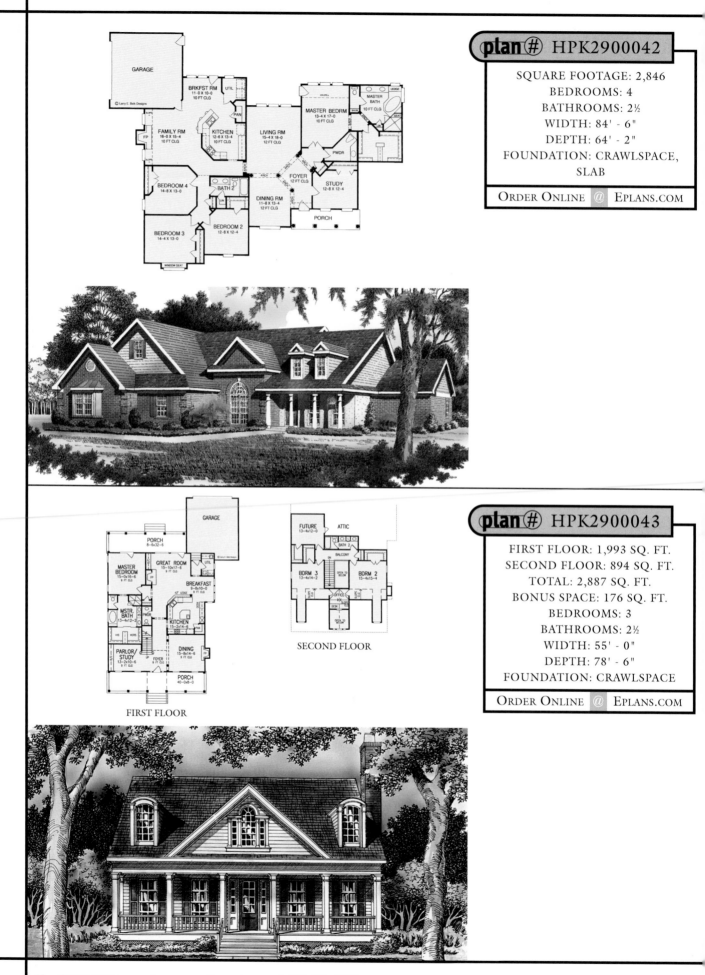

plan # HPK2900042

SQUARE FOOTAGE: 2,846
BEDROOMS: 4
BATHROOMS: 2½
WIDTH: 84' - 6"
DEPTH: 64' - 2"
FOUNDATION: CRAWLSPACE,
SLAB

ORDER ONLINE @ EPLANS.COM

plan # HPK2900043

FIRST FLOOR: 1,993 SQ. FT.
SECOND FLOOR: 894 SQ. FT.
TOTAL: 2,887 SQ. FT.
BONUS SPACE: 176 SQ. FT.
BEDROOMS: 3
BATHROOMS: 2½
WIDTH: 55' - 0"
DEPTH: 78' - 6"
FOUNDATION: CRAWLSPACE

ORDER ONLINE @ EPLANS.COM

SECOND FLOOR

FIRST FLOOR

plan # HPK2900044

SQUARE FOOTAGE: 2,946
BEDROOMS: 4
BATHROOMS: 3
WIDTH: 94' - 1"
DEPTH: 67' - 4"
FOUNDATION: SLAB

ORDER ONLINE @ EPLANS.com

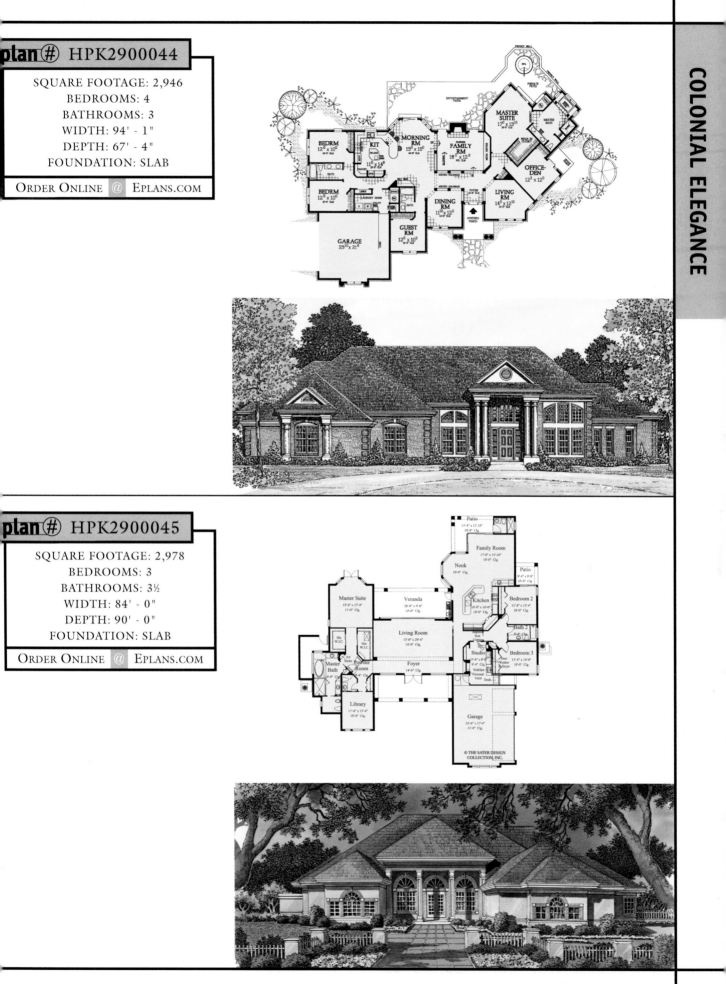

plan # HPK2900045

SQUARE FOOTAGE: 2,978
BEDROOMS: 3
BATHROOMS: 3½
WIDTH: 84' - 0"
DEPTH: 90' - 0"
FOUNDATION: SLAB

ORDER ONLINE @ EPLANS.com

plan# HPK2900046

FIRST FLOOR: 2,101 SQ. FT.
SECOND FLOOR: 877 SQ. FT.
TOTAL: 2,978 SQ. FT.
BEDROOMS: 4
BATHROOMS: 3
WIDTH: 66' - 0"
DEPTH: 51' - 0"

ORDER ONLINE @ EPLANS.COM

The centerpiece of this home's facade is its imposing arch. Inside, the foyer is flanked by a dining room and living room, and the spacious family room—with a porch out back—is straight ahead. Bedroom 2 and the master suite occupy the left wing. An ample playroom/study complements the two bedrooms upstairs.

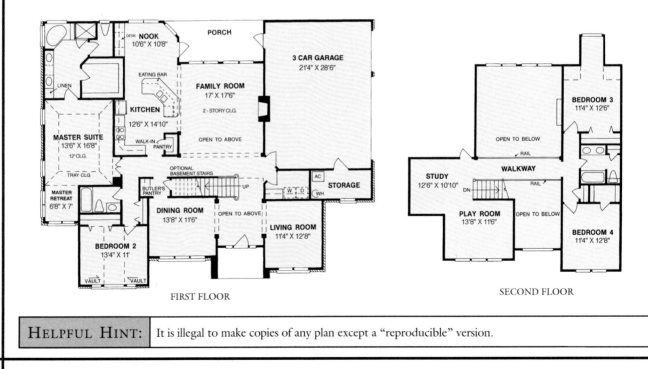

FIRST FLOOR

SECOND FLOOR

HELPFUL HINT: It is illegal to make copies of any plan except a "reproducible" version.

plan(#) HPK2900047

FIRST FLOOR: 1,995 SQ. FT.
SECOND FLOOR: 1,062 SQ. FT.
TOTAL: 3,057 SQ. FT.
BONUS SPACE: 459 SQ. FT.
BEDROOMS: 4
BATHROOMS: 3½
WIDTH: 71' - 0"
DEPTH: 57' - 4"
FOUNDATION: UNFINISHED
BASEMENT

ORDER ONLINE @ EPLANS.COM

Wood siding, muntin window dormers, and a double-decker porch exemplify Southern Country style in this welcoming plan. Slide off your porch swing and enter through the foyer, flanked by the bayed living room and dining room. The family room flows effortlessly into the breakfast area and the kitchen, complete with an island. The master bedroom wows with a closet designed for a true clotheshorse. Three upstairs bedrooms enjoy access to the upper porch and space for a future recreation room.

FIRST FLOOR

SECOND FLOOR

plan# HPK2900048

FIRST FLOOR: 2,194 SQ. FT.
SECOND FLOOR: 973 SQ. FT.
TOTAL: 3,167 SQ. FT.
BONUS SPACE: 281 SQ. FT.
BEDROOMS: 4
BATHROOMS: 3½
WIDTH: 71' - 11"
DEPTH: 54' - 4"

ORDER ONLINE @ EPLANS.COM

This updated farmhouse has been given additional custom-styled features. Twin gables, sidelights, and an arched entryway accent the facade; decorative ceiling treatments, bay windows, and French doors adorn the interior. From an abundance of counter space and large walk-in pantry to the built-ins and storage areas, this design makes the most of space. Supported by columns, a curved balcony overlooks the stunning two-story great room. The powder room is easily accessible from the common rooms, and angled corners soften the dining room. The well-equipped private bath and twin closets in the master suite are welcome luxuries.

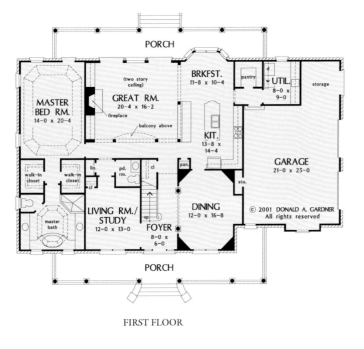

FIRST FLOOR

SECOND FLOOR

plan # HPK2900049

SQUARE FOOTAGE: 3,190
BONUS SPACE: 305 SQ. FT.
BEDROOMS: 4
BATHROOMS: 3½
WIDTH: 74' - 0"
DEPTH: 84' - 6"
FOUNDATION: CRAWLSPACE,
UNFINISHED WALKOUT
BASEMENT

ORDER ONLINE @ EPLANS.COM

This Southern Colonial beauty will be the showpiece of any neighborhood, with prominent columns, multipane window dormers, and flower-box accents. Inside, it is instantly clear that this luxurious home is designed with your ultimate comfort in mind. Columns define the dining room from the raised-ceiling foyer; both the dining room and nearby guest suite have French-door access to the front porch. The vaulted great room makes an elegant statement with a bookshelf-framed fireplace and rear French doors topped by a radius window. The island kitchen is definitely made for gourmet entertaining, complete with a butler's pantry and a serving bar to the bayed breakfast nook. The adjacent vaulted keeping room is perfect for cozy gatherings. The left wing is devoted to the master suite, decadent with a sitting bay and a vaulted bath with a step-up tub. Expansion options include a fifth bedroom and full bath.

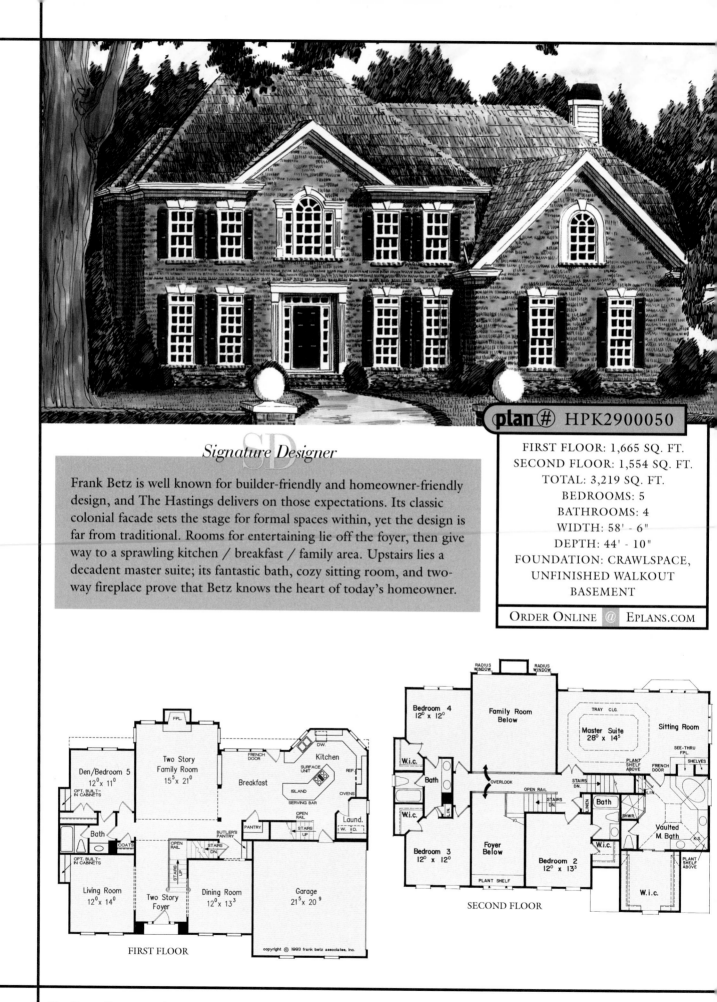

plan # HPK2900050

FIRST FLOOR: 1,665 SQ. FT.
SECOND FLOOR: 1,554 SQ. FT.
TOTAL: 3,219 SQ. FT.
BEDROOMS: 5
BATHROOMS: 4
WIDTH: 58' - 6"
DEPTH: 44' - 10"
FOUNDATION: CRAWLSPACE,
UNFINISHED WALKOUT
BASEMENT

ORDER ONLINE @ EPLANS.COM

Signature Designer

Frank Betz is well known for builder-friendly and homeowner-friendly design, and The Hastings delivers on those expectations. Its classic colonial facade sets the stage for formal spaces within, yet the design is far from traditional. Rooms for entertaining lie off the foyer, then give way to a sprawling kitchen / breakfast / family area. Upstairs lies a decadent master suite; its fantastic bath, cozy sitting room, and two-way fireplace prove that Betz knows the heart of today's homeowner.

plan # HPK2900051

FIRST FLOOR: 2,127 SQ. FT.
SECOND FLOOR: 1,110 SQ. FT.
TOTAL: 3,237 SQ. FT.
BEDROOMS: 5
BATHROOMS: 3½
WIDTH: 69' - 0"
DEPTH: 67' - 4"
FOUNDATION: CRAWLSPACE,
SLAB, UNFINISHED
BASEMENT

ORDER ONLINE @ EPLANS.COM

With an unmistakable country appeal, this home is sure to please. The open layout creates a natural flow through the home without the use of unnecessary walls. Meal preparation is now a family affair, as the cook is able to interact with others seated in the breakfast area, at the snack bar, or in the adjoining great room. A rear porch allows for outdoor dining and entertaining. Two first-floor bedrooms share a full bath, and the master suite sits in seclusion on the opposite side of the plan. The second floor houses two additional family bedrooms, a full bath, and a game room. Storage space in the garage is an added bonus.

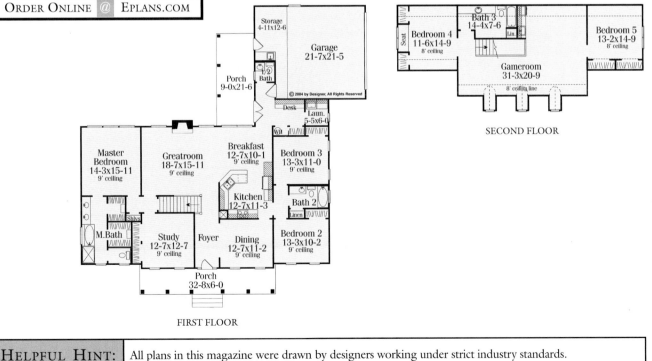

FIRST FLOOR

SECOND FLOOR

HELPFUL HINT: All plans in this magazine were drawn by designers working under strict industry standards.

FIRST FLOOR: 1,754 SQ. FT.
SECOND FLOOR: 1,502 SQ. FT.
TOTAL: 3,256 SQ. FT.
BONUS SPACE: 588 SQ. FT.
BEDROOMS: 4
BATHROOMS: 3½
WIDTH: 70' - 4"
DEPTH: 48' - 0"
FOUNDATION: CRAWLSPACE

Behind its elegant Palladian facade, this plan offers a delightful arrangement of rooms for both formal and casual living. In the foyer, look up through the open stairwell to the tray ceiling two stories above. To the right, a formal dining room also boasts a striking ceiling treatment, and to the left, double doors open to a study or parlor. Pocket doors allow this room to be open or closed to the family room, where a fireplace, built-in cabinetry, and a wall of windows create an exciting space for gatherings. The huge kitchen includes an L-shaped island, complete with cooktop and snack counter. Laundry facilities are found in the mudroom-style entry from the three-car garage, along with a back stair to the spacious bonus room. This room's proximity to the fourth suite's bath would allow it to be used as a permanent or occasional bedroom. Two additional bedrooms share a compartmented bath, while the homeowners enjoy the privacy of their luxury suite.

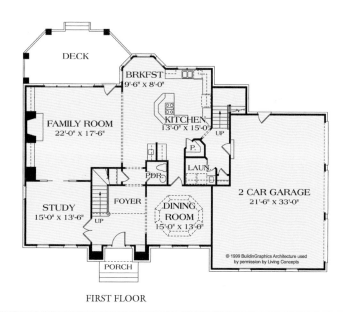

FIRST FLOOR

SECOND FLOOR

plan# HPK2900053

FIRST FLOOR: 2,055 SQ. FT.
SECOND FLOOR: 1,229 SQ. FT.
TOTAL: 3,284 SQ. FT.
BEDROOMS: 4
BATHROOMS: 3½
WIDTH: 65' - 0"
DEPTH: 60' - 10"
FOUNDATION: CRAWLSPACE, SLAB

ORDER ONLINE @ EPLANS.com

A pedimented entry, shingle accents, and shutters blend modern and traditional looks on this southern design. The foyer features a two-story ceiling and opens to the formal dining room, which has a lovely tray ceiling. A gallery hall connects the formal living room with all areas of the home. French doors open the living space to the back property. The master wing includes two walk-in closets, an angled garden tub, a separate shower with a seat, and a knee-space vanity. Second-floor sleeping quarters are connected by a balcony hall that leads to a sizable game room.

FIRST FLOOR

SECOND FLOOR

© William E. Poole Designs, Inc.

plan# HPK2900054

FIRST FLOOR: 2,320 SQ. FT.
SECOND FLOOR: 1,009 SQ. FT.
TOTAL: 3,329 SQ. FT.
BONUS SPACE: 521 SQ. FT.
BEDROOMS: 4
BATHROOMS: 3½
WIDTH: 80' - 4"
DEPTH: 58' - 0"
FOUNDATION: CRAWLSPACE

ORDER ONLINE @ EPLANS.COM

Sturdy columns on a spacious, welcoming front porch lend a Greek Revival feel to this design, and three dormer windows provide a relaxed country look. The living and dining rooms, each with a fireplace, flank the two-story foyer; the family room also includes a fireplace, as well as built-in shelves and a wall of windows. The L-shaped kitchen, conveniently near the breakfast area, features a work island and a large pantry. Two walk-in closets highlight the lavish master suite, which offers a private bath with a soothing whirlpool tub. Three family bedrooms—all with dormer alcoves and two with walk-in closets—sit upstairs, along with a future recreation room.

FIRST FLOOR

SECOND FLOOR

© William E. Poole Designs, Inc.

plan # HPK2900055

FIRST FLOOR: 2,191 SQ. FT.
SECOND FLOOR: 1,220 SQ. FT.
TOTAL: 3,411 SQ. FT.
BONUS SPACE: 280 SQ. FT.
BEDROOMS: 4
BATHROOMS: 3½
WIDTH: 75' - 8"
DEPTH: 54' - 4"
FOUNDATION: CRAWLSPACE,
UNFINISHED BASEMENT

ORDER ONLINE @ EPLANS.COM

This Colonial farmhouse will be the showpiece of your neighborhood. Come in from the wide front porch through French doors topped by a sunburst window. Continue past the formal dining and living rooms to a columned gallery and a large family room with a focal fireplace. The kitchen astounds with a unique layout, an island, and abundant counter and cabinet space. The master bath balances luxury with efficiency. Three upstairs bedrooms enjoy amenities such as dormer windows or walk-in closets. Bonus space is ready for expansion as your needs change.

FIRST FLOOR

SECOND FLOOR

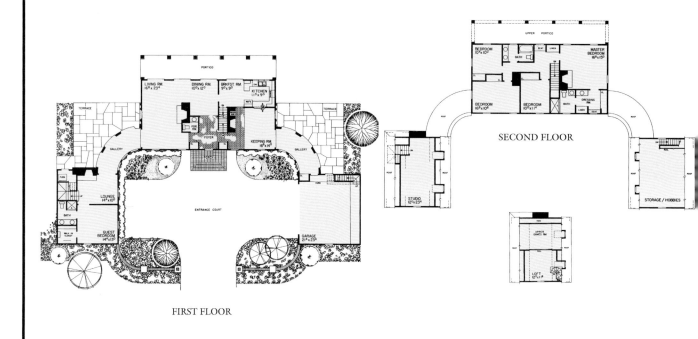

plan# HPK2900056

FIRST FLOOR: 1,992 SQ. FT.
SECOND FLOOR: 1,458 SQ. FT.
TOTAL: 3,450 SQ. FT.
BONUS SPACE: 380 SQ. FT.
BEDROOMS: 5
BATHROOMS: 3½
WIDTH: 108' - 0"
DEPTH: 64' - 0"
FOUNDATION: UNFINISHED
BASEMENT

ORDER ONLINE @ EPLANS.COM

The origin of this house dates back to 1787 and George Washington's stately Mount Vernon. The unusual design features curved galleries leading to matching wings. In the main house, the living and dining rooms provide a large open area, with access to the rear porch for additional entertaining possibilities. A keeping room features a pass-through to the kitchen and a fireplace with a built-in wood box. Four bedrooms, including a master suite with a fireplace, are found upstairs. One wing contains separate guest quarters with a full bath, a lounge area, and an upstairs studio, which features a spiral staircase and a loft area. On the other side of the house, the second floor over the garage can be used for storage or as a hobby room.

FIRST FLOOR

SECOND FLOOR

plan # HPK2900057

FIRST FLOOR: 2,033 SQ. FT.
SECOND FLOOR: 1,447 SQ. FT.
TOTAL: 3,480 SQ. FT.
BONUS SPACE: 411 SQ. FT.
BEDROOMS: 3
BATHROOMS: 3½
WIDTH: 67' - 10"
DEPTH: 64' - 4"
FOUNDATION: CRAWLSPACE,
UNFINISHED BASEMENT,
UNFINISHED WALKOUT
BASEMENT

ORDER ONLINE @ EPLANS.COM

Southern grandeur is evident in this wonderful two-story design with its magnificent second-floor balcony. The formal living spaces—dining room and living room—flank the impressive foyer with its stunning staircase. The family room resides in the rear, opening to the terrace. The sunny breakfast bay adjoins the island kitchen for efficient planning. The right wing holds the two-car garage, utility room, a secondary staircase, and a study that can easily be converted to a guest suite with a private bath. The master suite and Bedrooms 2 and 3 are placed on the second floor.

SECOND FLOOR

FIRST FLOOR

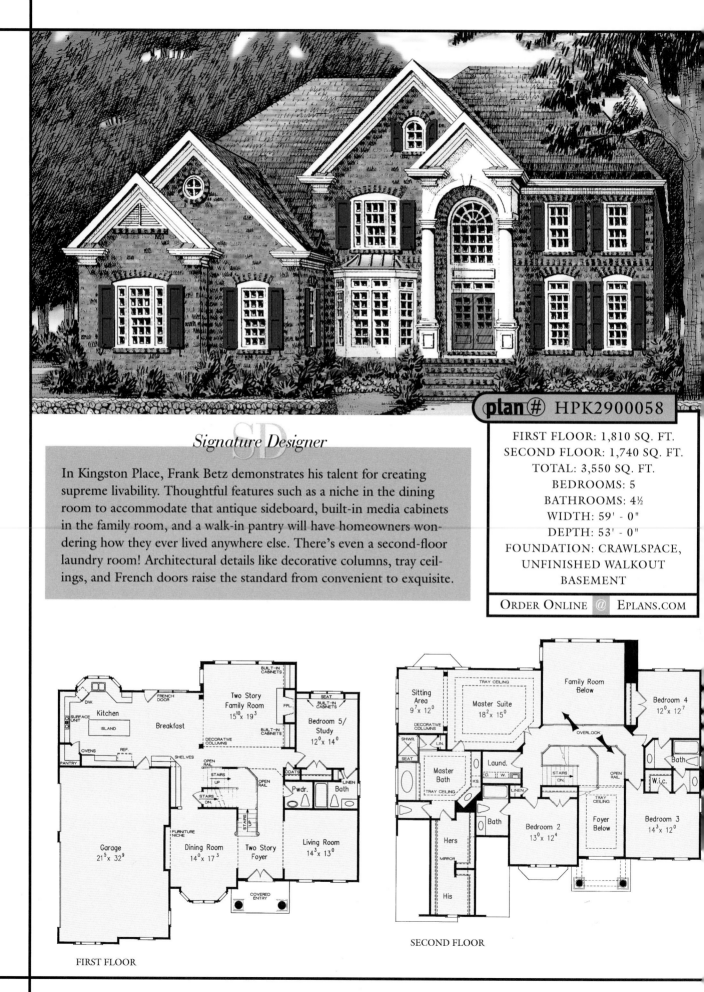

plan# HPK2900058

FIRST FLOOR: 1,810 SQ. FT.
SECOND FLOOR: 1,740 SQ. FT.
TOTAL: 3,550 SQ. FT.
BEDROOMS: 5
BATHROOMS: 4½
WIDTH: 59' - 0"
DEPTH: 53' - 0"
FOUNDATION: CRAWLSPACE,
UNFINISHED WALKOUT
BASEMENT

ORDER ONLINE @ EPLANS.COM

Signature Designer

In Kingston Place, Frank Betz demonstrates his talent for creating supreme livability. Thoughtful features such as a niche in the dining room to accommodate that antique sideboard, built-in media cabinets in the family room, and a walk-in pantry will have homeowners wondering how they ever lived anywhere else. There's even a second-floor laundry room! Architectural details like decorative columns, tray ceilings, and French doors raise the standard from convenient to exquisite.

FIRST FLOOR

SECOND FLOOR

plan # HPK2900059

FIRST FLOOR: 2,483 SQ. FT.
SECOND FLOOR: 1,127 SQ. FT.
TOTAL: 3,610 SQ. FT.
BONUS SPACE: 332 SQ. FT.
BEDROOMS: 4
BATHROOMS: 3½
WIDTH: 83' - 0"
DEPTH: 71' - 8"
FOUNDATION: SLAB

ORDER ONLINE @ EPLANS.COM

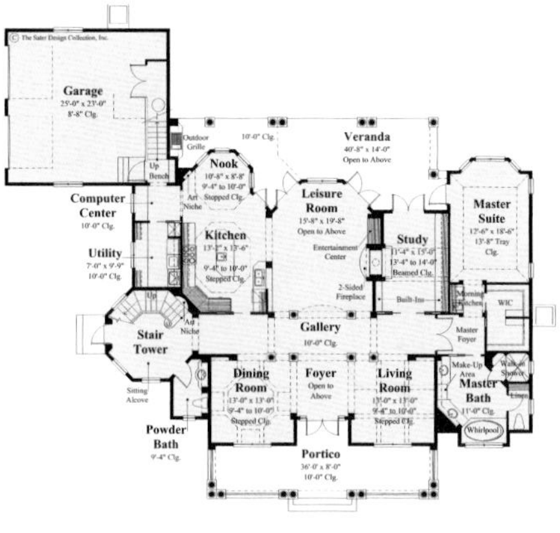

FIRST FLOOR

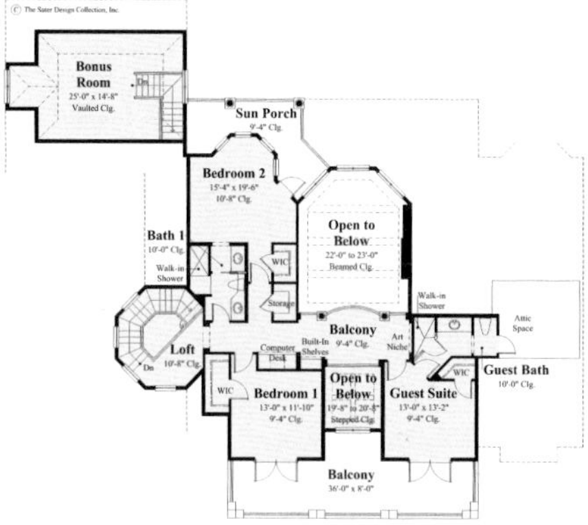

SECOND FLOOR

© The Sater Design Collection, Inc.

plan # HPK2900060

FIRST FLOOR: 2,484 SQ. FT.
SECOND FLOOR: 1,127 SQ. FT.
TOTAL: 3,611 SQ. FT.
BONUS SPACE: 332 SQ. FT.
BEDROOMS: 4
BATHROOMS: 3½
WIDTH: 83' - 0"
DEPTH: 71' - 8"
FOUNDATION: SLAB

ORDER ONLINE @ EPLANS.COM

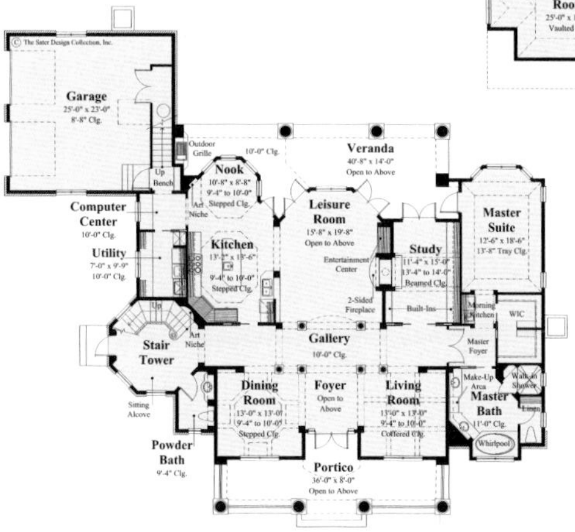

FIRST FLOOR

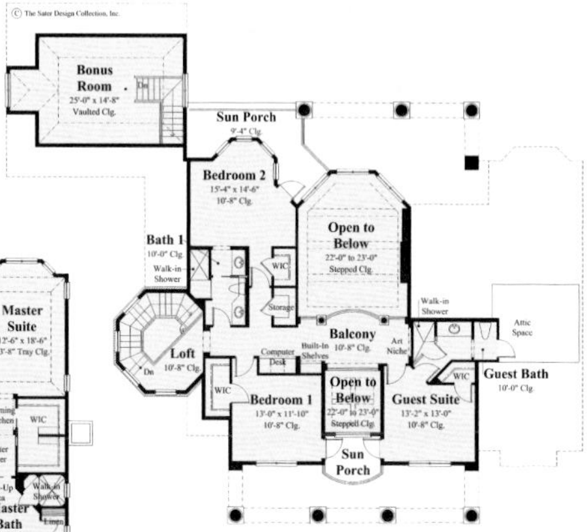

SECOND FLOOR

© The Sater Design Collection, Inc.

FIRST FLOOR

SECOND FLOOR

plan# HPK2900061

FIRST FLOOR: 2,772 SQ. FT.
SECOND FLOOR: 933 SQ. FT.
TOTAL: 3,705 SQ. FT.
BEDROOMS: 4
BATHROOMS: 4½
WIDTH: 74' - 8"
DEPTH: 61' - 10"
FOUNDATION: CRAWLSPACE,
SLAB

ORDER ONLINE @ Eplans.com

plan# HPK2900062

SQUARE FOOTAGE: 3,790
BEDROOMS: 4
BATHROOMS: 3½
WIDTH: 80' - 8"
DEPTH: 107' - 8"
FOUNDATION: SLAB

ORDER ONLINE @ Eplans.com

OPTIONAL LAYOUT

© The Sater Design Collection, Inc.

plan # HPK2900063

FIRST FLOOR: 2,608 SQ. FT.
SECOND FLOOR: 1,432 SQ. FT.
TOTAL: 4,040 SQ. FT.
BEDROOMS: 4
BATHROOMS: 3½
WIDTH: 89' - 10"
DEPTH: 63' - 8"
FOUNDATION: CRAWLSPACE,
SLAB

ORDER ONLINE @ EPLANS.COM

A distinctively French flair is the hallmark of this European design. Inside, the two-story foyer provides views to the huge great room beyond. A well-placed study off the foyer provides space for a home office. The kitchen, breakfast room, and sunroom are adjacent and lend a spacious feel. The great room is visible from this area through decorative arches. The master suite includes a roomy sitting area and a lovely bath with a centerpiece whirlpool tub flanked by half-columns. Upstairs, Bedrooms 2 and 3 share a bath that includes separate dressing areas.

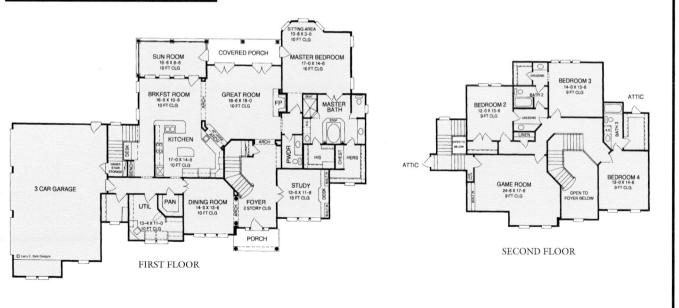

FIRST FLOOR

SECOND FLOOR

HELPFUL HINT: Bonus rooms generally are not calculated in the total square footage of a home.

© William E. Poole Designs, Inc.

plan# HPK2900064

FIRST FLOOR: 2,603 SQ. FT.
SECOND FLOOR: 1,660 SQ. FT.
TOTAL: 4,263 SQ. FT.
BONUS SPACE: 669 SQ. FT.
BEDROOMS: 4
BATHROOMS: 4½ + ½
WIDTH: 98' - 0"
DEPTH: 56' - 8"
FOUNDATION: UNFINISHED
BASEMENT

ORDER ONLINE @ EPLANS.COM

This fine example of the Georgian style of architecture offers a wonderful facade with Southern charm. The foyer is flanked by the formal dining room and the living room. The efficient kitchen is situated between the sunny breakfast nook and the dining room. The family room opens to the backyard. The master suite enjoys an opulent bath and large walk-in closet. The second floor presents three bedrooms and two baths.

FIRST FLOOR

SECOND FLOOR

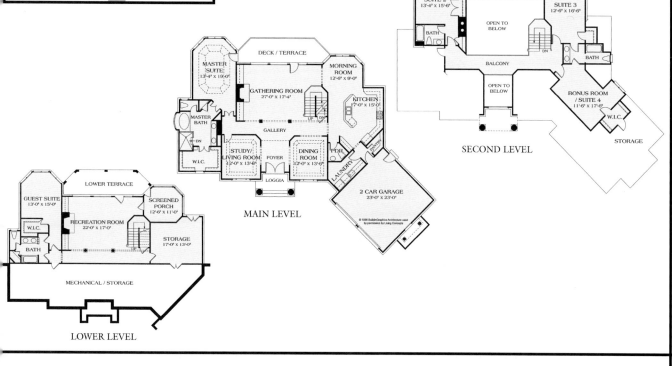

plan# HPK2900065

MAIN LEVEL: 2,293 SQ. FT.
SECOND LEVEL: 949 SQ. FT.
LOWER LEVEL: 1,088 SQ. FT.
TOTAL: 4,330 SQ. FT.
BONUS SPACE: 373 SQ. FT.
BEDROOMS: 4
BATHROOMS: 4½
WIDTH: 82' - 6"
DEPTH: 67' - 2"
FOUNDATION: FINISHED
WALKOUT BASEMENT

ORDER ONLINE @ Eplans.com

From its dramatic front entry to its rear twin turrets, this design is as traditional as it is historic. A two-story foyer opens through a gallery to an expansive gathering room, which shares its natural light with a bumped-out morning nook. A formal living room or study offers a coffered ceiling and a private door to the gallery hall that leads to the master suite. The dining room opens to more casual living space, including the kitchen with its angled island counter. Bonus space may be developed later.

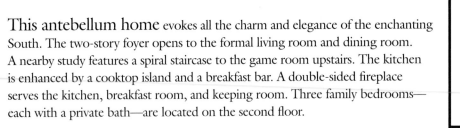

This antebellum home evokes all the charm and elegance of the enchanting South. The two-story foyer opens to the formal living room and dining room. A nearby study features a spiral staircase to the game room upstairs. The kitchen is enhanced by a cooktop island and a breakfast bar. A double-sided fireplace serves the kitchen, breakfast room, and keeping room. Three family bedrooms— each with a private bath—are located on the second floor.

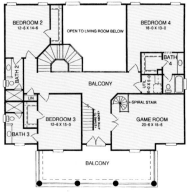

SECOND FLOOR

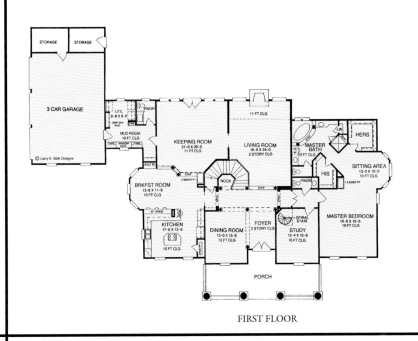

FIRST FLOOR

plan ⊕ HPK2900067

FIRST FLOOR: 3,170 SQ. FT.
SECOND FLOOR: 1,914 SQ. FT.
TOTAL: 5,084 SQ. FT.
BONUS SPACE: 445 SQ. FT.
BEDROOMS: 4
BATHROOMS: 3½
WIDTH: 100' - 10"
DEPTH: 65' - 5"
FOUNDATION: CRAWLSPACE

ORDER ONLINE @ EPLANS.COM

This elegantly appointed home is a beauty inside and out. A centerpiece stair rises gracefully from the two-story grand foyer. The kitchen, breakfast room, and family room provide open space for the gathering of family and friends. The beam-ceilinged study and the dining room flank the grand foyer, and each includes a fireplace. The master bedroom features a cozy sitting area and a luxury master bath with His and Hers vanities and walk-in closets. Three large bedrooms and a game room complete the second floor. A large expandable area is available at the top of the rear stair.

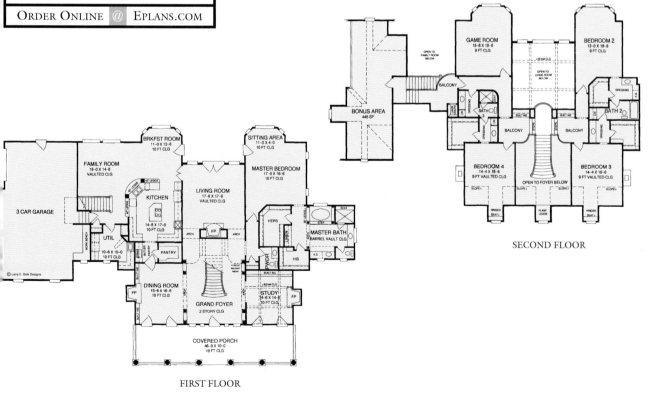

FIRST FLOOR

SECOND FLOOR

plan # HPK2900068

FIRST FLOOR: 3,599 SQ. FT.
SECOND FLOOR: 1,621 SQ. FT.
TOTAL: 5,220 SQ. FT.
BONUS SPACE: 537 SQ. FT.
BEDROOMS: 4
BATHROOMS: 5½
WIDTH: 108' - 10"
DEPTH: 53' - 10"
FOUNDATION: SLAB,
UNFINISHED BASEMENT

ORDER ONLINE @ EPLANS.COM

A grand facade detailed with brick corner quoins, stucco flourishes, arched windows, and an elegant entrance presents this home. A spacious foyer is accented by curving stairs and flanked by a formal living room and a formal dining room. For cozy times, a through-fireplace is located between a large family room and a quiet study. The master bedroom is designed to pamper, with two walk-in closets, a two-sided fireplace, a bayed sitting area, and a lavish private bath. Upstairs, three secondary bedrooms each have a private bath and a walk-in closet. Also on this level is a spacious recreation room, perfect for a game room or children's playroom.

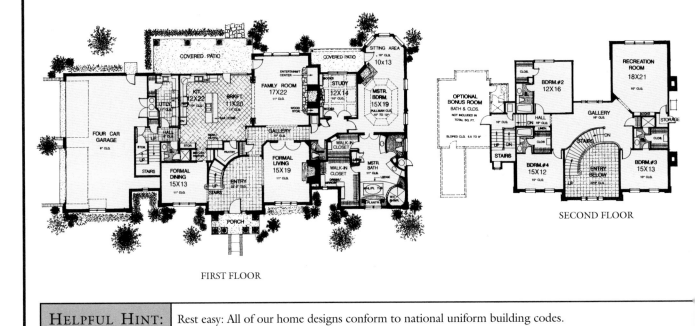

FIRST FLOOR

SECOND FLOOR

| HELPFUL HINT: | Rest easy: All of our home designs conform to national uniform building codes. |

plan# HPK2900069

FIRST FLOOR 3,413 SQ. FT.
SECOND FLOOR: 2,076 SQ. FT.
TOTAL: 5,489 SQ. FT.
BEDROOMS: 4
BATHROOMS: 3½
WIDTH: 90' - 6"
DEPTH: 63' - 6"
FOUNDATION: UNFINISHED
BASEMENT

ORDER ONLINE @ EPLANS.COM

Classic design combined with dynamite interiors make this executive home a real gem. Inside, a free-floating curved staircase rises majestically to the second floor. The enormous living room, great for formal entertaining, features a dramatic two-story window wall. The family room, breakfast room, and kitchen are conveniently grouped. A large pantry and a companion butler's pantry serve both the dining room and kitchen. Privately located, the master suite includes a sitting area and a sumptuous master bath. The second floor contains Bedroom 2, which has a private bath. Bedrooms 3 and 4 share a bath that includes two private dressing areas. A large game room is accessed from a rear stair.

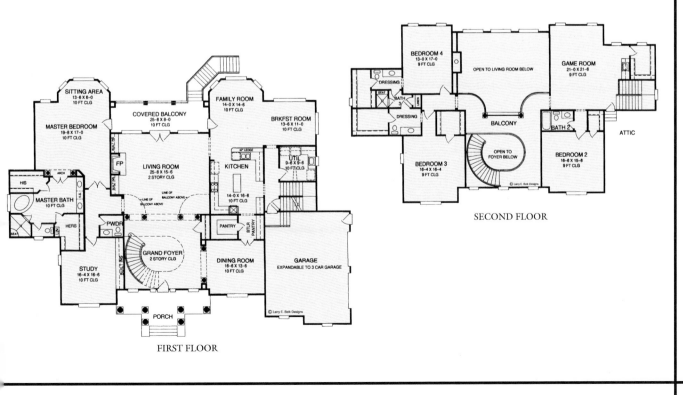

FIRST FLOOR

SECOND FLOOR

A richly detailed entrance sets the elegant tone of this luxurious design. Rising gracefully from the two-story foyer, the staircase is a fine prelude to the great room beyond, where a fantastic span of windows on the back wall overlooks the rear grounds. The dining room is located off the entry and has a lovely coffered ceiling. The kitchen, breakfast room, and sunroom are conveniently grouped for casual entertaining. The elaborate master suite enjoys a coffered ceiling, private sitting room, and spa-style bath. The second level consists of four bedrooms with private baths and a large game room featuring a rear stair.

STYLE: NEW AMERICAN
FIRST FLOOR: 3,722 SQ. FT.
SECOND FLOOR: 1,859 SQ. FT.
TOTAL: 5,581 SQ. FT.
BEDROOMS: 5
BATHROOMS: 4½
WIDTH: 127' - 10"
DEPTH: 83' - 9"
FOUNDATION: SLAB

ORDER ONLINE @ EPLANS.COM

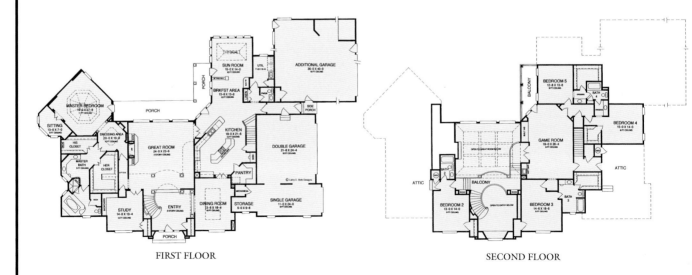

FIRST FLOOR

SECOND FLOOR

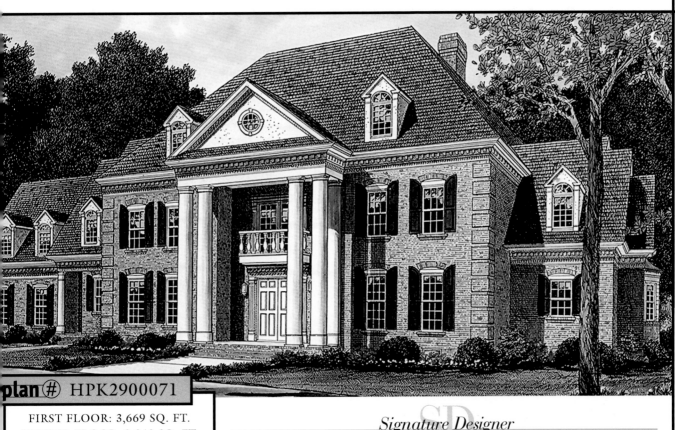

plan # HPK2900071

FIRST FLOOR: 3,669 SQ. FT.
SECOND FLOOR: 2,048 SQ. FT.
TOTAL: 5,717 SQ. FT.
BONUS SPACE: 375 SQ. FT.
BEDROOMS: 5
BATHROOMS: 4½ + ½
WIDTH: 108' - 10"
DEPTH: 72' - 0"
FOUNDATION: CRAWLSPACE

ORDER ONLINE @ EPLANS.COM

Signature Designer

Living Concepts's reputation for designing homes in a grand style is demonstrated in the Augusta. The name alone evokes images of columned porticos and sweeping stairways, and the plan delivers on those sweet Southern promises. The home is designed for entertaining as well as luxurious living. Both public and private spaces are well-planned and exquisitely detailed.

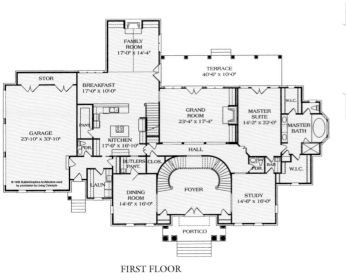

FIRST FLOOR

SECOND FLOOR

This farmhouse encompasses all the comforts country style has to offer, and more. A front porch is a welcome site on many of these plans, and the matching dormer windows on Stephen Fuller's Meadowview—complete with flower boxes—adds that touch of country charm.

Part of what makes this style so comforting is the abundance of casual spaces, designed with the intent of warm family gatherings and conversation among friends. The Meadowview creates this atmosphere with a hearth-warmed keeping room that fully opens to the island kitchen and a game room on the second floor. The formal spaces are not lacking warmth, either. Even the dining room, a space often dedicated for special occasions, has a welcoming openness about it,

Hearth Warming

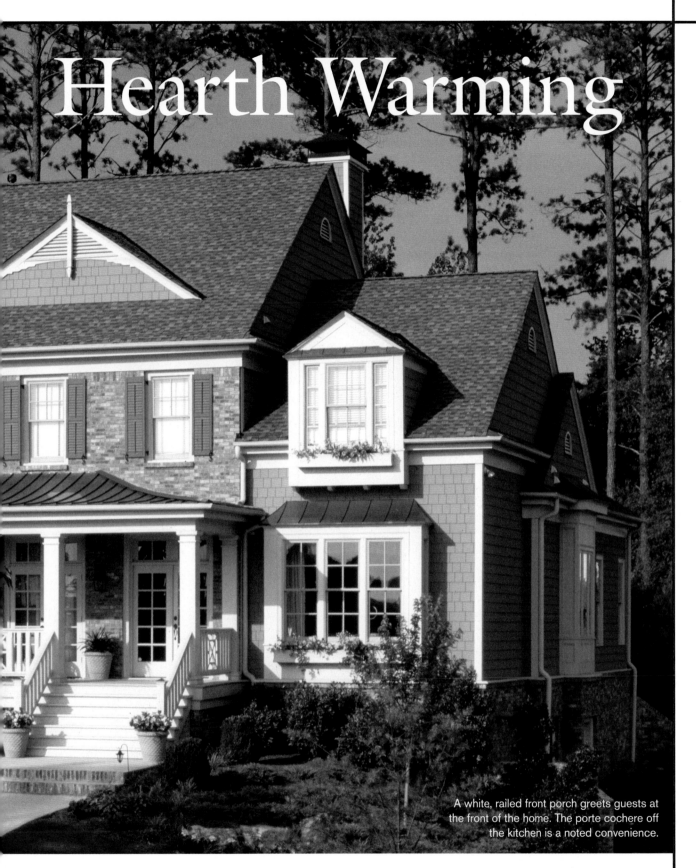

A white, railed front porch greets guests at the front of the home. The porte cochere off the kitchen is a noted convenience.

with two sets of French doors that open onto the front porch and little more than a couple of columns separating it from the foyer.

Country style is also found in details. Low coffered ceilings keep rooms cozy, and there can never be enough fireplaces; Meadowview has one in the keeping room, study, and living room. The heart of every country home is the kitchen, and this one has all the latest appliances and plenty of counter space so multiple cooks can help.

Because at the core of this style is family togetherness, plans in the section also include abundant outdoor spaces for entertaining. The requisite front porch is reserved for greeting guests and chit-chatting with neighbors, while a back deck or patio accommodates cookouts and festivities under the stars.

ABOVE: A box-bay window off the kitchen is the perfect spot to house a casual dining table for breakfast and other laid-back meals. RIGHT: A larger-than-life kitchen is equipped to serve the family brood plus a houseful of visitors. TOP LEFT: One of three fireplaces in the Meadowview warms the front-facing study. TOP RIGHT: The L shape of the rear facade and three-car garage borders an in-ground pool.

plan # HPK2900072

FIRST FLOOR: 3,132 SQ. FT.
SECOND FLOOR: 2,280 SQ. FT.
TOTAL: 5,412 SQ. FT.
BEDROOMS: 4
BATHROOMS: 3½
WIDTH: 99' - 3"
DEPTH: 93' - 6"
FOUNDATION: UNFINISHED
BASEMENT

ORDER ONLINE @ EPLANS.COM

FIRST FLOOR

Three Car Garage 24'⁹ x 33'⁰
Porte Cochere
Office 8'⁰ x 9'⁰
Kitchen 13'⁶ x 10'⁰
Keeping Room 16'⁰ x 12'⁶
Dining Room 16' x 14'⁰
Great Room 19'⁶ x 20'³
Master Suite 16'³ x 16'⁶
Study 12'⁰ x 13'⁰
Porch

SECOND FLOOR

Bonus
Bedroom #2 16' x 13'⁰
Game Room 22' x 18'⁰
Bedroom #3 16' x 14'⁰
Bedroom #4 15'⁶ x 13'⁰

plan # HPK2900073

SQUARE FOOTAGE: 1,093
BEDROOMS: 2
BATHROOMS: 2
WIDTH: 35' - 0"
DEPTH: 56' - 0"
FOUNDATION: SLAB

ORDER ONLINE @ EPLANS.COM

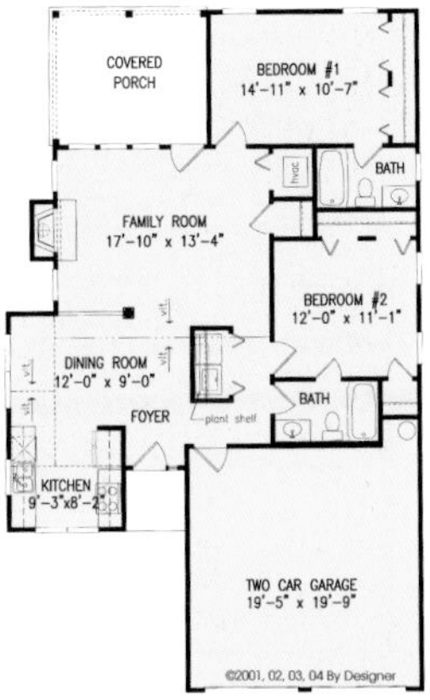

plan # HPK2900074

SQUARE FOOTAGE: 1,295
BEDROOMS: 2
BATHROOMS: 2
WIDTH: 48' - 0"
DEPTH: 59' - 0"
FOUNDATION: UNFINISHED BASEMENT

ORDER ONLINE @ EPLANS.COM

HELPFUL HINT:

Reproducible plans are printed on vellum or Mylar.

plan # HPK2900075

SQUARE FOOTAGE: 1,342
BONUS SPACE: 350 SQ. FT.
BEDROOMS: 3
BATHROOMS: 2
WIDTH: 52' - 6"
DEPTH: 39' - 10"
FOUNDATION: CRAWLSPACE,
SLAB, UNFINISHED WALKOUT
BASEMENT

ORDER ONLINE @ EPLANS.COM

plan # HPK2900076

SQUARE FOOTAGE: 1,360
BEDROOMS: 3
BATHROOMS: 2
WIDTH: 40' - 0"
DEPTH: 49' - 10"
FOUNDATION: SLAB

ORDER ONLINE @ EPLANS.COM

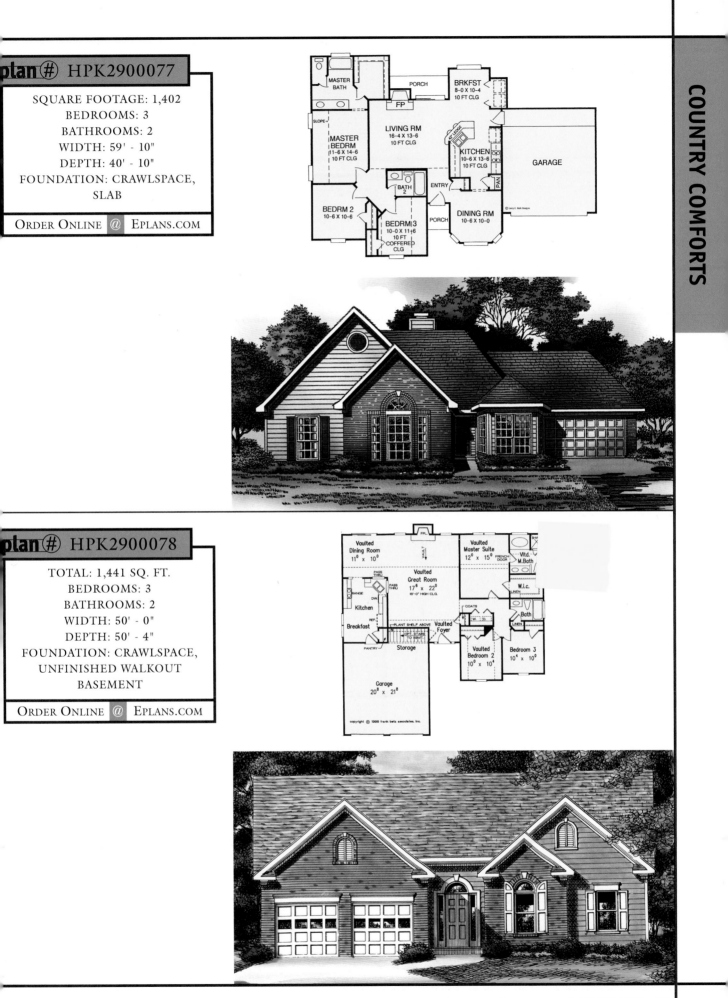

eplan(#) HPK2900077

SQUARE FOOTAGE: 1,402
BEDROOMS: 3
BATHROOMS: 2
WIDTH: 59' - 10"
DEPTH: 40' - 10"
FOUNDATION: CRAWLSPACE,
SLAB

ORDER ONLINE @ EPLANS.COM

MASTER BATH

PORCH

BRKFST
8-0 X 10-4
10 FT CLG

FP

LIVING RM
16-4 X 13-6
10 FT CLG

MASTER BEDRM
11-6 X 14-6
10 FT CLG

SLOPE

KITCHEN
10-6 X 13-6
10 FT CLG

GARAGE

BATH 2

ENTRY

PAN

BEDRM 2
10-6 X 10-6

BEDRM 3
10-0 X 11-6
10 FT COFFERED CLG

PORCH

DINING RM
10-6 X 10-0

eplan(#) HPK2900078

TOTAL: 1,441 SQ. FT.
BEDROOMS: 3
BATHROOMS: 2
WIDTH: 50' - 0"
DEPTH: 50' - 4"
FOUNDATION: CRAWLSPACE,
UNFINISHED WALKOUT
BASEMENT

ORDER ONLINE @ EPLANS.COM

FPL

Vaulted Dining Room
11⁰ x 10⁰

VAULT

Vaulted Master Suite
12⁰ x 15⁰

Vltd. M.Bath

PASS THRU

Vaulted Great Room
17⁶ x 22⁰
15'-0" HIGH CLG.

FRENCH DOOR

RANGE

PASS THRU

W.i.c.

Kitchen

LINEN

COATS

REF.

Breakfast

PLANT SHELF ABOVE

W. S.D.

Bath

LINEN

OPT. STAIRS TO BSMT.

Vaulted Foyer

Vaulted Bedroom 2
10⁰ x 10⁴

Bedroom 3
10⁴ x 10⁰

PANTRY

Storage

Garage
20⁸ x 21⁸

copyright © 1999 frank betz associates, inc.

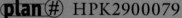

plan # HPK2900079

FIRST FLOOR: 685 SQ. FT.
SECOND FLOOR: 760 SQ. FT.
TOTAL: 1,445 SQ. FT.
BEDROOMS: 3
BATHROOMS: 2½
WIDTH: 21' - 0"
DEPTH: 36' - 0"
FOUNDATION: UNFINISHED
BASEMENT

ORDER ONLINE @ EPLANS.COM

Here's a plan with lots of flexibility. It comes with two garage alternatives—rear-loading or front-loading—and open space to organize the living and dining areas to suit your needs. There's also an option of adding a fireplace. The kitchen is marked off from the living/dining area by a handy snack bar. Upstairs, a master suite with a dual-sink vanity enjoys a private bath; two family bedrooms share a bath. This plan is well-suited for a narrow lot.

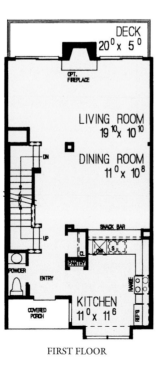

FIRST FLOOR

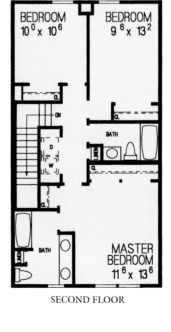

SECOND FLOOR

plan # HPK2900080

SQUARE FOOTAGE: 1,455
BEDROOMS: 3
BATHROOMS: 2
WIDTH: 50' - 6"
DEPTH: 38' - 0"
FOUNDATION: CRAWLSPACE,
UNFINISHED BASEMENT

ORDER ONLINE @ EPLANS.COM

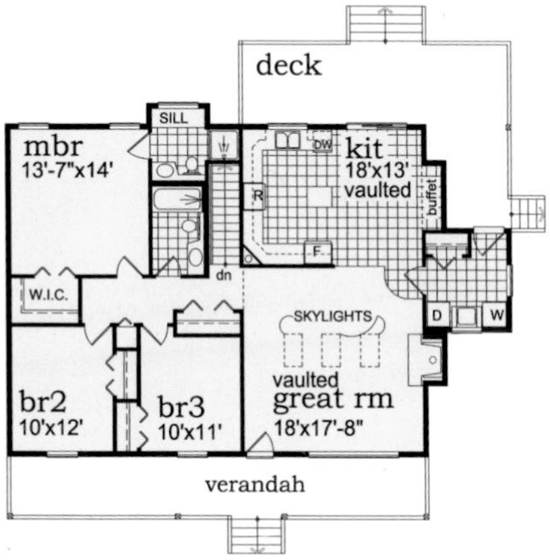

plan # HPK2900081

SQUARE FOOTAGE: 1,456
BEDROOMS: 3
BATHROOMS: 2
WIDTH: 54' - 0"
DEPTH: 45' - 6"
FOUNDATION: CRAWLSPACE

ORDER ONLINE @ EPLANS.COM

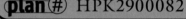

plan# HPK2900082

FIRST FLOOR: 768 SQ. FT.
SECOND FLOOR: 690 SQ. FT.
TOTAL: 1,458 SQ. FT.
BEDROOMS: 3
BATHROOMS: 2½
WIDTH: 32' - 0"
DEPTH: 24' - 0"
FOUNDATION: UNFINISHED
BASEMENT

ORDER ONLINE @ EPLANS.COM

This cottage, complete with sweeping rooflines, is dazzled with country allure. The covered front porch is perfect for rocking chairs on cool summer nights. Enter into the foyer, which features a coat closet. To the right, the dining room connects to an island-cooktop kitchen. To the left, the spacious living room overlooks the front yard. A laundry room is located at the rear of the plan, near a secondary coat closet and a back door to the outside. Upstairs, the master bedroom contains a large walk-in closet and a private bath. Two additional bedrooms share a hall bath.

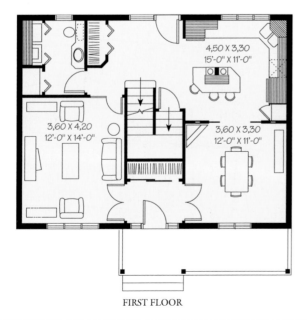

FIRST FLOOR

SECOND FLOOR

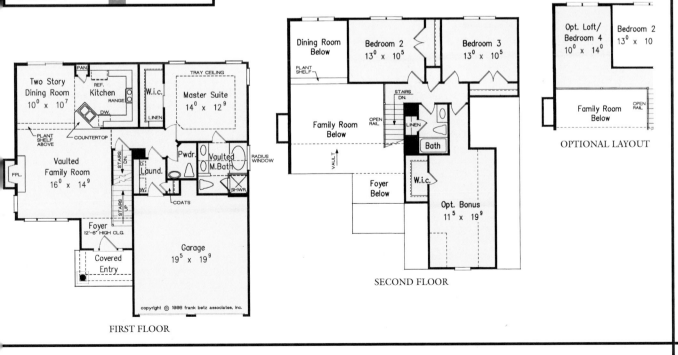

plan # HPK2900083

FIRST FLOOR: 1,001 SQ. FT.
SECOND FLOOR: 466 SQ. FT.
TOTAL: 1,467 SQ. FT.
BONUS SPACE: 292 SQ. FT.
BEDROOMS: 3
BATHROOMS: 2½
WIDTH: 42' - 0"
DEPTH: 42' - 0"
FOUNDATION: CRAWLSPACE, SLAB, UNFINISHED WALKOUT BASEMENT

ORDER ONLINE @ EPLANS.COM

Signature Designer

A street-side beauty, this home provides all the amenities one could desire in 1,500 square feet. Designer Frank Betz keeps it simple, creating an ideal home for a couple of empty-nesters or first-time home-owners who still crave a degree of luxury. A lack of superfluous rooms lends more space to the vital gathering, dining, and kitchen areas. The master bath is perfectly designed for sharing. Upstairs, Betz demonstrates his ability to create flexible plans, offering an option for a fourth bedroom as well as a bonus space for future expansion.

FIRST FLOOR

SECOND FLOOR

OPTIONAL LAYOUT

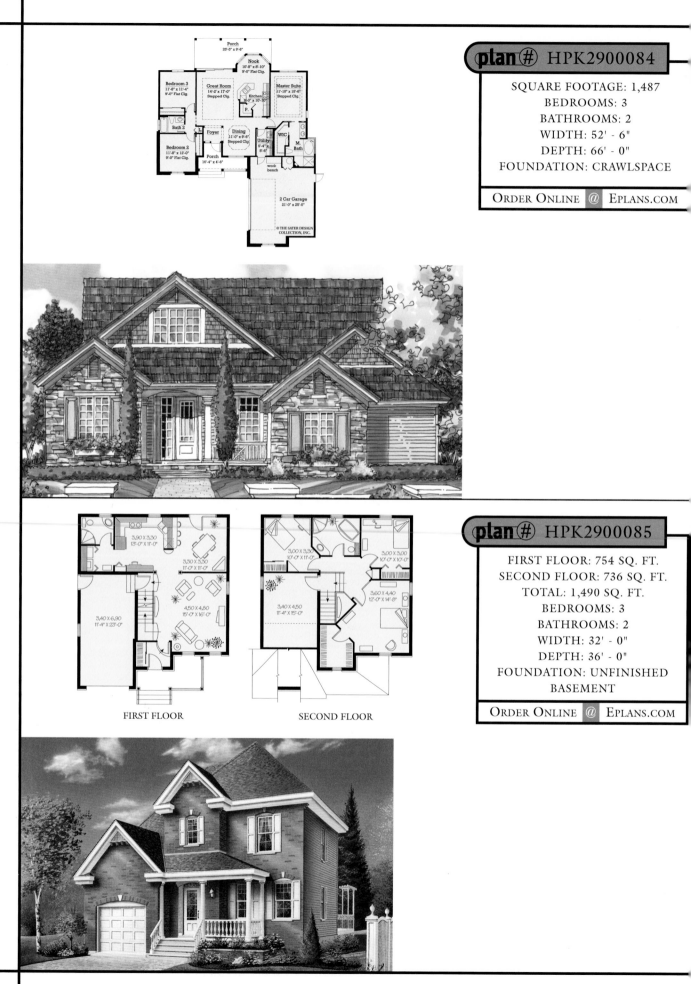

plan # HPK2900084

SQUARE FOOTAGE: 1,487
BEDROOMS: 3
BATHROOMS: 2
WIDTH: 52' - 6"
DEPTH: 66' - 0"
FOUNDATION: CRAWLSPACE

ORDER ONLINE @ EPLANS.COM

FIRST FLOOR

SECOND FLOOR

plan # HPK2900085

FIRST FLOOR: 754 SQ. FT.
SECOND FLOOR: 736 SQ. FT.
TOTAL: 1,490 SQ. FT.
BEDROOMS: 3
BATHROOMS: 2
WIDTH: 32' - 0"
DEPTH: 36' - 0"
FOUNDATION: UNFINISHED BASEMENT

ORDER ONLINE @ EPLANS.COM

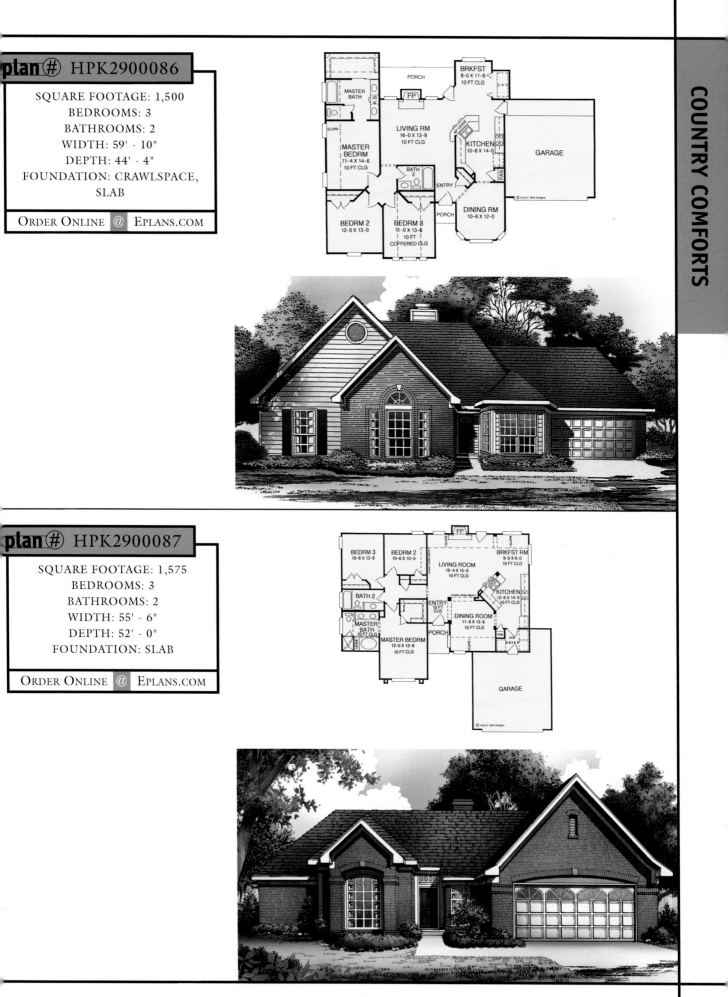

plan # HPK2900086

SQUARE FOOTAGE: 1,500
BEDROOMS: 3
BATHROOMS: 2
WIDTH: 59' - 10"
DEPTH: 44' - 4"
FOUNDATION: CRAWLSPACE,
SLAB

ORDER ONLINE @ EPLANS.COM

plan # HPK2900087

SQUARE FOOTAGE: 1,575
BEDROOMS: 3
BATHROOMS: 2
WIDTH: 55' - 6"
DEPTH: 52' - 0"
FOUNDATION: SLAB

ORDER ONLINE @ EPLANS.COM

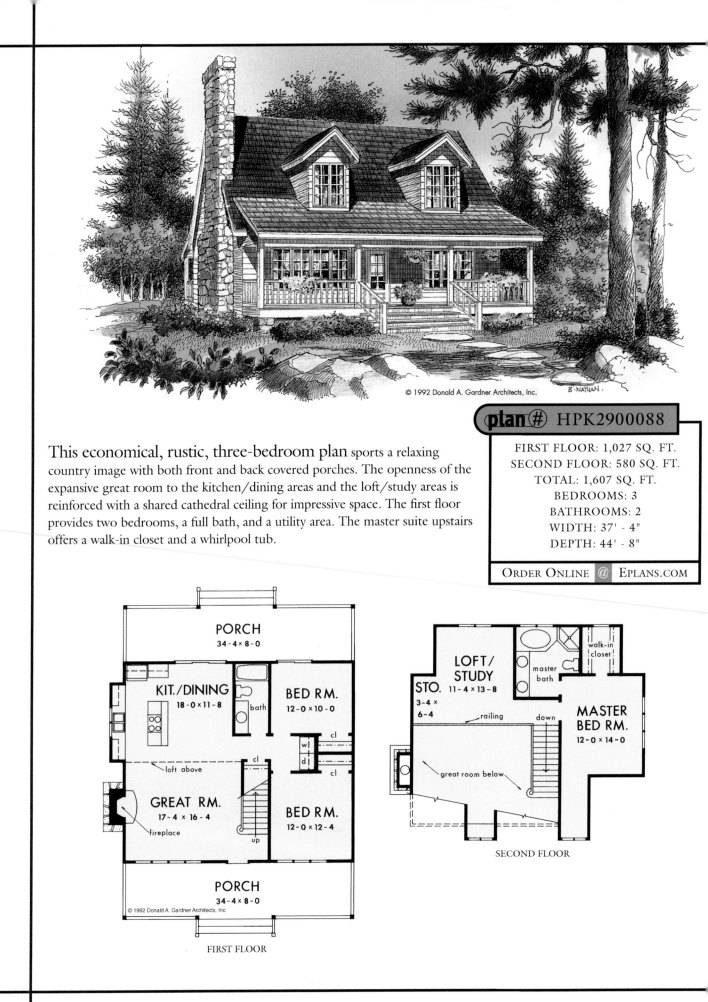

© 1992 Donald A. Gardner Architects, Inc.

B·NATHAN

This economical, rustic, three-bedroom plan sports a relaxing country image with both front and back covered porches. The openness of the expansive great room to the kitchen/dining areas and the loft/study areas is reinforced with a shared cathedral ceiling for impressive space. The first floor provides two bedrooms, a full bath, and a utility area. The master suite upstairs offers a walk-in closet and a whirlpool tub.

plan# HPK2900088

FIRST FLOOR: 1,027 SQ. FT.
SECOND FLOOR: 580 SQ. FT.
TOTAL: 1,607 SQ. FT.
BEDROOMS: 3
BATHROOMS: 2
WIDTH: 37' - 4"
DEPTH: 44' - 8"

ORDER ONLINE @ EPLANS.com

PORCH
34-4 × 8-0

KIT./DINING
18-0 × 11-8

bath

BED RM.
12-0 × 10-0

cl

w/
d

cl

cl

loft above

GREAT RM.
17-4 × 16-4

fireplace

BED RM.
12-0 × 12-4

up

PORCH
34-4 × 8-0

© 1992 Donald A. Gardner Architects, Inc.

FIRST FLOOR

STO.
3-4 ×
6-4

LOFT/ STUDY
11-4 × 13-8

master bath

walk-in closet

railing

down

MASTER BED RM.
12-0 × 14-0

great room below

SECOND FLOOR

plan # HPK2900089

SQUARE FOOTAGE: 1,611
BEDROOMS: 3
BATHROOMS: 2
WIDTH: 66' - 4"
DEPTH: 43' - 10"
FOUNDATION: UNFINISHED
BASEMENT

ORDER ONLINE @ EPLANS.COM

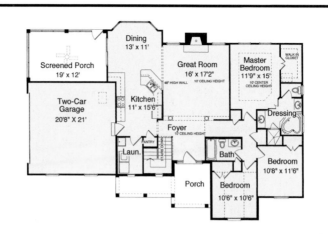

plan # HPK2900090

SQUARE FOOTAGE: 1,627
BEDROOMS: 3
BATHROOMS: 2
WIDTH: 37' - 0"
DEPTH: 66' - 0"
FOUNDATION: SLAB

ORDER ONLINE @ EPLANS.COM

HELPFUL HINT:

A Smart House design enables universal control of home theater, security, and audio systems.

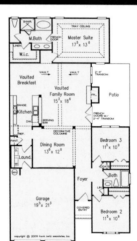

© 2003 Donald A. Gardner, Inc.

plan # HPK2900091

A Palladian window, stately columns, and gables create an abundance of style to this facade. A front-entry garage adds convenience, and front and rear porches take living to the outdoors. An open floor plan makes for easy, family-efficient living. Versatility can be found in the study/bedroom and bonus room. Special elements include decorative ceiling treatments, built-in cabinetry, and a fireplace in the great room. A column helps distinguish the formal dining room, which is located directly across from the efficient kitchen. With direct access to the rear porch through French doors, the master bedroom features a large walk-in closet, linen closet, and pampering master bath with double vanity, private toilet, and a separate shower and garden tub.

SQUARE FOOTAGE: 1,628
BONUS SPACE: 300 SQ. FT.
BEDROOMS: 3
BATHROOMS: 2
WIDTH: 56' - 0"
DEPTH: 50' - 4"

ORDER ONLINE @ EPLANS.COM

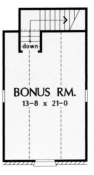

plan # HPK2900092

SQUARE FOOTAGE: 1,632
BEDROOMS: 3
BATHROOMS: 2
WIDTH: 62' - 4"
DEPTH: 55' - 2"

ORDER ONLINE @ EPLANS.COM

REAR EXTERIOR

Signature Designer

A classic Don Gardner design, the Stratford is equally appealing from the street and the backyard. This country cottage offers the kind of amenities and special touches typically found in much larger homes: elegant ceiling treatments, interior columns, and a grand fireplace. A secluded master suite is a stroke of genius, offering ultimate privacy and proving that one does not have to sacrifice luxury for sensible living.

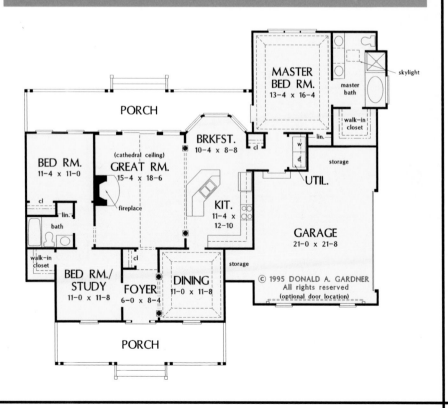

plan# HPK2900093

FIRST FLOOR: 1,177 SQ. FT.
SECOND FLOOR: 457 SQ. FT.
TOTAL: 1,634 SQ. FT.
BONUS SPACE: 249 SQ. FT.
BEDROOMS: 3
BATHROOMS: 2½
WIDTH: 41' - 0"
DEPTH: 48' - 4"
FOUNDATION: CRAWLSPACE,
UNFINISHED WALKOUT
BASEMENT

ORDER ONLINE @ EPLANS.COM

Influenced by Early American architecture, this petite rendition offers all of the amenities you love in a space designed for small lots. A two-story foyer is lit by surrounding sidelights and a multipane dormer window. The dining room flows conveniently into the efficient kitchen, which opens to the breakfast nook, brightened by sliding glass doors. The vaulted family room is warmed by an extended-hearth fireplace. Past a well-concealed laundry room, the master suite pampers with a vaulted spa bath and immense walk-in closet. Two bedrooms upstairs access future bonus space.

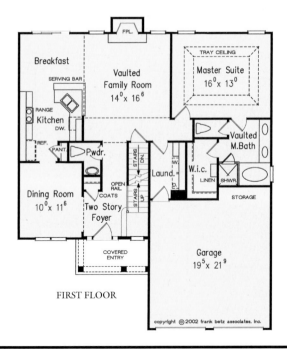

FIRST FLOOR

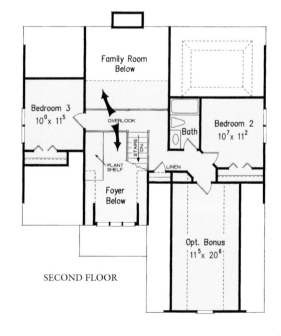

SECOND FLOOR

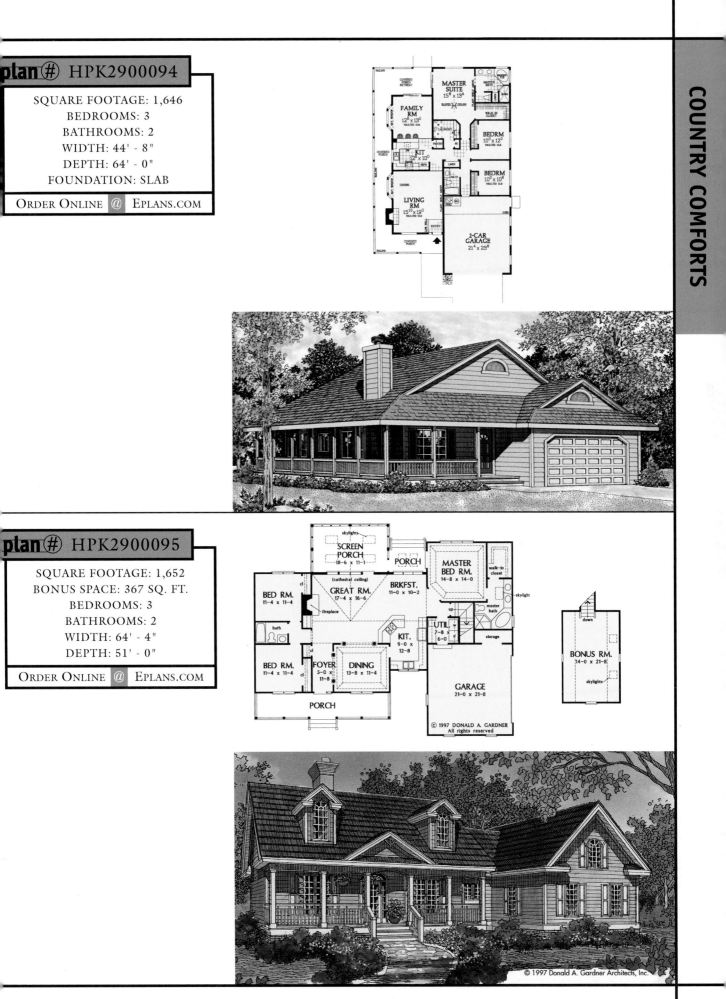

plan # HPK2900094

SQUARE FOOTAGE: 1,646
BEDROOMS: 3
BATHROOMS: 2
WIDTH: 44' - 8"
DEPTH: 64' - 0"
FOUNDATION: SLAB

ORDER ONLINE @ EPLANS.COM

plan # HPK2900095

SQUARE FOOTAGE: 1,652
BONUS SPACE: 367 SQ. FT.
BEDROOMS: 3
BATHROOMS: 2
WIDTH: 64' - 4"
DEPTH: 51' - 0"

ORDER ONLINE @ EPLANS.COM

© 1997 Donald A. Gardner Architects, Inc.

plan # HPK2900096

SQUARE FOOTAGE: 1,654
BEDROOMS: 3
BATHROOMS: 2
WIDTH: 54' - 10"
DEPTH: 69' - 10"
FOUNDATION: CRAWLSPACE, SLAB

ORDER ONLINE @ EPLANS.COM

plan # HPK2900097

FIRST FLOOR: 630 SQ. FT.
SECOND FLOOR: 1,039 SQ. FT.
TOTAL: 1,669 SQ. FT.
BEDROOMS: 3
BATHROOMS: 2
WIDTH: 44' - 6"
DEPTH: 32' - 0"
FOUNDATION: SLAB

ORDER ONLINE @ EPLANS.COM

HELPFUL HINT:

Reproducible sets include a license to build the home once.

FIRST FLOOR

SECOND FLOOR

plan # HPK2900098

FIRST FLOOR: 1,093 SQ. FT.
SECOND FLOOR: 576 SQ. FT.
TOTAL: 1,669 SQ. FT.
BEDROOMS: 3
BATHROOMS: 2
WIDTH: 52' - 0"
DEPTH: 46' - 0"
FOUNDATION: CRAWLSPACE

ORDER ONLINE @ EPLANS.COM

Here's a great country farmhouse with a lot of contemporary appeal. The generous use of windows—including two sets of triple muntin windows in the front—adds exciting visual elements to the exterior as well as plenty of natural light to the interior. An impressive tiled entry opens to a two-story great room with a raised hearth and views to the front and side grounds. The U-shaped kitchen conveniently combines with this area and offers a snack counter in addition to a casual dining nook with rear-porch access. The family bedrooms reside on the main level. An expansive master suite with an adjacent study creates a resplendent retreat upstairs, complete with a private balcony, walk-in closet, and bath.

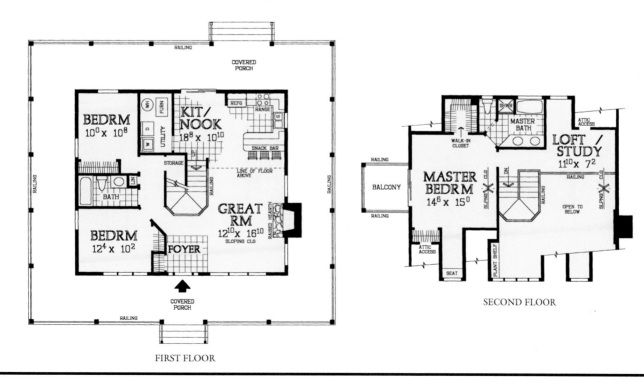

FIRST FLOOR

SECOND FLOOR

Comfortable covered porches lead you into a home that's tailor-made for casual living. The foyer offers access to a front-facing great room with a raised-hearth fireplace. The great room then flows into the breakfast nook, with outdoor access, and on to the efficient kitchen. Two family bedrooms, a shared bath, and a utility room complete the first floor. Curved stairs lead you to the upstairs master bedroom with its private balcony, large walk-in closet, and amenity-filled bath.

plan # HPK2900099

FIRST FLOOR: 1,093 SQ. FT.
SECOND FLOOR: 580 SQ. FT.
TOTAL: 1,673 SQ. FT.
BEDROOMS: 3
BATHROOMS: 2
WIDTH: 46' - 0"
DEPTH: 52' - 0"
FOUNDATION: CRAWLSPACE

ORDER ONLINE @ Eplans.com

FIRST FLOOR

SECOND FLOOR

plan # HPK2900100

SQUARE FOOTAGE: 1,688
BEDROOMS: 3
BATHROOMS: 2
WIDTH: 60' - 8"
DEPTH: 46' - 2"
FOUNDATION: CRAWLSPACE,
SLAB, UNFINISHED
BASEMENT

ORDER ONLINE @ EPLANS.COM

Stucco and siding bring a fresh new look to a traditional country home. Inside, a cathedral ceiling adds height to the great room, and a fireplace makes the room a cozy spot for relaxing. Ahead, wraparound counters make kitchen preparations a breeze. A sunny breakfast nook with porch access invites alfresco dining. Two secondary bedrooms share a full hall bath to the left; to the right, the master suite has a relaxing private bath and His and Hers closets. Future space is ready to grow as your family does.

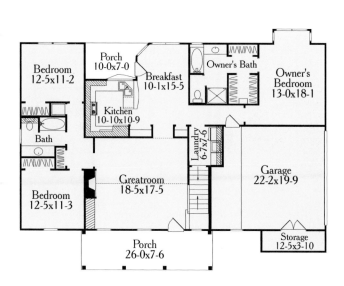

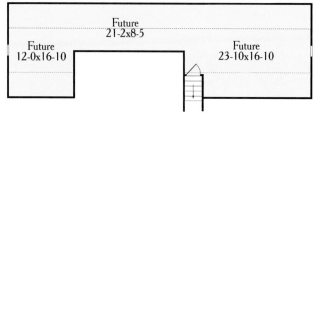

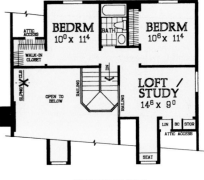

plan# HPK2900101

FIRST FLOOR: 1,093 SQ. FT.
SECOND FLOOR: 603 SQ. FT.
TOTAL: 1,696 SQ. FT.
BEDROOMS: 3
BATHROOMS: 2½
WIDTH: 52' - 0"
DEPTH: 46' - 0"
FOUNDATION: CRAWLSPACE

ORDER ONLINE @ EPLANS.COM

This two-story home's rustic design reflects thoughtful planning, including a porch that fully wraps the house in comfort and provides lots of room for rocking chairs. A stone chimney and arched windows set in dormers further enhance this home's country appeal. Inside, the floor plan is designed for maximum efficiency. A great room with a sloped ceiling enjoys a raised-hearth fireplace whose warmth radiates into the kitchen/nook. The master suite is located on the first floor and includes plenty of closet space and a private bath filled with amenities. A utility room and a powder room complete this level. The second floor contains two secondary bedrooms, a full bath, and a loft/study with a window seat.

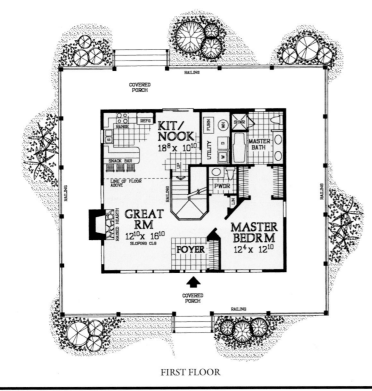

FIRST FLOOR

SECOND FLOOR

plan # HPK2900102

SQUARE FOOTAGE: 1,725
BEDROOMS: 3
BATHROOMS: 2
WIDTH: 56' - 4"
DEPTH: 72' - 8"
FOUNDATION: CRAWLSPACE,
SLAB

ORDER ONLINE @ EPLANS.COM

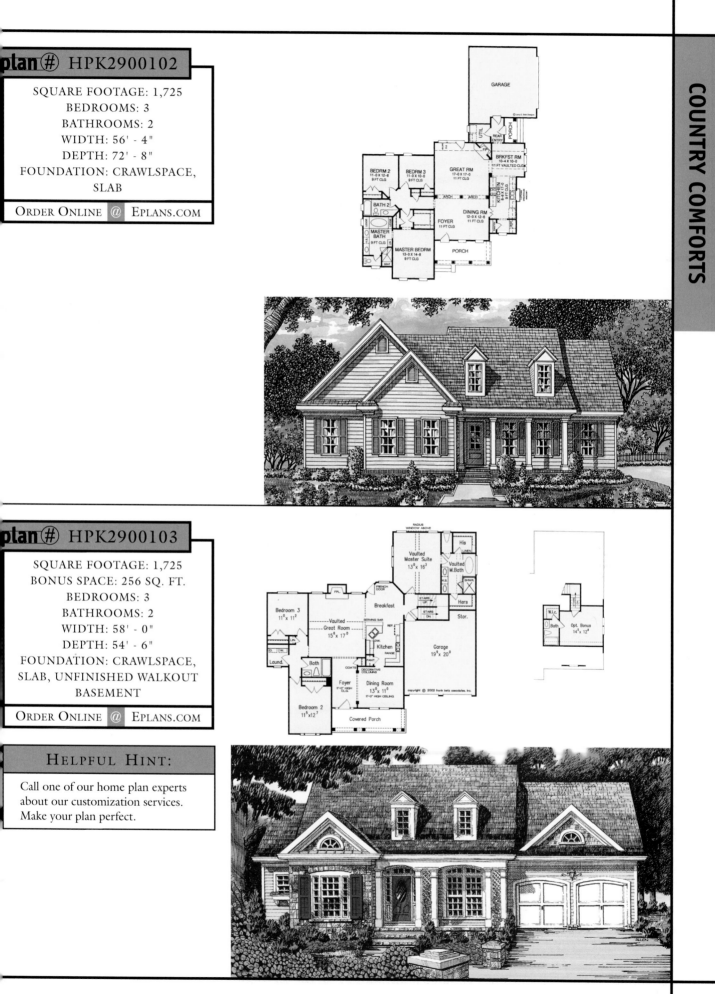

plan # HPK2900103

SQUARE FOOTAGE: 1,725
BONUS SPACE: 256 SQ. FT.
BEDROOMS: 3
BATHROOMS: 2
WIDTH: 58' - 0"
DEPTH: 54' - 6"
FOUNDATION: CRAWLSPACE,
SLAB, UNFINISHED WALKOUT
BASEMENT

ORDER ONLINE @ EPLANS.COM

HELPFUL HINT:

Call one of our home plan experts
about our customization services.
Make your plan perfect.

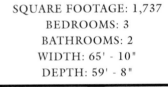

plan # HPK2900104

SQUARE FOOTAGE: 1,737
BEDROOMS: 3
BATHROOMS: 2
WIDTH: 65' - 10"
DEPTH: 59' - 8"

ORDER ONLINE @ EPLANS.COM

Signature Designer

Behind the unsophisticated charm and sensible layout of this home is architect Donald Gardner, arguably the most accomplished designer of predrawn house plans working today. This design shows an ingenious problem-solver at work: bedrooms that find great privacy in a small home and meaningful separations between the semi-formal great room and family-style kitchen. By contrast, the bayed dining room has been designed to impress. The recessed garage can be modified easily to load from the front, side, or rear.

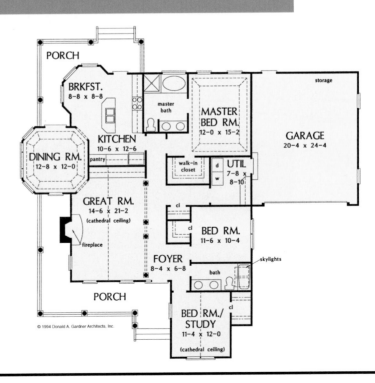

plan # HPK2900105

SQUARE FOOTAGE: 1,749
BONUS SPACE: 327 SQ. FT.
BEDROOMS: 3
BATHROOMS: 2
WIDTH: 54' - 0"
DEPTH: 56' - 6"
FOUNDATION: CRAWLSPACE,
SLAB, UNFINISHED WALKOUT
BASEMENT

ORDER ONLINE @ EPLANS.COM

This cozy country cottage is enhanced with a front-facing planter box above the garage and a charming covered porch. The foyer leads to a vaulted great room, complete with a fireplace and radius windows. Decorative columns complement the entrance to the dining room, as does the arched opening. On the left side of the plan resides the master suite, which is resplendent with amenities including a vaulted sitting room with an arched entryway, tray ceiling, and French doors to the vaulted full bath. On the right side, two additional bedrooms share a full bath.

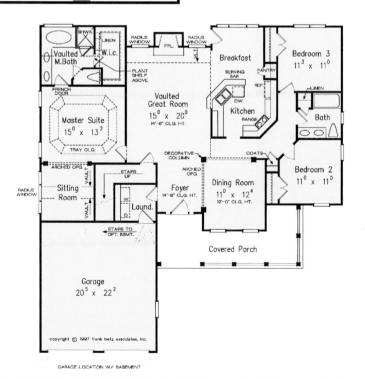

GARAGE LOCATION W/ BASEMENT

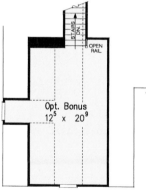

OPTIONAL BONUS ROOM PLAN

This attractive Georgian-inspired home incorporates a classic look with modern amenities for a family home that is sure to please. Follow a 14-foot ceiling from the foyer into the great room, where a warming fireplace is framed by radius windows. A creative use of counter space places the kitchen between the dining room, with decorative columns and a box-bay window, and the sunny breakfast nook. Two bedrooms on this side of the home share a full hall bath. On the far left, the master suite reigns. The bedroom is surrounded by luxurious touches, including an octagonal tray ceiling and an arched opening to the sitting room. In the vaulted bath, a garden tub will relax any stress away.

plan # HPK2900106

SQUARE FOOTAGE: 1,768
BONUS SPACE: 354 SQ. FT.
BEDROOMS: 3
BATHROOMS: 2
WIDTH: 54' - 0"
DEPTH: 59' - 6"
FOUNDATION: CRAWLSPACE,
SLAB, UNFINISHED WALKOUT
BASEMENT

ORDER ONLINE @ EPLANS.COM

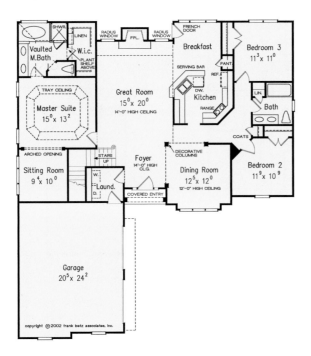

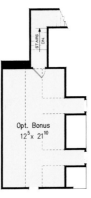

OPTIONAL LAYOUT

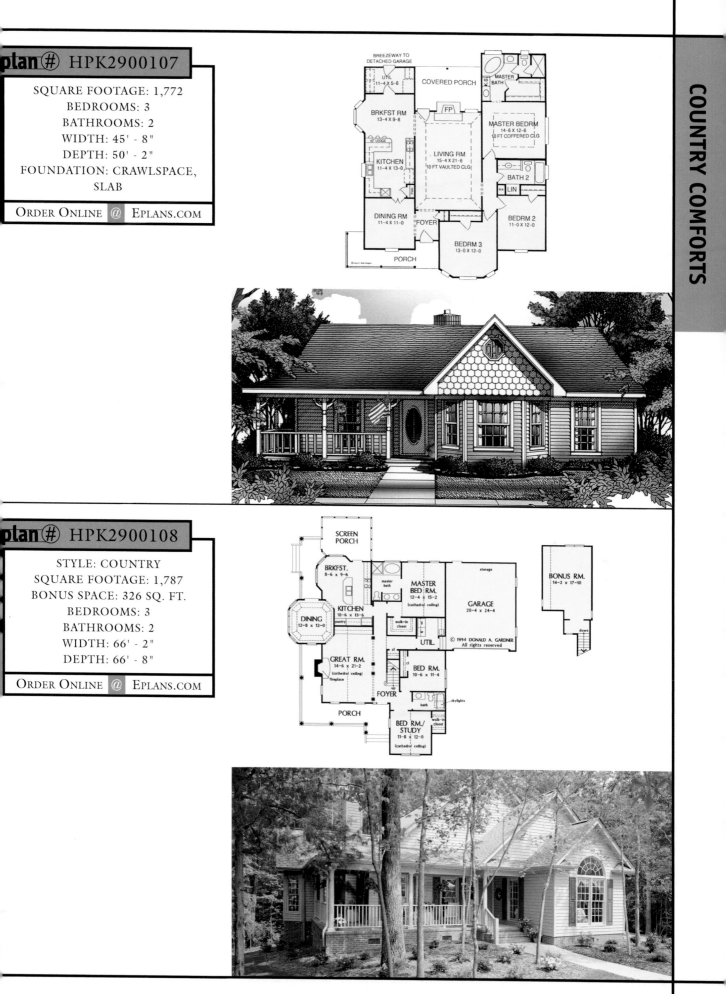

plan # HPK2900107

SQUARE FOOTAGE: 1,772
BEDROOMS: 3
BATHROOMS: 2
WIDTH: 45' - 8"
DEPTH: 50' - 2"
FOUNDATION: CRAWLSPACE,
SLAB

ORDER ONLINE @ EPLANS.COM

plan # HPK2900108

STYLE: COUNTRY
SQUARE FOOTAGE: 1,787
BONUS SPACE: 326 SQ. FT.
BEDROOMS: 3
BATHROOMS: 2
WIDTH: 66' - 2"
DEPTH: 66' - 8"

ORDER ONLINE @ EPLANS.COM

SQUARE FOOTAGE: 1,815
BONUS SPACE: 336 SQ. FT.
BEDROOMS: 3
BATHROOMS: 2
WIDTH: 70' - 8"
DEPTH: 70' - 2"

ORDER ONLINE @ EPLANS.COM

Dormers, arched windows, and covered porches lend this home its country appeal. Inside, the foyer opens to the dining room on the right and leads through a columned entrance to the great room. The open kitchen easily serves the great room, the breakfast area, and the dining room. A cathedral ceiling graces the master suite, which is complete with a walk-in closet and a private bath. Two family bedrooms share a hall bath.

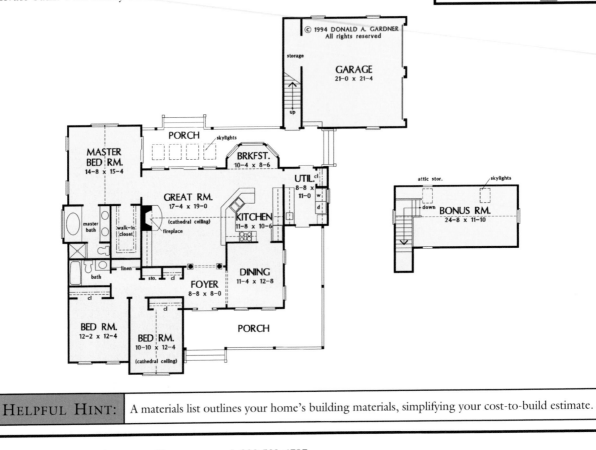

HELPFUL HINT: A materials list outlines your home's building materials, simplifying your cost-to-build estimate.

© 1999 Donald A. Gardner, Inc.

plan# HPK2900110

FIRST FLOOR: 1,293 SQ. FT.
SECOND FLOOR: 528 SQ. FT.
TOTAL: 1,821 SQ. FT.
BONUS SPACE: 355 SQ. FT.
BEDROOMS: 3
BATHROOMS: 2½
WIDTH: 48' - 8"
DEPTH: 50' - 0"

ORDER ONLINE @ EPLANS.COM

This nostalgic cottage's facade is enhanced by a charming gable, twin dormers, and a wrapping front porch. Bay windows enlarge both the dining room and the master bedroom, and the vaulted great room receives additional light from a front clerestory window. The kitchen features a practical design and includes a handy pantry and ample cabinets. A nearby utility room boasts a sink and additional cabinet and countertop space. Located on the first floor for convenience, the master suite enjoys a private bath and a walk-in closet. Upstairs, two more bedrooms and a generous bonus room share a full bath.

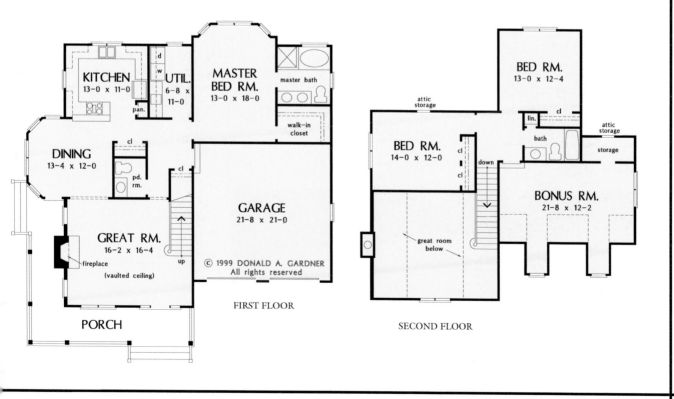

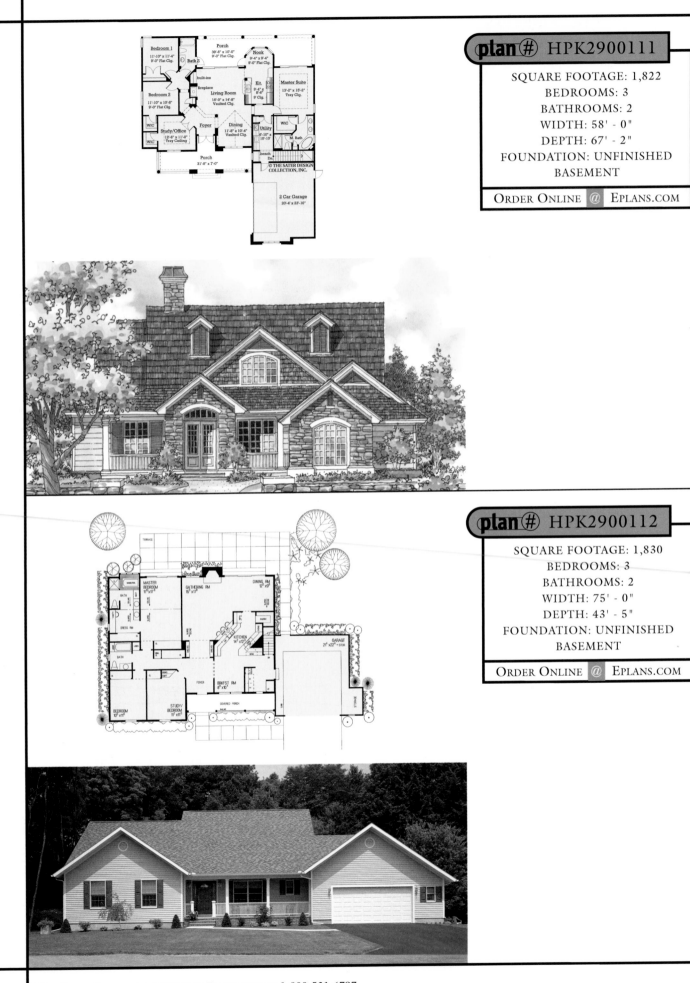

plan # HPK2900111

SQUARE FOOTAGE: 1,822
BEDROOMS: 3
BATHROOMS: 2
WIDTH: 58' - 0"
DEPTH: 67' - 2"
FOUNDATION: UNFINISHED BASEMENT

ORDER ONLINE @ EPLANS.COM

plan # HPK2900112

SQUARE FOOTAGE: 1,830
BEDROOMS: 3
BATHROOMS: 2
WIDTH: 75' - 0"
DEPTH: 43' - 5"
FOUNDATION: UNFINISHED BASEMENT

ORDER ONLINE @ EPLANS.COM

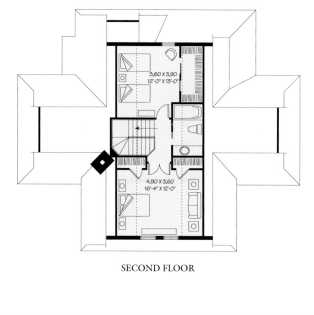

plan # HPK2900113

FIRST FLOOR: 1,212 SQ. FT.
SECOND FLOOR: 620 SQ. FT.
TOTAL: 1,832 SQ. FT.
BEDROOMS: 3
BATHROOMS: 2
WIDTH: 38' - 0"
DEPTH: 40' - 0"
FOUNDATION: FINISHED
WALKOUT BASEMENT

ORDER ONLINE @ EPLANS.COM

This comfortable vacation design provides two levels of relaxing family space. The main level offers a spacious wrapping front porch and an abundance of windows, filling interior spaces with the summer sunshine. A two-sided fireplace warms the living room/dining room combination and a master bedroom that features a roomy walk-in closet. Nearby, the hall bath offers a relaxing whirlpool tub. The kitchen is open and features an island snack bar and pantry storage. A cozy sunroom accesses the wrapping deck. Upstairs, two additional bedrooms feature ample closet space and share a second-floor bath.

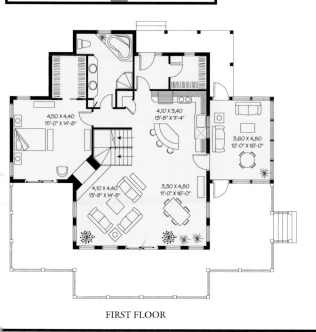

FIRST FLOOR

SECOND FLOOR

© 1995 Donald A. Gardner Architects, Inc.

plan# HPK2900114

SQUARE FOOTAGE: 1,832
BONUS SPACE: 425 SQ. FT.
BEDROOMS: 3
BATHROOMS: 2
WIDTH: 65' - 4"
DEPTH: 62' - 0"

ORDER ONLINE @ EPLANS.COM

Signature Designer

The Georgetown is another design by Donald Gardner that goes straight for the heart of the small-family home buyer. Packed into a 1,832-square-foot layout are two, well-defined formal spaces (one of which converts into a third bedroom), expansive shared spaces that face rearward views, and great privacy for the owners. The back porch is ready for a complementing deck design, for outdoor enjoyment. Lastly, the side-gabled country exterior will be a welcome sight in any neighborhood.

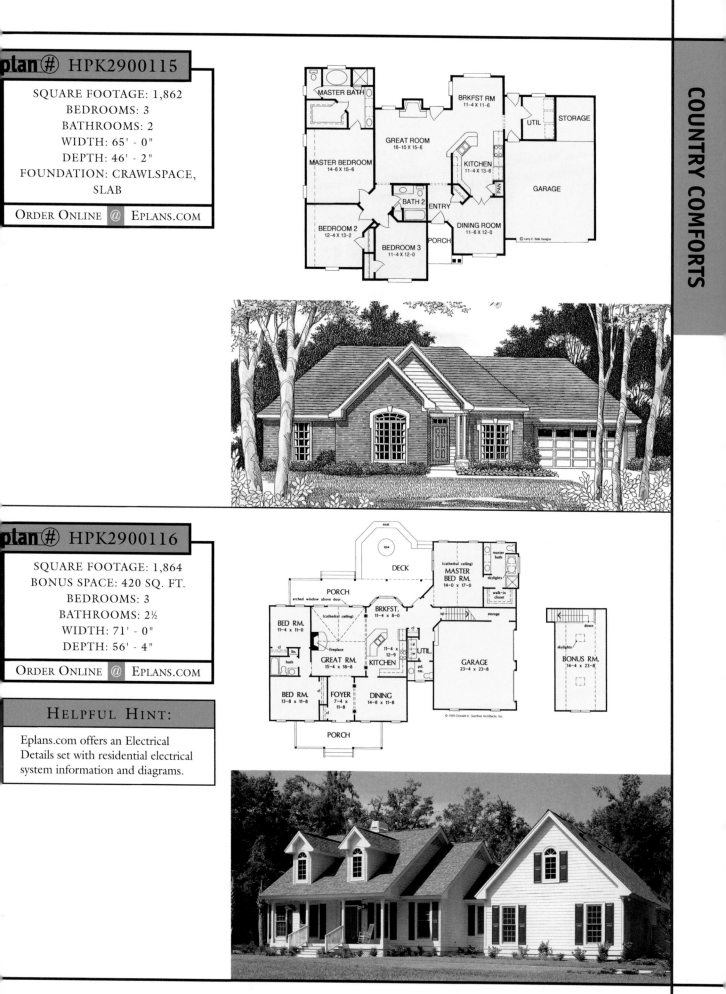

plan # HPK2900115

SQUARE FOOTAGE: 1,862
BEDROOMS: 3
BATHROOMS: 2
WIDTH: 65' - 0"
DEPTH: 46' - 2"
FOUNDATION: CRAWLSPACE,
SLAB

ORDER ONLINE @ EPLANS.COM

plan # HPK2900116

SQUARE FOOTAGE: 1,864
BONUS SPACE: 420 SQ. FT.
BEDROOMS: 3
BATHROOMS: 2½
WIDTH: 71' - 0"
DEPTH: 56' - 4"

ORDER ONLINE @ EPLANS.COM

HELPFUL HINT:

Eplans.com offers an Electrical Details set with residential electrical system information and diagrams.

plan# HPK2900117

SQUARE FOOTAGE: 1,879
BONUS SPACE: 360 SQ. FT.
BEDROOMS: 3
BATHROOMS: 2
WIDTH: 66' - 4"
DEPTH: 55' - 2"

ORDER ONLINE @ EPLANS.COM

Dormers cast light into the foyer for a grand first impression that sets the tone in this home full of today's amenities. The great room, articulated by columns, features a cathedral ceiling and is conveniently located adjacent to the breakfast room and kitchen. Tray ceilings and arch-top picture windows accent the front bedroom and dining room. A secluded master suite, highlighted by a tray ceiling in the bedroom, includes a bath with a skylight, a garden tub, a separate shower, a double-bowl vanity, and a spacious walk-in closet.

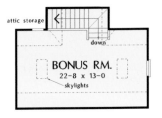

REAR EXTERIOR

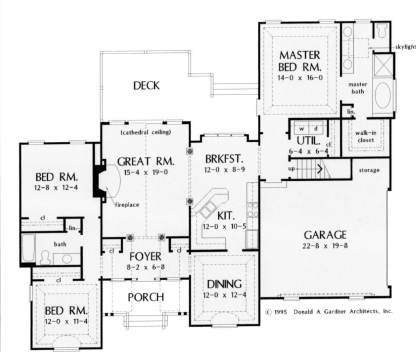

© 1995 Donald A Gardner Architects, Inc.

© 1999 Donald A. Gardner, Inc.

plan # HPK2900118

SQUARE FOOTAGE: 1,882
BONUS SPACE: 363 SQ. FT.
BEDROOMS: 3
BATHROOMS: 2½
WIDTH: 61' - 4"
DEPTH: 55' - 0"

ORDER ONLINE @ EPLANS.COM

An arched window in a center front-facing gable lends style and beauty to the facade of this three-bedroom home. An open common area features a great room with a cathedral ceiling, a formal dining room with a tray ceiling, a functional kitchen, and an informal breakfast area that separates the master suite from the secondary bedrooms for privacy. The master suite provides a dramatic vaulted ceiling, access to the back porch, and abundant closet space. Access to a versatile bonus room is near the master bedroom.

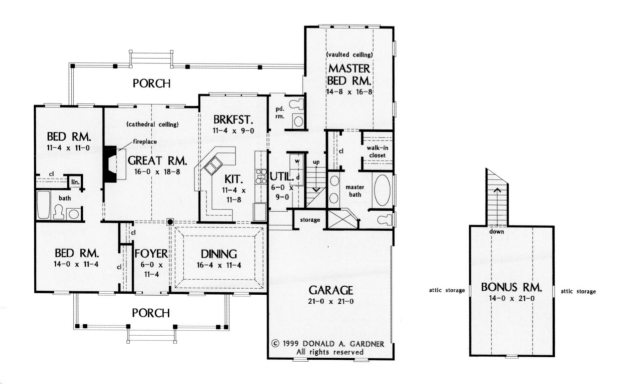

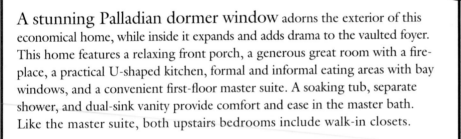

© 1999 Donald A. Gardner, Inc.

plan# HPK2900119

FIRST FLOOR: 1,309 SQ. FT.
SECOND FLOOR: 582 SQ. FT.
TOTAL: 1,891 SQ. FT.
BONUS SPACE: 572 SQ. FT.
BEDROOMS: 3
BATHROOMS: 2½
WIDTH: 65' - 8"
DEPTH: 39' - 4"
FOUNDATION: CRAWLSPACE

ORDER ONLINE @ EPLANS.COM

A stunning Palladian dormer window adorns the exterior of this economical home, while inside it expands and adds drama to the vaulted foyer. This home features a relaxing front porch, a generous great room with a fireplace, a practical U-shaped kitchen, formal and informal eating areas with bay windows, and a convenient first-floor master suite. A soaking tub, separate shower, and dual-sink vanity provide comfort and ease in the master bath. Like the master suite, both upstairs bedrooms include walk-in closets.

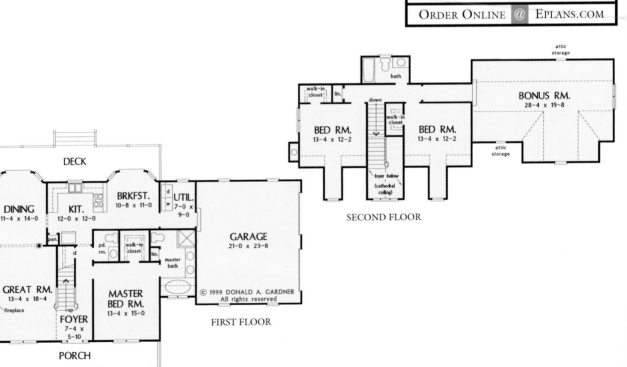

SECOND FLOOR

FIRST FLOOR

plan # HPK2900120

FIRST FLOOR: 1,295 SQ. FT.
SECOND FLOOR: 600 SQ. FT.
TOTAL: 1,895 SQ. FT.
BEDROOMS: 3
BATHROOMS: 2½
WIDTH: 50' - 0"
DEPTH: 55' - 3"
FOUNDATION: UNFINISHED
BASEMENT

ORDER ONLINE @ EPLANS.COM

This Southern Country farmhouse extends a warm welcome with a wraparound porch and a bayed entry. An unrestrained floor plan, replete with soaring, open space as well as sunny bays and charming niches, invites traditional festivities and cozy family gatherings. Colonial columns introduce the two-story great room, which boasts an extended-hearth fireplace and French doors to the wraparound porch, and opens through a wide arch to the tiled country kitchen with a cooktop island counter and snack bar. The first-floor master suite enjoys its own bay window, private access to the wraparound porch, and a sumptuous bath with a clawfoot tub and separate vanities. Upstairs, two family bedrooms share a full bath and a balcony hall that overlooks the great room and the entry.

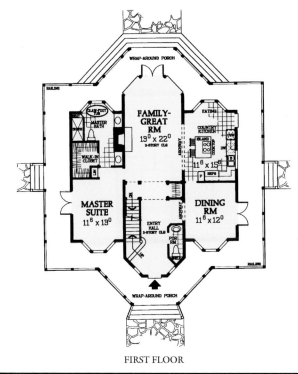

FIRST FLOOR

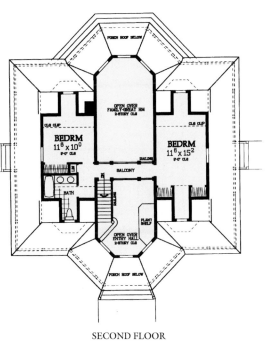

SECOND FLOOR

plan # HPK2900121

FIRST FLOOR: 1,007 SQ. FT.
SECOND FLOOR: 917 SQ. FT.
TOTAL: 1,924 SQ. FT.
BONUS SPACE: 325 SQ. FT.
BEDROOMS: 3
BATHROOMS: 2½
WIDTH: 53' - 0"
DEPTH: 44' - 0"
FOUNDATION: CRAWLSPACE,
UNFINISHED BASEMENT

ORDER ONLINE @ EPLANS.COM

This charming country exterior conceals an elegant interior, starting with formal living and dining rooms, each with a bay window. Decorative columns help define an elegant dining room. The gourmet kitchen features a work island and a breakfast area with its own bay window. A fireplace warms the family room, which opens to the rear porch through French doors. Upstairs, two family bedrooms share a full bath and a gallery hall with a balcony overlook to the foyer. Also on this floor, a master suite boasts a vaulted ceiling, a walk-in closet, and a tiled bath.

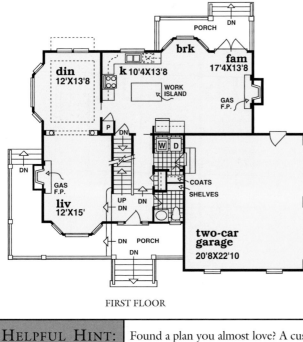

FIRST FLOOR

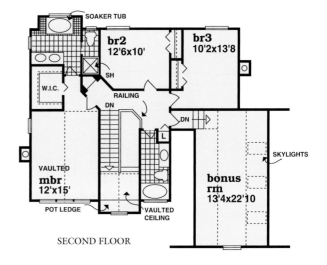

SECOND FLOOR

HELPFUL HINT:	Found a plan you almost love? A customization estimate for $50 is money well spent.

plan # HPK2900122

FIRST FLOOR: 1,044 SQ. FT.
SECOND FLOOR: 892 SQ. FT.
TOTAL: 1,936 SQ. FT.
BONUS SPACE: 228 SQ. FT.
BEDROOMS: 3
BATHROOMS: 2½
WIDTH: 58' - 0"
DEPTH: 43' - 6"
FOUNDATION: UNFINISHED
BASEMENT

ORDER ONLINE @ EPLANS.COM

This charming country traditional home provides a well-lit home office harbored in a beautiful bay with three windows. The second-floor bay brightens the master bath, which has a double-bowl vanity, a step-up tub, and a dressing area. The living and dining rooms share a two-sided fireplace. The gourmet kitchen has a cooktop island counter and enjoys outdoor views through sliding glass doors in the breakfast area. A sizable bonus room above the two-car garage can be developed into hobby space or a recreation room.

FIRST FLOOR

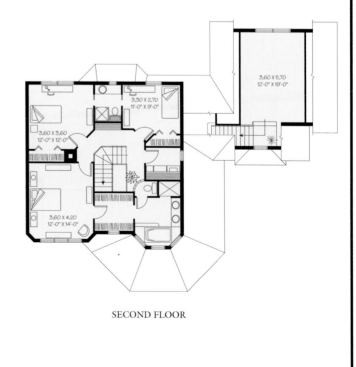

SECOND FLOOR

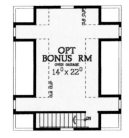

plan # HPK2900123

SQUARE FOOTAGE: 1,937
BONUS SPACE: 414 SQ. FT.
BEDROOMS: 3
BATHROOMS: 2
WIDTH: 62' - 8"
DEPTH: 56' - 0"
FOUNDATION: CRAWLSPACE

ORDER ONLINE @ EPLANS.COM

Country living in a unique floor plan makes this design the perfect choice for a family. The covered front porch opens to an angled foyer that leads to a large great room with a sloped ceiling and fireplace. To the right is the formal dining room, defined by columns and plenty of windows overlooking the porch. Two secondary bedrooms share a full bath at the front of the plan. Connecting to the two-car garage via a laundry area, the kitchen provides an island cooktop and a quaint morning room. The master suite offers a retreat with a sloped ceiling, walk-in closet, and a bath with a whirlpool tub.

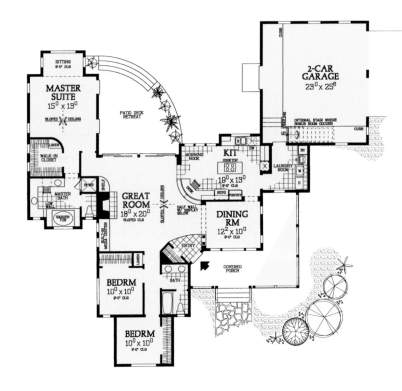

plan # HPK2900124

SQUARE FOOTAGE: 1,957
BONUS SPACE: 479 SQ. FT.
BEDROOMS: 3
BATHROOMS: 2
WIDTH: 66' - 0"
DEPTH: 55' - 0"
FOUNDATION: CRAWLSPACE, SLAB, UNFINISHED BASEMENT

ORDER ONLINE @ EPLANS.COM

An arched front window, a brick-and-siding facade, and a covered porch make this home look elegant yet comfortable. The foyer opens to a formal dining room, which leads into a kitchen with plenty of counter space. The great room, with its warming fireplace and boxed ceiling, truly is the center of this home. It offers easy access to all three bedrooms, the cozy breakfast room and a second covered porch. The master suite also features a boxed ceiling, and boasts its own lavish bath and access to a covered porch. A handy storage area can be accessed from the garage. Upstairs, a bonus room and an optional full bath wait to be developed.

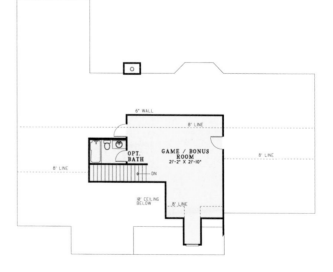

plan# HPK2900125

FIRST FLOOR: 1,374 SQ. FT.
SECOND FLOOR: 600 SQ. FT.
TOTAL: 1,974 SQ. FT.
BEDROOMS: 3
BATHROOMS: 2½
WIDTH: 51' - 8"
DEPTH: 50' - 8"
FOUNDATION: UNFINISHED
BASEMENT

ORDER ONLINE @ EPLANS.com

Balustrades and brackets, dual balconies, and a wraparound porch create a country-style exterior reminiscent of soft summer evenings spent watching fireflies and sipping tea. The tiled foyer opens to the two-story great room filled with light from six windows and a fireplace. The sunny bayed nook shares its natural light with the snack counter and kitchen. A spacious master suite occupies a bay window and offers a sumptuous bath. Upstairs, two family bedrooms—each with a private balcony and a walk-in closet—share a full bath.

FIRST FLOOR

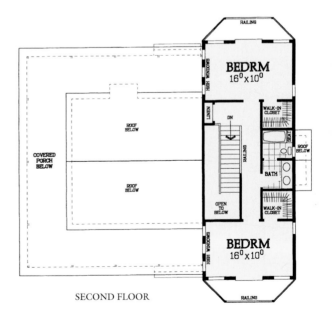

SECOND FLOOR

plan # HPK2900126

FIRST FLOOR: 1,529 SQ. FT.
SECOND FLOOR: 448 SQ. FT.
TOTAL: 1,977 SQ. FT.
BONUS SPACE: 292 SQ. FT.
BEDROOMS: 3
BATHROOMS: 2½
WIDTH: 49' - 0"
DEPTH: 59' - 0"

ORDER ONLINE @ EPLANS.COM

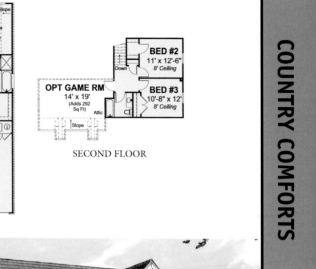

FIRST FLOOR

SECOND FLOOR

plan # HPK2900127

SQUARE FOOTAGE: 1,979
BEDROOMS: 3
BATHROOMS: 2
WIDTH: 67' - 2"
DEPTH: 44' - 2"
FOUNDATION: UNFINISHED
WALKOUT BASEMENT

ORDER ONLINE @ EPLANS.COM

HELPFUL HINT:

Want to Mirror Reverse a design? It's
an easy change to make for only $55.

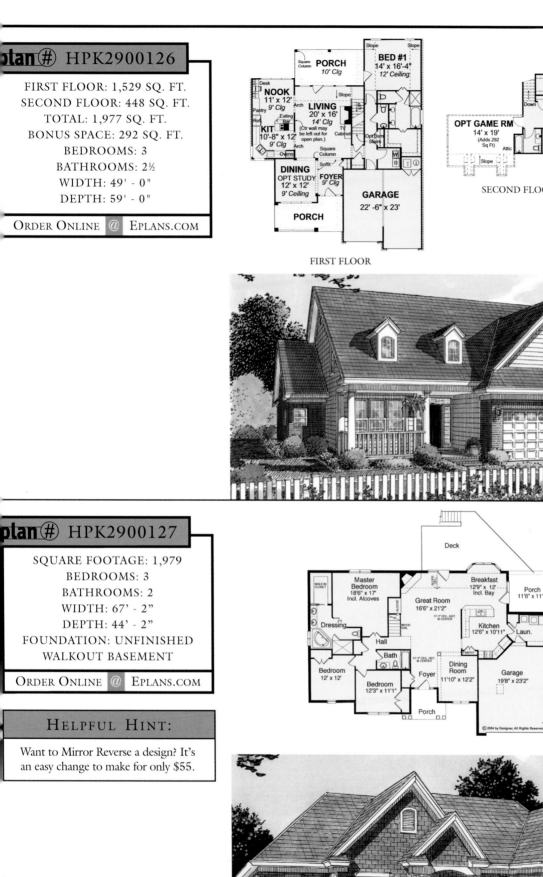

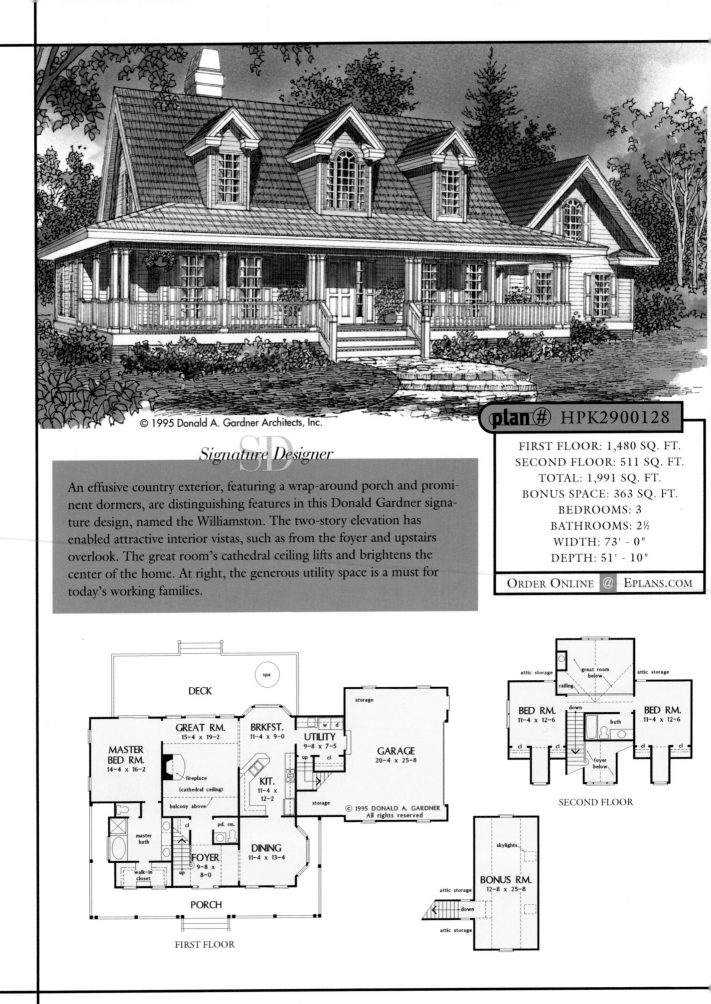

© 1995 Donald A. Gardner Architects, Inc.

Signature Designer SD

An effusive country exterior, featuring a wrap-around porch and prominent dormers, are distinguishing features in this Donald Gardner signature design, named the Williamston. The two-story elevation has enabled attractive interior vistas, such as from the foyer and upstairs overlook. The great room's cathedral ceiling lifts and brightens the center of the home. At right, the generous utility space is a must for today's working families.

plan# HPK2900128

FIRST FLOOR: 1,480 SQ. FT.
SECOND FLOOR: 511 SQ. FT.
TOTAL: 1,991 SQ. FT.
BONUS SPACE: 363 SQ. FT.
BEDROOMS: 3
BATHROOMS: 2½
WIDTH: 73' - 0"
DEPTH: 51' - 10"

ORDER ONLINE @ EPLANS.COM

DECK

spa

GREAT RM.
15-4 x 19-2

BRKFST.
11-4 x 9-0

UTILITY
9-8 x 7-5

storage

w d

MASTER BED RM.
14-4 x 16-2

fireplace
(cathedral ceiling)

balcony above

KIT.
11-4 x 12-2

GARAGE
20-4 x 25-8

up

cl

storage

master bath

cl

pd. rm.

© 1995 DONALD A. GARDNER
All rights reserved

walk-in closet

FOYER
9-8 x 8-0

up

DINING
11-4 x 13-4

PORCH

FIRST FLOOR

attic storage

great room below

attic storage

railing

BED RM.
11-4 x 12-6

down

bath

BED RM.
11-4 x 12-6

cl

cl

cl

cl

foyer below

SECOND FLOOR

skylights

attic storage

BONUS RM.
12-8 x 25-8

attic storage

down

plan# HPK2900129

SQUARE FOOTAGE: 1,993
BONUS SPACE: 307 SQ. FT.
BEDROOMS: 3
BATHROOMS: 2
WIDTH: 66' - 10"
DEPTH: 71' - 5"
FOUNDATION: CRAWLSPACE,
SLAB

ORDER ONLINE @ EPLANS.COM

A gabled roof, flanked by attractive dormers, tops the welcoming covered front porch of this country charmer. Inside, a formal dining room opens directly off the foyer, announced by decorative columns. The nearby living room offers a warming fireplace and access to the rear covered porch. Angled counters in the kitchen contribute to easy food preparation, while a snack counter accommodates quick meals. Nestled in its own wing, the master suite opens through double doors from a private vestibule and offers a relaxing retreat for the homeowner. On the other side of the plan, two family bedrooms share a full hall bath.

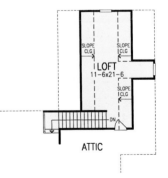

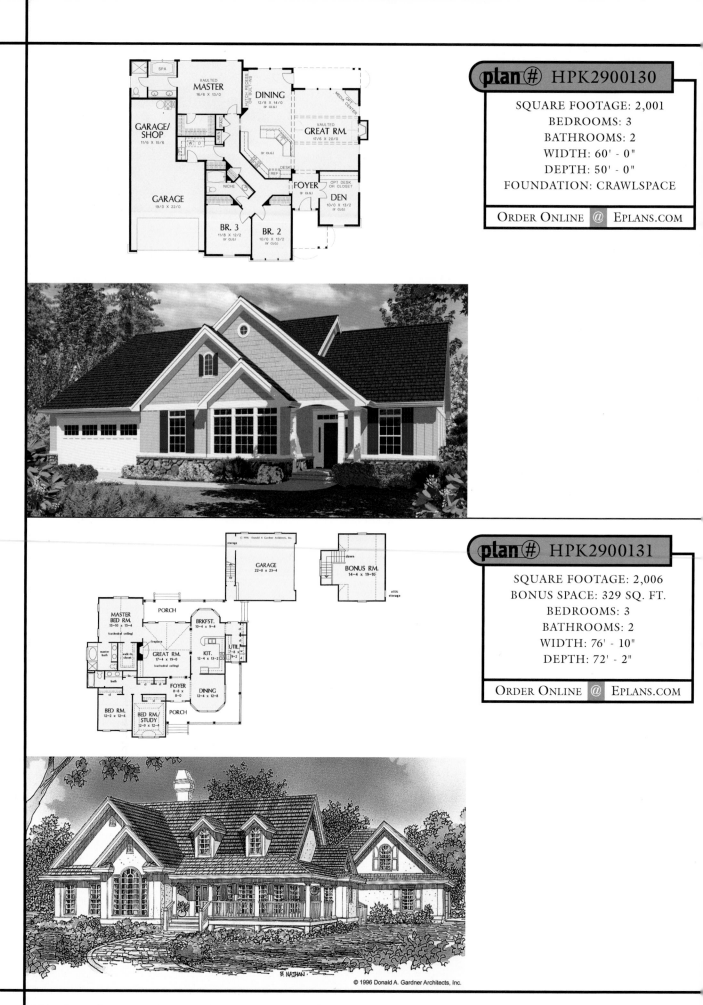

plan # HPK2900130

SQUARE FOOTAGE: 2,001
BEDROOMS: 3
BATHROOMS: 2
WIDTH: 60' - 0"
DEPTH: 50' - 0"
FOUNDATION: CRAWLSPACE

ORDER ONLINE @ EPLANS.COM

plan # HPK2900131

SQUARE FOOTAGE: 2,006
BONUS SPACE: 329 SQ. FT.
BEDROOMS: 3
BATHROOMS: 2
WIDTH: 76' - 10"
DEPTH: 72' - 2"

ORDER ONLINE @ EPLANS.COM

© 1996 Donald A. Gardner Architects, Inc.

plan ⊛ # HPK2900132

FIRST FLOOR: 971 SQ. FT.
SECOND FLOOR: 1,057 SQ. FT.
TOTAL: 2,028 SQ. FT.
BONUS SPACE: 305 SQ. FT.
BEDROOMS: 3
BATHROOMS: 2½
WIDTH: 46' - 0"
DEPTH: 40' - 0"
FOUNDATION: UNFINISHED
BASEMENT

ORDER ONLINE @ EPLANS.COM

This two-story farmhouse-style plan is not only stunning on the outside, it is well-designed inside for the growing family. Upstairs, three bedrooms and two baths, with extra space for a fourth bedroom or playroom, highlight the possibilities offered by this home. A walk-in closet and lavish bath with a huge shower, tub, and dual-sink vanity make the master suite deluxe quality. The other bedrooms share a bath with a large double-basin vanity and access to a laundry. An open layout for the living room, dining area, and kitchen make it possible to arrange the space to best suit your family's needs. A study or home office at the front also marks this plan's versatility.

FIRST FLOOR

SECOND FLOOR

plan# HPK2900133

FIRST FLOOR: 1,347 SQ. FT.
SECOND FLOOR: 690 SQ. FT.
TOTAL: 2,037 SQ. FT.
BEDROOMS: 4
BATHROOMS: 2
WIDTH: 55' - 0"
DEPTH: 41' - 0"
FOUNDATION: UNFINISHED
BASEMENT

ORDER ONLINE @ EPLANS.COM

Perfect for waterfront property, the home is designed for great views from the rear of the plan. Inside, open planning can be found in the living room, which offers a corner fireplace for cool evenings and blends beautifully into the dining and kitchen areas. For chores and storage, the laundry room is conveniently nestled between the kitchen and the two-car garage. The master suite features a walk-through closet and sumptuous bath. Upstairs, three uniquely shaped bedrooms share a full bath.

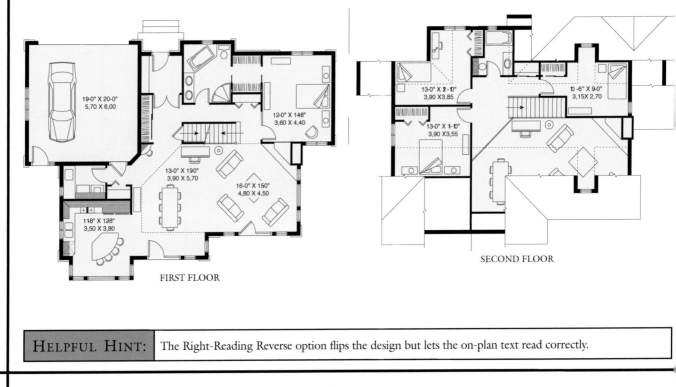

FIRST FLOOR

SECOND FLOOR

HELPFUL HINT: The Right-Reading Reverse option flips the design but lets the on-plan text read correctly.

Donald A. Gardner Architects, Inc.

plan # HPK2900134

SQUARE FOOTAGE: 2,057
BONUS SPACE: 444 SQ. FT.
BEDROOMS: 3
BATHROOMS: 3
WIDTH: 80' - 10"
DEPTH: 61' - 6"

ORDER ONLINE @ EPLANS.COM

With its clean lines and symmetry, this home radiates grace and style. Inside, cathedral and tray ceilings add volume and elegance. The L-shaped kitchen includes a snack bar angled toward the breakfast bay and great room. Secluded at the back of the house, the vaulted master suite includes a skylit bath. Of the two secondary bedrooms, one acts as a "second" master suite, and an alternate bath design creates a wheelchair-accessible option. The bonus room makes a great craft room, playroom, office, or optional fourth bedroom with a bath. The two-car garage loads to the side.

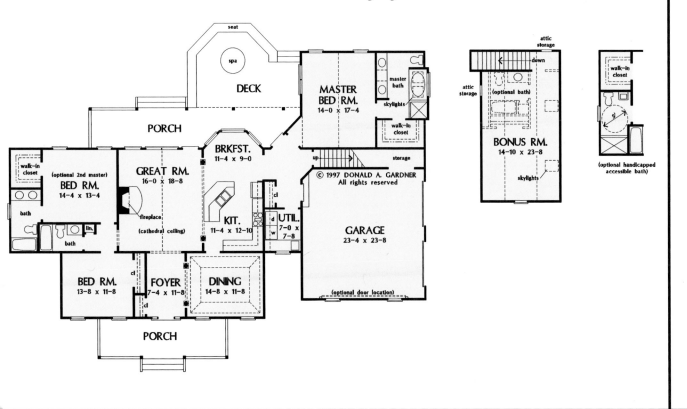

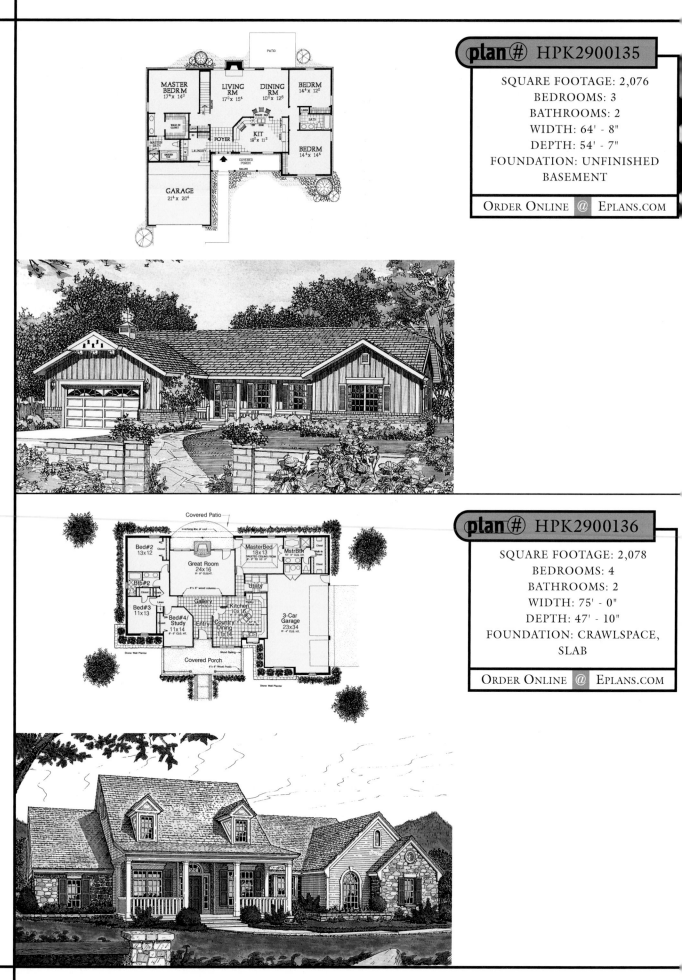

plan # HPK2900135

SQUARE FOOTAGE: 2,076
BEDROOMS: 3
BATHROOMS: 2
WIDTH: 64' - 8"
DEPTH: 54' - 7"
FOUNDATION: UNFINISHED
BASEMENT

ORDER ONLINE @ EPLANS.COM

plan # HPK2900136

SQUARE FOOTAGE: 2,078
BEDROOMS: 4
BATHROOMS: 2
WIDTH: 75' - 0"
DEPTH: 47' - 10"
FOUNDATION: CRAWLSPACE,
SLAB

ORDER ONLINE @ EPLANS.COM

© 1999 Donald A. Gardner, Inc.

plan # HPK2900137

SQUARE FOOTAGE: 2,078
BONUS SPACE: 339 SQ. FT.
BEDROOMS: 3
BATHROOMS: 2½
WIDTH: 62' - 2"
DEPTH: 47' - 8"

ORDER ONLINE @ EPLANS.COM

Signature Designer

A skilled designer can do a lot with 2,078 square feet. Donald Gardner's Northwyke is a cross-gabled country cottage that skimps little in the way of style or livability. The full-sized formal dining room suits the plan for families that enjoy dinner guests. After, the family retreats to one of three comfortable bedrooms, including a master suite with excellent views of the side property.

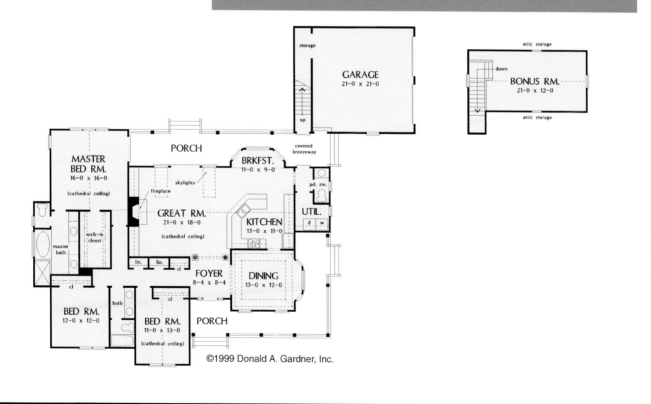

©1999 Donald A. Gardner, Inc.

plan # HPK2900138

FIRST FLOOR: 1,488 SQ. FT.
SECOND FLOOR: 602 SQ. FT.
TOTAL: 2,090 SQ. FT.
BONUS SPACE: 1,321 SQ. FT.
BEDROOMS: 2
BATHROOMS: 2
WIDTH: 60' - 0"
DEPTH: 44' - 0"
FOUNDATION: FINISHED
BASEMENT

ORDER ONLINE @ EPLANS.COM

A truly original angle at the entrance of this country home belies a much more traditionally designed floor plan. There are two sets of stairs in the foyer, one leading to the second level and the other to the basement. The island kitchen and dining room enjoy the glow of the living room fireplace. The master suite with walk-in closet and bathroom are on the main level and situated next to the two-car garage. Up the short flight of stairs you'll find a convenient home office, or make it a sitting room to create a truly lavish second bedroom with a roomy closet and private bath. Finish the bonus space as a third bedroom if you wish.

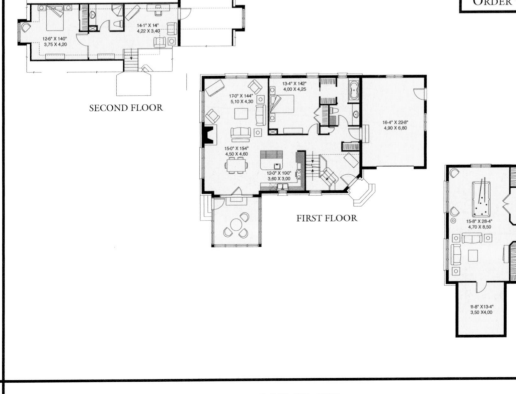

SECOND FLOOR

FIRST FLOOR

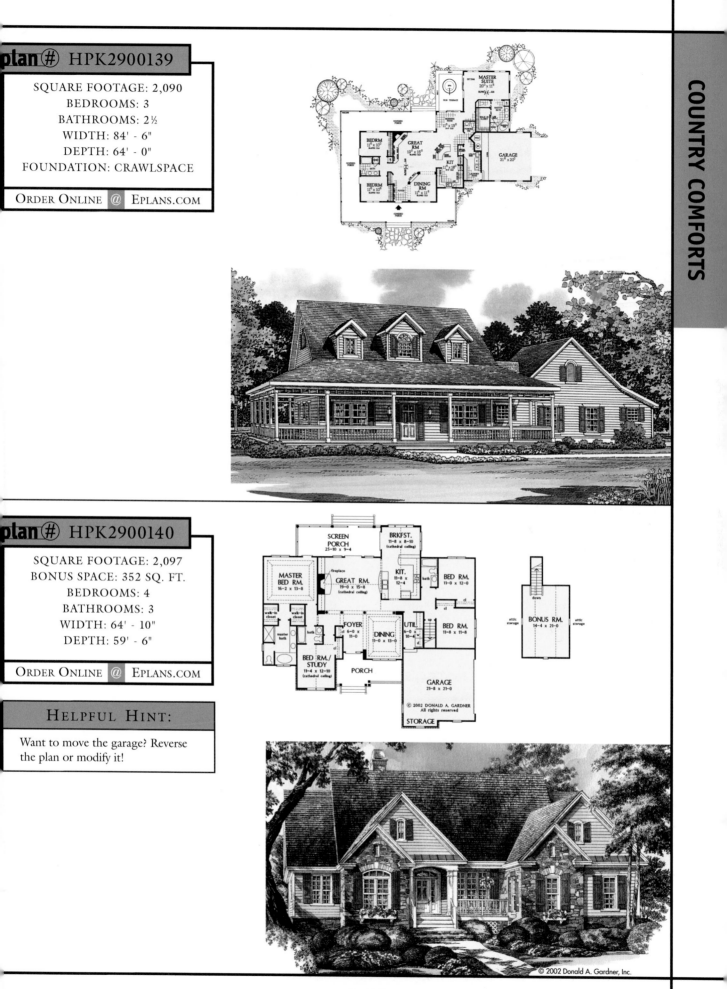

plan # HPK2900139

SQUARE FOOTAGE: 2,090
BEDROOMS: 3
BATHROOMS: 2½
WIDTH: 84' - 6"
DEPTH: 64' - 0"
FOUNDATION: CRAWLSPACE

ORDER ONLINE @ EPLANS.COM

plan # HPK2900140

SQUARE FOOTAGE: 2,097
BONUS SPACE: 352 SQ. FT.
BEDROOMS: 4
BATHROOMS: 3
WIDTH: 64' - 10"
DEPTH: 59' - 6"

ORDER ONLINE @ EPLANS.COM

HELPFUL HINT:

Want to move the garage? Reverse
the plan or modify it!

© 2002 Donald A. Gardner, Inc.

plan# HPK2900141

FIRST FLOOR: 1,060 SQ. FT.
SECOND FLOOR: 1,039 SQ. FT.
TOTAL: 2,099 SQ. FT.
BEDROOMS: 4
BATHROOMS: 2½
WIDTH: 50' - 8"
DEPTH: 39' - 4"
FOUNDATION: UNFINISHED
BASEMENT

ORDER ONLINE @ EPLANS.COM

This lovely country design features a stunning wrapping porch and plenty of windows to provide the interior with natural light. The living room boasts a centered fireplace that helps to define this spacious open area. A nine-foot ceiling on the first floor adds a sense of spaciousness and light. The casual living room leads outdoors to a rear porch. Upstairs, four bedrooms cluster around a central hall. The master suite sports a walk-in closet and a deluxe bath with an oval tub and a separate shower.

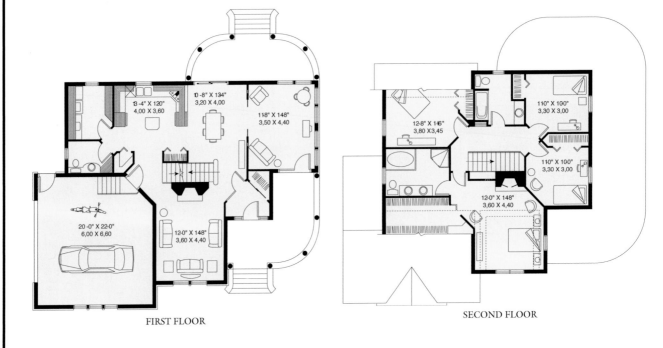

FIRST FLOOR

SECOND FLOOR

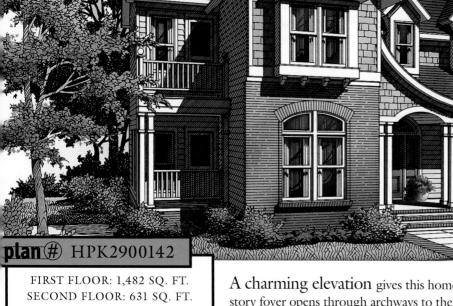

plan # HPK2900142

FIRST FLOOR: 1,482 SQ. FT.
SECOND FLOOR: 631 SQ. FT.
TOTAL: 2,113 SQ. FT.
BEDROOMS: 3
BATHROOMS: 2½
WIDTH: 41' - 10"
DEPTH: 56' - 5"
FOUNDATION: CRAWLSPACE,
SLAB

ORDER ONLINE @ EPLANS.COM

A charming elevation gives this home its curbside appeal. Inside, the two-story foyer opens through archways to the living and dining rooms. Clerestory windows flood the living room with natural light. The kitchen and breakfast room are nearby. An angled sink, with a serving ledge and pass-through, opens the kitchen to the living room beyond. An old-time side porch off the kitchen enhances the look of the home and provides convenient access to the outside. The master bath has all the frills and includes roomy His and Hers walk-in closets. Two bedrooms and a bath are located upstairs. A lovely balcony is located off Bedroom 2. This plan includes a two-car detached garage.

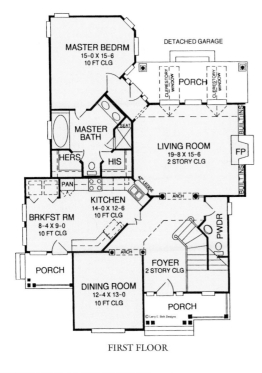

FIRST FLOOR

SECOND FLOOR

An arched clerestory, multipane windows, and a balustered porch splash this classic country exterior with an extraordinary new spirit. Inside, the two-story foyer is flanked by the sunny formal dining room and an elegant stairway. The great room offers a fireplace with a tiled hearth, a built-in media center, and a snack bar that it shares with the large island kitchen and breakfast room. Ceramic tiles dress up the L-shaped kitchen, which boasts a built-in desk, extra closet space, and double ovens. The first-floor master suite is appointed with a sitting area and enjoys private access to the rear covered porch, and the master bath boasts an angled whirlpool tub and twin lavatories. Upstairs two secondary bedrooms, each with its own balcony, share a full bath that includes ample linen storage.

plan # HPK2900143

FIRST FLOOR: 1,655 SQ. FT.
SECOND FLOOR: 515 SQ. FT.
TOTAL: 2,170 SQ. FT.
BEDROOMS: 3
BATHROOMS: 2½
WIDTH: 68' - 6"
DEPTH: 66' - 5"
FOUNDATION: UNFINISHED
BASEMENT

ORDER ONLINE @ EPLANS.COM

FIRST FLOOR

SECOND FLOOR

plan（#） HPK2900144

FIRST FLOOR: 1,186 SQ. FT.
SECOND FLOOR: 988 SQ. FT.
TOTAL: 2,174 SQ. FT.
BEDROOMS: 4
BATHROOMS: 2½
WIDTH: 72' - 0"
DEPTH: 50' - 10"
FOUNDATION: UNFINISHED
BASEMENT

ORDER ONLINE @ EPLANS.COM

A Palladian window, fish-scale shingles, and turret-style bays set off this country-style Victorian exterior. Muntin windows and a quintessential wraparound porch dress up an understated theme and introduce an unrestrained floor plan with plenty of bays and niches. An impressive tiled entry opens to the formal rooms that nestle to the left side of the plan and receive natural light from an abundance of windows. The turret houses a secluded study on the first floor and provides a sunny bay window for a family bedroom upstairs. The second-floor master suite boasts its own fireplace, a dressing area with a walk-in closet, and a lavish bath with a garden tub and twin vanities. The two-car garage offers space for a workshop or extra storage and leads to a service entrance to the walk-through utility room.

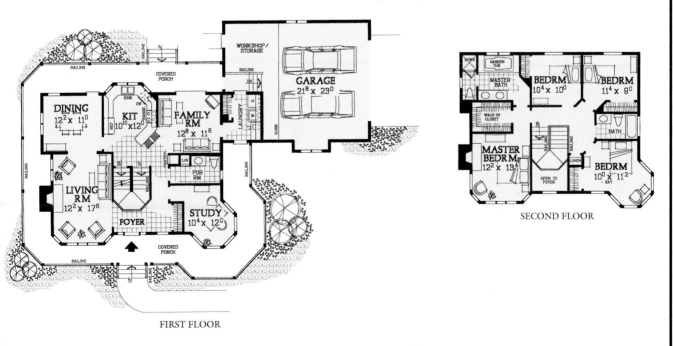

FIRST FLOOR

SECOND FLOOR

plan# HPK2900145

Horizontal siding with corner boards, muntin windows, and a raised veranda enhance the appeal of this country home. Twin carriage lamps flank the sheltered entrance. Inside, the central foyer delights with its two sets of columns at the openings to the formal living and dining rooms. In the L-shaped kitchen, an adjacent snack bar offers everyday ease. Open to the kitchen, the great room boasts a centered fireplace, a high ceiling, and access to the veranda. Sleeping accommodations start off with the master bedroom; a connecting bath with a whirlpool tub will be a favorite spot. Upstairs, three bedrooms share a full bath that includes twin lavatories. The storage room is also added to the second floor.

FIRST FLOOR: 1,186 SQ. FT.
SECOND FLOOR: 988 SQ. FT.
TOTAL: 2,174 SQ. FT.
BEDROOMS: 4
BATHROOMS: 2½
WIDTH: 72' - 4"
DEPTH: 51' - 2"
FOUNDATION: UNFINISHED BASEMENT

ORDER ONLINE @ EPLANS.COM

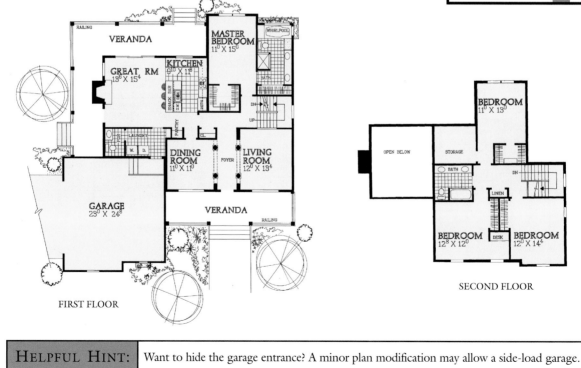

FIRST FLOOR

SECOND FLOOR

HELPFUL HINT: Want to hide the garage entrance? A minor plan modification may allow a side-load garage.

plan # HPK2900146

FIRST FLOOR: 1,232 SQ. FT.
SECOND FLOOR: 951 SQ. FT.
TOTAL: 2,183 SQ. FT.
BONUS SPACE: 365 SQ. FT.
BEDROOMS: 3
BATHROOMS: 2½
WIDTH: 56' - 0"
DEPTH: 38' - 0"
FOUNDATION: UNFINISHED
BASEMENT

ORDER ONLINE @ EPLANS.COM

This beautiful three-bedroom home boasts many attractive features. Two covered porches will entice you outside; inside, a special sunroom on the first floor brings the outdoors in. The foyer opens on the right to a comfortable family room that may be used as a home office. On the left, the living area is warmed by the sunroom and a cozy corner fireplace. A formal dining area lies adjacent to an efficient kitchen with a central island and breakfast nook overlooking the back porch. The second level offers two family bedrooms served by a full bath. A spacious master suite with a walk-in closet and luxurious bath completes the second floor.

FIRST FLOOR

SECOND FLOOR

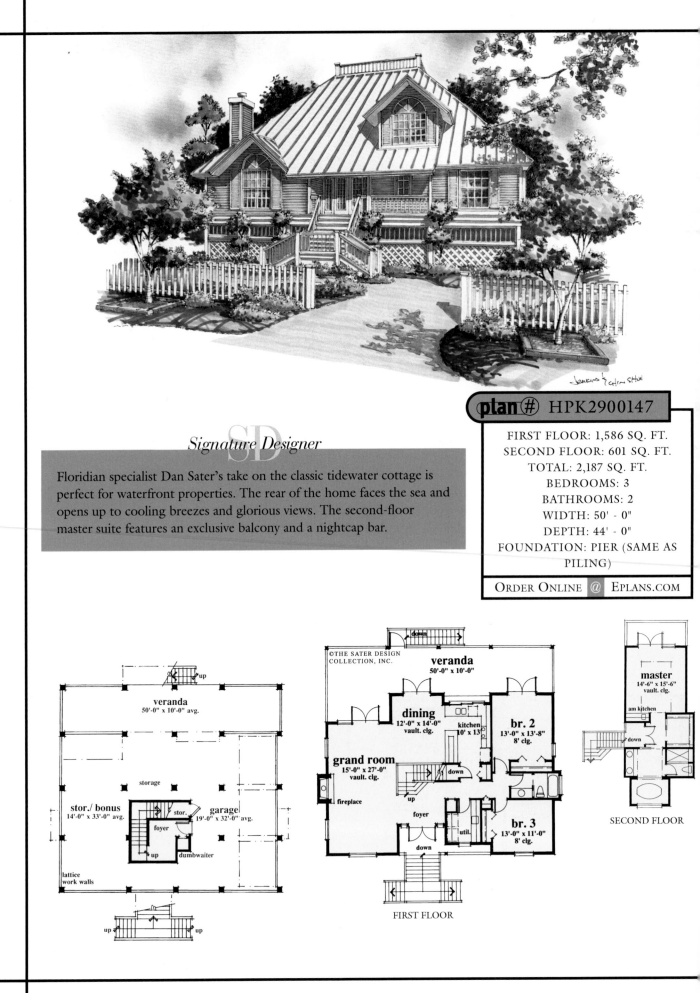

Signature Designer

Floridian specialist Dan Sater's take on the classic tidewater cottage is perfect for waterfront properties. The rear of the home faces the sea and opens up to cooling breezes and glorious views. The second-floor master suite features an exclusive balcony and a nightcap bar.

plan# HPK2900147

FIRST FLOOR: 1,586 SQ. FT.
SECOND FLOOR: 601 SQ. FT.
TOTAL: 2,187 SQ. FT.
BEDROOMS: 3
BATHROOMS: 2
WIDTH: 50' - 0"
DEPTH: 44' - 0"
FOUNDATION: PIER (SAME AS PILING)

ORDER ONLINE @ EPLANS.COM

veranda
50'-0" x 10'-0" avg.

storage

stor./ bonus
14'-0" x 33'-0" avg.

foyer

stor.

garage
19'-0" x 32'-0" avg.

dumbwaiter

lattice work walls

up   up

©THE SATER DESIGN COLLECTION, INC.

down

veranda
50'-0" x 10'-0"

dining
12'-0" x 14'-0"
vault. clg.

kitchen
10' x 13'

br. 2
13'-0" x 13'-8"
8' clg.

grand room
15'-0" x 27'-0"
vault. clg.

down

fireplace

up

foyer

util.

br. 3
13'-0" x 11'-0"
8' clg.

down

FIRST FLOOR

master
14'-6" x 15'-6"
vault. clg.

am kjtchen

down

SECOND FLOOR

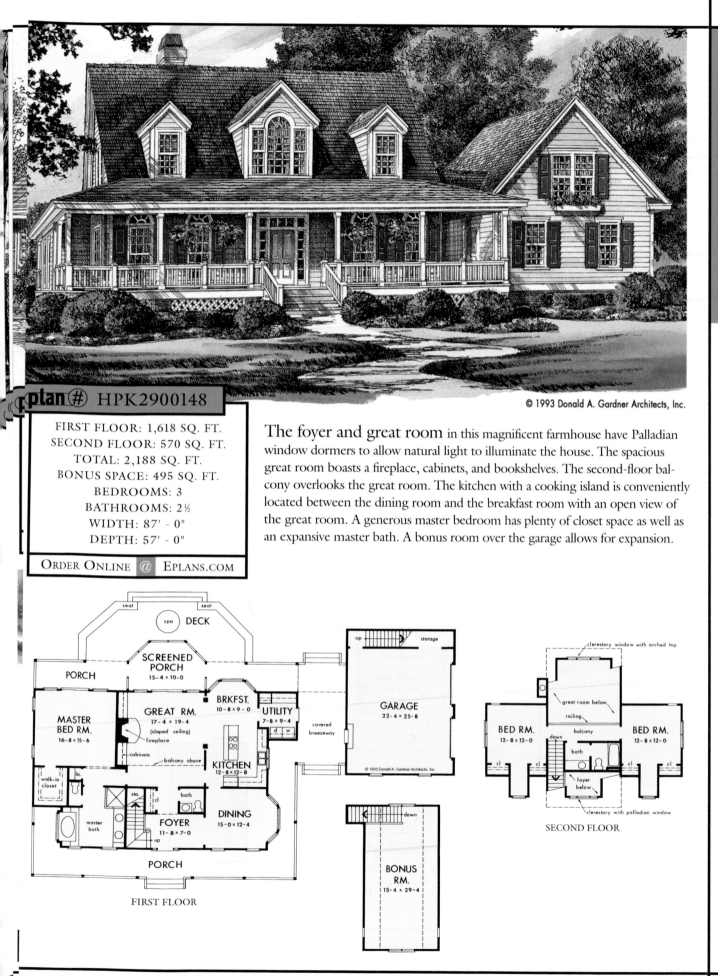

© 1993 Donald A. Gardner Architects, Inc.

plan# HPK2900148

FIRST FLOOR: 1,618 SQ. FT.
SECOND FLOOR: 570 SQ. FT.
TOTAL: 2,188 SQ. FT.
BONUS SPACE: 495 SQ. FT.
BEDROOMS: 3
BATHROOMS: 2½
WIDTH: 87' - 0"
DEPTH: 57' - 0"

ORDER ONLINE @ EPLANS.COM

The foyer and great room in this magnificent farmhouse have Palladian window dormers to allow natural light to illuminate the house. The spacious great room boasts a fireplace, cabinets, and bookshelves. The second-floor balcony overlooks the great room. The kitchen with a cooking island is conveniently located between the dining room and the breakfast room with an open view of the great room. A generous master bedroom has plenty of closet space as well as an expansive master bath. A bonus room over the garage allows for expansion.

The traditional charm of this family home offers a distinct American flavor. Horizontal siding and a quaint wraparound front porch are sure signs of country styling. To the left of the foyer, the home office is a quiet retreat. To the right is a combined living and dining room area. The gourmet kitchen features a snack bar overlooking the rear porch and is open to a casual family area with a fireplace. A two-car garage, laundry room, and half-bath complete the first floor. Upstairs, the master suite offers a private bath and massive walk-in closet.

plan # HPK2900161

FIRST FLOOR: 1,319 SQ. FT.
SECOND FLOOR: 1,107 SQ. FT.
TOTAL: 2,426 SQ. FT.
BEDROOMS: 3
BATHROOMS: 2½
WIDTH: 52' - 0"
DEPTH: 46' - 8"
FOUNDATION: UNFINISHED BASEMENT

ORDER ONLINE @ EPLANS.COM

FIRST FLOOR

SECOND FLOOR

plan # HPK2900162

FIRST FLOOR: 1,841 SQ. FT.
SECOND FLOOR: 594 SQ. FT.
TOTAL: 2,435 SQ. FT.
BONUS SPACE: 391 SQ. FT.
BEDROOMS: 4
BATHROOMS: 3
WIDTH: 82' - 2"
DEPTH: 48' - 10"

ORDER ONLINE @ EPLANS.COM

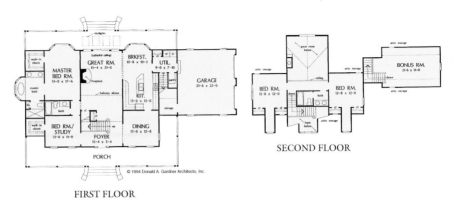

FIRST FLOOR

SECOND FLOOR

© 1994 Donald A. Gardner Architects, Inc.

© 1994 Donald A. Gardner Architects, Inc.

plan # HPK2900163

SQUARE FOOTAGE: 2,439
BEDROOMS: 3
BATHROOMS: 2 ½
WIDTH: 81' - 2"
DEPTH: 67' - 10"
FOUNDATION: CRAWLSPACE,
SLAB

ORDER ONLINE @ EPLANS.COM

plan # HPK2900164

SQUARE FOOTAGE: 2,454
BONUS SPACE: 256 SQ. FT.
BEDROOMS: 3
BATHROOMS: 2
WIDTH: 80' - 6"
DEPTH: 66' - 6"
FOUNDATION: CRAWLSPACE

ORDER ONLINE @ EPLANS.COM

Garage
19'-2" x 23'-0"
10'-4" Clg.

Bonus Room
13'-10" x 12'-0"

Master Suite
13'-0" x 19'-6"
10'-0" to 11'-4"
Tray Clg.

Porch
10'-0" Clg.

Dining
11'-4" x 14'-0"
10'-0" to 11'-0"
Stepped Clg.

Study
12'-4" x 13'-0"
10'-0" to 11'-0"
Stepped Clg.

Great Room
18'-4" x 19'-0"
11'-0" to 12'-0"
Coffered Clg.

Kitchen
14'-4" x 13'-8"
10'-0" to 11'-0"
Stepped Clg.

Bedroom 2
11'-2" x 11'-6"
10'-0" Clg.

Her WIC

His WIC

Master Bath
10'-0" Clg.

Foyer
10'-0" Clg.

Porch
20'-8" x 6'-0"
12'-0" Clg.

Bedroom 1
12'-8" x 11'-8"
10'-0" Clg.

plan # HPK2900168

SQUARE FOOTAGE: 2,487
BEDROOMS: 4
BATHROOMS: 3
WIDTH: 86' - 2"
DEPTH: 51' - 8"

ORDER ONLINE @ EPLANS.COM

(optional 2nd master)
BED RM.
13-8 x 15-0

PORCH

BRKFST.
11-4 x 9-4

MASTER BED RM.
14-0 x 17-4

master bath

walk-in closet

GREAT RM.
19-10 x 18-8
(cathedral ceiling)

KIT.
11-4 x 12-6

storage

walk-in closet

bath

BED RM.
11-6 x 13-4

BED RM.
14-0 x 11-8

FOYER
8-4 x 11-8

DINING
16-4 x 11-8

UTIL.
7-0 x 7-8

GARAGE
24-4 x 23-0

PORCH

plan# HPK2900165

SQUARE FOOTAGE: 2,500
BEDROOMS: 3
BATHROOMS: 3
WIDTH: 64' - 0"
DEPTH: 52' - 0"
FOUNDATION: UNFINISHED
BASEMENT

ORDER ONLINE @ EPLANS.COM

This Florida "Cracker"-style home is warm and inviting. Unpretentious use of space is the hallmark of the Florida Cracker. This design shows the style at its best; private baths for each of the bedrooms are a fine example. The huge great room, which sports a volume ceiling, opens to the expansive rear porch for extended entertaining. Traditional Cracker homes had sparse master suites. Not this one! It has a lavish bedchamber and a luxurious bath with His and Hers closets and a corner soaking tub. Perfect for a sloping lot, this home can be expanded with a lower garage and bonus space in the basement.

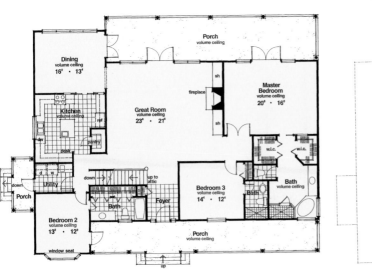

plan# HPK2900166

FIRST FLOOR: 1,319 SQ. FT.
SECOND FLOOR: 1,181 SQ. FT.
TOTAL: 2,500 SQ. FT.
BONUS SPACE: 371 SQ. FT.
BEDROOMS: 4
BATHROOMS: 2½
WIDTH: 60' - 0"
DEPTH: 42' - 0"
FOUNDATION: CRAWLSPACE

ORDER ONLINE @ EPLANS.COM

A stunning Shingle home with stone accents (including a stone fire-place!), this Cape Cod-style design will complement any neighborhood. Inside, the two-story foyer presents a grand staircase and high ceilings throughout. Multipane windows light up the living room and an archway connects it to the family room. Here, a lateral fireplace allows rear views. The breakfast nook has French doors to the rear property, inviting outdoor dining. The island kitchen is designed with lots of extra space to accommodate two cooks. A butler's pantry makes entertaining a breeze. Upstairs, three bedrooms (or make one a den) share a full bath and a bonus room. The master suite is graced with a vaulted ceiling and a private bath with a Roman spa tub.

FIRST FLOOR

SECOND FLOOR

HELPFUL HINT: Eplans.com offers a Plumbing Details set with general residential plumbing information and diagrams.

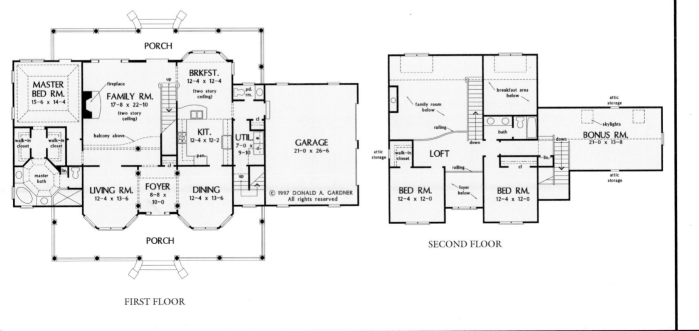

1997 Donald A. Gardner, Inc.

plan # HPK2900167

FIRST FLOOR: 1,914 SQ. FT.
SECOND FLOOR: 597 SQ. FT.
TOTAL: 2,511 SQ. FT.
BONUS SPACE: 487 SQ. FT.
BEDROOMS: 3
BATHROOMS: 2½
WIDTH: 79' - 2"
DEPTH: 51' - 6"

ORDER ONLINE @ EPLANS.COM

Filled with the charm of farmhouse details, such as twin dormers and bay windows, this design begins with a classic covered porch. The entry leads to a foyer flanked by columns that separate it from the formal dining and living rooms. The U-shaped kitchen separates the dining room from the bayed breakfast room. The first-floor master suite features a bedroom with a tray ceiling and a luxurious private bath.

plan# HPK2900169

FIRST FLOOR: 1,542 SQ. FT.
SECOND FLOOR: 971 SQ. FT.
TOTAL: 2,513 SQ. FT.
BEDROOMS: 3
BATHROOMS: 3
WIDTH: 46' - 0"
DEPTH: 51' - 0"
FOUNDATION: ISLAND
BASEMENT

ORDER ONLINE @ EPLANS.COM

Signature Designer

A two-story elevation and a tight footprint mean plenty of views and sun for this vacation design by Dan Sater. Get a load of all those out-door spaces, as well as the two-story great room that soars through the middle of the plan. The casually minded kitchen and dining room work well to provide a comfortable shared space for the relaxing family.

© THE SATER DESIGN COLLECTION, INC.

Lower Porch
28'-8" x 16'-10"

Bonus/
Storage

Up.
Up.

2 Car Garage

Storage

Bedroom 2
11'-4" x 13'-0"
10'-0" Clg.

© THE SATER DESIGN COLLECTION, INC.

Covered Porch
28'-8" x 16'-0"

Closet

Great Room
19'-0" x 18'-0"
2-Story Clg.

Fireplace

Bath

Tub

Dining
12'-0" x 14'-0"
10'-0" Clg.

Up.   Dn.

Up.

Kitchen
10'-8" x 13'-6"
10'-4" Clg.

Built-ins

Foyer
11'-4" x 13'-6"

Butler
Pantry   Util.

Study
13'-4" x 12'-0"
10'-0" Vaulted Clg.

Entry Porch
10'-4" Clg.

FIRST FLOOR

br. 3
11'-4" x 13'-0"
vaulted clg.

deck

open to below

sitting

dn

overlook

master
suite
16'-0" x 14'-0"
vaulted clg.

dn   open

master
bath

w.i.c.

SECOND FLOOR

plan # HPK2900170

FIRST FLOOR: 1,324 SQ. FT.
SECOND FLOOR: 1,192 SQ. FT.
TOTAL: 2,516 SQ. FT.
BEDROOMS: 4
BATHROOMS: 2½
WIDTH: 67' - 6"
DEPTH: 47' - 6"
FOUNDATION: CRAWLSPACE,
UNFINISHED BASEMENT

ORDER ONLINE @ EPLANS.COM

A turret, wood detailing, and a wraparound veranda signal desirable Victorian style for this home. The double-door entry opens to a foyer with a lovely curved staircase and leads into the living and dining rooms on the right and the den on the left. All three rooms have attractive tray ceilings. The living room boasts a fireplace, and the formal dining room features a buffet alcove. Sliding glass doors in the dining room open to the veranda. Four bedrooms occupy the second floor. A tray ceiling highlights the master suite, and the private bath and walk-in closet give it a luxurious feel. Bedroom 2 includes a cozy window seat.

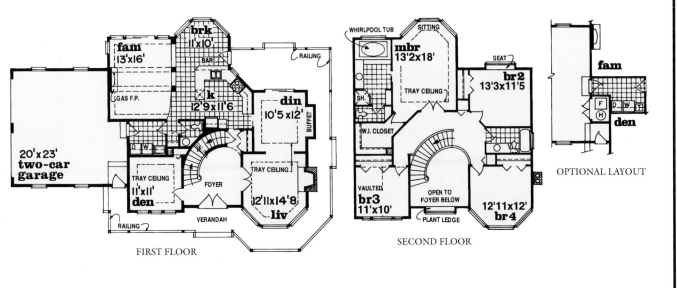

FIRST FLOOR

SECOND FLOOR

OPTIONAL LAYOUT

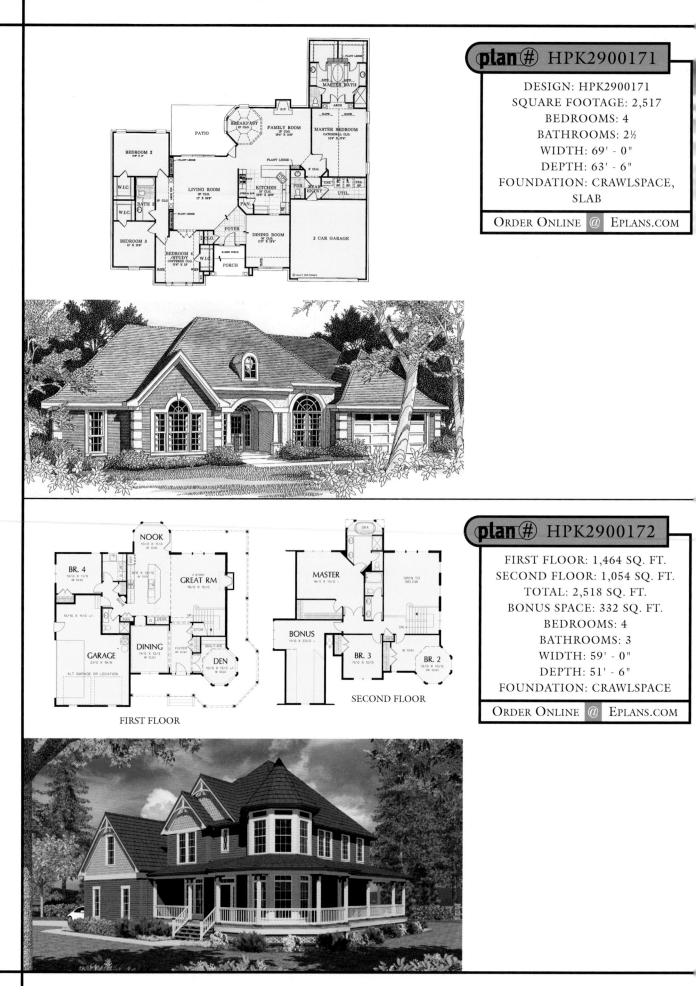

plan # HPK2900171

DESIGN: HPK2900171
SQUARE FOOTAGE: 2,517
BEDROOMS: 4
BATHROOMS: 2½
WIDTH: 69' - 0"
DEPTH: 63' - 6"
FOUNDATION: CRAWLSPACE,
SLAB

ORDER ONLINE @ EPLANS.COM

plan # HPK2900172

FIRST FLOOR: 1,464 SQ. FT.
SECOND FLOOR: 1,054 SQ. FT.
TOTAL: 2,518 SQ. FT.
BONUS SPACE: 332 SQ. FT.
BEDROOMS: 4
BATHROOMS: 3
WIDTH: 59' - 0"
DEPTH: 51' - 6"
FOUNDATION: CRAWLSPACE

ORDER ONLINE @ EPLANS.COM

FIRST FLOOR

SECOND FLOOR

© 2002 Donald A. Gardner, Inc.

plan (#) HPK2900173

FIRST FLOOR: 1,798 SQ. FT.
SECOND FLOOR: 723 SQ. FT.
TOTAL: 2,521 SQ. FT.
BONUS SPACE: 349 SQ. FT.
BEDROOMS: 4
BATHROOMS: 3½
WIDTH: 66' - 8"
DEPTH: 49' - 8"

ORDER ONLINE @ EPLANS.COM

With spacious front and rear porches, twin gables, and an arched entrance, this home has charm and curb appeal. Columns make a grand impression both inside and outside, and transoms above French doors brighten both the front and rear of the floor plan. An angled counter separates the kitchen from the great room and breakfast area, and the mudroom/utility area is complete with a sink. A tray ceiling tops the master bedroom, and the formal living room/study and bonus room are flexible spaces, tailoring to family needs. A balcony overlooks the foyer and great room; an additional upstairs bedroom has its own bath and can be used as a guest suite.

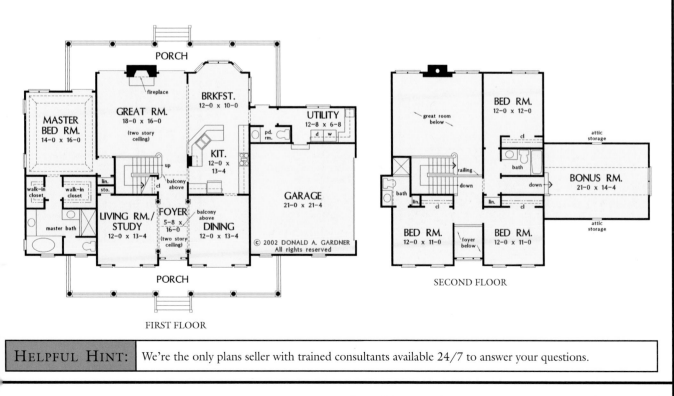

HELPFUL HINT: We're the only plans seller with trained consultants available 24/7 to answer your questions.

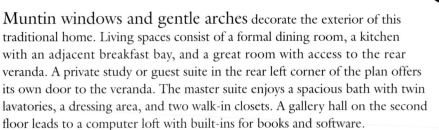

© The Sater Design Collection, ▶

plan# HPK2900174

FIRST FLOOR: 1,676 SQ. FT.
SECOND FLOOR: 851 SQ. FT.
TOTAL: 2,527 SQ. FT.
BEDROOMS: 4
BATHROOMS: 2½
WIDTH: 55' - 0"
DEPTH: 50' - 0"
FOUNDATION: SLAB

ORDER ONLINE @ EPLANS.COM

Muntin windows and gentle arches decorate the exterior of this traditional home. Living spaces consist of a formal dining room, a kitchen with an adjacent breakfast bay, and a great room with access to the rear veranda. A private study or guest suite in the rear left corner of the plan offers its own door to the veranda. The master suite enjoys a spacious bath with twin lavatories, a dressing area, and two walk-in closets. A gallery hall on the second floor leads to a computer loft with built-ins for books and software.

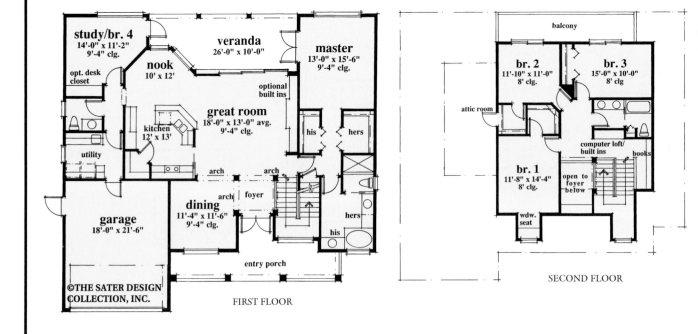

©THE SATER DESIGN COLLECTION, INC.

FIRST FLOOR

SECOND FLOOR

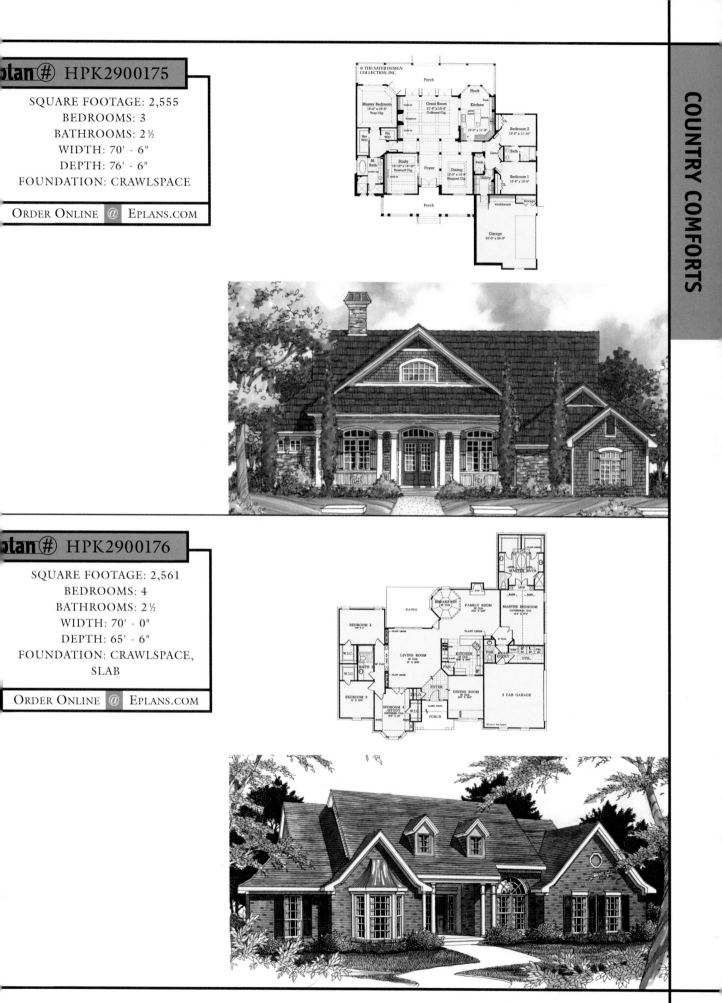

PLAN # HPK2900175

SQUARE FOOTAGE: 2,555
BEDROOMS: 3
BATHROOMS: 2 ½
WIDTH: 70' - 6"
DEPTH: 76' - 6"
FOUNDATION: CRAWLSPACE

ORDER ONLINE @ EPLANS.COM

PLAN # HPK2900176

SQUARE FOOTAGE: 2,561
BEDROOMS: 4
BATHROOMS: 2 ½
WIDTH: 70' - 0"
DEPTH: 65' - 6"
FOUNDATION: CRAWLSPACE,
SLAB

ORDER ONLINE @ EPLANS.COM

Perfectly proportionate and definitely distinctive, this country home offers an open floor plan, abundant natural light, and plenty of space to kick back and relax. The plan begins with a two-story foyer that leads ahead to a family room lit by second-floor radius windows. Decorative columns define the nearby dining room, and a freestanding pantry is all that separates the family room from the welcoming island kitchen. The breakfast nook flows easily into the vaulted keeping room, surrounded by sparkling windows. Two bedrooms reside on this level, including a secondary bedroom with a box-bay window and a master suite with a sitting bay and a vaulted bath. Upstairs, two bedrooms enjoy privacy and share a full bath and a loft. Optional bonus space is available to expand as your family's needs change.

FIRST FLOOR: 1,894 SQ. FT.
SECOND FLOOR: 683 SQ. FT.
TOTAL: 2,577 SQ. FT.
BONUS SPACE: 210 SQ. FT.
BEDROOMS: 4
BATHROOMS: 3
WIDTH: 57' - 0"
DEPTH: 53' - 6"
FOUNDATION: CRAWLSPACE,
UNFINISHED WALKOUT
BASEMENT

ORDER ONLINE @ EPLANS.COM

FIRST FLOOR

SECOND FLOOR

plan # HPK2900178

FIRST FLOOR: 2,028 SQ. FT.
SECOND FLOOR: 558 SQ. FT.
TOTAL: 2,586 SQ. FT.
BONUS SPACE: 272 SQ. FT.
BEDROOMS: 4
BATHROOMS: 3
WIDTH: 64' - 10"
DEPTH: 61' - 0"
FOUNDATION: CRAWLSPACE,
SLAB, UNFINISHED
BASEMENT

ORDER ONLINE @ EPLANS.COM

Double columns and an arch-top clerestory window create an inviting entry to this fresh interpretation of traditional style. Decorative columns and arches open to the formal dining room and to the octagonal great room, which has a 10-foot tray ceiling. The U-shaped kitchen looks over an angled counter to a breakfast bay that brings in the outdoors and shares a through-fireplace with the great room. A sitting area and a lavish bath set off the secluded master suite. A nearby secondary bedroom with its own bath could be used as a guest suite. Upstairs, two family bedrooms share a full bath and a hall that leads to an expandable area.

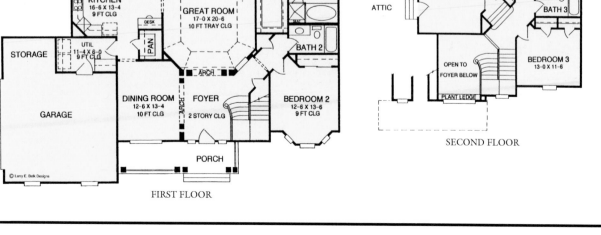

FIRST FLOOR

SECOND FLOOR

Varying roof planes, gables, and dormers help create the unique character of this house. Inside, the family/great room gains attention with its high ceiling, fireplace/media-center wall, view of the upstairs balcony, and French doors to the sunroom. In the U-shaped kitchen, an island work surface, a planning desk, and a pantry are added conveniences. The spacious master suite can function with the home office, library, or private sitting room. Its direct access to the huge raised veranda provides an ideal private outdoor haven for relaxation. The second floor contains two bedrooms and a bath. The garage features a workshop area and stairway to a second-floor storage or multipurpose room.

plan # HPK2900179

FIRST FLOOR: 1,969 SQ. FT.
SECOND FLOOR: 660 SQ. FT.
TOTAL: 2,629 SQ. FT.
BONUS SPACE: 360 SQ. FT.
BEDROOMS: 4
BATHROOMS: 3
WIDTH: 90' - 8"
DEPTH: 80' - 4"
FOUNDATION: UNFINISHED
BASEMENT

ORDER ONLINE @ EPLANS.COM

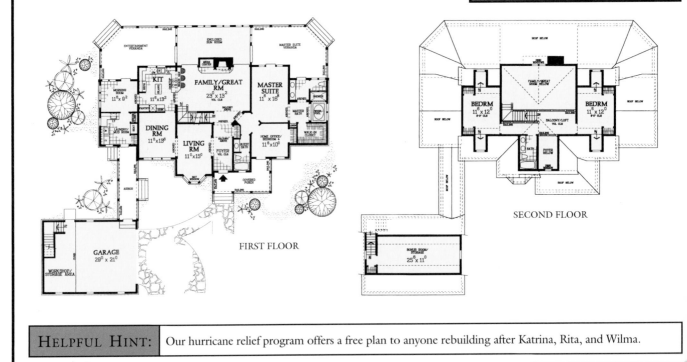

FIRST FLOOR

SECOND FLOOR

HELPFUL HINT: Our hurricane relief program offers a free plan to anyone rebuilding after Katrina, Rita, and Wilma.

plan (#) **HPK2900180**

FIRST FLOOR: 1,362 SQ. FT.
SECOND FLOOR: 1,270 SQ. FT.
TOTAL: 2,632 SQ. FT.
BEDROOMS: 4
BATHROOMS: 2 ½
WIDTH: 79' - 0"
DEPTH: 44' - 0"
FOUNDATION: CRAWLSPACE,
UNFINISHED BASEMENT

ORDER ONLINE @ EPLANS.com

Rich with Victorian details—scalloped shingles, a wraparound veranda, and turrets—this beautiful facade conceals a modern floor plan. Archways announce a distinctive tray-ceilinged living room and help define the dining room. An octagonal den across from the foyer provides a private spot for reading or studying. The U-shaped island kitchen holds an octagonal breakfast bay and a pass-through breakfast bar to the family room. Upstairs, three family bedrooms share a hall bath—one bedroom is within a turret. The master suite is complete with a bayed sitting room along with a fancy bath set in another of the turrets.

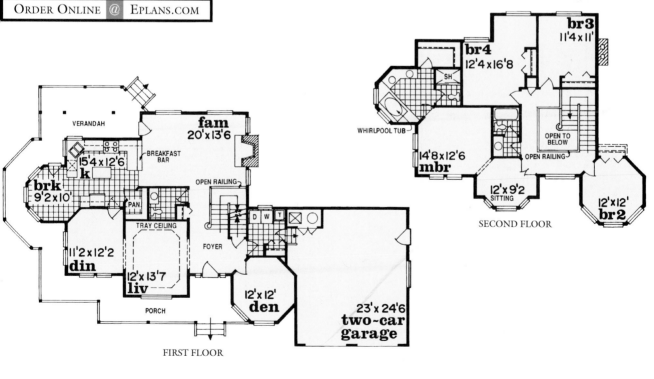

Signature Designer

Amenities abound in this mid-sized luxury plan with European touches. Designer Frank Betz infused everyday spaces with custom details, such as the richly coffered ceiling in the dining room and the private porch attending the master bedroom. Long hallways and transition spaces help define the relationships between the hand-crafted rooms. The cross-gabled exterior leaves room for an attractive courtyard design.

plan# HPK2900181

SQUARE FOOTAGE: 2,656
BONUS SPACE: 484 SQ. FT.
BEDROOMS: 3
BATHROOMS: 2 ½
WIDTH: 63' - 0"
DEPTH: 76' - 6"
FOUNDATION: CRAWLSPACE, UNFINISHED WALKOUT BASEMENT

ORDER ONLINE @ EPLANS.COM

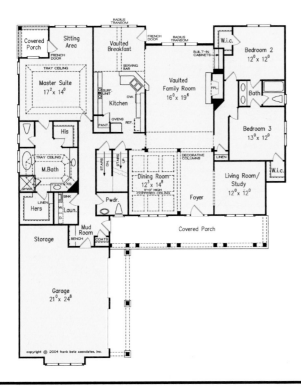

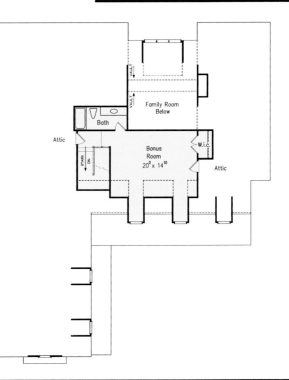

© 1993 Donald A. Gardner Architects, Inc.

B. NATHAN.

plan# HPK2900182

FIRST FLOOR: 2,064 SQ. FT.
SECOND FLOOR: 594 SQ. FT.
TOTAL: 2,658 SQ. FT.
BONUS SPACE: 483 SQ. FT.
BEDROOMS: 4
BATHROOMS: 3½
WIDTH: 92' - 0"
DEPTH: 57' - 8"

ORDER ONLINE @ EPLANS.COM

Meandering through this four-bedroom farmhouse with its wraparound porch, you'll find country living at its best. A front Palladian dormer window and rear clerestory windows in the great room add exciting visual elements to the exterior and provide natural light to the interior. The large great room boasts a fireplace, bookshelves, and a raised cathedral ceiling, allowing a curved balcony overlook above. The great room, master bedroom, and breakfast room are accessible to the rear porch for greater circulation and flexibility. Special features, such as the large cooktop island in the kitchen, the wet bar, the bedroom/study, the generous bonus room over the garage, and ample storage space, set this plan apart.

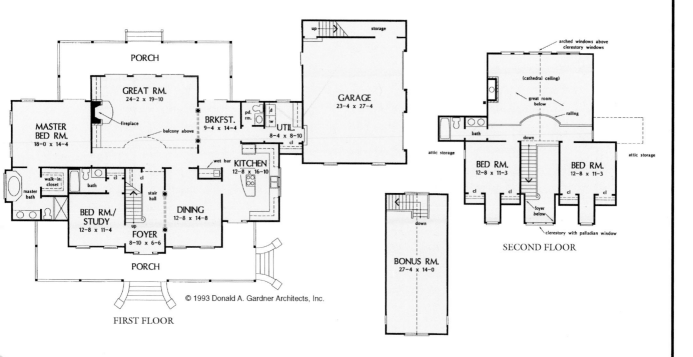

© 1993 Donald A. Gardner Architects, Inc.

FIRST FLOOR

SECOND FLOOR

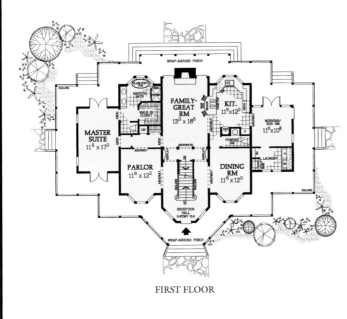

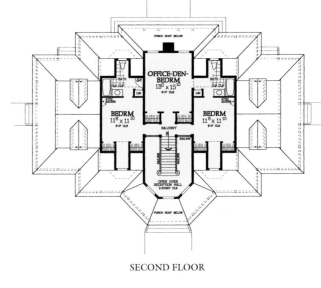

plan# HPK2900183

FIRST FLOOR: 1,752 SQ. FT.
SECOND FLOOR: 906 SQ. FT.
TOTAL: 2,658 SQ. FT.
BEDROOMS: 4
BATHROOMS: 3½
WIDTH: 74' - 0"
DEPTH: 51' - 7"
FOUNDATION: UNFINISHED
BASEMENT

ORDER ONLINE @ EPLANS.COM

Delightfully proportioned and superbly symmetrical, this Victorian farmhouse has lots of curb appeal. The wraparound porch offers rustic columns and railings, and broad steps present easy access to the front, rear, and side yards. Archways, display niches, and columns help define the great room, which offers a fireplace framed by views to the rear property. A formal parlor and a dining room flank the reception hall, and each offers a bay window. The master suite boasts two sets of French doors to the wraparound porch and a private bath with a clawfoot tub, twin lavatories, a walk-in closet, and a stall shower. Upstairs, a spacious office/den adjoins two family bedrooms and can serve as a guest room.

FIRST FLOOR

SECOND FLOOR

plan (#) HPK2900184

SQUARE FOOTAGE: 2,663
BONUS SPACE: 653 SQ. FT.
BEDROOMS: 4
BATHROOMS: 2½
WIDTH: 72' - 7"
DEPTH: 71' - 5"

ORDER ONLINE @ EPLANS.COM

This home's personality is reflected in charming arch-top windows, set off with keystones and decorative shutters. A columned foyer enjoys natural light from a clerestory window and opens to the great room, which boasts a cathedral ceiling and sliding glass doors to the sunroom. An extended-hearth fireplace adds warmth to the living area. Open planning allows the nearby gourmet kitchen to share the glow of the hearth. The breakfast room really lets the sunshine in with a triple window to the rear property. The master suite offers private access to the rear deck with a spa and features a cozy fireplace, a relaxing bath, and a generous walk-in closet. Three family bedrooms—or make one a study—share a full bath and a powder room on the other side of the plan.

© 1993 Donald A. Gardner Architects, Inc.

HELPFUL HINT: Many of our plans come with optional landscape or deck plans.

An inviting entry porch on this fine home impresses with a warm welcome. Upon entering the foyer, notice the formal living room to the right and a casual den area to the left. The open family room boasts a fireplace and overlooks the rear patio. An island cooktop kitchen is conveniently located between the dining room and the breakfast nook. A laundry room is available on the first floor, and a workshop area sits inside the two-car garage. Secluded on the first floor for privacy, the master suite provides a luxurious private bath, a spacious walk-in closet, and private access to the rear patio. On the second floor, two additional family bedrooms, each with walk-in closets, share access to a bathroom. A spacious loft area completes the upper floor.

plan# HPK2900185

FIRST FLOOR: 1,907 SQ. FT.
SECOND FLOOR: 758 SQ. FT.
TOTAL: 2,665 SQ. FT.
BEDROOMS: 3
BATHROOMS: 2½
WIDTH: 50' - 0"
DEPTH: 86' - 0"
FOUNDATION: SLAB

ORDER ONLINE @ EPLANS.COM

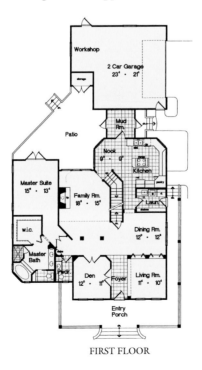

FIRST FLOOR

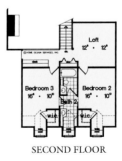

SECOND FLOOR

plan # HPK2900186

FIRST FLOOR: 1,297 SQ. FT.
SECOND FLOOR: 1,390 SQ. FT.
TOTAL: 2,687 SQ. FT.
BONUS SPACE: 229 SQ. FT.
BEDROOMS: 3
BATHROOMS: 2½
WIDTH: 60' - 0"
DEPTH: 44' - 0"
FOUNDATION: FINISHED
BASEMENT

ORDER ONLINE @ EPLANS.COM

If sitting on the porch with your coffee in the morning, taking in the sunshine in the afternoon, and basking in the moonlight by evening is your idea of perfection, look no further than this plan. With a porch that wraps around three corners of the house, outdoor living is ideal. Two bedrooms even enjoy access to the second-floor balcony! Inside, spacious and open planning means that cooking in the kitchen and serving the dining area leads to entertaining in the living room without a hitch. A breakfast nook and a den provide more closed options. Upstairs are three bedrooms and two full baths—take a look at the space in the master bath! Another sitting area near the stairs is a treat.

FIRST FLOOR

SECOND FLOOR

This grand farmhouse design is anything but ordinary. Its lovely details—a Palladian window, a covered veranda, and shutters—put it a cut above the rest. The interior features classic floor planning with a vaulted center-hall foyer and staircase to the second floor. Formal areas—a living room and a dining room—reside on the right; a cozy den and the large family room are on the left. A full bath sits near the den so that it can double as guest space. Four bedrooms on the second floor include a luxurious master suite.

plan # HPK2900189

FIRST FLOOR: 1,639 SQ. FT.
SECOND FLOOR: 1,158 SQ. FT.
TOTAL: 2,797 SQ. FT.
BEDROOMS: 4
BATHROOMS: 3
WIDTH: 80' - 0"
DEPTH: 44' - 0"
FOUNDATION: CRAWLSPACE,
UNFINISHED BASEMENT

ORDER ONLINE @ EPLANS.COM

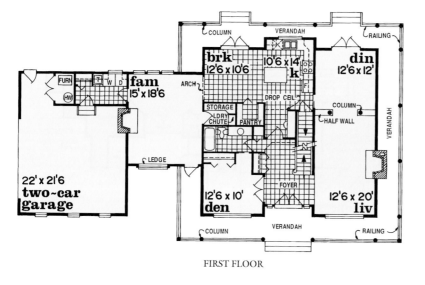

FIRST FLOOR

SECOND FLOOR

HELPFUL HINT: The national cost-to-build average, based on the heated living space of the home, is $110 per sq. ft.

Plan # HPK2900190

SQUARE FOOTAGE: 2,818
BEDROOMS: 4
BATHROOMS: 3
WIDTH: 70' - 0"
DEPTH: 69' - 10"

ORDER ONLINE @ EPLANS.COM

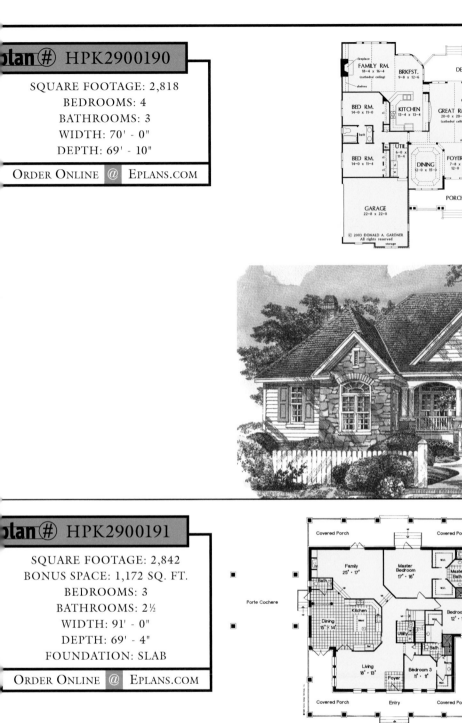

Plan # HPK2900191

SQUARE FOOTAGE: 2,842
BONUS SPACE: 1,172 SQ. FT.
BEDROOMS: 3
BATHROOMS: 2½
WIDTH: 91' - 0"
DEPTH: 69' - 4"
FOUNDATION: SLAB

ORDER ONLINE @ EPLANS.COM

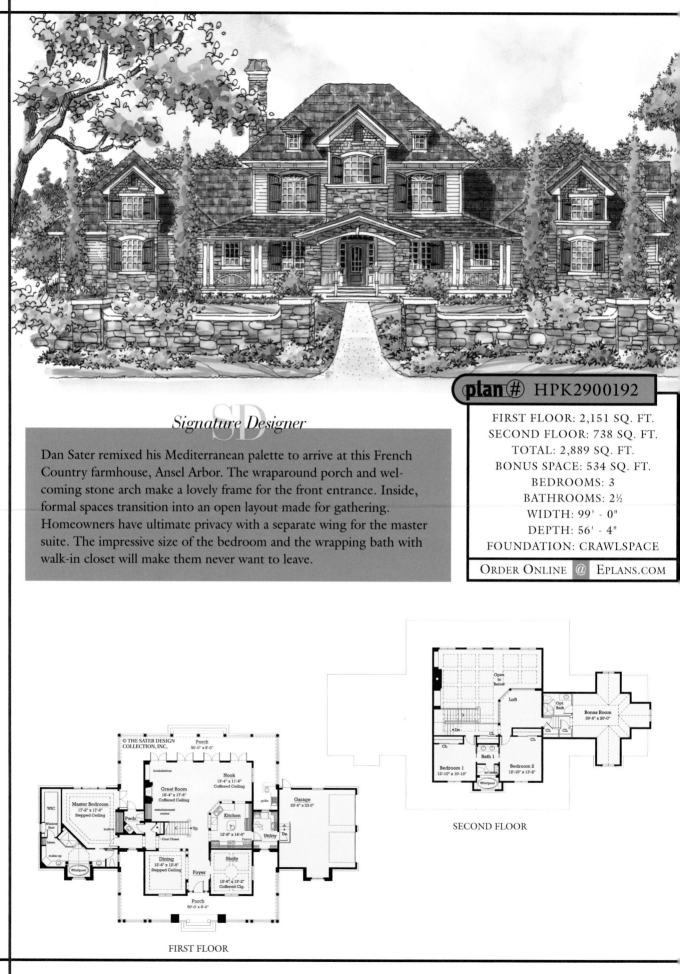

plan # HPK2900192

Signature Designer

Dan Sater remixed his Mediterranean palette to arrive at this French Country farmhouse, Ansel Arbor. The wraparound porch and welcoming stone arch make a lovely frame for the front entrance. Inside, formal spaces transition into an open layout made for gathering. Homeowners have ultimate privacy with a separate wing for the master suite. The impressive size of the bedroom and the wrapping bath with walk-in closet will make them never want to leave.

FIRST FLOOR: 2,151 SQ. FT.
SECOND FLOOR: 738 SQ. FT.
TOTAL: 2,889 SQ. FT.
BONUS SPACE: 534 SQ. FT.
BEDROOMS: 3
BATHROOMS: 2½
WIDTH: 99' - 0"
DEPTH: 56' - 4"
FOUNDATION: CRAWLSPACE

ORDER ONLINE @ EPLANS.COM

SECOND FLOOR

FIRST FLOOR

plan # HPK2900503

FIRST FLOOR: 1,804 SQ. FT.
SECOND FLOOR: 1,041 SQ. FT.
TOTAL: 2,845 SQ. FT.
BEDROOMS: 4
BATHROOMS: 3½
WIDTH: 57' - 3"
DEPTH: 71' - 0"
FOUNDATION: FINISHED
WALKOUT BASEMENT

ORDER ONLINE @ EPLANS.COM

FIRST FLOOR

SECOND FLOOR

REAR EXTERIOR

plan # HPK2900193

FIRST FLOOR: 1,913 SQ. FT.
SECOND FLOOR: 997 SQ. FT.
TOTAL: 2,910 SQ. FT.
BONUS SPACE: 377 SQ. FT.
BEDROOMS: 4
BATHROOMS: 3½
WIDTH: 63' - 0"
DEPTH: 59' - 4"
FOUNDATION: CRAWLSPACE,
UNFINISHED BASEMENT

ORDER ONLINE @ EPLANS.COM

FIRST FLOOR

SECOND FLOOR

plan# HPK2900194

FIRST FLOOR: 2,316 SQ. FT.
SECOND FLOOR: 721 SQ. FT.
TOTAL: 3,037 SQ. FT.
BONUS SPACE: 545 SQ. FT.
BEDROOMS: 4
BATHROOMS: 3½
WIDTH: 95' - 4"
DEPTH: 54' - 10"

ORDER ONLINE @ EPLANS.COM

Three dormers top a covered wraparound porch on this attractive country home. The entrance with Palladian clerestory window lends an abundance of natural light into the foyer. The great room furthers this feeling of airiness with a balcony above the great room and two sets of sliding glass doors leading to the back porch. For privacy, the master suite occupies the right side of the first floor. With a sitting bay and all the amenities of a modern master bath, this lavish retreat will be a welcome haven for the homeowner. Two family bedrooms reside upstairs, sharing a full hall bath.

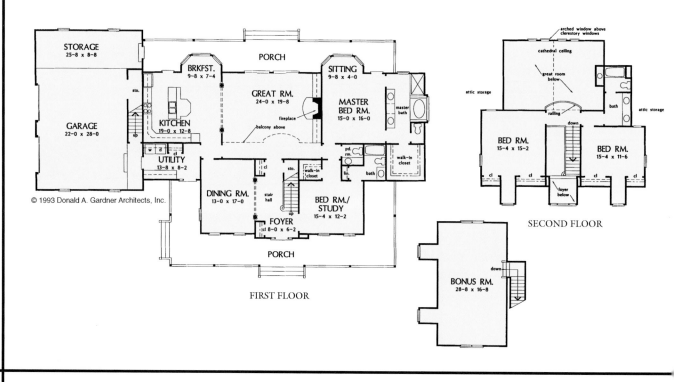

plan # HPK2900195

FIRST FLOOR: 2,194 SQ. FT.
SECOND FLOOR: 870 SQ. FT.
TOTAL: 3,064 SQ. FT.
BONUS SPACE: 251 SQ. FT.
BEDROOMS: 3
BATHROOMS: 2½
WIDTH: 50' - 11"
DEPTH: 91' - 2"
FOUNDATION: CRAWLSPACE

ORDER ONLINE @ EPLANS.COM

With equally appealing front and side entrances, a charming Victorian facade invites entry to this stunning home. The foyer showcases the characteristic winding staircase and opens to the large great room with masonry fireplace. An enormous kitchen features a cooktop island and a breakfast bar large enough to seat four. A lovely bay window distinguishes the nearby dining room. The master suite with masonry fireplace is located on the first floor. The amenity-filled master bath features double vanities, a whirlpool tub, a separate shower, and a gigantic walk-in closet with an additional cedar closet. The second floor contains two bedrooms—one with access to the outdoor balcony on the side of the home. The third floor is completely expandable.

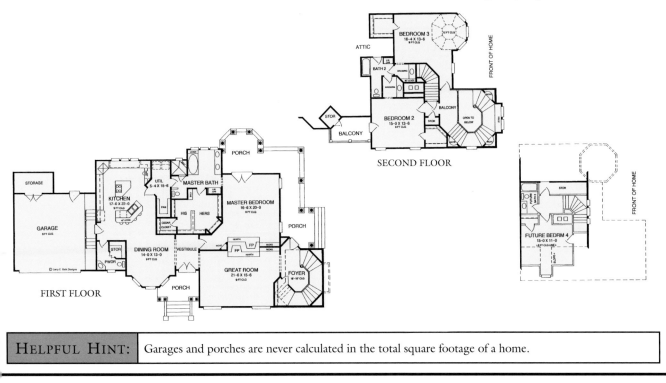

HELPFUL HINT: Garages and porches are never calculated in the total square footage of a home.

©The Sater Design Collection, Inc.

A circular front porch and an abundance of arched windows welcome both sunshine and guests to this brick Victorian home. A radius staircase adorns the entry and leads gracefully up to three secondary bedrooms. The first-floor master suite includes porch access and a deluxe bath featuring a whirlpool tub. Other unique features on the first floor include a study with a window seat and built-in cabinetry, an island kitchen, a nook and a butler's pantry, a utility room, and an outdoor kitchen. The relaxing leisure room sports a built-in entertainment center. Two sets of double doors lead from the leisure room to the outdoor kitchen on the wraparound porch.

plan# HPK2900196

FIRST FLOOR: 2,083 SQ. FT.
SECOND FLOOR: 1,013 SQ. FT.
TOTAL: 3,096 SQ. FT.
BEDROOMS: 4
BATHROOMS: 3½
WIDTH: 74' - 0"
DEPTH: 88' - 6"
FOUNDATION: CRAWLSPACE

ORDER ONLINE @ Eplans.com

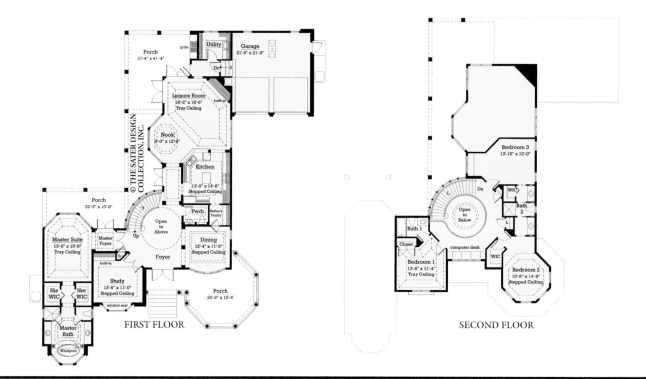

FIRST FLOOR

SECOND FLOOR

© William E. Poole Designs, Inc.

plan# HPK2900197

FIRST FLOOR: 1,480 SQ. FT.
SECOND FLOOR: 1,651 SQ. FT.
TOTAL: 3,131 SQ. FT.
BEDROOMS: 4
BATHROOMS: 3½
WIDTH: 67' - 5"
DEPTH: 61' - 5"
FOUNDATION: CRAWLSPACE

ORDER ONLINE @ EPLANS.com

This design incorporates Victorian touches with the masterful use of a turret and a gazebo. With a wealth of windows, this home never lacks natural light. Inside, divergent room shapes offer interesting appeal. The family room is centrally located with a fireplace and a built-in entertainment center on the left wall. The island kitchen features a built-in desk, abundant counter space, and a butler's pantry. A separate utility room houses the washer/dryer, fold-down ironing board, and sink. The second floor houses the sleeping quarters, including the lavish master suite, complete with a private sitting area and fireplace, and three additional family bedrooms sharing two full baths.

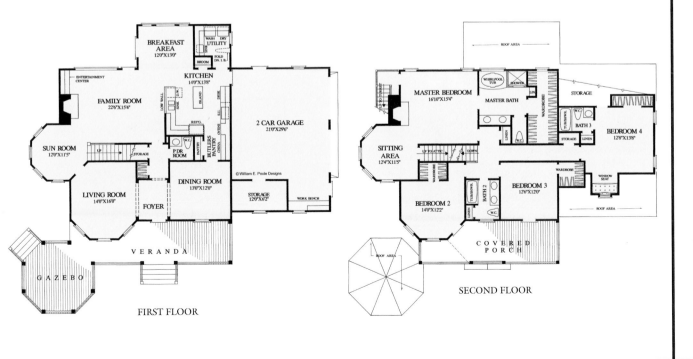

plan# HPK2900198

FIRST FLOOR: 2,086 SQ. FT.
SECOND FLOOR: 1,077 SQ. FT.
TOTAL: 3,163 SQ. FT.
BONUS SPACE: 403 SQ. FT.
BEDROOMS: 4
BATHROOMS: 3½
WIDTH: 81' - 10"
DEPTH: 51' - 8"

ORDER ONLINE @ EPLANS.COM

This beautiful farmhouse, with its prominent twin gables and bays, adds just the right amount of country style. The master suite is quietly tucked away downstairs with no rooms directly above. The family cook will love the spacious U-shaped kitchen and adjoining bayed breakfast nook. A bonus room awaits expansion on the second floor, where three large bedrooms share two full baths. Storage space abounds with walk-ins, half-shelves, and linen closets. A curved balcony borders a versatile loft/study, which overlooks the stunning two-story family room.

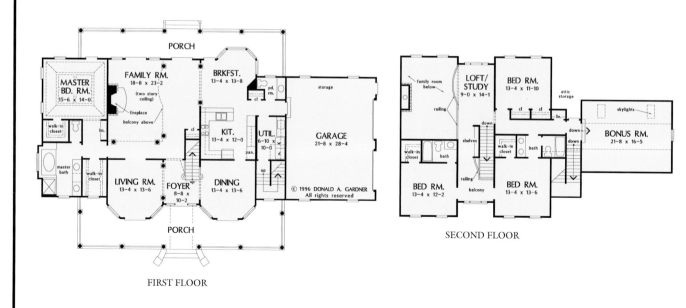

FIRST FLOOR

SECOND FLOOR

plan # HPK2900199

FIRST FLOOR: 1,670 SQ. FT.
SECOND FLOOR: 1,590 SQ. FT.
TOTAL: 3,260 SQ. FT.
BEDROOMS: 5
BATHROOMS: 4
WIDTH: 53' - 4"
DEPTH: 50' - 0"
FOUNDATION: UNFINISHED
BASEMENT

ORDER ONLINE @ EPLANS.COM

Designed for living comfort and entertaining, this fetching plan may be exactly what you are looking for. Step into the two-story foyer and formal dining and living rooms are immediately on either side. Straight ahead, the grand room soars two stories and sweeps around a curved bar into the informal family breakfast alcove. On the other side of the bar/counter, the spacious kitchen opens to a keeping room with a charming fireplace. A bedroom with a private bath is situated on the first floor—perfect for sleepover guests—and four more bedrooms, all with walk-in closets, and three baths are upstairs. The resplendent master suite has a sitting room with an inviting view of the backyard and gardens. Optional space that could be used for an exercise room, office, or hobby area is also on this floor.

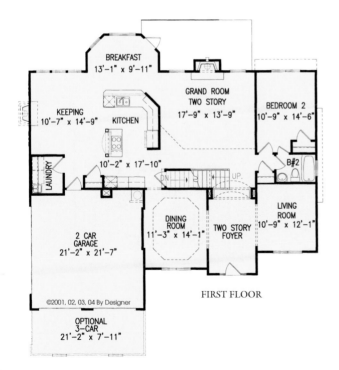

FIRST FLOOR

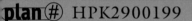

SECOND FLOOR

Dormered windows, a covered porch, and symmetrical balustrades provide a warm country welcome. Inside, formal living and dining rooms flank the foyer. To the left of the dining room and down a step is a spacious family room with a raised-hearth fireplace. The nearby breakfast/kitchen area features an island cooktop, a pantry, and a planning desk. French doors in the breakfast area, the study (or optional guest room), and the master suite's sitting area provide access to the rear porch. A lavish master bath is complete with a whirlpool tub and separate His and Hers dressing areas. The second floor contains two family bedrooms and a full bath with separate vanities.

plan# HPK2900200

FIRST FLOOR: 2,426 SQ. FT.
SECOND FLOOR: 876 SQ. FT.
TOTAL: 3,302 SQ. FT.
BEDROOMS: 4
BATHROOMS: 3
WIDTH: 83' - 0"
DEPTH: 69' - 6"
FOUNDATION: UNFINISHED BASEMENT

ORDER ONLINE @ EPLANS.COM

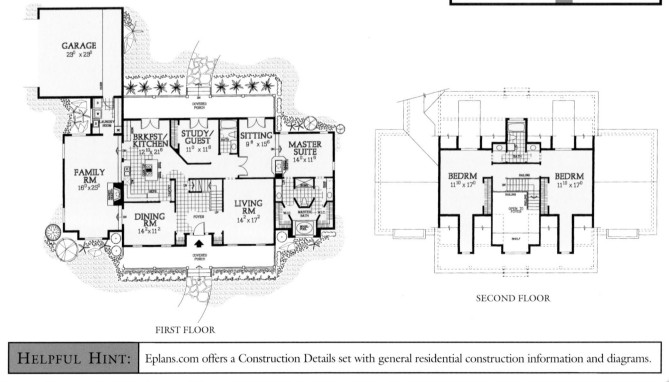

FIRST FLOOR

SECOND FLOOR

HELPFUL HINT: Eplans.com offers a Construction Details set with general residential construction information and diagrams.

plan # HPK2900201

MAIN LEVEL: 1,944 SQ. FT.
SECOND LEVEL: 1,196 SQ. FT.
LOWER LEVEL: 195 SQ. FT.
TOTAL: 3,335 SQ. FT.
BEDROOMS: 4
BATHROOMS: 4½
WIDTH: 68' - 0"
DEPTH: 54' - 0"
FOUNDATION: SLAB

ORDER ONLINE @ EPLANS.COM

In the deluxe grand room of this Floridian home, family and friends will enjoy the ambiance created by arches and access to a veranda. Two guest rooms flank a full bath; one of the guest rooms also sports a private deck. The kitchen serves a circular breakfast nook. Upstairs, a balcony overlook furthers the drama of the grand room. The master suite, with a deck and a private bath opening through a pocket door, will be a pleasure to occupy. Another bedroom—or use this room for a study—sits at the other side of this floor. It extends the wing with a curved bay window, an expansive deck, built-ins, and a full bath. The lower level contains enough room for two cars in its carport and offers plenty of storage and bonus room.

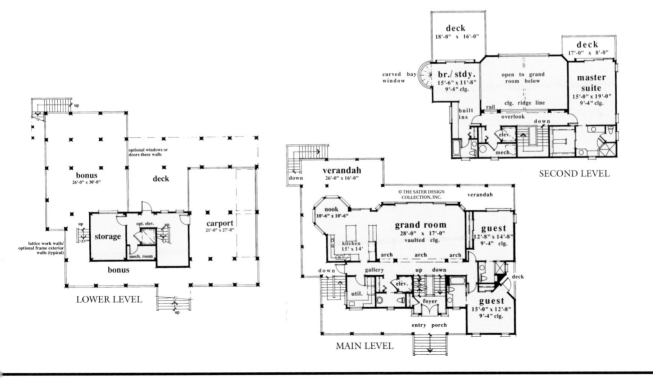

Dutch-gable rooflines and a gabled wraparound porch provide an extra measure of farmhouse style. The foyer opens on the left to the study or guest bedroom that leads to the master suite. To the right is the formal dining room; the massive great room is in the center. The kitchen combines with the great room, the breakfast nook, and the dining room for entertaining options. The master suite includes access to the covered patio, a spacious walk-in closet, and a full bath with a whirlpool tub.

plan # HPK2900202

FIRST FLOOR: 2,347 SQ. FT.
SECOND FLOOR: 1,087 SQ. FT.
TOTAL: 3,434 SQ. FT.
BEDROOMS: 4
BATHROOMS: 2½
WIDTH: 93' - 6"
DEPTH: 61' - 0"
FOUNDATION: UNFINISHED BASEMENT

ORDER ONLINE @ EPLANS.COM

FIRST FLOOR

SECOND FLOOR

plan # HPK2900203

FIRST FLOOR: 1,329 SQ. FT.
SECOND FLOOR: 1,917 SQ. FT.
THIRD FLOOR: 189 SQ. FT.
TOTAL: 3,435 SQ. FT.
BEDROOMS: 3
BATHROOMS: 2½
WIDTH: 40' - 4"
DEPTH: 62' - 0"
FOUNDATION: SLAB

ORDER ONLINE @ EPLANS.COM

While speaking clearly of the past, the inside of this Victorian home coincides with the open, flowing interiors of today. Have meals in the elegant dining room with its tray ceiling, or move through the double French doors between the formal living room and informal family room to sense the comfort of this charming home. The kitchen boasts a large pantry and a corner sink with a window. The lovely master suite resides upstairs. The raised sitting area off the master bedroom provides the owner with a mini retreat for reading and relaxing. The second floor also includes two large bedrooms and a library/music room.

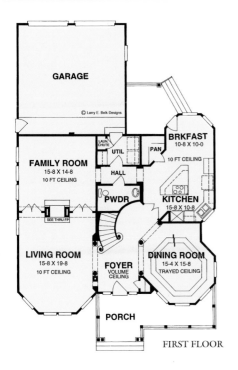

FIRST FLOOR

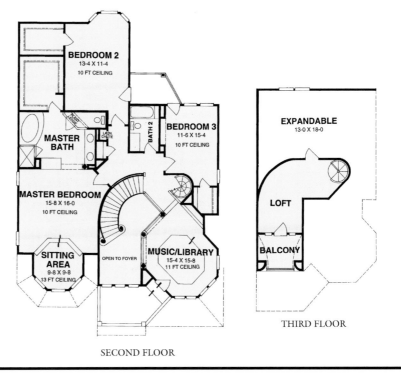

SECOND FLOOR

THIRD FLOOR

plan # HPK2900204

This country farmhouse is accented by exterior features that really stand out—a steep roof gable, shuttered muntin windows, stone siding, and the double-columned, covered front porch. Inside, the entry is flanked by the study/Bedroom 2 and the dining room. Across the tiled gallery, the great room provides an impressive fireplace and overlooks the rear veranda. The island kitchen opens to a bayed breakfast room. The right side of the home includes a utility room and a three-car garage, and two family bedrooms that share a bath. The master wing of the home has a bayed sitting area, a sumptuous bath, and an enormous walk-in closet. The second-floor bonus room is cooled by a ceiling fan and makes a perfect guest suite.

SQUARE FOOTAGE: 3,439
BONUS SPACE: 514 SQ. FT.
BEDROOMS: 4
BATHROOMS: 3½
WIDTH: 100' - 0"
DEPTH: 67' - 11"
FOUNDATION: CRAWLSPACE, SLAB, UNFINISHED BASEMENT

ORDER ONLINE @ EPLANS.COM

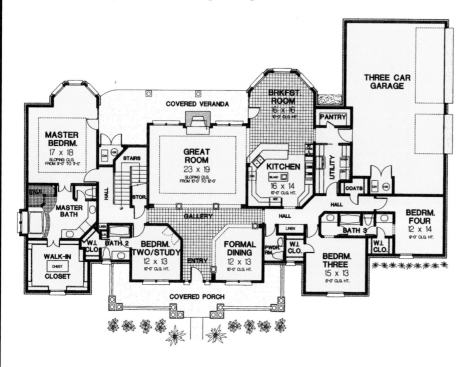

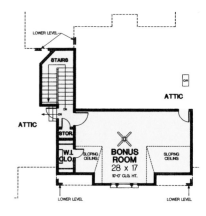

plan # HPK2900205

FIRST FLOOR: 2,202 SQ. FT.
SECOND FLOOR: 1,355 SQ. FT.
TOTAL: 3,557 SQ. FT.
BONUS SPACE: 523 SQ. FT.
BEDROOMS: 4
BATHROOMS: 3½
WIDTH: 66' - 0"
DEPTH: 65' - 10"
FOUNDATION: CRAWLSPACE

ORDER ONLINE @ EPLANS.COM

Signature Designer

Expansive living space with well-appointed amenities, homes by Living Concepts lend a touch of luxury to any neighborhood. Columns and arches distinguish the front porch of this attractive, shingle-sided home. Named the Amhurst by the designer, the rustic exterior of this hillside home is well-suited for a crisp autumn day in any town.

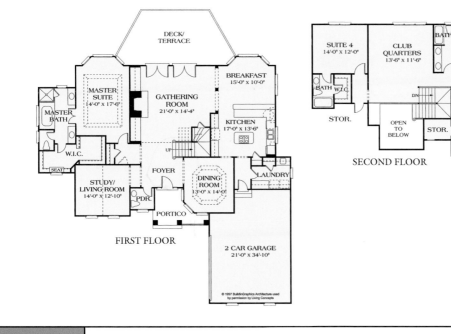

FIRST FLOOR

SECOND FLOOR

HELPFUL HINT: A local engineer can ensure your plan meets local building codes.

plan# HPK2900206

FIRST FLOOR: 2,589 SQ. FT.
SECOND FLOOR: 981 SQ. FT.
TOTAL: 3,570 SQ. FT.
BEDROOMS: 4
BATHROOMS: 3½
WIDTH: 70' - 8"
DEPTH: 61' - 10"
FOUNDATION: CRAWLSPACE

ORDER ONLINE @ EPLANS.COM

Decidedly rustic with exposed truss work and wood exterior, this home has natural appeal. A spacious floor plan maximizes open space with formal rooms flanking the foyer and giving way to a comfortable living room with fireplace and rear deck access. A casual room grouping that includes an island kitchen, family room, office, eating area, and utility room will be the hub of family activity. Let the master suite entice you to relax in privacy and enjoy a hot bath or a great view of the rear landscape and deck. Three family bedrooms are outfitted with walk-in closets and access to two full baths.

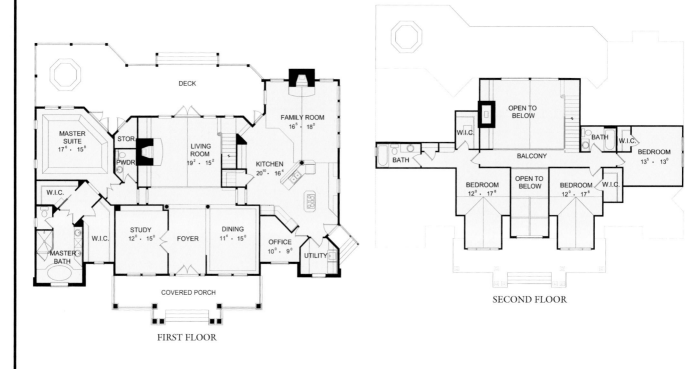

FIRST FLOOR

SECOND FLOOR

© William E. Poole Designs, Inc.

plan # HPK2900207

FIRST FLOOR: 2,442 SQ. FT.
SECOND FLOOR: 1,286 SQ. FT.
TOTAL: 3,728 SQ. FT.
BONUS SPACE: 681 SQ. FT.
BEDROOMS: 4
BATHROOMS: 3½ + ½
WIDTH: 84' - 8"
DEPTH: 60' - 0"
FOUNDATION: CRAWLSPACE

ORDER ONLINE @ EPLANS.COM

With a gazebo-style corner and careful exterior details, you can't help but imagine tea parties, porch swings, and lazy summer evenings spent on this covered porch. Inside, a living room/library will comfort with its fireplace and built-ins. The family room is graced with a fireplace and a curved, two-story ceiling with an overlook above. The master bedroom is a private retreat with a lovely bath, twin walk-in closets, and rear-porch access. Upstairs, three bedrooms with sizable closets—one bedroom would make an excellent guest suite or alternate master suite—share access to expandable space.

FIRST FLOOR

SECOND FLOOR

This luxury countryside cottage is at home in New England-style neighborhoods—perfect for the ideal American home. The foyer is flanked by a dining room and study. The great room is central, while the kitchen and breakfast nook are located to the left of the plan. A luxurious bath and walk-in closet are featured in the master suite. Three additional bedrooms and a media room are upstairs. A bonus room is above the garage.

FIRST FLOOR: 2,513 SQ. FT.
SECOND FLOOR: 1,421 SQ. FT.
TOTAL: 3,934 SQ. FT.
BONUS SPACE: 596 SQ. FT.
BEDROOMS: 4
BATHROOMS: 4½
WIDTH: 72' - 0"
DEPTH: 93' - 0"
FOUNDATION: CRAWLSPACE

ORDER ONLINE @ EPLANS.COM

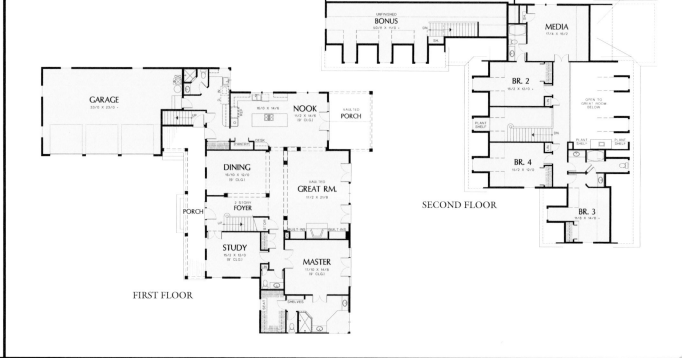

FIRST FLOOR

SECOND FLOOR

plan #️ HPK2900209

FIRST FLOOR: 2,931 SQ. FT.
SECOND FLOOR: 1,319 SQ. FT.
TOTAL: 4,250 SQ. FT.
BEDROOMS: 4
BATHROOMS: 4½
WIDTH: 103' - 7"
DEPTH: 63' - 9"
FOUNDATION: CRAWLSPACE

ORDER ONLINE @ EPLANS.COM

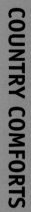

SECOND FLOOR

FIRST FLOOR

plan #️ HPK2900210

FIRST FLOOR: 3,219 SQ. FT.
SECOND FLOOR: 1,202 SQ. FT.
TOTAL: 4,421 SQ. FT.
BEDROOMS: 4
BATHROOMS: 4½
WIDTH: 86' - 1"
DEPTH: 76' - 10"
FOUNDATION: CRAWLSPACE

ORDER ONLINE @ EPLANS.COM

SECOND FLOOR

FIRST FLOOR

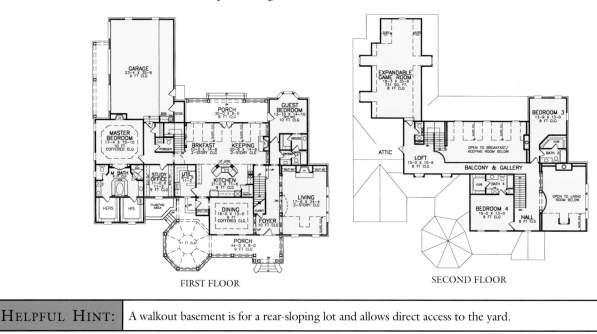

Unusual rooflines characterize this four-bedroom family design. The front porch, with a gazebo-style sitting area, adds a country touch. Interior space begins with an entrance leading directly through the two-story foyer to a living room with a vaulted ceiling and a fireplace with flanking built-ins. The snack-bar kitchen easily serves the dining and breakfast rooms. The combined breakfast and keeping room is warmed by a fireplace and accesses the rear porch through double doors. The master bedroom is also warmed by a fireplace and boasts a luxurious master bath with His and Hers walk-in closets. A study/office is located nearby. On the opposite side of the home, a bay-windowed guest bedroom offers private access to a hall bath. Upstairs, Bedrooms 3 and 4 have their own baths and walk-in closets. A balcony overlooking the breakfast/keeping room leads to a loft area that accesses an expandable game room.

plan# HPK2900211

FIRST FLOOR: 3,211 SQ. FT.
SECOND FLOOR: 1,246 SQ. FT.
TOTAL: 4,457 SQ. FT.
BONUS SPACE: 731 SQ. FT.
BEDROOMS: 4
BATHROOMS: 4½ + ½
WIDTH: 87' - 2"
DEPTH: 90' - 6"
FOUNDATION: CRAWLSPACE

ORDER ONLINE @ EPLANS.COM

FIRST FLOOR

SECOND FLOOR

HELPFUL HINT: A walkout basement is for a rear-sloping lot and allows direct access to the yard.

plan # HPK2900212

FIRST FLOOR: 3,471 SQ. FT.
SECOND FLOOR: 1,221 SQ. FT.
TOTAL: 4,692 SQ. FT.
BEDROOMS: 4
BATHROOMS: 4½ + ½
WIDTH: 100' - 2"
DEPTH: 82' - 6"
FOUNDATION: CRAWLSPACE

ORDER ONLINE @ EPLANS.COM

Multiple dormers and a covered front porch are sure signs that family and friends are welcome to this four-bedroom home. The two-story foyer leads through arches into the formal dining room, living room, and hallway to the first floor sleeping wing. Here, a deluxe master suite has many amenities to offer: a two-sided fireplace, a sitting room, His and Hers walk-in closets, and a lavish bath. On the other end of the home, a spacious kitchen features a cook-top island and has direct access to the adjacent keeping and breakfast rooms. Note the huge walk-in pantry and the sun room. A private study offers a walk-in closet. Upstairs are two more family bedrooms, two-and-a-half baths, and a large game room.

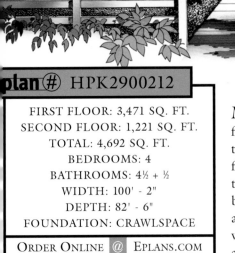

FIRST FLOOR

SECOND FLOOR

A front porch and dormers embellish the side-gabled roof. The wings of the wide floor plan frame a courtyard entry.

Natural Beauty

A pleasing blend of unique details and a lively floor plan recommend this spirited design by Donald Gardner, called the Crowne Canyon. The rest of the section offers a similar blend of crisp rectilinear forms and natural textures that are the hallmarks of the uniquely American and very popular Craftsman style. Other signature details include exposed rafter tails and beams, stone fireplaces, prominent porches, and transom-topped windows and doors, all found in Gardner's design.

The Crowne Canyon's great room, enhanced by an exposed-beam ceiling, a fireplace, and wet bar, shows the Craftsman style at best advantage. The contrast of textures and geometries feels peaceful and meditative, easily creating a space for gathering and casual entertainment. A wall of windows lets natural light into the room, which helps to justify its extraordinary height.

To the left of the great room, informal columns define the dining room, which opens to a charming gourmet kitchen with a pantry, an island cooktop, and a box-bay window over a double sink. The screened porch, also accessible through the dining room, includes a second fireplace and opens to the side and rear covered porches. It is to the designer's credit that outdoor spaces emerge throughout the home with ease and surprise.

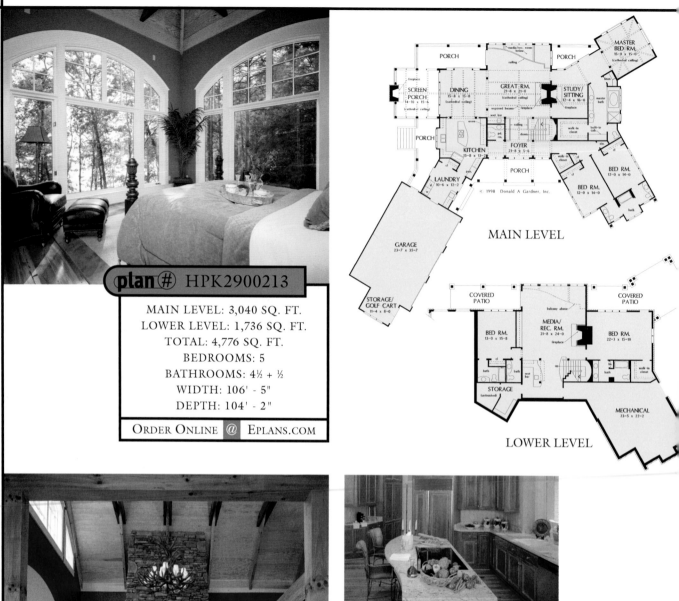

plan# HPK2900213

MAIN LEVEL: 3,040 SQ. FT.
LOWER LEVEL: 1,736 SQ. FT.
TOTAL: 4,776 SQ. FT.
BEDROOMS: 5
BATHROOMS: 4½ + ½
WIDTH: 106' - 5"
DEPTH: 104' - 2"

ORDER ONLINE @ EPLANS.COM

MAIN LEVEL

LOWER LEVEL

TOP: Picture windows provide panoramic views from the master bedroom, which is further enhanced by a cathedral ceiling.
ABOVE: A massive stone hearth is the focal point of the home's centerpiece: the great room. ABOVE RIGHT: The distressed finish of the cabinets complements the hardwood floor. The layout provides plenty of workspace and storage. RIGHT: Rearward views from the great room are framed in spectacular fashion.

plan ⊕ HPK2900214

SQUARE FOOTAGE: 1,404
BONUS SPACE: 256 SQ. FT.
BEDROOMS: 2
BATHROOMS: 2
WIDTH: 54' - 7"
DEPTH: 46' - 6"
FOUNDATION: CRAWLSPACE

ORDER ONLINE @ EPLANS.COM

This rustic Craftsman-style cottage provides an open interior with good flow to the outdoors. The front covered porch invites casual gatherings; inside, the dining area is set for both everyday and formal occasions. Meal preparations are a breeze with a cooktop/snack-bar island in the kitchen. A centered fireplace in the great room shares its warmth with the dining room. A rear hall leads to the master bedroom and a secondary bedroom; upstairs, a loft has space for computers.

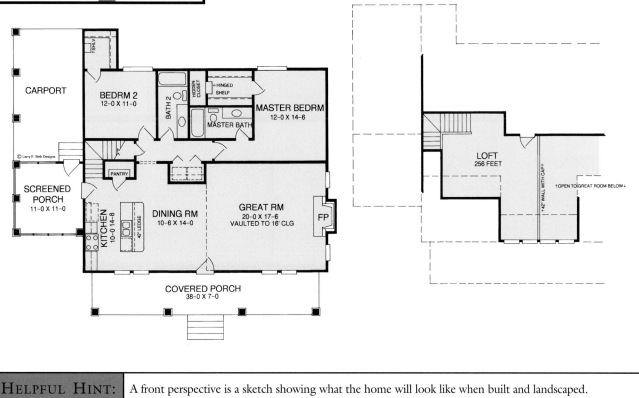

HELPFUL HINT: A front perspective is a sketch showing what the home will look like when built and landscaped.

plan # HPK2900215

FIRST FLOOR: 1,024 SQ. FT.
SECOND FLOOR: 456 SQ. FT.
TOTAL: 1,480 SQ. FT.
BEDROOMS: 2
BATHROOMS: 2
WIDTH: 32' - 0"
DEPTH: 40' - 0"
FOUNDATION: FINISHED
WALKOUT BASEMENT

ORDER ONLINE @ EPLANS.COM

Multi-pane windows lend subtle Craftsman flavor to this lovely country cottage. Inside, the entry room has a coat closet and an interior entry door to eliminate drafts. The light-filled L-shaped kitchen lies conveniently near the entrance. A large room adjacent to the kitchen serves as a dining and living area where a fireplace adds warmth. A master suite boasts a walk-in closet and full bath. The second floor holds a loft, a second bedroom, and a full bath.

FIRST FLOOR

SECOND FLOOR

plan# HPK2900216

FIRST FLOOR: 1,024 SQ. FT.
SECOND FLOOR: 456 SQ. FT.
TOTAL: 1,480 SQ. FT.
BEDROOMS: 2
BATHROOMS: 2
WIDTH: 32' - 0"
DEPTH: 40' - 0"
FOUNDATION: UNFINISHED
BASEMENT

ORDER ONLINE @ EPLANS.COM

A conservative and charming traditional plan delivers easy living and awaits a personal touch. The two-story great room and dining area handles family gatherings, apart from the master bedroom at the top of the plan. The second bedroom resides upstairs, along with a reading room or media room. Full baths accompany both bedrooms. A classic front porch frames the entryway and brings interest to the cross-gabled design. A small mudroom/utility space receives traffic from the rear entry.

FIRST FLOOR

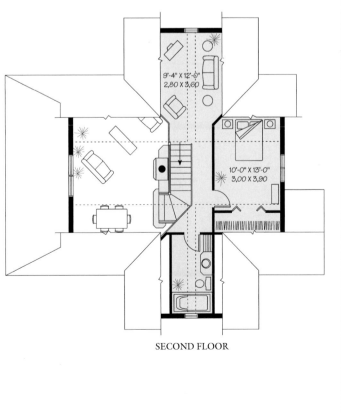

SECOND FLOOR

FIRST FLOOR

3,00 X 3,30
10'-0" X 11'-0"

4,30 X 3,00
14'-4" X 10'-0"

3,80 X 3,80
12'-0" X 12'-8"

3,80 X 3,50
12'-8" X 11'-8"

4,20 X 3,50
14'-0" X 11'-8"

SECOND FLOOR

4,30 X 3,30
14'-4" X 11'-0"

4,30 X 3,80
14'-4" X 12'-8"

plan # HPK2900217

FIRST FLOOR: 908 SQ. FT.
SECOND FLOOR: 576 SQ. FT.
TOTAL: 1,484 SQ. FT.
BEDROOMS: 3
BATHROOMS: 2
WIDTH: 26' - 0"
DEPTH: 36' - 0"
FOUNDATION: FINISHED
WALKOUT BASEMENT

ORDER ONLINE @ EPLANS.COM

Dining
11'6" x 14'2"

Covered
Porch

Great Room
16'10" x 17'

Master Bedroom
14' x 11'8"

Kitchen
18'2" x 10'10"

Two-Car
Garage
22' x 20'

Laun.
6'9" x 7'

Foyer

Bath

Bedroom
10'6" x 10'4"

Porch

Bedroom
11' x 10'6"

plan # HPK2900218

SQUARE FOOTAGE: 1,509
BEDROOMS: 3
BATHROOMS: 2
WIDTH: 59' - 4"
DEPTH: 46' - 4"
FOUNDATION: UNFINISHED
BASEMENT

ORDER ONLINE @ EPLANS.COM

plan# HPK2900219

SQUARE FOOTAGE: 1,526
BONUS SPACE: 336 SQ. FT.
BEDROOMS: 3
BATHROOMS: 2
WIDTH: 65' - 0"
DEPTH: 54' - 0"
FOUNDATION: CRAWLSPACE

ORDER ONLINE @ EPLANS.COM

Signature Designer SD

Craftsman influences guide the work of celebrated designer Dan Sater. Mansions to cottages alike impress with abundant detail and superior amenities. The Davenport, as named by the designer, is a perfect plan for a couple that desires all the luxuries without excess space. Rich warm stone adorns the facade of this home and upscale touches such as elegant ceiling treatments, built-in cabinets, and decorative columns enhance the efficient design.

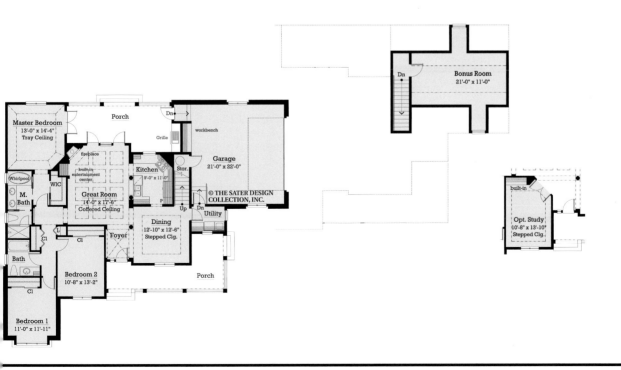

© THE SATER DESIGN COLLECTION, INC.

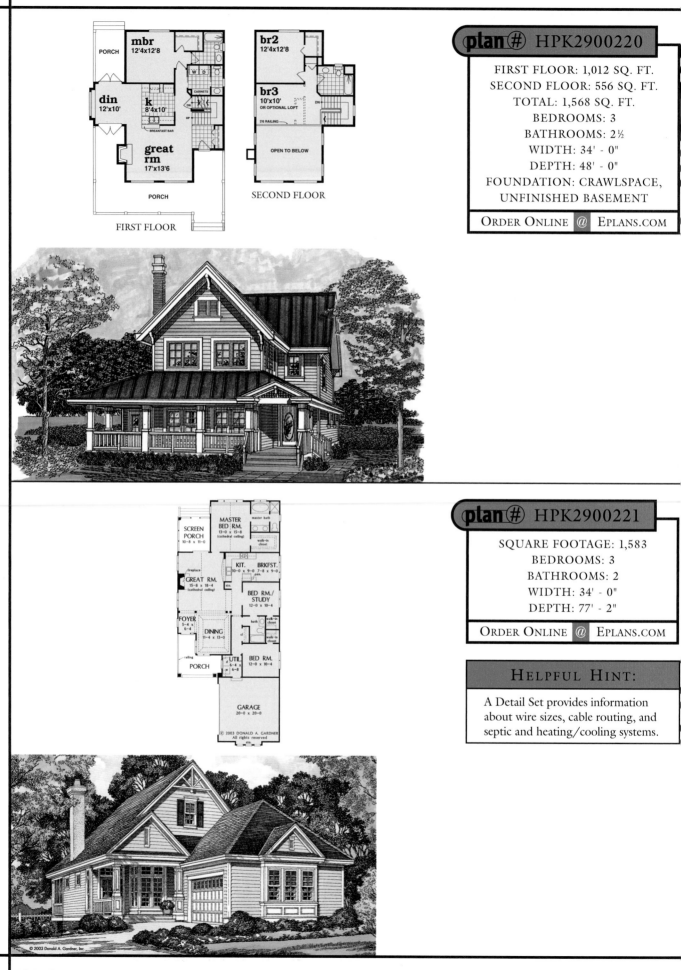

FIRST FLOOR

PORCH

mbr
12'4x12'8

din
12'x10'

k
8'4x10'

W D

CABINETS

BREAKFAST BAR

great
rm
17'x13'6

PORCH

SECOND FLOOR

br2
12'4x12'8

br3
10'x10'
OR OPTIONAL LOFT

DN

3'6 RAILING

OPEN TO BELOW

plan # HPK2900220

FIRST FLOOR: 1,012 SQ. FT.
SECOND FLOOR: 556 SQ. FT.
TOTAL: 1,568 SQ. FT.
BEDROOMS: 3
BATHROOMS: 2½
WIDTH: 34' - 0"
DEPTH: 48' - 0"
FOUNDATION: CRAWLSPACE,
UNFINISHED BASEMENT

ORDER ONLINE @ EPLANS.COM

SCREEN
PORCH
10-8 x 11-0

MASTER
BED RM.
13-0 x 15-8
(cathedral ceiling)

master bath

walk-in
closet

fireplace

GREAT RM.
15-8 x 18-4
(cathedral ceiling)

KIT.
10-0 x 9-0

BRKFST.
7-8 x 9-0

BED RM./
STUDY
12-0 x 10-4

FOYER
5-4 x
6-4

bath
walk-in
closet

DINING
11-4 x 13-0

walk-in
closet

cl

railing

PORCH

UTIL.
6-4 x
6-8

BED RM.
12-0 x 10-4

GARAGE
20-0 x 20-0

© 2003 Donald A. Gardner
All rights reserved

plan # HPK2900221

SQUARE FOOTAGE: 1,583
BEDROOMS: 3
BATHROOMS: 2
WIDTH: 34' - 0"
DEPTH: 77' - 2"

ORDER ONLINE @ EPLANS.COM

HELPFUL HINT:

A Detail Set provides information
about wire sizes, cable routing, and
septic and heating/cooling systems.

© 2003 Donald A. Gardner, Inc.

plan # HPK2900222

FIRST FLOOR: 1,108 SQ. FT.
SECOND FLOOR: 517 SQ. FT.
TOTAL: 1,625 SQ. FT.
BEDROOMS: 3
BATHROOMS: 2
WIDTH: 36' - 0"
DEPTH: 36' - 0"
FOUNDATION: UNFINISHED
BASEMENT

ORDER ONLINE @ EPLANS.COM

Stone-and-wood siding echo the great outdoors in this design. A small porch is perfect for dusting off the snow and stargazing on dark winter nights. Inside, a fireplace warms up the living room. The kitchen provides an area for a dining table, plenty of work space, and storage with a corner window sink. The master bedroom has a spacious walk-in closet and has a full bath with a dual-sink vanity. On the second level, two family bedrooms share a full bath and the loft overlook to the living room.

REAR EXTERIOR

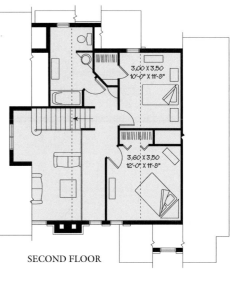

SECOND FLOOR

FIRST FLOOR

plan # HPK2900223

FIRST FLOOR: 1,094 SQ. FT.
SECOND FLOOR: 576 SQ. FT.
TOTAL: 1,670 SQ. FT.
BEDROOMS: 3
BATHROOMS: 2
WIDTH: 43' - 0"
DEPTH: 35' - 4"
FOUNDATION: CRAWLSPACE

ORDER ONLINE @ EPLANS.COM

A covered veranda with covered deck above opens through French doors to the living/dining area of this vacation cottage. A masonry fireplace with a wood storage bin warms this area. A modified U-shaped kitchen serves the dining room; a laundry room is just across the hall near a side veranda. The master bedroom is on the first floor and has the use of a full bath. Sliding glass doors in the master bedroom and the living room lead to still another veranda. The second floor has two family bedrooms, a full bath, a family room with a balcony overlooking the living room and dining room, a fireplace, and double doors to a patio. A large storage area on this level adds convenience.

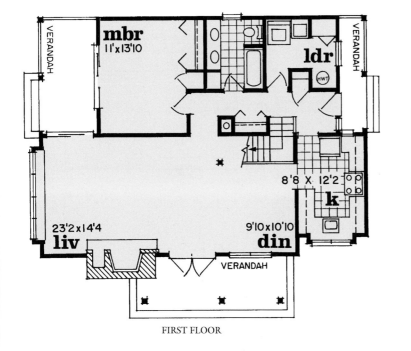

FIRST FLOOR

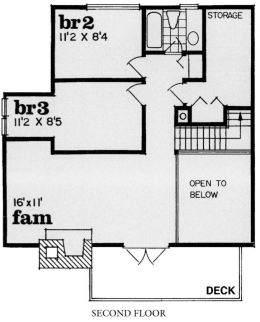

SECOND FLOOR

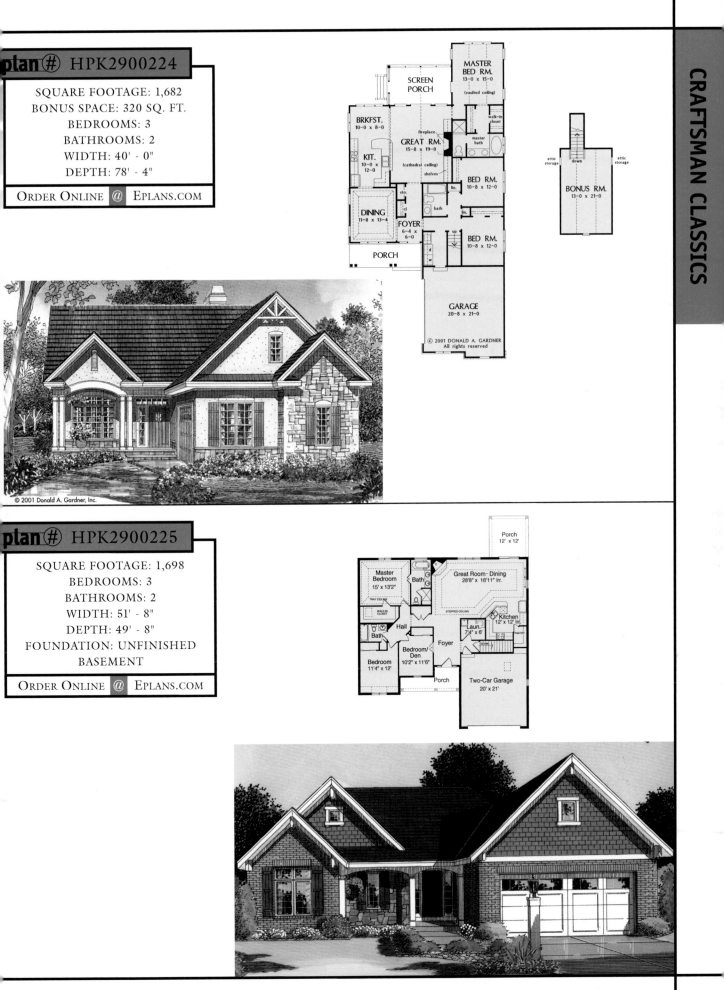

plan# HPK2900224

SQUARE FOOTAGE: 1,682
BONUS SPACE: 320 SQ. FT.
BEDROOMS: 3
BATHROOMS: 2
WIDTH: 40' - 0"
DEPTH: 78' - 4"

ORDER ONLINE @ EPLANS.COM

MASTER BED RM.
13-0 x 15-0
(vaulted ceiling)

SCREEN PORCH

walk-in closet

BRKFST.
10-0 x 8-0

GREAT RM.
15-8 x 19-0
(cathedral ceiling)

KIT.
10-0 x 12-0

fireplace

master bath

shelves

BED RM.
10-8 x 12-0

lin.

DINING
11-8 x 13-4

sto.
cl.

bath

lin.

FOYER
6-4 x 6-0

up

BED RM.
10-8 x 12-0

PORCH

d
w

GARAGE
20-8 x 21-0

© 2001 DONALD A. GARDNER
All rights reserved

attic storage

down

attic storage

BONUS RM.
13-0 x 21-0

plan# HPK2900225

SQUARE FOOTAGE: 1,698
BEDROOMS: 3
BATHROOMS: 2
WIDTH: 51' - 8"
DEPTH: 49' - 8"
FOUNDATION: UNFINISHED BASEMENT

ORDER ONLINE @ EPLANS.COM

Porch
12' x 12'

Master Bedroom
15' x 13'2"

Bath

Great Room- Dining
28'8" x 16'11" irr.

TRAY CEILING

WALK-IN CLOSET

STEPPED CEILING

Kitchen
12' x 12' irr.

Bath

Hall

Laun.
7'4" x 6'

PANTRY

Bedroom
11'4" x 12'

Bedroom/ Den
10'2" x 11'6"

Foyer

DOWN

Porch

Two-Car Garage
20' x 21'

plan# HPK2900226

FIRST FLOOR: 1,230 SQ. FT.
SECOND FLOOR: 477 SQ. FT.
TOTAL: 1,707 SQ. FT.
BONUS SPACE: 195 SQ. FT.
BEDROOMS: 3
BATHROOMS: 2½
WIDTH: 40' - 0"
DEPTH: 52' - 10"
FOUNDATION: CRAWLSPACE

ORDER ONLINE @ EPLANS.COM

With windows throughout and a wonderfully open living space, this one-and-a-half-story bungalow feels larger than its modest square footage. The great room is highlighted with a corner window, fireplace, and soaring ceiling. The dining room continues the open feeling and is easily served from the kitchen. A bayed nook complements the island kitchen that also has a stylish wraparound counter. The master bedroom suite has a lofty vaulted ceiling. Upstairs, two family bedrooms share a full hall bath; a bonus room can be developed as needed.

FIRST FLOOR

SECOND FLOOR

plan # HPK2900227

SQUARE FOOTAGE: 1,724
BONUS SPACE: 375 SQ. FT.
BEDROOMS: 3
BATHROOMS: 2
WIDTH: 53' - 6"
DEPTH: 58' - 6"
FOUNDATION: CRAWLSPACE,
SLAB, UNFINISHED WALKOUT
BASEMENT

ORDER ONLINE @ EPLANS.COM

Signature Designer

Designer Frank Betz has responded to the resurgence of Craftsman and Bungalow style homes with innovative designs that blend the distinct facade with modern interior touches. Inherent to the style, tapered square columns adorn the partial-width porch of the Oxnard. The open, interior layout is enhanced by upgraded ceiling treatments, built-ins, and French doors.

HELPFUL HINT: Each plan includes a Specification Outline listing 166 items crucial to the building process.

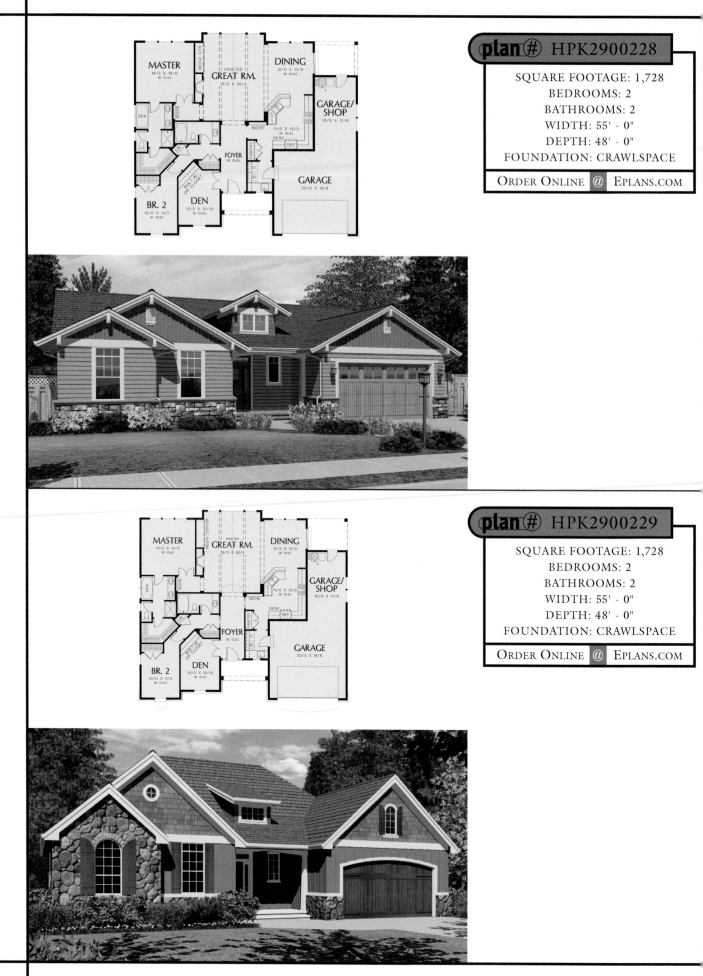

plan # HPK2900228

SQUARE FOOTAGE: 1,728
BEDROOMS: 2
BATHROOMS: 2
WIDTH: 55' - 0"
DEPTH: 48' - 0"
FOUNDATION: CRAWLSPACE

ORDER ONLINE @ EPLANS.COM

plan # HPK2900229

SQUARE FOOTAGE: 1,728
BEDROOMS: 2
BATHROOMS: 2
WIDTH: 55' - 0"
DEPTH: 48' - 0"
FOUNDATION: CRAWLSPACE

ORDER ONLINE @ EPLANS.COM

plan # HPK2900230

FIRST FLOOR: 1,342 SQ. FT.
SECOND FLOOR: 511 SQ. FT.
TOTAL: 1,853 SQ. FT.
BEDROOMS: 3
BATHROOMS: 2
WIDTH: 44' - 0"
DEPTH: 40' - 0"
FOUNDATION: UNFINISHED
BASEMENT

ORDER ONLINE @ EPLANS.COM

Matchstick details and a careful blend of stone and siding lend a special style and spirit to this stately retreat. Multipane windows take in the scenery and deck out the refined exterior of this cabin-style home, designed for a life of luxury. An open foyer shares its natural light with the great room—a bright reprieve filled with its own outdoor light. Dinner guests may wander from the coziness of the hearth space into the crisp night air through lovely French doors. The master retreat is an entire wing of the main level.

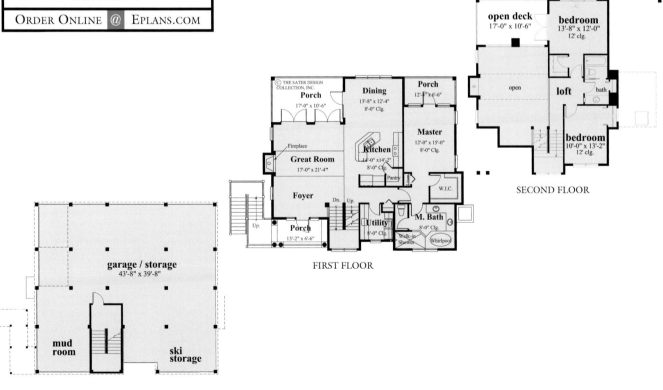

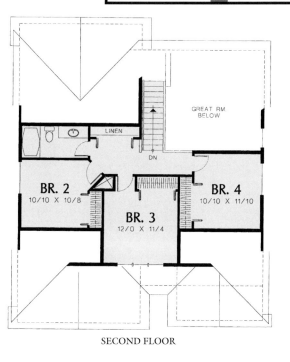

plan # HPK2900231

FIRST FLOOR: 1,198 SQ. FT.
SECOND FLOOR: 668 SQ. FT.
TOTAL: 1,866 SQ. FT.
BEDROOMS: 4
BATHROOMS: 2½
WIDTH: 40' - 0"
DEPTH: 47' - 0"
FOUNDATION: CRAWLSPACE

ORDER ONLINE @ EPLANS.COM

A fine example of a Craftsman bungalow, this four-bedroom home will be a delight to own. The efficient kitchen offers a serving island to the dining area, while the glow from the corner fireplace in the great room adds cheer to the entire area. Located on the first floor for privacy, the vaulted master bedroom features a walk-in closet, a private bath with a dual-bowl vanity, and access to the rear yard. Upstairs, three secondary bedrooms share a full hall bath and a large linen closet. The two-car garage will easily shelter the family fleet.

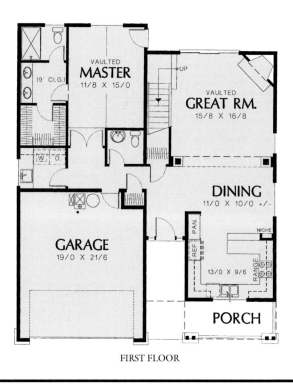

FIRST FLOOR

SECOND FLOOR

plan # HPK2900232

FIRST FLOOR: 1,097 SQ. FT.
SECOND FLOOR: 807 SQ. FT.
TOTAL: 1,904 SQ. FT.
BEDROOMS: 3
BATHROOMS: 2½
WIDTH: 40' - 0"
DEPTH: 45' - 0"
FOUNDATION: CRAWLSPACE

ORDER ONLINE @ EPLANS.COM

The combination of rafter tails and stone-and-siding gabled rooflines gives this home plenty of curb appeal. Inside, a vaulted den is entered through double doors, just to the left of the foyer. A spacious vaulted great room features a fireplace and is located near the dining room. The kitchen offers an octagonal island, a corner sink with a window, and a pantry. Up the angled staircase are the sleeping quarters. Here, two secondary bedrooms share a hall bath, and the master suite is enhanced with a private bath and a walk-in closet.

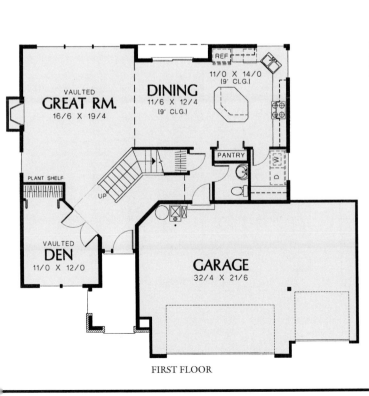

FIRST FLOOR

SECOND FLOOR

This home would look great in any neighborhood! From the covered front porch with a bench to rest on to the trio of gables, this design has a lot of appeal. Inside, the Craftsman styling continues with built-in shelves in the study, a warming fireplace in the great room, and plenty of windows to bring in the outdoors. The L-shaped kitchen is open to the nook and great room, and offers easy access to the formal dining area. Upstairs, two family bedrooms share a full bath and access to both a laundry room and a large bonus room. A vaulted master suite rounds out this floor with class. Complete with a walk-in closet and a pampering bath, this suite will be a haven for any homeowner.

FIRST FLOOR: 1,082 SQ. FT.
SECOND FLOOR: 864 SQ. FT.
TOTAL: 1,946 SQ. FT.
BONUS SPACE: 358 SQ. FT.
BEDROOMS: 3
BATHROOMS: 2½
WIDTH: 40' - 0"
DEPTH: 52' - 0"
FOUNDATION: CRAWLSPACE

ORDER ONLINE @ EPLANS.COM

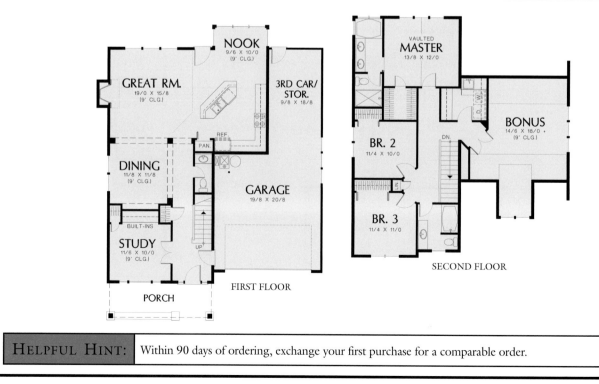

FIRST FLOOR

SECOND FLOOR

HELPFUL HINT: Within 90 days of ordering, exchange your first purchase for a comparable order.

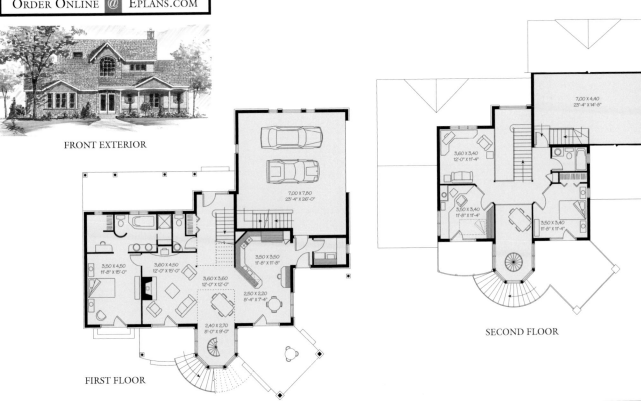

plan # HPK2900234

FIRST FLOOR: 1,301 SQ. FT.
SECOND FLOOR: 652 SQ. FT.
TOTAL: 1,953 SQ. FT.
BONUS SPACE: 342 SQ. FT.
BEDROOMS: 3
BATHROOMS: 2½
WIDTH: 58' - 0"
DEPTH: 55' - 0"
FOUNDATION: UNFINISHED
BASEMENT

ORDER ONLINE @ EPLANS.COM

Country finesse and stylish charm present a lovely siding-and-stone exterior. The rear of the house encourages outdoor relaxation with abundant porches, an elegant bayed turret, and a graceful curved stairway cascading from a second-floor porch to the rear patio. Inside, the family room is warmed by a large fireplace, and the dining room is illuminated by the spectacular turret bay. The first-floor master suite is enchanting with a walk-in closet and a private bath. Upstairs, two family bedrooms share a full hall bath and a study loft area.

FRONT EXTERIOR

FIRST FLOOR

SECOND FLOOR

A sensible floor plan, with living spaces on the first floor and bedrooms on the second floor, is the essence of this Craftsman home. Elegance reigns in the formal living room, with a vaulted ceiling and columned entry; this room is open to the dining room, which is brightened by natural light from two tall windows. Ideal for informal gatherings, the family room boasts a fireplace flanked by built-in shelves. The efficient kitchen includes a central island and double sink, and the nearby nook features easy access to the outdoors through sliding glass doors. The master suite includes a lavish bath with a corner spa tub and compartmented toilet; two additional bedrooms, one with a walk-in closet, share a full bath.

plan # HPK2900235

FIRST FLOOR: 970 SQ. FT.
SECOND FLOOR: 988 SQ. FT.
TOTAL: 1,958 SQ. FT.
BEDROOMS: 3
BATHROOMS: 2½
WIDTH: 40' - 0"
DEPTH: 43' - 0"
FOUNDATION: CRAWLSPACE

ORDER ONLINE @ EPLANS.COM

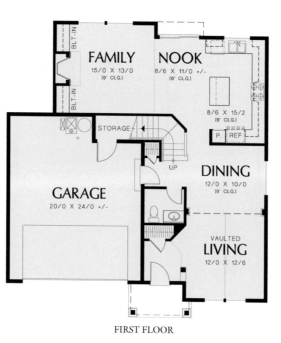

FIRST FLOOR

SECOND FLOOR

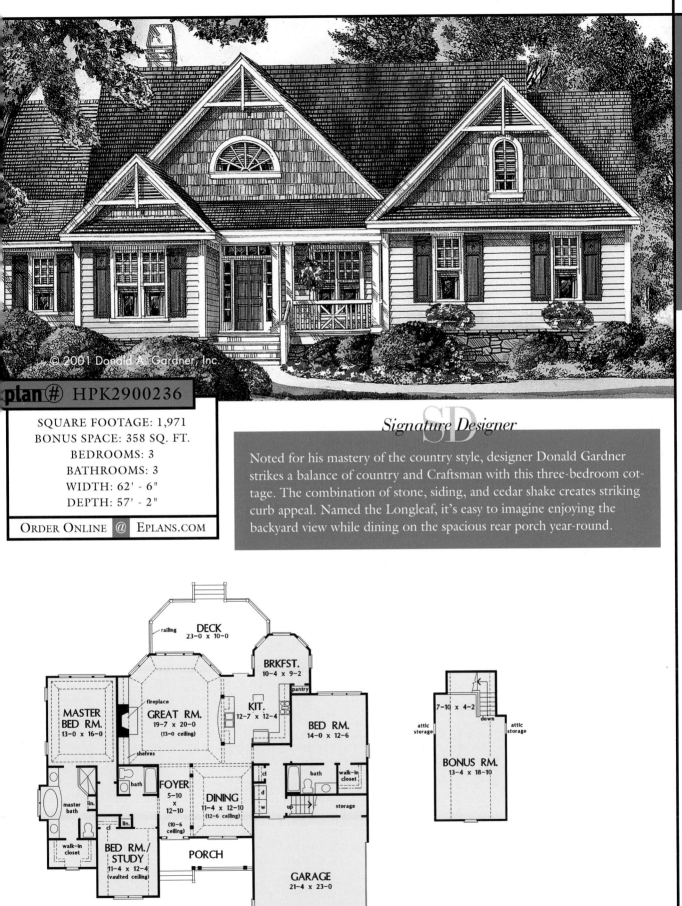

© 2001 Donald A. Gardner, Inc.

plan # HPK2900236

SQUARE FOOTAGE: 1,971
BONUS SPACE: 358 SQ. FT.
BEDROOMS: 3
BATHROOMS: 3
WIDTH: 62' - 6"
DEPTH: 57' - 2"

ORDER ONLINE @ EPLANS.COM

Signature Designer SD

Noted for his mastery of the country style, designer Donald Gardner strikes a balance of country and Craftsman with this three-bedroom cottage. The combination of stone, siding, and cedar shake creates striking curb appeal. Named the Longleaf, it's easy to imagine enjoying the backyard view while dining on the spacious rear porch year-round.

DECK
23-0 x 10-0
railing

BRKFST.
10-4 x 9-2

pantry

MASTER BED RM.
13-0 x 16-0

fireplace

GREAT RM.
19-7 x 20-0
(13-0 ceiling)

KIT.
12-7 x 12-4

BED RM.
14-0 x 12-6

shelves

bath

master bath

lin.

FOYER
5-10 x 12-10
(10-6 ceiling)

DINING
11-4 x 12-10
(12-6 ceiling)

cl

d

w

bath

walk-in closet

up

storage

walk-in closet

cl

lin.

lin.

BED RM./ STUDY
11-4 x 12-4
(vaulted ceiling)

PORCH

GARAGE
21-4 x 23-0

7-10 x 4-2

attic storage

down

attic storage

BONUS RM.
13-4 x 18-10

© 2001 DONALD A. GARDNER
All rights reserved

plan# HPK2900237

FIRST FLOOR: 1,106 SQ. FT.
SECOND FLOOR: 872 SQ. FT.
TOTAL: 1,978 SQ. FT.
BEDROOMS: 3
BATHROOMS: 2½
WIDTH: 38' - 0"
DEPTH: 35' - 0"
FOUNDATION: SLAB,
UNFINISHED BASEMENT

ORDER ONLINE @ EPLANS.COM

Although this home gives the impression of the Northwest, it will be the winner of any neighborhood. From the foyer, the two-story living room is just a couple of steps up and features a through-fireplace. The U-shaped kitchen has a cooktop work island, an adjacent nook, and easy access to the formal dining room. A spacious family room shares the fireplace with the living room, is enhanced by built-ins, and offers a quiet deck for stargazing. The upstairs consists of two family bedrooms sharing a full bath and a vaulted master suite complete with a walk-in closet and sumptuous bath. A two-car, drive-under garage has plenty of room for storage.

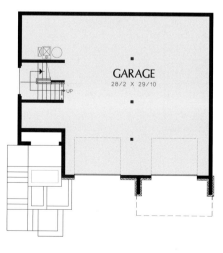

GARAGE
28/2 X 29/10

FIRST FLOOR

SECOND FLOOR

plan # HPK2900238

SQUARE FOOTAGE: 1,997
BONUS SPACE: 310 SQ. FT.
BEDROOMS: 2
BATHROOMS: 2½
WIDTH: 64' - 4"
DEPTH: 63' - 0"
FOUNDATION: CRAWLSPACE,
UNFINISHED BASEMENT

ORDER ONLINE @ EPLANS.COM

REAR EXTERIOR

The hub of this charming plan is the spacious kitchen with an island and a serving bar. The nearby breakfast nook accesses the greenhouse with its wall of windows and three large skylights. A built-in media center beside a warming fireplace is the focal point of the family room. Bedroom 2 shares a full bath with the den/study, which might also be a third bedroom. The master suite features large His and Hers vanity sinks, a corner tub with an open walk-in shower, and a supersized walk-in closet. Future space over the garage can expand the living space as your family grows.

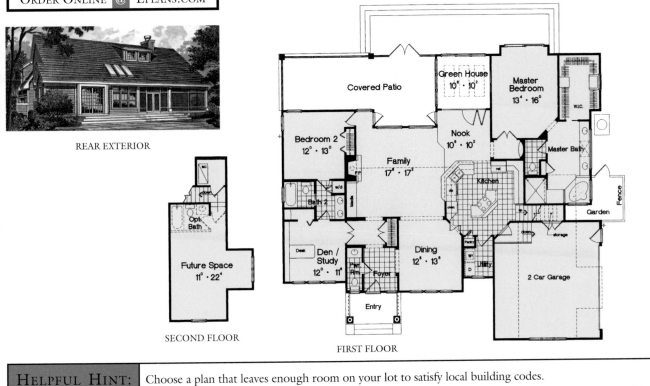

SECOND FLOOR

FIRST FLOOR

HELPFUL HINT: Choose a plan that leaves enough room on your lot to satisfy local building codes.

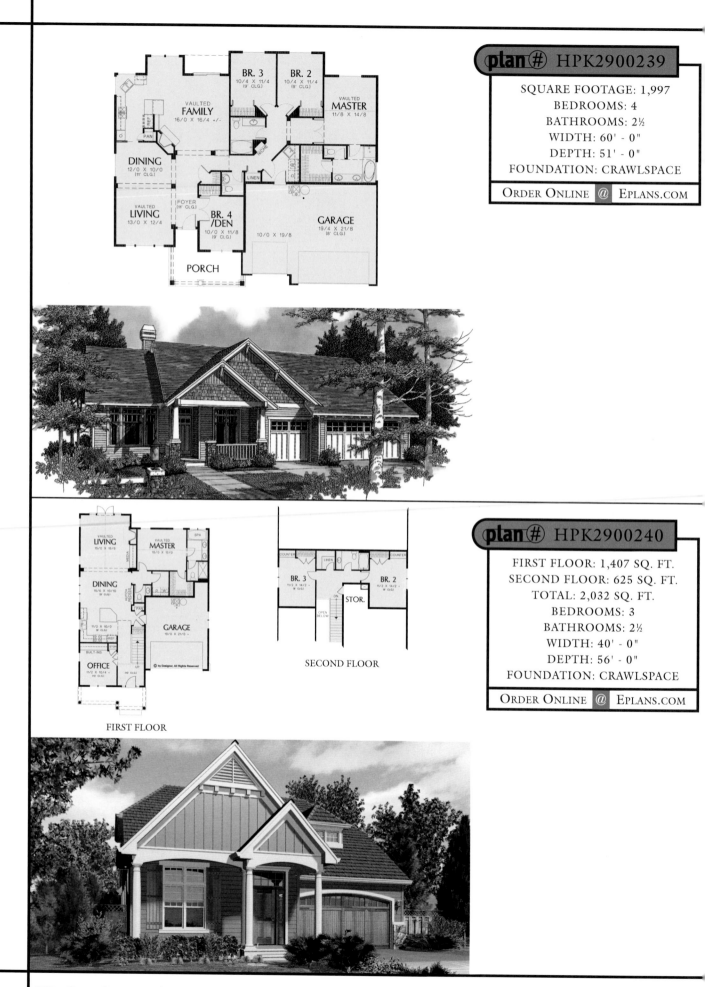

BR. 3
10/4 X 11/4
(9' CLG.)

BR. 2
10/4 X 11/4
(9' CLG.)

VAULTED
FAMILY
16/0 X 16/4 +/-

VAULTED
MASTER
11/8 X 14/8

DINING
12/0 X 10/0
(11' CLG.)

LIVING
13/0 X 12/4

VAULTED

FOYER
(11' CLG.)

BR. 4
/DEN
10/0 X 11/8
(9' CLG.)

10/0 X 19/8

GARAGE
19/4 X 21/8
(8' CLG.)

LINEN

PORCH

plan # HPK2900239

SQUARE FOOTAGE: 1,997
BEDROOMS: 4
BATHROOMS: 2½
WIDTH: 60' - 0"
DEPTH: 51' - 0"
FOUNDATION: CRAWLSPACE

ORDER ONLINE @ EPLANS.COM

VAULTED
LIVING
15/0 X 15/8

VAULTED
MASTER
15/0 X 17/0

SPA

DINING
15/6 X 10/10
(9' CLG.)

GARAGE
19/0 X 21/4

11/2 X 10/0
(9' CLG.)

OFFICE
11/2 X 10/4 +
(9' CLG.)

BUILT-INS

FIRST FLOOR

COUNTER

LINEN

COUNTER

BR. 3
11/2 X 14/2 -
(8' CLG.)

BR. 2
11/2 X 14/2
(8' CLG.)

STOR.

OPEN
DOWN

SECOND FLOOR

© by Designer, All Rights Reserved

plan # HPK2900240

FIRST FLOOR: 1,407 SQ. FT.
SECOND FLOOR: 625 SQ. FT.
TOTAL: 2,032 SQ. FT.
BEDROOMS: 3
BATHROOMS: 2½
WIDTH: 40' - 0"
DEPTH: 56' - 0"
FOUNDATION: CRAWLSPACE

ORDER ONLINE @ EPLANS.COM

plan # HPK2900241

FIRST FLOOR: 1,461 SQ. FT.
SECOND FLOOR: 584 SQ. FT.
TOTAL: 2,045 SQ. FT.
BEDROOMS: 3
BATHROOMS: 2½
WIDTH: 35' - 6"
DEPTH: 52' - 0"
FOUNDATION: CRAWLSPACE

ORDER ONLINE @ EPLANS.COM

Woodwork details and shaped columns decorate the porch of this charming three-bedroom cottage. Enter the home via the breakfast nook or the foyer from the porch. A hearth-warmed family room with built-in shelves sits to the right of the foyer and adjoins the dining area. His and Hers walk-in closets and a spacious bath ensure the master suite is a comfortable retreat. Two family bedrooms share a full bath on the second floor.

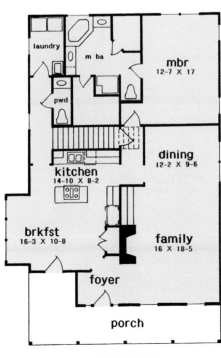

FIRST FLOOR

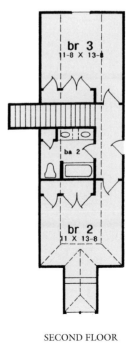

SECOND FLOOR

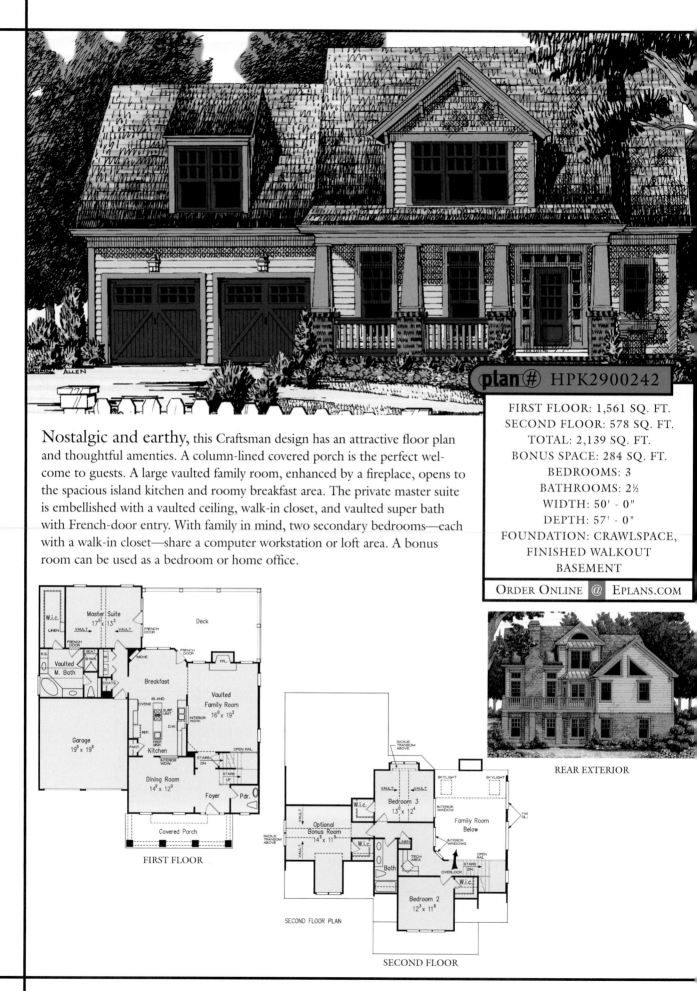

plan# HPK2900242

Nostalgic and earthy, this Craftsman design has an attractive floor plan and thoughtful amenties. A column-lined covered porch is the perfect welcome to guests. A large vaulted family room, enhanced by a fireplace, opens to the spacious island kitchen and roomy breakfast area. The private master suite is embellished with a vaulted ceiling, walk-in closet, and vaulted super bath with French-door entry. With family in mind, two secondary bedrooms—each with a walk-in closet—share a computer workstation or loft area. A bonus room can be used as a bedroom or home office.

FIRST FLOOR: 1,561 SQ. FT.
SECOND FLOOR: 578 SQ. FT.
TOTAL: 2,139 SQ. FT.
BONUS SPACE: 284 SQ. FT.
BEDROOMS: 3
BATHROOMS: 2½
WIDTH: 50' - 0"
DEPTH: 57' - 0"
FOUNDATION: CRAWLSPACE,
FINISHED WALKOUT
BASEMENT

ORDER ONLINE @ EPLANS.COM

REAR EXTERIOR

FIRST FLOOR

SECOND FLOOR PLAN

SECOND FLOOR

plan # HPK2900243

FIRST FLOOR: 1,561 SQ. FT.
SECOND FLOOR: 578 SQ. FT.
TOTAL: 2,139 SQ. FT.
BONUS SPACE: 238 SQ. FT.
BEDROOMS: 3
BATHROOMS: 2½
WIDTH: 50' - 0"
DEPTH: 56' - 6"
FOUNDATION: CRAWLSPACE,
SLAB, UNFINISHED WALKOUT
BASEMENT

ORDER ONLINE @ EPLANS.COM

Come home to this delightful bungalow, created with you in mind. From the covered front porch, the foyer opens to the dining room on the left and vaulted family room ahead. An elongated island in the well-planned kitchen makes meal preparation a joy. A sunny breakfast nook is perfect for casual pursuits. Tucked to the rear, the master suite enjoys ultimate privacy and a luxurious break from the world with a vaulted bath and garden tub. Secondary bedrooms share a full bath upstairs. A bonus room is ready to expand as your needs change.

FIRST FLOOR

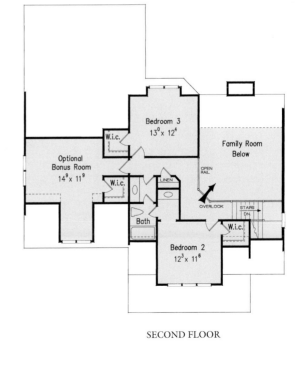

SECOND FLOOR

This cozy Craftsman plan conveniently separates living and sleeping quarters, with family living areas on the first floor and bedrooms on the second. The plan begins with a vaulted living/dining room and moves on to a great room that provides a fireplace flanked by built-ins. The adjacent kitchen includes a built-in desk and adjoins a breakfast nook that opens to the backyard. To the rear of the plan, the den can be converted to a fourth bedroom. Upstairs, a master suite—with a spa tub and walk-in closet with built-in shelves—joins two bedrooms and a vaulted bonus room.

FIRST FLOOR: 1,252 SQ. FT.
SECOND FLOOR: 985 SQ. FT.
TOTAL: 2,237 SQ. FT.
BONUS SPACE: 183 SQ. FT.
BEDROOMS: 4
BATHROOMS: 3
WIDTH: 40' - 0"
DEPTH: 51' - 0"
FOUNDATION: CRAWLSPACE

ORDER ONLINE @ EPLANS.COM

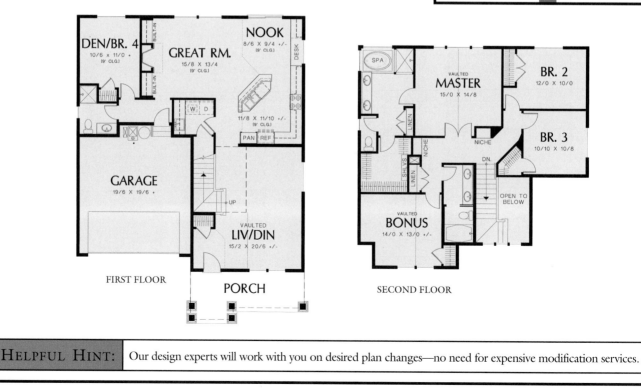

FIRST FLOOR

SECOND FLOOR

HELPFUL HINT: Our design experts will work with you on desired plan changes—no need for expensive modification services.

plan # HPK2900245

FIRST FLOOR: 1,302 SQ. FT.
SECOND FLOOR: 960 SQ. FT.
TOTAL: 2,262 SQ. FT.
BEDROOMS: 3
BATHROOMS: 2½
WIDTH: 40' - 0"
DEPTH: 40' - 0"
FOUNDATION: SLAB

ORDER ONLINE @ EPLANS.COM

This vacation home is certain to be a family favorite. The two-story great room boasts a built-in media center, access to a front deck, and a two-sided fireplace shared by the adjacent den. The spacious island kitchen is ideal for entertaining. The second floor houses the master suite, two additional family bedrooms, and a full bath. A workshop and extra storage space in the garage are added bonuses.

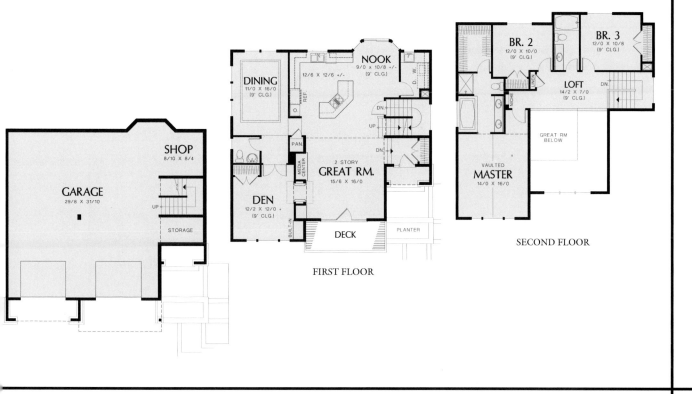

FIRST FLOOR

SECOND FLOOR

The decorative pillars and the wraparound porch are just the beginning of this comfortable home. Inside, an angled, U-shaped stairway leads to the second-floor sleeping zone. On the first floor, French doors lead to a bay-windowed den that shares a see-through fireplace with the two-story family room. The large island kitchen includes a writing desk, a corner sink, a breakfast nook, and access to the laundry room, the powder room, and the two-car garage. Upstairs, the master suite is a real treat with its French-door access, vaulted ceiling, and luxurious bath. Two other bedrooms and a full bath complete the second floor.

plan# HPK2900246

FIRST FLOOR: 1,371 SQ. FT.
SECOND FLOOR: 916 SQ. FT.
TOTAL: 2,287 SQ. FT.
BEDROOMS: 3
BATHROOMS: 2½
WIDTH: 43' - 0"
DEPTH: 69' - 0"
FOUNDATION: CRAWLSPACE

ORDER ONLINE @ EPLANS.COM

SECOND FLOOR

FIRST FLOOR

plan# HPK2900247

FIRST FLOOR: 1,774 SQ. FT.
SECOND FLOOR: 525 SQ. FT.
TOTAL: 2,299 SQ. FT.
BONUS SPACE: 300 SQ. FT.
BEDROOMS: 4
BATHROOMS: 3
WIDTH: 56' - 0"
DEPTH: 63' - 4"
FOUNDATION: CRAWLSPACE,
SLAB, UNFINISHED WALKOUT
BASEMENT

ORDER ONLINE @ EPLANS.COM

Signature Designer SD

Renowned for a variety of styles, designer Frank Betz revisits the Craftsman and Bungalow home. Distinctive Craftsman elements add exterior appeal while the ample interior is decorated with upgraded amenities, impressive ceiling treatments, and abundant built-ins. The charming appeal of this home makes it a welcome addition to any streetscape.

Screened Porch
11² x 11⁸

Breakfast

Bedroom 4
11³ x 11⁰

Master Suite
13² x 18⁰

Vaulted Family Room
16⁰ x 18⁴

Kitchen

Bath

Vaulted M.Bath

Laund.

Two Story Foyer

Dining Room
11⁹ x 12⁰

Garage
20⁵ x 22³

Covered Porch

FIRST FLOOR PLAN   FIRST FLOOR

copyright © 2004 frank betz associates, inc.

Bedroom 2
12⁵ x 13⁸

Bath

Bedroom 3
11³ x 13⁰

Foyer Below

Attic Storage

Opt. Bonus Room
12⁵ x 22³

SECOND FLOOR

Fine details like the shed dormer, open millwork accents, an arched entry, and a standing-seam roof will make this home a neighborhood favorite. A split-bedroom floor plan positions the family bedrooms to the left with a compartmented bath between them. The family room, with fireplace and built-ins, is a generous and open space that works with the huge island kitchen, bright sunroom, and breakfast nook. A more formal dining space is found to the right of the foyer. Seclusion is just one amenity the master suite boasts; others include an oversized walk-in closet, super bath, and French doors to the deck.

plan# HPK2900248

SQUARE FOOTAGE: 2,326
BONUS SPACE: 358 SQ. FT.
BEDROOMS: 3
BATHROOMS: 2½
WIDTH: 64' - 0"
DEPTH: 72' - 4"
FOUNDATION: UNFINISHED BASEMENT

ORDER ONLINE @ EPLANS.com

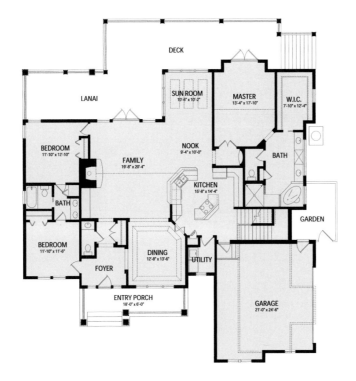

plan(#) HPK2900249

SQUARE FOOTAGE: 2,326
BONUS SPACE: 358 SQ. FT.
BEDROOMS: 3
BATHROOMS: 2½
WIDTH: 64' - 0"
DEPTH: 72' - 4"
FOUNDATION: FINISHED
WALKOUT BASEMENT

ORDER ONLINE @ EPLANS.COM

This sensible plan flouts tradition and delivers high-end amenities in a well-balanced design. A full-sized formal dining room, featuring a tray ceiling, enables homeowners to host elegant dinners made to perfection in the gourmet kitchen. The combined space of the great room, breakfast nook, and sun room is enhanced even further by the lanai and deck. Homeowners will know just how pleasing this home can be as they retire each night to a deluxe master suite. The bedroom features exclusive access to the deck, and a private garden beautifies the corner whirlpool tub.

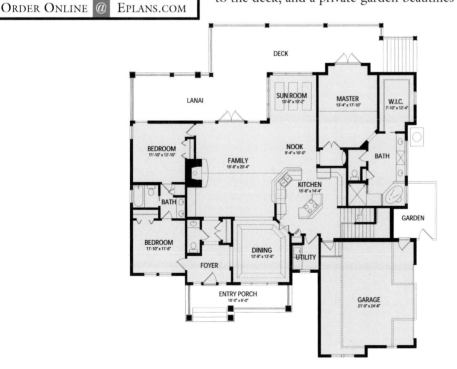

HELPFUL HINT: Reproducible sets allow for changes without redrawing the plans.

A covered porch, multipane windows, and shingle-with-stone siding combine to give this bungalow plenty of curb appeal. Inside, the foyer is flanked by the formal living room and an angled staircase. The formal dining room adjoins the living room, and the kitchen is accessible through double doors. A large family room is graced by a fireplace and opens off a cozy eating nook. The second level presents many attractive angles. The master suite has a spacious walk-in closet and a sumptuous bath complete with a garden tub and separate shower. Three family bedrooms share a full hall bath.

plan# HPK2900250

FIRST FLOOR: 1,205 SQ. FT.
SECOND FLOOR: 1,123 SQ. FT.
TOTAL: 2,328 SQ. FT.
BEDROOMS: 4
BATHROOMS: 2½
WIDTH: 57' - 2"
DEPTH: 58' - 7"
FOUNDATION: CRAWLSPACE

ORDER ONLINE @ EPLANS.COM

FIRST FLOOR

SECOND FLOOR

plan # HPK2900251

SQUARE FOOTAGE: 2,400
BONUS SPACE: 845 SQ. FT.
BEDROOMS: 3
BATHROOMS: 2½
WIDTH: 61' - 0"
DEPTH: 70' - 6"
FOUNDATION: CRAWLSPACE, SLAB, UNFINISHED WALKOUT BASEMENT

ORDER ONLINE @ EPLANS.COM

Decorative columns can be found throughout, beginning with the covered front porch. Once inside, the foyer opens to the dining room on the right and the family room straight ahead. Enhanced by a coffered ceiling and built-in cabinets, a fireplace warms the space. A bay window view of the backyard extends private living space to the outdoors. Entry to the vaulted master suite reveals a walk-in closet, roomy bath with dual-sink vanities, separate shower and tub, and a private toilet. A serving bar in the kitchen allows for casual meals and easy interaction between the breakfast area and family room. Two additional family bedrooms share a full bath. Upstairs, a fourth bedroom and full bath, possible guest quarters, and a bonus room complete the plan.

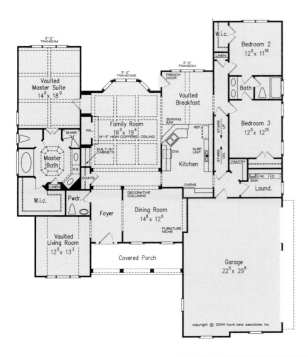

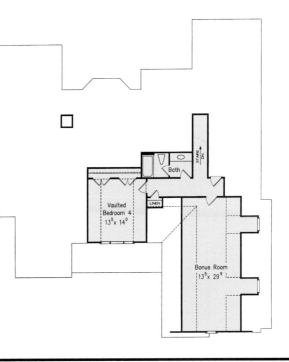

From the covered porch to the two-story window in the great room, this design is sure to please. The two-story foyer is flanked by a cozy den on the right and a formal dining room with a bay window on the left. A sunny nook is adjacent to the efficient kitchen, which offers a snack bar and a corner sink. The first-floor master suite features a double-door entry, a tray ceiling, a walk-in closet, and a bath with a corner tub and separate shower. Upstairs, two family bedrooms—each with a walk-in closet—share a full hall bath. A bonus room completes this level and is available for future development. A three-car garage easily shelters the family fleet.

plan# HPK2900252

FIRST FLOOR: 1,786 SQ. FT.
SECOND FLOOR: 690 SQ. FT.
TOTAL: 2,476 SQ. FT.
BONUS SPACE: 204 SQ. FT.
BEDROOMS: 3
BATHROOMS: 2½
WIDTH: 50' - 0"
DEPTH: 52' - 0"
FOUNDATION: CRAWLSPACE

ORDER ONLINE @ EPLANS.com

FIRST FLOOR

SECOND FLOOR

plan # HPK2900253

SQUARE FOOTAGE: 2,487
BONUS SPACE: 306 SQ. FT.
BEDROOMS: 3
BATHROOMS: 2½
WIDTH: 61' - 6"
DEPTH: 67' - 6"
FOUNDATION: CRAWLSPACE,
SLAB, UNFINISHED WALKOUT
BASEMENT

ORDER ONLINE @ EPLANS.COM

Vertical siding and stone details create the facade of this home. One story, measuring just under 2,500 square feet, is all you need when the floor plan is as perfect as this one. Family and friends will feel right at home in the family room topped with a gorgeous coffered ceiling and embellished with a warming fireplace flanked by built-in shelves. The nearby kitchen with corner pantry connects to a convenient breakfast room and is only a hop away from the formal dining area. The master suite and bath are spectacular—feel free to turn the living room into a master sitting room for more space. Two more bedrooms are on the opposite side of the plan and share a full bath. The dual sinks here will ensure quick and painless morning/evening routines. A laundry room and powder room provide the finishing touches.

The modern rustic look of this cottage lends a unique charm to the overall plan. Inside, the foyer faces a formal area made up of the combined living and dining rooms. The island kitchen expands into a bayed nook. The study/office is placed just off the entry. Two family bedrooms share a hall bath. Double doors open into the master suite, which offers two walk-in closets and a private bath.

plan# HPK2900254

SQUARE FOOTAGE: 2,487
BEDROOMS: 3
BATHROOMS: 2
WIDTH: 70' - 0"
DEPTH: 72' - 0"
FOUNDATION: SLAB

ORDER ONLINE @ EPLANS.COM

HELPFUL HINT: Choose a foundation based on your region, budget, and personal preference.

plan # HPK2900255

MAIN LEVEL: 1,544 SQ. FT.
LOWER LEVEL: 1,018 SQ. FT.
TOTAL: 2,562 SQ. FT.
BEDROOMS: 4
BATHROOMS: 3
WIDTH: 40' - 0"
DEPTH: 60' - 0"
FOUNDATION: FINISHED
WALKOUT BASEMENT

ORDER ONLINE @ EPLANS.com

This Cape Cod design is enhanced with shingles, stone detailing, and muntin windows.

The entry is flanked on the left by a bedroom/den, perfect for overnight guests or as a cozy place to relax. The hearth-warmed great room enjoys expansive views of the rear deck area. The dining room is nestled next to the island kitchen, which boasts plenty of counter space. The master bedroom is positioned at the rear of the home for privacy and accesses its own bath. Two family bedrooms and a spacious games room complete the finished basement.

MAIN LEVEL

LOWER LEVEL

With Craftsman detail and traditional charm, this four-bedroom home captures the comfort and style you've been searching for. From a wrapping porch enter the two-story foyer with a decorative niche that displays special photos or treasures to all your guests. Continue to a beautiful family room, graced with a two-story ceiling and second-floor radius windows. The kitchen is open and spacious, leading to a breakfast area, hearth-warmed keeping room, and elegant dining room. A bedroom on this level also serves as an ideal den or home office. Upstairs, two secondary bedrooms share a full bath. The master suite is ready for relaxation with a sunny sitting room and soothing vaulted bath. A laundry room on this level makes wash day a breeze.

plan # HPK2900256

FIRST FLOOR: 1,322 SQ. FT.
SECOND FLOOR: 1,262 SQ. FT.
TOTAL: 2,584 SQ. FT.
BEDROOMS: 4
BATHROOMS: 3
WIDTH: 48' - 0"
DEPTH: 50' - 0"
FOUNDATION: CRAWLSPACE, SLAB, UNFINISHED WALKOUT BASEMENT

ORDER ONLINE @ EPLANS.COM

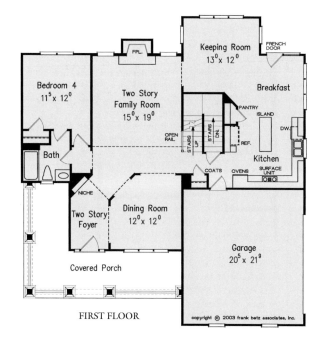

FIRST FLOOR

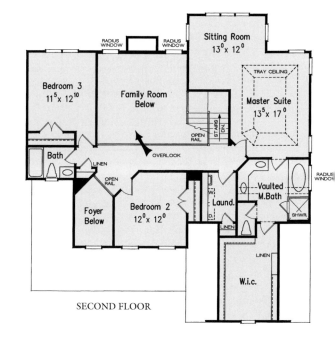

SECOND FLOOR

plan # HPK2900257

FIRST FLOOR: 1,755 SQ. FT.
SECOND FLOOR: 864 SQ. FT.
TOTAL: 2,619 SQ. FT.
BEDROOMS: 4
BATHROOMS: 3½
WIDTH: 56' - 0"
DEPTH: 53' - 0"
FOUNDATION: CRAWLSPACE,
SLAB, UNFINISHED WALKOUT
BASEMENT

ORDER ONLINE @ EPLANS.COM

Signature Designer

Emerging as a Craftsman favorite, Kensington Park is another brilliant design from Frank Betz's extensive collection. Blending historical flourishes reminiscent of the Craftsman style with a surprisingly modern interior is the genius of the design. Open-face gables, broad white trim, and double-hung window sashes create appeal on this cottage's exterior while the open floor plan is adorned with high ceilings that expand the interior space.

FIRST FLOOR

SECOND FLOOR

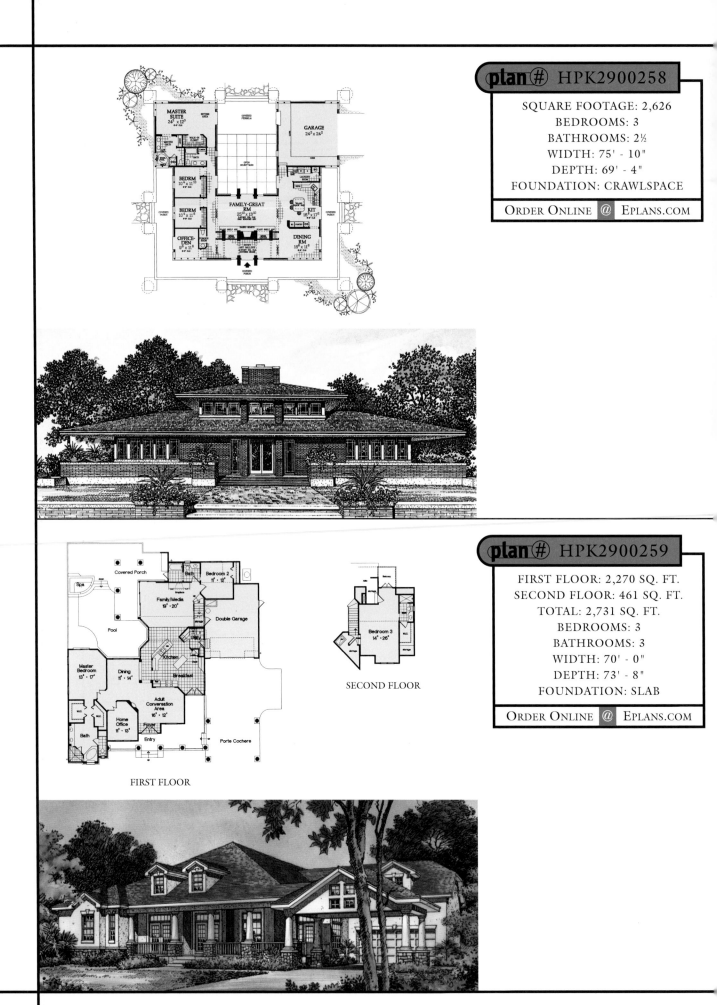

plan # HPK2900258

SQUARE FOOTAGE: 2,626
BEDROOMS: 3
BATHROOMS: 2½
WIDTH: 75' - 10"
DEPTH: 69' - 4"
FOUNDATION: CRAWLSPACE

ORDER ONLINE @ EPLANS.COM

plan # HPK2900259

FIRST FLOOR: 2,270 SQ. FT.
SECOND FLOOR: 461 SQ. FT.
TOTAL: 2,731 SQ. FT.
BEDROOMS: 3
BATHROOMS: 3
WIDTH: 70' - 0"
DEPTH: 73' - 8"
FOUNDATION: SLAB

ORDER ONLINE @ EPLANS.COM

SECOND FLOOR

FIRST FLOOR

plan (#) HPK2900260

FIRST FLOOR: 1,578 SQ. FT.
SECOND FLOOR: 1,159 SQ. FT.
TOTAL: 2,737 SQ. FT.
BEDROOMS: 4
BATHROOMS: 3
WIDTH: 63' - 0"
DEPTH: 53' - 0"
FOUNDATION: CRAWLSPACE

ORDER ONLINE @ EPLANS.COM

Stone and siding, gables and rafter tails, window detail, and a wonderful floor plan—all elements of a fantastic Craftsman home. This two-story four-bedroom home is designed for today's active family. The foyer is flanked by a spacious living room with a fireplace to the right and a cozy den entered through double doors to the left. At the rear of the home, a large family room offers a corner fireplace and a wall of windows. A huge kitchen is enhanced by plenty of counter and cabinet space, a large cooktop work island, a corner sink, and an adjacent sunny nook with access to the rear yard. Upstairs, three family bedrooms share a full hall bath, while the master bedroom is filled with amenities.

FIRST FLOOR

SECOND FLOOR

HELPFUL HINT: Eplans.com offers a Mechanical Details set with general mechanical system information and diagrams.

This rustic farmhouse design features a variety of today's most up-to-date amenities. A country front porch welcomes you inside through a set of double doors. The foyer is flanked on either side by the formal dining room and the study with built-in bookshelves. The grand room boasts a fireplace flanked by built-ins—decorative art niches are found here and in the dining room. A wall of double doors opens from the grand room to the rear porch. The kitchen opens to a nook, accessing both back porches. The master suite is enhanced by a private bath and His and Hers walk-in closets. Upstairs, two family bedrooms share a hall bath with the bonus room—a perfect home office or fourth bedroom.

plan # HPK2900261

FIRST FLOOR: 2,215 SQ. FT.
SECOND FLOOR: 708 SQ. FT.
TOTAL: 2,923 SQ. FT.
BONUS SPACE: 420 SQ. FT.
BEDROOMS: 3
BATHROOMS: 3
WIDTH: 76' - 4"
DEPTH: 69' - 10"
FOUNDATION: CRAWLSPACE

ORDER ONLINE @ EPLANS.COM

FIRST FLOOR

© THE SATER DESIGN COLLECTION, INC.

SECOND FLOOR

plan # HPK2900262

MAIN LEVEL: 1,268 SQ. FT.
SECOND LEVEL: 931 SQ. FT.
LOWER LEVEL: 949 SQ. FT.
TOTAL: 3,148 SQ. FT.
BEDROOMS: 4
BATHROOMS: 3½
WIDTH: 53' - 6"
DEPTH: 73' - 0"
FOUNDATION: FINISHED
WALKOUT BASEMENT

ORDER ONLINE @ EPLANS.COM

A covered front porch provides a welcoming entry for this Craftsman design, which features a stunning, amenity-filled interior. Vaulted ceilings adorn the great room, office, and even the garage; the dining room includes a built-in hutch, and the kitchen boasts a walk-in pantry. Upstairs, the master suite offers a walk-in closet with built-in shelves, along with a private bath that contains a spa tub; two additional bedrooms also have walk-in closets. A fourth bedroom, a recreation room with a fireplace and wet bar, and a wine cellar reside on the lower level.

REAR EXTERIOR

LOWER LEVEL

MAIN LEVEL

SECOND LEVEL

This incredible home evokes images of stately Southwestern ranches with classic wood detailing and deep eaves. An arched entryway mimics the large clerestory above it, and a trio of dormers and multiple gables add architectural interest. Equally impressive, the interior boasts three fireplaces—one within a screened porch—while a long cathedral ceiling extends from the great room and is highlighted by exposed beams. An art niche complements the foyer, and a wet bar enhances the great room. Columns help distinguish rooms without enclosing space. The extraordinary master suite features a large study/sitting area, bedroom with exposed beams in a hipped cathedral ceiling, huge walk-in closet, and spacious master bath.

SQUARE FOOTAGE: 3,188
BONUS SPACE: 615 SQ. FT.
BEDROOMS: 3
BATHROOMS: 2½
WIDTH: 106' - 4"
DEPTH: 104' - 1"

ORDER ONLINE @ EPLANS.COM

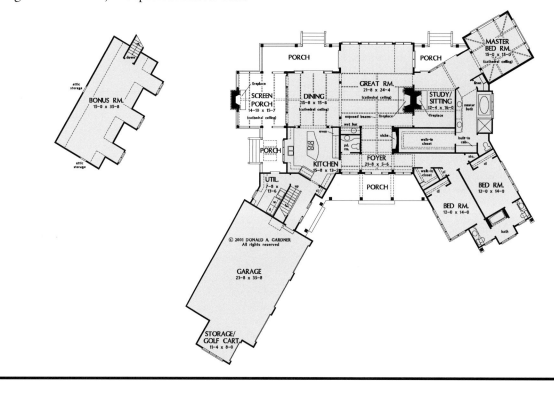

plan # HPK2900264

MAIN LEVEL: 2,170 SQ. FT.
LOWER LEVEL: 1,076 SQ. FT.
TOTAL: 3,246 SQ. FT.
BEDROOMS: 3
BATHROOMS: 2½
WIDTH: 74' - 0"
DEPTH: 54' - 0"
FOUNDATION: SLAB,
FINISHED WALKOUT
BASEMENT

ORDER ONLINE @ EPLANS.COM

Perfect for a sloping lot, this Craftsman design boasts two levels of living space. Plenty of special amenities—vaulted ceilings in the living, dining, and family rooms, as well as in the master bedroom; built-ins in the family room and den; a large island cooktop in the kitchen; and an expansive rear deck—make this plan stand out. All three of the bedrooms—a main-level master suite and two lower-level bedrooms—include walk-in closets. Also on the lower level, find a recreation room with built-ins and a fireplace.

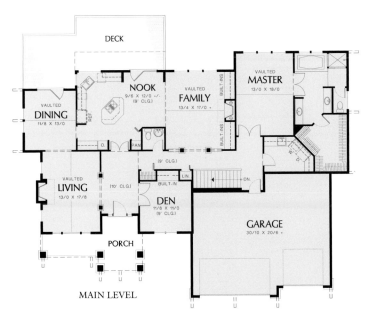

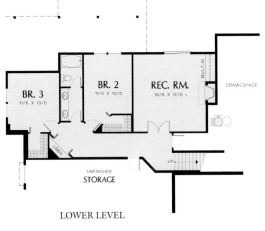

© 1999 Donald A. Gardner, Inc.

plan# HPK2900265

A Craftsman combination of cedar shingles and wood siding lends warmth and style to this four-bedroom home. A stunning cathedral ceiling spans the open great room and spacious island kitchen for exceptional volume. A deep tray ceiling heightens the formal dining room, while the breakfast room is enhanced by a vaulted ceiling. Two rear decks and a screened porch augment the home's ample living space. The master bedroom is topped by a tray ceiling and features two walk-in closets and a generous private bath. A second bedroom is located on the main level and two more can be found on the lower level.

MAIN LEVEL: 2,122 SQ. FT.
LOWER LEVEL: 1,150 SQ. FT.
TOTAL: 3,272 SQ. FT.
BEDROOMS: 4
BATHROOMS: 3
WIDTH: 83' - 0"
DEPTH: 74' - 4"

ORDER ONLINE @ EPLANS.COM

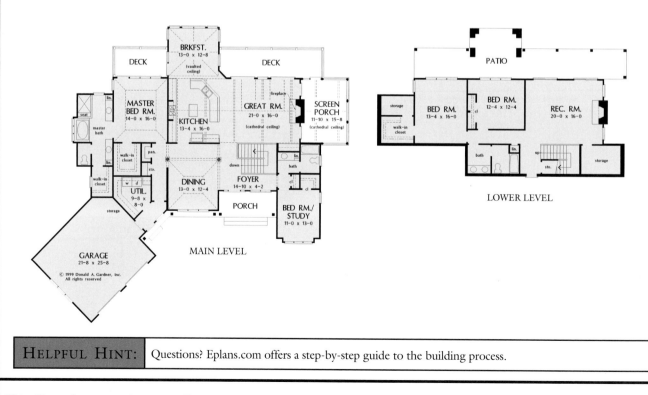

HELPFUL HINT: Questions? Eplans.com offers a step-by-step guide to the building process.

plan# HPK2900266

MAIN LEVEL: 1,451 SQ. FT.
LOWER LEVEL: 2,035 SQ. FT.
TOTAL: 3,486 SQ. FT.
BEDROOMS: 4
BATHROOMS: 3½
WIDTH: 56' - 0"
DEPTH: 65' - 0"
FOUNDATION: FINISHED
WALKOUT BASEMENT

ORDER ONLINE @ EPLANS.COM

This charming vacation retreat will feel like home in the mountains as well as by a wooded lakefront. With a covered deck, screened porch, and spacious patio, this home is designed for lovers of the outdoors. Inside, a comfy, rustic aura dominates. On the main level, a lodge-like living area with an extended-hearth fireplace and snack bar dominates. A library, easy-to-use kitchen, and enchanting master suite are also located on this floor. Downstairs, there are two more bedrooms, a huge recreation room, a hobby room (or make it into another bedroom), and lots of storage space.

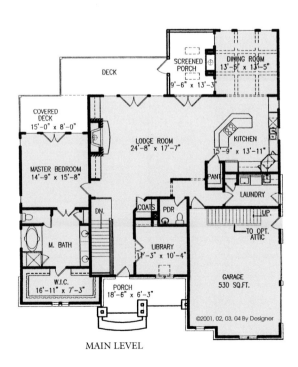

MAIN LEVEL

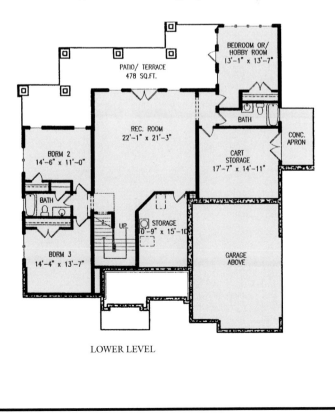

LOWER LEVEL

plan# HPK2900267

FIRST FLOOR: 2,597 SQ. FT.
SECOND FLOOR: 2,171 SQ. FT.
TOTAL: 4,768 SQ. FT.
BEDROOMS: 4
BATHROOMS: 4½
WIDTH: 76' - 6"
DEPTH: 68' - 6"
FOUNDATION: CRAWLSPACE

ORDER ONLINE @ EPLANS.COM

This splendid Craftsman home will look good in any neighborhood. Inside, the foyer offers a beautiful wooden bench to the right, flanked by built-in curio cabinets. On the left, double French doors lead to a cozy study. The formal dining room is complete with beamed ceilings, a built-in hutch, and cabinets. The large L-shaped kitchen includes a work island/snack bar, plenty of storage, and an adjacent sunny nook. The two-story great room surely lives up to its name, with a massive stone fireplace and a two-story wall of windows. Upstairs, two family bedrooms share a full bath, and the guest suite features its own bath. The lavish master bedroom suite pampers the homeowner with two walk-in closets, a fireplace, and a private deck.

FIRST FLOOR

SECOND FLOOR

© Larry E. Belk Designs

plan # HPK2900268

FIRST FLOOR: 3,253 SQ. FT.
SECOND FLOOR: 1,747 SQ. FT.
TOTAL: 5,000 SQ. FT.
BEDROOMS: 4
BATHROOMS: 4½
WIDTH: 112' - 9"
DEPTH: 89' - 10"
FOUNDATION: CRAWLSPACE

ORDER ONLINE @ EPLANS.COM

This impressive two-story Craftsman design features a modern layout filled with abundant rooms and amenities. A wide front porch welcomes you inside to an entry flanked on either side by formal living and dining rooms. Built-ins enhance the dining room, while the living room shares a see-through fireplace with the library/study. The island kitchen offers a utility room and food pantry nearby, and it overlooks the breakfast and family rooms. The mudroom accesses the rear porch and sunroom. The luxurious master suite contains a sitting area, His and Hers walk-in closets, a private bath, and an exercise room. At the rear, planters enhance the raised patio area. The second floor features three additional bedrooms. A study between Bedrooms 3 and 4 is perfect for the kids. A game room, sleep loft, and rear balcony complete this floor.

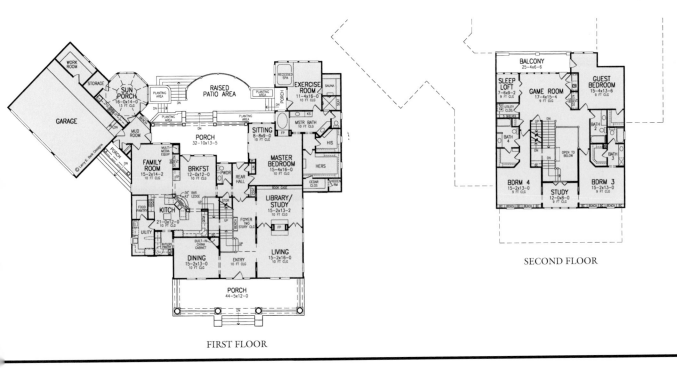

FIRST FLOOR

SECOND FLOOR

Designer Stephen Fuller recalled quintessential Neoclassical and Colonial Revival elements to conceive Hedgewood Heights. Asymmetrical gables and a pedimented entry supported by double columns lend visual interest to the blended exterior. The presence of a bay window is characteristic of both styles. The wealth of natural light in this stunning home is sure to please.

The cross-gabled roof and
mix of materials make
for a very dynamic exterior.

Home Grown

The New American style exemplified by designer Stephen Fuller's Hedgewood Heights draws on familiar period elements—such as the Colonial details surrounding the entry—without formalizing a single, historically established style. The result in this case is an eclectic mix of stonework, siding, columns, gables, and dormers that come together with balance and asymmetry. The footprint of the home—narrow, as in a townhouse with a side-loading garage at rear—anticipates siting on an established neighborhood, but can also take command of larger lots.

Arched pass-throughs gently separate the formal spaces from the foyer. BELOW LEFT: Panoramic views from the bedroom match those of the family room. The decorative ceiling is an elegant touch. BELOW RIGHT: Tile backsplashes and a custom range hood keep the kitchen design on theme.

Freed from the constraints of established form, New American styles offer great functional versatility. In the Hedgewood Heights, family members can easily access the kitchen from the porte cochere (not pictured) or the garage by way of the laundry room when carrying luggage or groceries. Homeowners will find that they can't live without the well-situated utility area, available as a mudroom, laundry room, pantry, or a multi-purpose crash pad for incoming family members.

Reserve the front-porch door for guests, who are met by the formal living room with a bay window and a full dining room—two

Visible at moment of entry, full-height windows frame views of the rear property

nods to tradition. By contrast, the family room works close to the kitchen and features a fireplace flanked by built-ins, forming a cohesive shared space for everyday gatherings. Wide views of the rear property brighten and beautify the entire first level.

Private spaces are generously proportioned and comfortable. Two of the upstairs bedrooms partly share a full bath, while the third is a suite. Downstairs, the master suite affords luxury amenities not usually found in a 3,000 square-foot home.

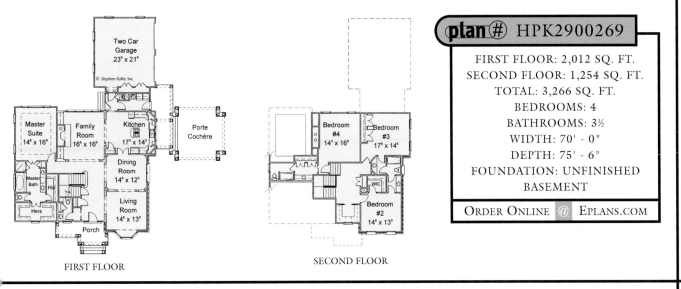

FIRST FLOOR

SECOND FLOOR

plan # HPK2900269

FIRST FLOOR: 2,012 SQ. FT.
SECOND FLOOR: 1,254 SQ. FT.
TOTAL: 3,266 SQ. FT.
BEDROOMS: 4
BATHROOMS: 3½
WIDTH: 70' - 0"
DEPTH: 75' - 6"
FOUNDATION: UNFINISHED BASEMENT

ORDER ONLINE @ EPLANS.COM

A stone-and-siding exterior brings dimension and color to this charming home. A two-story foyer greets you upon entry, and the great room, with views to the rear and side yards, offers a 12-foot ceiling. The breakfast bay and entry to a covered porch create a bright and cheery place to start the day. Counter space that wraps around the kitchen provides additional storage and a convenient writing desk. A furniture alcove adds space to the formal dining room and a rear entry hall offers storage closets and a large laundry room. A second-floor master bedroom, with a ceiling that slopes to nine feet, keeps the parents close at hand to younger family members. This home has a full basement that can be developed for additional square footage.

plan# HPK2900271

FIRST FLOOR: 941 SQ. FT.
SECOND FLOOR: 786 SQ. FT.
BEDROOMS: 3
BATHROOMS: 2½
WIDTH: 57' - 10"
DEPTH: 42' - 4"
FOUNDATION: UNFINISHED BASEMENT

ORDER ONLINE @ EPLANS.COM

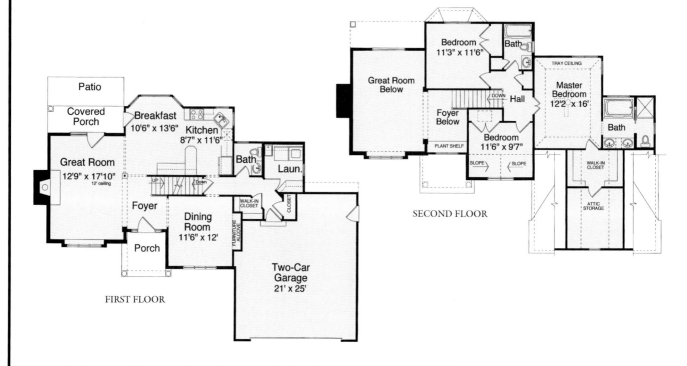

FIRST FLOOR

SECOND FLOOR

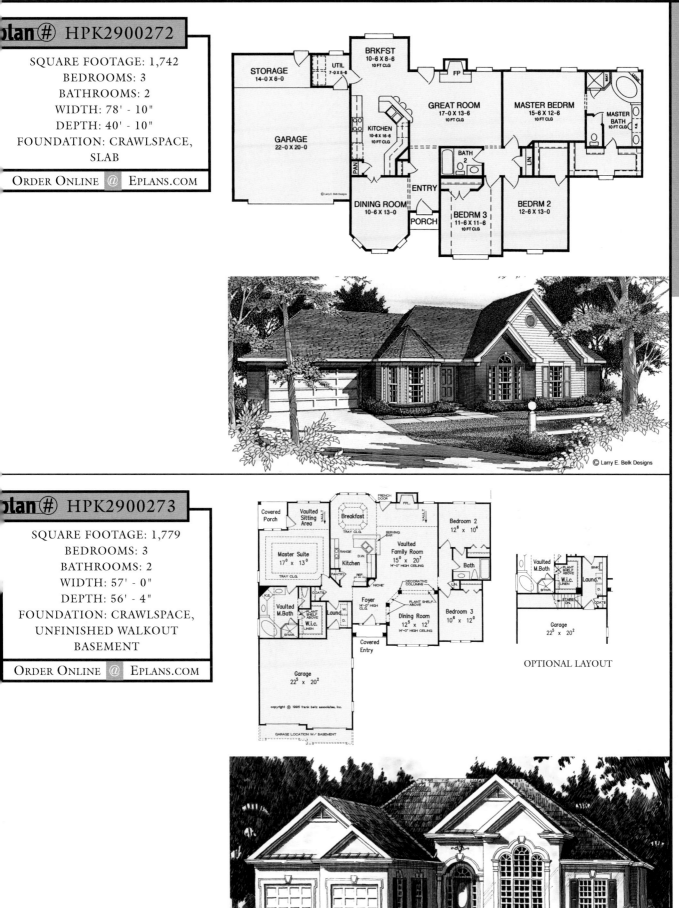

plan # HPK2900272

SQUARE FOOTAGE: 1,742
BEDROOMS: 3
BATHROOMS: 2
WIDTH: 78' - 10"
DEPTH: 40' - 10"
FOUNDATION: CRAWLSPACE,
SLAB

ORDER ONLINE @ EPLANS.com

STORAGE
14-0 X 6-0

UTIL
7-0 X 5-6

BRKFST
10-6 X 8-6
10 FT CLG

FP

GARAGE
22-0 X 20-0

KITCHEN
10-6 X 16-6
10 FT CLG

GREAT ROOM
17-0 X 13-6
10 FT CLG

MASTER BEDRM
15-6 X 12-6
10 FT CLG

MASTER
BATH
10 FT CLG

PAN

BATH
2

LIN

ENTRY

DINING ROOM
10-6 X 13-0

PORCH

BEDRM 3
11-6 X 11-6
10 FT CLG

BEDRM 2
12-6 X 13-0

© Larry E. Belk Designs

plan # HPK2900273

SQUARE FOOTAGE: 1,779
BEDROOMS: 3
BATHROOMS: 2
WIDTH: 57' - 0"
DEPTH: 56' - 4"
FOUNDATION: CRAWLSPACE,
UNFINISHED WALKOUT
BASEMENT

ORDER ONLINE @ EPLANS.com

Covered
Porch

Vaulted
Sitting
Area

Breakfast

TRAY CLG.

FRENCH
DOOR

FPL.

VAULT

VAULT

Master Suite
17⁰ x 13⁰

TRAY CLG.

Kitchen

D.W.

RANGE

SERVING
BAR

Vaulted
Family Room
15⁰ x 20⁷
14'-0" HIGH CEILING

Bedroom 2
12⁸ x 10⁴

Bath

REF.

PANTRY

NICHE

DECORATIVE
COLUMNS

LIN.

K.S.

Vaulted
M.Bath

PLANT
SHELF
ABOVE

Laund.

W.
D.

W.i.c.

LINEN

COATS

Foyer
14'-0" HIGH
CLG.

PLANT SHELF
ABOVE

Dining Room
12⁵ x 12⁷
14'-0" HIGH CEILING

Bedroom 3
10⁸ x 12⁰

Vaulted
M.Bath

PLANT
SHELF
ABOVE

SINK

W.i.c.

LINEN

Laund.

SH.WR.

STAIRS
DN.

COATS

SHWR.

Covered
Entry

Garage
22⁸ x 20²

Garage
22⁸ x 20²

copyright © 1995 frank betz associates, inc.

GARAGE LOCATION W/ BASEMENT

OPTIONAL LAYOUT

© 2002 Donald A. Gardner, Inc.

FIRST FLOOR: 1,345 SQ. FT.
SECOND FLOOR: 452 SQ. FT.
TOTAL: 1,797 SQ. FT.
BONUS SPACE: 349 SQ. FT.
BEDROOMS: 3
BATHROOMS: 2½
WIDTH: 63' - 0"
DEPTH: 40' - 0"

ORDER ONLINE @ EPLANS.COM

Incorporating Old World style and elements, this house combines stone and stucco with gable peaks and arched windows for a stunning European facade. The grand portico leads to an open floor plan, which is equally impressive. Built-in cabinetry, French doors, and a fireplace enhance the great room; an angled counter separates the kitchen from the breakfast nook. The first-floor master suite is located in the quiet zone with no rooms above it. Upstairs, a balcony overlooks the great room. The bonus room features convenient second-floor access and shares a full bath with two upstairs bathrooms.

SECOND FLOOR

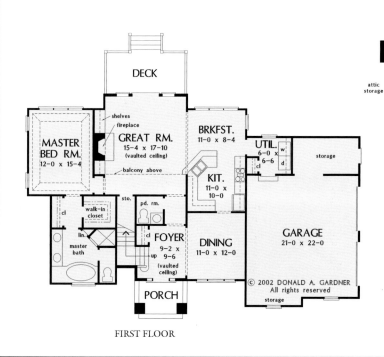

FIRST FLOOR

plan # HPK2900275

FIRST FLOOR: 972 SQ. FT.
SECOND FLOOR: 843 SQ. FT.
TOTAL: 1,815 SQ. FT.
BONUS SPACE: 180 SQ. FT.
BEDROOMS: 3
BATHROOMS: 2½
WIDTH: 45' - 0"
DEPTH: 37' - 0"
FOUNDATION: CRAWLSPACE

ORDER ONLINE @ EPLANS.COM

A brick arch and a two-story bay window adorn the facade of this comfortable family home. Inside, the formal bayed living room and dining room combine to make entertaining a breeze. At the rear of the home, family life is easy with the open floor plan of the family room, breakfast nook, and efficient kitchen. A fireplace graces the family room, and sliding glass doors access the outdoors from the nook. A powder room is conveniently located in the entry hall. Upstairs, three bedrooms include the master suite with a pampering bath. A full hall bath with twin vanities is shared by the family bedrooms. A bonus room is available for future development as a study, library, or fourth bedroom.

FIRST FLOOR

SECOND FLOOR

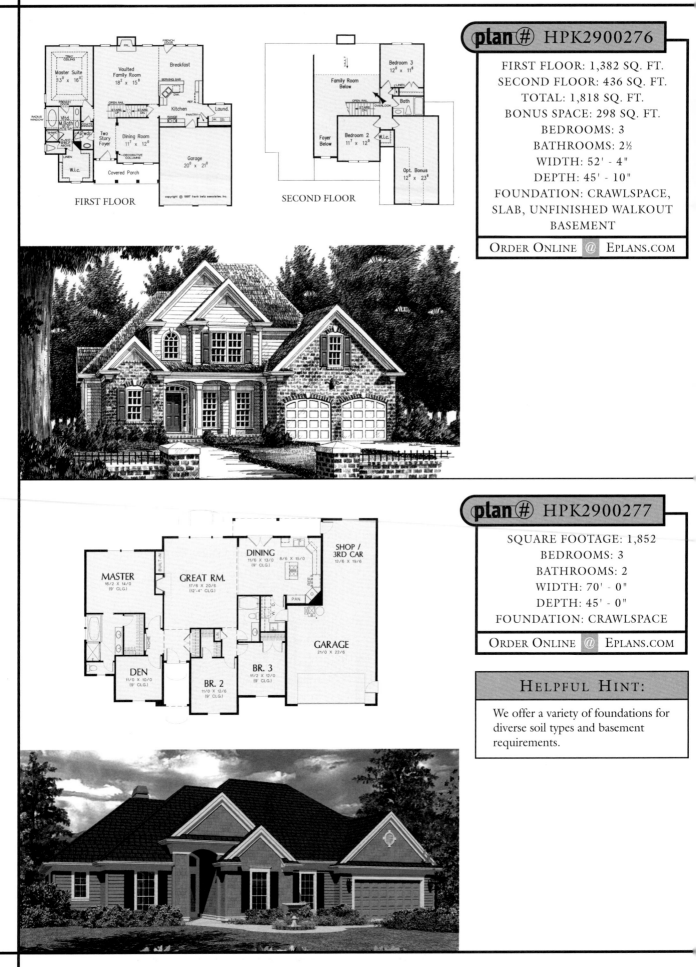

FIRST FLOOR

SECOND FLOOR

plan # HPK2900276

FIRST FLOOR: 1,382 SQ. FT.
SECOND FLOOR: 436 SQ. FT.
TOTAL: 1,818 SQ. FT.
BONUS SPACE: 298 SQ. FT.
BEDROOMS: 3
BATHROOMS: 2½
WIDTH: 52' - 4"
DEPTH: 45' - 10"
FOUNDATION: CRAWLSPACE,
SLAB, UNFINISHED WALKOUT
BASEMENT

ORDER ONLINE @ EPLANS.COM

plan # HPK2900277

SQUARE FOOTAGE: 1,852
BEDROOMS: 3
BATHROOMS: 2
WIDTH: 70' - 0"
DEPTH: 45' - 0"
FOUNDATION: CRAWLSPACE

ORDER ONLINE @ EPLANS.COM

HELPFUL HINT:

We offer a variety of foundations for diverse soil types and basement requirements.

© The Sater Design Collection, Inc.

plan# HPK2900278

FIRST FLOOR: 1,342 SQ. FT.
SECOND FLOOR: 511 SQ. FT.
TOTAL: 1,853 SQ. FT.
BEDROOMS: 3
BATHROOMS: 2
WIDTH: 44' - 0"
DEPTH: 40' - 0"
FOUNDATION: PIER
(SAME AS PILING)

ORDER ONLINE @ EPLANS.COM

Amenities abound in this delightful two-story home. The foyer opens directly into the fantastic grand room, which offers a warming fireplace and two sets of double doors to the rear deck. The dining room also accesses this deck and a second deck shared with Bedroom 2. A convenient kitchen and another bedroom also reside on this level. Upstairs, the master bedroom reigns supreme. Entered through double doors, it pampers with a luxurious bath, walk-in closet, morning kitchen, and private observation deck.

SECOND FLOOR

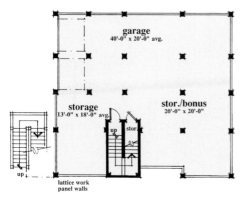

REAR EXTERIOR

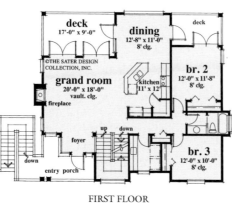

FIRST FLOOR

© The Sater Design Collection, Inc.

Detailed fretwork complements a standing-seam roof on this tropical cottage. An arch-top transom provides an absolutely perfect highlight to the classic clapboard facade. An unrestrained floor plan offers cool digs for kicking back and a sensational retreat for guests—whether the occasion is formal or casual. French doors open to a rear porch from the great room letting in fresh air and the sights and sounds of the great outdoors. Inside, the master bedroom leads to a dressing space with linen storage and a walk-in closet. The lavish bath includes a garden tub, oversized shower, and a wraparound vanity with two sinks. Two secondary bedrooms on the upper level share a spacious loft that overlooks the great room. One of the bedrooms opens to a private deck.

plan # HPK2900279

FIRST FLOOR: 1,342 SQ. FT.
SECOND FLOOR: 511 SQ. FT.
TOTAL: 1,853 SQ. FT.
BEDROOMS: 3
BATHROOMS: 2½
WIDTH: 44' - 0"
DEPTH: 44' - 0"
FOUNDATION: ISLAND BASEMENT

ORDER ONLINE @ EPLANS.com

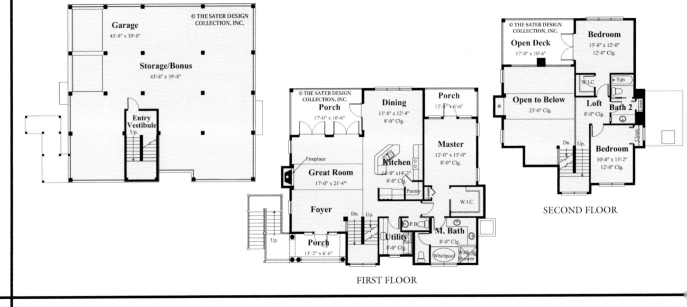

FIRST FLOOR

SECOND FLOOR

plan # HPK2900280

FIRST FLOOR: 1,416 SQ. FT.
SECOND FLOOR: 445 SQ. FT.
TOTAL: 1,861 SQ. FT.
BONUS SPACE: 284 SQ. FT.
BEDROOMS: 3
BATHROOMS: 2½
WIDTH: 58' - 3"
DEPTH: 68' - 6"

ORDER ONLINE @ EPLANS.COM

Arched windows and triple gables provide a touch of elegance to this traditional home. An entrance supported by columns welcomes family and guests inside. On the main level, the dining room offers round columns at the entrance. The great room boasts a cathedral ceiling, a fireplace, and an arched window over the doors to the deck. The kitchen features an island cooktop and an adjoining breakfast nook for informal dining. The master suite offers twin walk-in closets and a lavish bath that includes a whirlpool tub and a double-basin vanity.

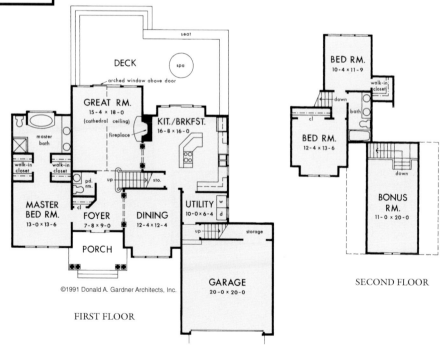

©1991 Donald A. Gardner Architects, Inc.

FIRST FLOOR

SECOND FLOOR

plan # HPK2900281

FIRST FLOOR: 1,320 SQ. FT.
SECOND FLOOR: 554 SQ. FT.
TOTAL: 1,874 SQ. FT.
BONUS SPACE: 155 SQ. FT.
BEDROOMS: 4
BATHROOMS: 2½
WIDTH: 54' - 6"
DEPTH: 42' - 4"
FOUNDATION: CRAWLSPACE,
UNFINISHED WALKOUT
BASEMENT

ORDER ONLINE @ EPLANS.COM

This plan combines a traditional, stately exterior with an updated floor plan to create a house that will please the entire family. The heart of the plan is surely the wide-open living space consisting of the vaulted family room, breakfast area, and gourmet kitchen. Highlights here are a full-length fireplace, a French door to the rear yard, and an island cooktop. The master suite has a tray ceiling and a vaulted master bath with a garden tub and walk-in closet. The family sleeping area on the upper level gives the option of two bedrooms and a loft overlooking the family room or three bedrooms.

FIRST FLOOR

SECOND FLOOR

plan (#) HPK2900282

SQUARE FOOTAGE: 1,977
BONUS SPACE: 430 SQ. FT.
BEDROOMS: 3
BATHROOMS: 2
WIDTH: 69' - 8"
DEPTH: 59' - 6"

ORDER ONLINE @ EPLANS.COM

A two-story foyer with a Palladian window above sets the tone for this sunlit home. Columns mark the passage from the foyer to the great room, where a central fireplace and built-in cabinets stretch the length of one wall. A screened porch with four skylights above and a wet bar provides a pleasant place to start the day or wind down after work. The kitchen is flanked by the formal dining room and the breakfast room. Hidden quietly at the rear, the master suite includes a bath with dual vanities and skylights. Two family bedrooms (one an optional study) share a bath with twin sinks.

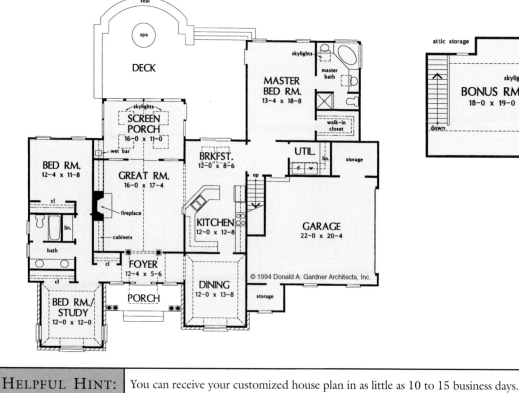

HELPFUL HINT: You can receive your customized house plan in as little as 10 to 15 business days.

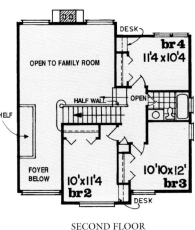

plan# HPK2900283

A portico entry, graceful arches, and brick detailing provide appeal and a low-maintenance exterior for this design. A half-circle transom over the entry lights the two-story foyer and a plant shelf lines the hallway to the sunken family room. This living space holds a vaulted ceiling, masonry fireplace, and French-door access to the railed patio. The nearby kitchen has a center prep island, built-in desk overlooking the family room, and extensive pantries in the breakfast area. The formal dining room has a tray ceiling and access to the foyer and the central hall. The master suite is on the first level for privacy and convenience. It features a walk-in closet and lavish bath with twin vanities, a whirlpool tub, and separate shower. Three family bedrooms, two of which feature built-in desks, are on the second floor.

FIRST FLOOR: 1,445 SQ. FT.
SECOND FLOOR: 652 SQ. FT.
TOTAL: 2,097 SQ. FT.
BEDROOMS: 4
BATHROOMS: 2½
WIDTH: 56' - 8"
DEPTH: 48' - 4"
FOUNDATION: CRAWLSPACE,
UNFINISHED BASEMENT

ORDER ONLINE @ EPLANS.COM

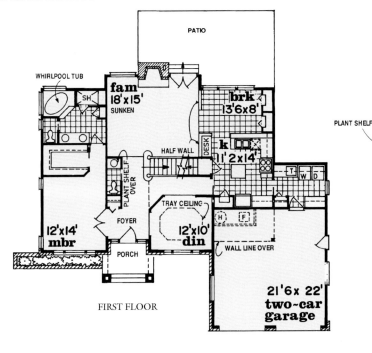

FIRST FLOOR

SECOND FLOOR

plan # HPK2900284

FIRST FLOOR: 1,688 SQ. FT.
SECOND FLOOR: 558 SQ. FT.
TOTAL: 2,246 SQ. FT.
BONUS SPACE: 269 SQ. FT.
BEDROOMS: 4
BATHROOMS: 3
WIDTH: 54' - 0"
DEPTH: 48' - 0"
FOUNDATION: CRAWLSPACE,
SLAB, UNFINISHED WALKOUT
BASEMENT

ORDER ONLINE @ EPLANS.COM

Graceful details combine with a covered entryway to welcome friends and family to come on in. The canted bay sitting area in the master suite provides sunny respite and quiet solitude. To be the center of attention, invite everyone to party in the vaulted great room, which spills over into the big, airy kitchen. Guests can make use of the optional study/bedroom. Upstairs, secondary bedrooms share a full bath and a balcony overlook. A spacious central hall leads to a bonus room that provides wardrobe space.

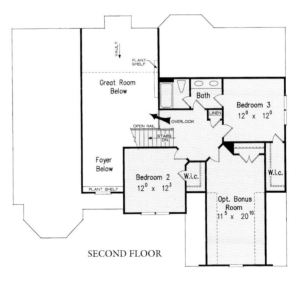

SECOND FLOOR

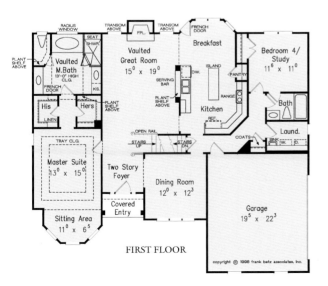

FIRST FLOOR

copyright © 1998 frank betz associates, Inc.

plan # HPK2900285

SQUARE FOOTAGE: 2,282
BONUS SPACE: 629 SQ. FT.
BEDROOMS: 3
BATHROOMS: 2½
WIDTH: 60' - 0"
DEPTH: 75' - 4"
FOUNDATION: CRAWLSPACE,
UNFINISHED WALKOUT
BASEMENT

ORDER ONLINE @ EPLANS.COM

Columns and keystone lintels lend a European aura to this stone-and-siding home. Arched openings and decorative columns define the formal dining room to the left of the foyer. A ribbon of windows with transoms above draws sunshine into the living room. The master suite opens from a short hallway and enjoys a tray ceiling and a vaulted bathroom with shelving, compartmented toilet, separate shower, and garden tub. Transoms abound in the open informal living areas of this home. A bay-windowed breakfast nook adjoins the kitchen with a central serving bar and the family room with a warming fireplace. Two additional bedrooms share a full bath to the left of the plan.

FIRST FLOOR

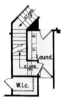

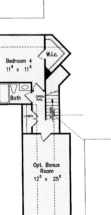

OPTIONAL LAYOUT

plan # HPK2900286

SQUARE FOOTAGE: 2,292
BEDROOMS: 4
BATHROOMS: 2½
WIDTH: 80' - 7"
DEPTH: 50' - 6"
FOUNDATION: CRAWLSPACE,
SLAB

ORDER ONLINE @ EPLANS.COM

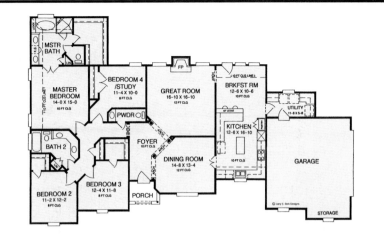

plan # HPK2900287

FIRST FLOOR: 1,715 SQ. FT.
SECOND FLOOR: 620 SQ. FT.
TOTAL: 2,335 SQ. FT.
BONUS SPACE: 265 SQ. FT.
BEDROOMS: 3
BATHROOMS: 2½
WIDTH: 58' - 6"
DEPTH: 50' - 3"

ORDER ONLINE @ EPLANS.COM

FIRST FLOOR

SECOND FLOOR

plan # HPK2900288

FIRST FLOOR: 1,687 SQ. FT.
SECOND FLOOR: 694 SQ. FT.
TOTAL: 2,381 SQ. FT.
BONUS SPACE: 407 SQ. FT.
BEDROOMS: 5
BATHROOMS: 3
WIDTH: 55' - 10"
DEPTH: 44' - 6"
FOUNDATION: CRAWLSPACE,
UNFINISHED WALKOUT
BASEMENT

ORDER ONLINE @ EPLANS.COM

Signature Designer

Stylistically defined as Traditional, there is nothing customary about the Wheaton. Classic clapboard siding with brick accents complements asymmetrical gables and a quaint covered porch on this 21st-Century design. Plentiful bedrooms and bonus space, a trademark for designer Frank Betz, ensure room for families to grow into. All this and a pleasing facade make this home one of our best sellers.

FIRST FLOOR

SECOND FLOOR

HELPFUL HINT: We'll typically deliver your standard plans within 2 to 3 days.

plan # HPK2900289

FIRST FLOOR: 1,814 SQ. FT.
SECOND FLOOR: 580 SQ. FT.
TOTAL: 2,394 SQ. FT.
BONUS SPACE: 259 SQ. FT.
BEDROOMS: 4
BATHROOMS: 3
WIDTH: 55' - 4"
DEPTH: 52' - 0"
FOUNDATION: CRAWLSPACE,
UNFINISHED WALKOUT
BASEMENT

ORDER ONLINE @ EPLANS.COM

Keystone arches and double-hung windows decorate a comfortably elegant elevation in this traditional home. Open living space creates harmony with a breakfast nook, well lit with a radius window, and an island kitchen with a pass-through to the vaulted family room. A tray ceiling and a vaulted bath with a plant shelf highlight the first-floor master suite, which boasts two ample walk-in closets. Upstairs, Bedrooms 2 and 3 share a full bath with twin vanities and a central hall with a balcony overlook.

FIRST FLOOR

SECOND FLOOR

plan# HPK2900290

FIRST FLOOR: 1,317 SQ. FT.
SECOND FLOOR: 1,146 SQ. FT.
TOTAL: 2,463 SQ. FT.
BEDROOMS: 4
BATHROOMS: 2½
WIDTH: 40' - 0"
DEPTH: 54' - 0"
FOUNDATION: CRAWLSPACE

ORDER ONLINE @ EPLANS.COM

This striking stucco home incorporates fine design elements throughout the plan, including a columned formal living and dining area with a boxed ceiling and a fireplace. A gourmet kitchen accommodates the most elaborate—as well as the simplest—meals. The large family room is just off the kitchen for easy casual living. A lovely curved staircase leads to a balcony overlooking the foyer. The master bedroom contains many fine design features, including a luxury bath with a vaulted ceiling and a spa-style bath. Three comfortable family bedrooms share a full hall bath.

FIRST FLOOR

SECOND FLOOR

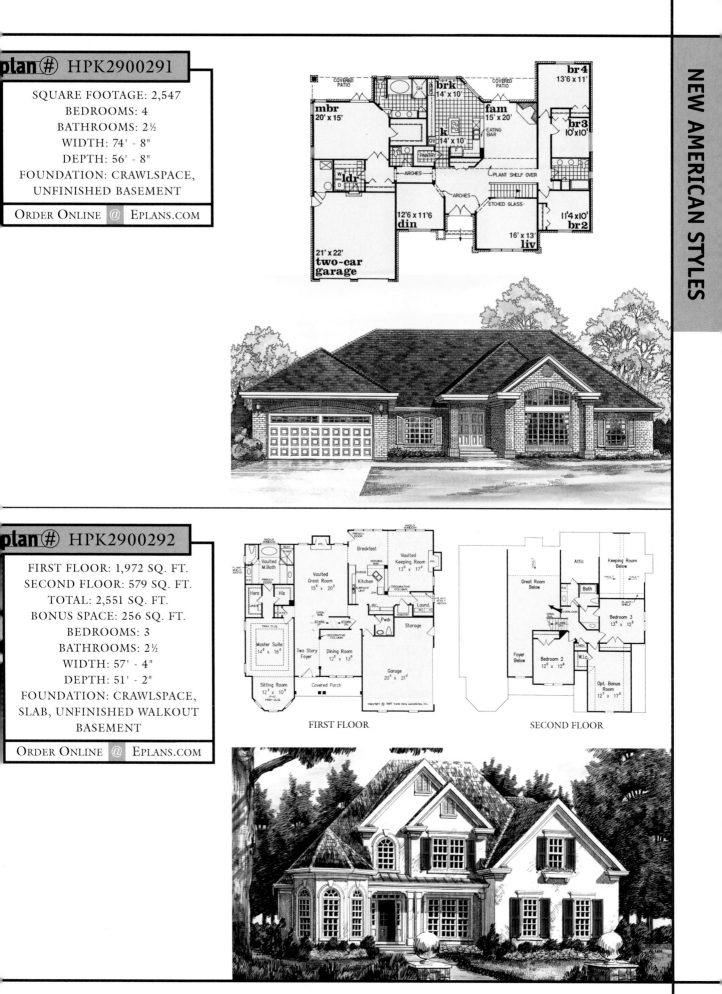

plan # HPK2900291

SQUARE FOOTAGE: 2,547
BEDROOMS: 4
BATHROOMS: 2½
WIDTH: 74' - 8"
DEPTH: 56' - 8"
FOUNDATION: CRAWLSPACE,
UNFINISHED BASEMENT

ORDER ONLINE @ EPLANS.COM

plan # HPK2900292

FIRST FLOOR: 1,972 SQ. FT.
SECOND FLOOR: 579 SQ. FT.
TOTAL: 2,551 SQ. FT.
BONUS SPACE: 256 SQ. FT.
BEDROOMS: 3
BATHROOMS: 2½
WIDTH: 57' - 4"
DEPTH: 51' - 2"
FOUNDATION: CRAWLSPACE,
SLAB, UNFINISHED WALKOUT
BASEMENT

ORDER ONLINE @ EPLANS.COM

FIRST FLOOR

SECOND FLOOR

Designed to take full advantage of panoramic rear vistas, this home possesses some great visual effects of its own. Its unusual and creative use of space includes an angled gathering room, expansive grand room, and continuous covered lanai. High ceilings throughout create an air of spaciousness. A tray ceiling reflects the pentagonal shape of the open dining room. The master retreat features a sitting area and a bath that includes both His and Hers vanities and walk-in closets. A private staircase leads to a large bonus room.

plan# HPK2900293

SQUARE FOOTAGE: 2,585
BONUS SPACE: 519 SQ. FT.
BEDROOMS: 3
BATHROOMS: 2½
WIDTH: 62' - 6"
DEPTH: 83' - 10"
FOUNDATION: CRAWLSPACE

ORDER ONLINE @ EPLANS.com

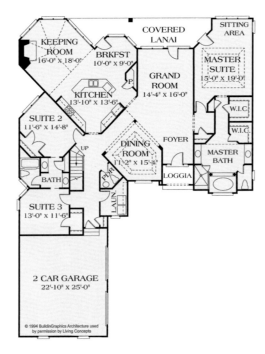

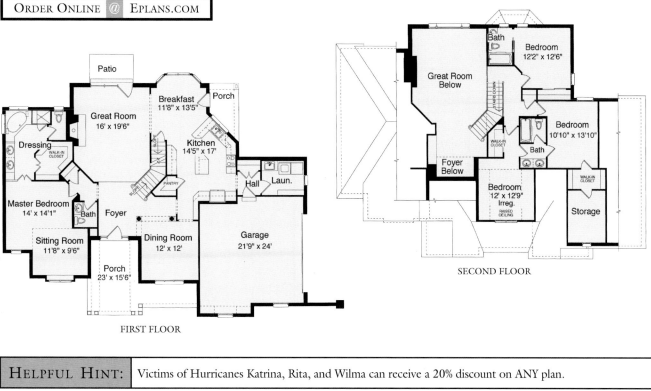

plan # HPK2900294

FIRST FLOOR: 1,790 SQ. FT.
SECOND FLOOR: 797 SQ. FT.
TOTAL: 2,587 SQ. FT.
BEDROOMS: 4
BATHROOMS: 3½
WIDTH: 64' - 4"
DEPTH: 50' - 0"
FOUNDATION: UNFINISHED
BASEMENT

ORDER ONLINE @ EPLANS.COM

A brick-and-stone facade with arched windows, a covered porch, and shingle siding, decorate the exterior of this exciting home. The foyer showcases an angled staircase and opens generously to the great room, which enjoys a spectacular rear view. The spacious kitchen serves the breakfast alcove and dining room with equal ease and enjoys a bar with seating, a window above the sink, and a walk-in pantry. The master suite boasts a sitting area and a deluxe dressing area. The whirlpool tub, double-bowl vanity, and walk-in closet offer a luxurious retreat. Three bedrooms, one with a private bath, reside upstairs.

FIRST FLOOR

SECOND FLOOR

HELPFUL HINT: Victims of Hurricanes Katrina, Rita, and Wilma can receive a 20% discount on ANY plan.

©The Sater Design Collection, Inc.

This Floridian-style home boasts an impressive balcony that is sure to catch the eye. A large veranda borders two sides of the home. The entry leads into a long foyer, which runs from the entrance to the rear of the design. The coffered great room enjoys a fireplace, built-in cabinetry, and French doors to the veranda; the dining room also accesses the veranda. The island kitchen leads into a bayed nook, perfect for Sunday morning breakfasting. The second floor is home to two family bedrooms—both with access to the deck—a study, and a luxurious master suite. A vaulted sitting area, full bath, and deck access are just some of the highlights of the master suite.

plan# HPK2900294

FIRST FLOOR: 1,266 SQ. FT.
SECOND FLOOR: 1,324 SQ. FT.
TOTAL: 2,590 SQ. FT.
BEDROOMS: 3
BATHROOMS: 2½
WIDTH: 34' - 0"
DEPTH: 63' - 2"
FOUNDATION: CRAWLSPACE

ORDER ONLINE @ EPLANS.COM

SECOND FLOOR

FIRST FLOOR

plan # HPK2900296

SQUARE FOOTAGE: 2,678
BEDROOMS: 4
BATHROOMS: 2½
WIDTH: 70' - 2"
DEPTH: 67' - 9"
FOUNDATION: CRAWLSPACE,
SLAB

ORDER ONLINE @ EPLANS.COM

plan # HPK2900297

FIRST FLOOR: 1,844 SQ. FT.
SECOND FLOOR: 841 SQ. FT.
TOTAL: 2,685 SQ. FT.
BONUS SPACE: 455 SQ. FT.
BEDROOMS: 4
BATHROOMS: 2½
WIDTH: 62' - 6"
DEPTH: 52' - 10"
FOUNDATION: SLAB

ORDER ONLINE @ EPLANS.COM

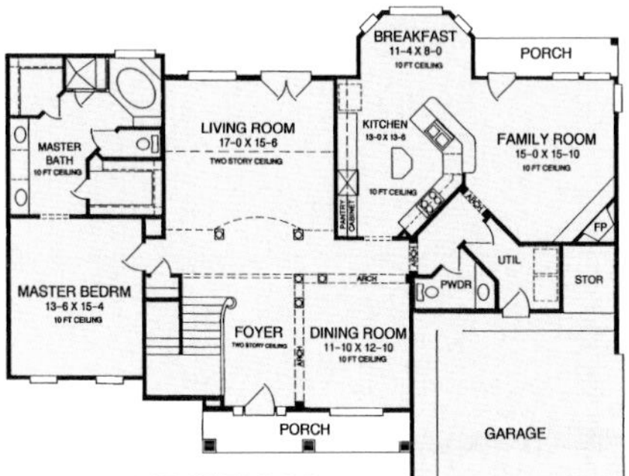

FIRST FLOOR

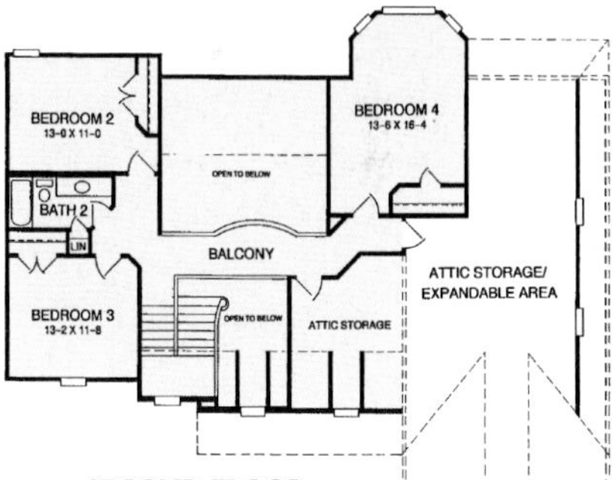

SECOND FLOOR

plan# HPK2900298

FIRST FLOOR: 1,809 SQ. FT.
SECOND FLOOR: 898 SQ. FT.
TOTAL: 2,707 SQ. FT.
BEDROOMS: 4
BATHROOMS: 3½
WIDTH: 54' - 4"
DEPTH: 46' - 0"
FOUNDATION: UNFINISHED
BASEMENT

ORDER ONLINE @ EPLANS.com

Nested, hipped gables create a dramatic effect on this beautiful two-story brick home. The arched doorway is echoed in the triple clerestory window that lights the two-story foyer. Columns decorate the formal dining room, which is open to the two-story grand room with a fireplace. The master suite is located on the first floor for privacy, while upstairs, three secondary bedrooms are joined by a gallery overlooking the grand room.

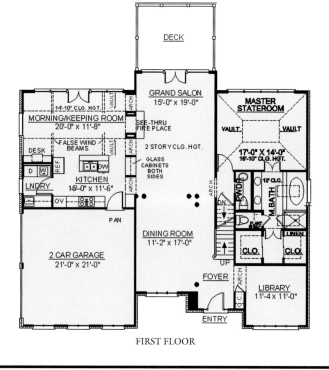

FIRST FLOOR

SECOND FLOOR

plan # HPK2900299

FIRST FLOOR: 1,930 SQ. FT.
SECOND FLOOR: 791 SQ. FT.
TOTAL: 2,721 SQ. FT.
BEDROOMS: 4
BATHROOMS: 3
WIDTH: 64' - 4"
DEPTH: 62' - 0"
FOUNDATION: CRAWLSPACE,
SLAB, UNFINISHED
BASEMENT

ORDER ONLINE @ EPLANS.COM

A **delightful facade** with a flared roof captures the eye and provides just the right touch for this inviting home. Inside, an angled foyer with a volume ceiling directs attention to the enormous great room. The detailed dining room includes massive round columns connected by arches and shares a through-fireplace with the great room. The master suite includes an upscale bath and access to a private covered porch. Nearby, Bedroom 2 is perfect for a nursery or home office/study. The kitchen features a large cooktop island and walk-in pantry. The second floor is dominated by an oversized game room. Two family bedrooms, a bath, and a linen closet complete the upstairs.

FIRST FLOOR

SECOND FLOOR

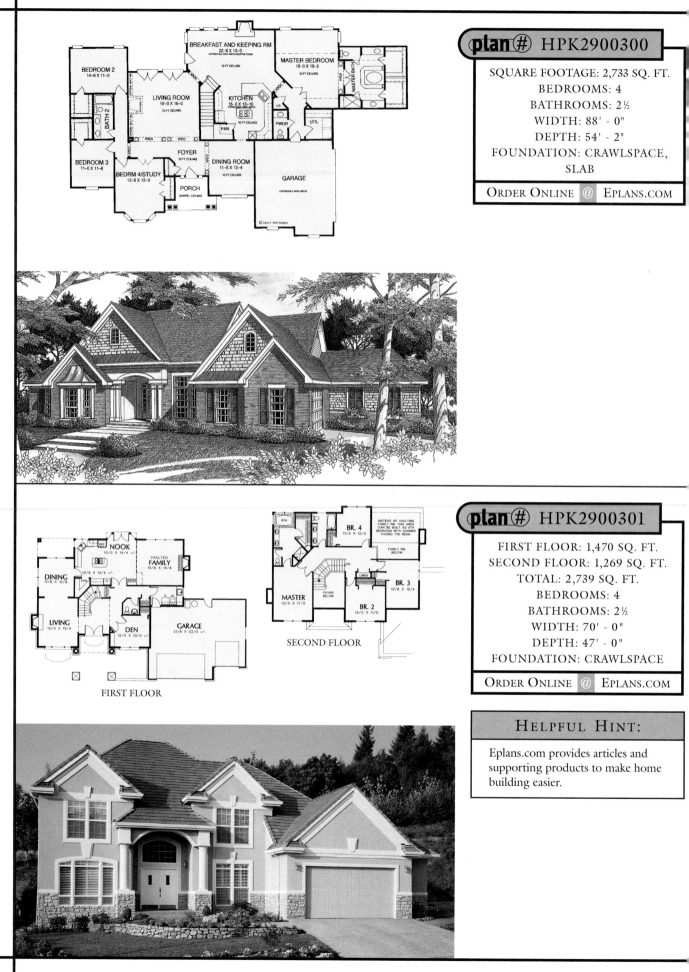

BEDROOM 2
14-6 X 11-0

BATH 2

BREAKFAST AND KEEPING RM
22-6 X 13-0
EXPANDABLE AREA ABOVE KEEPING ROOM
10 FT CEILING

MASTER BEDROOM
16-0 X 19-2
10 FT CEILING

MASTER BATH

LIVING ROOM
18-0 X 16-0
10 FT CEILING

KITCHEN
15-0 X 13-10
10 FT CEILING

LIN

PAN

PWDR

UTIL

ARCH

BEDROOM 3
11-0 X 11-6

FOYER
10 FT CEILING

DINING ROOM
11-8 13-4
10 FT CEILING

GARAGE
EXPANDABLE AREA ABOVE

BEDRM 4/STUDY
12-6 X 13-0

PORCH
BARREL CEILING

© Larry E. Belk Designs

NOOK
10/0 X 14/4

VAULTED FAMILY
15/6 X 14/4

DINING
11/8 X 12/8

PAN

LIVING
13/0 X 15/4

DEN
13/0 10/0 +/-

GARAGE
31/8 X 23/0 +/-

D. W.

FIRST FLOOR

SPA

BR. 4
11/0 X 12/4

INSTEAD OF VAULTING FAMILY RM, THIS AREA CAN BE BUILT AS 5TH BEDROOM WITH DORMER FACING THE REAR.

FAMILY RM. BELOW

MASTER
13/0 X 17/0

FOYER BELOW

LINEN

BR. 3
10/8 X 15/4

BR. 2
13/0 X 11/0

SECOND FLOOR

HELPFUL HINT:

Eplans.com provides articles and supporting products to make home building easier.

plan# HPK2900302

SQUARE FOOTAGE: 2,755
BONUS SPACE: 440 SQ. FT.
BEDROOMS: 4
BATHROOMS: 3
WIDTH: 73' - 0"
DEPTH: 82' - 8"
FOUNDATION: SLAB

ORDER ONLINE @ EPLANS.COM

The use of stone and stucco has created a very pleasant exterior that would fit in well with a traditional environment. The double-door entry, which leads to the foyer, welcomes guests to a formal living and dining room area. Upon entering the master suite through double doors, the master bed wall becomes the focal point. A stepped ceiling treatment adds excitement, with floor-length windows framing the bed. The sitting area created by the bayed door wall further enhances the opulence of the suite. The master bath comes complete with His and Hers walk-in closets, dual vanities with a makeup area, and a soaking tub balanced by the large shower and private toilet chamber.

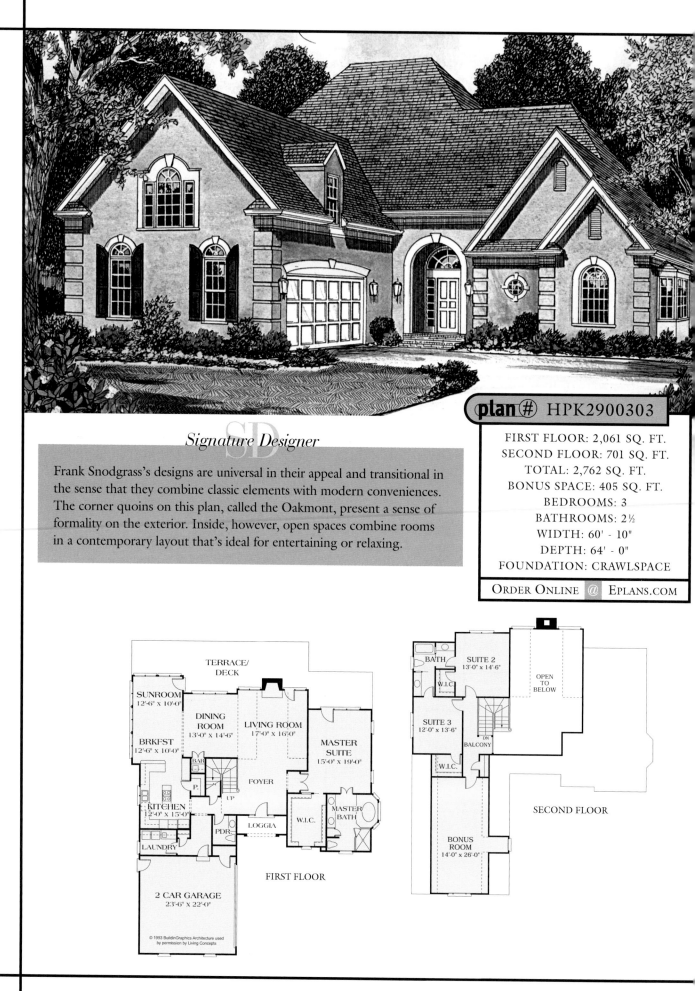

Signature Designer

Frank Snodgrass's designs are universal in their appeal and transitional in the sense that they combine classic elements with modern conveniences. The corner quoins on this plan, called the Oakmont, present a sense of formality on the exterior. Inside, however, open spaces combine rooms in a contemporary layout that's ideal for entertaining or relaxing.

plan# HPK2900303

FIRST FLOOR: 2,061 SQ. FT.
SECOND FLOOR: 701 SQ. FT.
TOTAL: 2,762 SQ. FT.
BONUS SPACE: 405 SQ. FT.
BEDROOMS: 3
BATHROOMS: 2½
WIDTH: 60' - 10"
DEPTH: 64' - 0"
FOUNDATION: CRAWLSPACE

ORDER ONLINE @ EPLANS.COM

TERRACE/ DECK

SUNROOM
12'-6" x 10'-0"

DINING ROOM
13'-0" x 14'-6"

LIVING ROOM
17'-0" x 16'-0"

BRKFST
12'-6" x 10'-0"

MASTER SUITE
15'-0" x 19'-0"

BAR

P.

FOYER

KITCHEN
12'-0" x 15'-0"

UP

PDR.

LOGGIA

W.I.C.

MASTER BATH

LAUNDRY

2 CAR GARAGE
23'-6" x 22'-0"

FIRST FLOOR

© 1993 BuildinGraphics Architecture used by permission by Living Concepts

BATH

SUITE 2
13'-0" x 14'-6"

W.I.C.

OPEN TO BELOW

SUITE 3
12'-0" x 13'-6"

DN BALCONY

W.I.C.

BONUS ROOM
14'-0" x 26'-0"

SECOND FLOOR

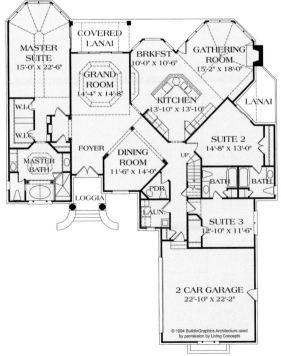

plan # HPK2900304

SQUARE FOOTAGE: 2,774
BONUS SPACE: 367 SQ. FT.
BEDROOMS: 3
BATHROOMS: 3½
WIDTH: 66' - 10"
DEPTH: 84' - 9"
FOUNDATION: CRAWLSPACE

ORDER ONLINE @ Eplans.com

Interesting room orientation distinguishes this unusual floor plan. The grand room's octagonal tray ceiling demonstrates that this is an elegant home inhabited by hospitable people. Beyond the grand room, a partially-covered lanai offers options for outdoor entertaining. The bay-shaped breakfast nook and gathering room play off the kitchen's angled countertops, creating an integrated, informal space. Note how the offset fireplace in the gathering room will ease furniture arrangement. The right wing of the home houses two bedroom suites, one with a private lanai, and a stair to the bonus room above the two-car garage. The master retreat occupies the left wing. More elegant ceiling treatments and a posh bath will make everyday living feel like a fantasy vacation!

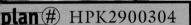

© 1994 BuildinGraphics Architecture used by permission by Living Concepts

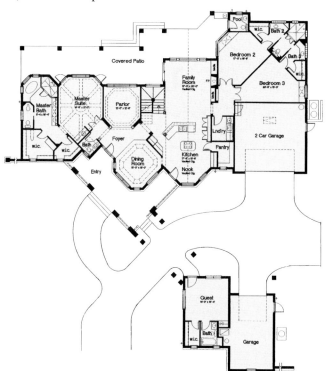

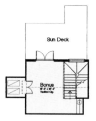

Though designed as a grand estate, this home retains the warmth of a country manor with intimate details on the inside and out. A one-of-a-kind drive court leads to private parking and ends in a two-car garage; a separate guest house is replete with angled walls and sculptured ceilings. A continuous vault follows from the family room through the kitchen and nook. The vault soars even higher in the bonus room with a sundeck upstairs. Two exquisitely appointed family bedrooms with window seats and walk-in closets share a full bath. The master suite has pampering details such as a juice bar and media wall, walk-in closets, and covered patio access.

plan # HPK2900305

SQUARE FOOTAGE: 2,816
BONUS SPACE: 290 SQ. FT.
BEDROOMS: 4
BATHROOMS: 3½ + ½
WIDTH: 94' - 0"
DEPTH: 70' - 5"
FOUNDATION: SLAB

ORDER ONLINE @ EPLANS.COM

plan # HPK2900306

FIRST FLOOR: 1,966 SQ. FT.
SECOND FLOOR: 872 SQ. FT.
TOTAL: 2,838 SQ. FT.
BEDROOMS: 5
BATHROOMS: 3
WIDTH: 79' - 10"
DEPTH: 63' - 10"
FOUNDATION: CRAWLSPACE,
SLAB, UNFINISHED
BASEMENT

ORDER ONLINE @ EPLANS.COM

This elegant two-story brick home, with its corner quoins, varied rooflines, and multipane windows, has so many amenities to offer! Enter the two-story foyer graced by an elegant, curved staircase. The formal dining room, defined by columns, is nearby and has double-door access to the efficient island kitchen. The large great room is enhanced by a warming fireplace and direct access to the rear patio. The first-floor master bedroom suite is nicely secluded for privacy and pampers with its own covered porch, His and Hers walk-in closets, and a lavish bath. Upstairs, all three family bedrooms have walk-in closets and share a full hall bath.

FIRST FLOOR

SECOND FLOOR

HELPFUL HINT:	Register on eplans.com to save searches and plans for later review.

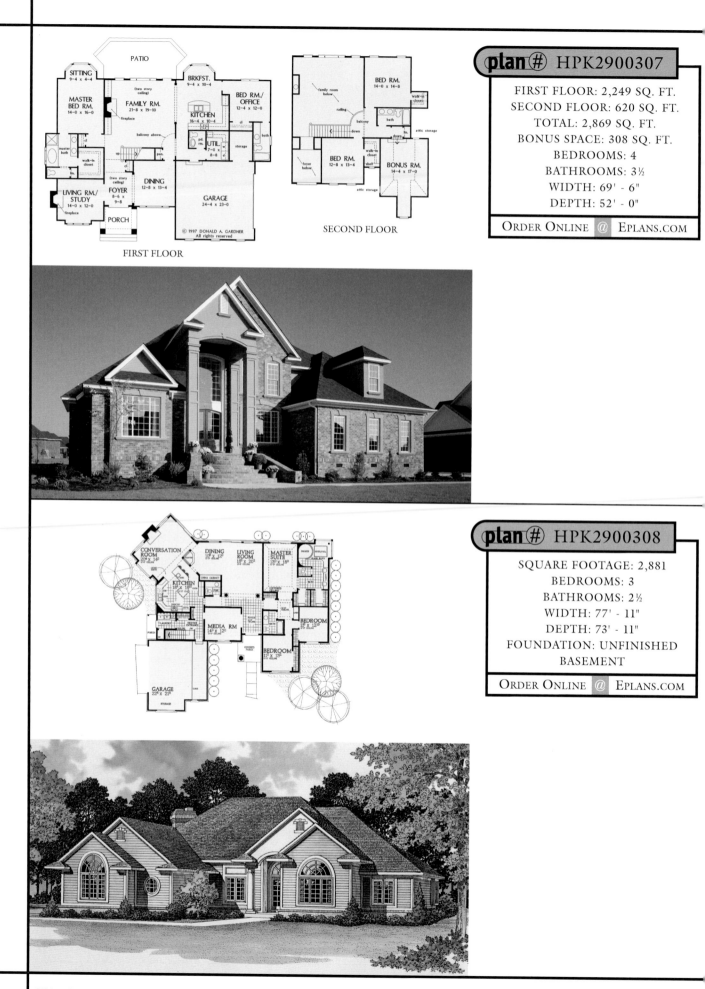

PATIO

SITTING
9-4 x 4-4

MASTER
BED RM.
14-0 x 16-0

(two story
ceiling)
FAMILY RM.
21-8 x 19-10

fireplace

balcony above.

BRKFST.
9-4 x 10-4

KITCHEN
16-4 x 10-4

BED RM./
OFFICE
12-4 x 12-0

cl

cl

bath

master
bath

cl

walk-in
closet

up

cl

(two story
ceiling)

pd.
rm.

pan.

UTIL.
7-0 x
8-8

w

d

storage

LIVING RM./
STUDY
14-0 x 12-0

fireplace

FOYER
8-6 x
9-8

DINING
12-8 x 13-4

GARAGE
24-4 x 23-0

© 1997 DONALD A. GARDNER
All rights reserved

PORCH

FIRST FLOOR

BED RM.
14-0 x 14-6

family room
below

railing

walk-in
closet

bath

balcony

down

BED RM.
12-8 x 13-4

foyer
below

down

walk-in
closet

shelf

lin.

attic storage

BONUS RM.
14-4 x 17-0

attic storage

SECOND FLOOR

CONVERSATION
ROOM
20⁴ x 14⁰

DINING
13⁰ x 12²

LIVING
ROOM
13² x 20²

MASTER
SUITE
13⁰ x 16⁰

KITCHEN
18³ x 16⁰

CHINA CABINET

BATH

BEDROOM
13⁰ x 12⁵⁰

MEDIA RM.
14⁰ x 12⁰

BATH

BEDROOM
11⁰ x 13⁰

COVERED PORCH

GARAGE
22⁸ x 21⁸

STORAGE

plan # HPK2900309

FIRST FLOOR: 2,247 SQ. FT.
SECOND FLOOR: 637 SQ. FT.
TOTAL: 2,884 SQ. FT.
BONUS SPACE: 235 SQ. FT.
BEDROOMS: 4
BATHROOMS: 4
WIDTH: 64' - 0"
DEPTH: 55' - 2"
FOUNDATION: CRAWLSPACE,
UNFINISHED WALKOUT
BASEMENT

ORDER ONLINE @ EPLANS.COM

This astonishing traditional home looks great with its gables, muntin windows, keystone lintels, and turret-style bay. Inside, the heart of the home is the vaulted family room with a fireplace. The kitchen conveniently connects to the dining room, breakfast room, and garage. The master bath leads into a walk-in closet. The home office or nursery near the hall bath is illuminated by a bayed wall of windows and could become an additional family bedroom. Family bedrooms upstairs share a loft that overlooks the family room.

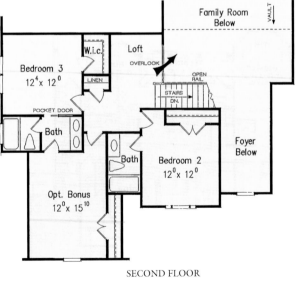

SECOND FLOOR

FIRST FLOOR

plan # HPK2900317

Brick and stone complement each other and the variety of windows to create a sophisticated facade on this traditional home. Three family bedrooms with large closets share two full baths on the second level, where you'll also find a playroom that can be finished at a later date. The master bedroom is situated to the far left of the lower level and includes a master bath with two sinks divided by a corner tub, a compartmented toilet, a separate shower, and access to an enormous walk-in closet. Living spaces range from casual—island kitchen, breakfast nook, family room with access to the covered patio—to the more formal living room and dining room.

FIRST FLOOR: 2,115 SQ. FT.
SECOND FLOOR: 947 SQ. FT.
TOTAL: 3,062 SQ. FT.
BONUS SPACE: 216 SQ. FT.
BEDROOMS: 4
BATHROOMS: 3½
WIDTH: 68' - 10"
DEPTH: 58' - 1"
FOUNDATION: CRAWLSPACE, SLAB, UNFINISHED BASEMENT

ORDER ONLINE @ EPLANS.COM

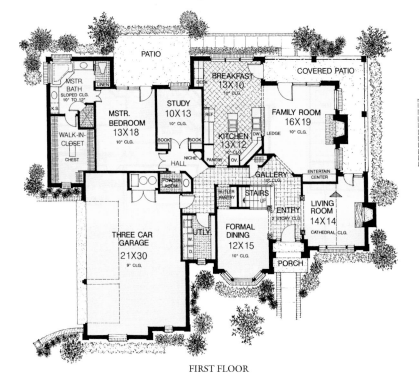

FIRST FLOOR

SECOND FLOOR

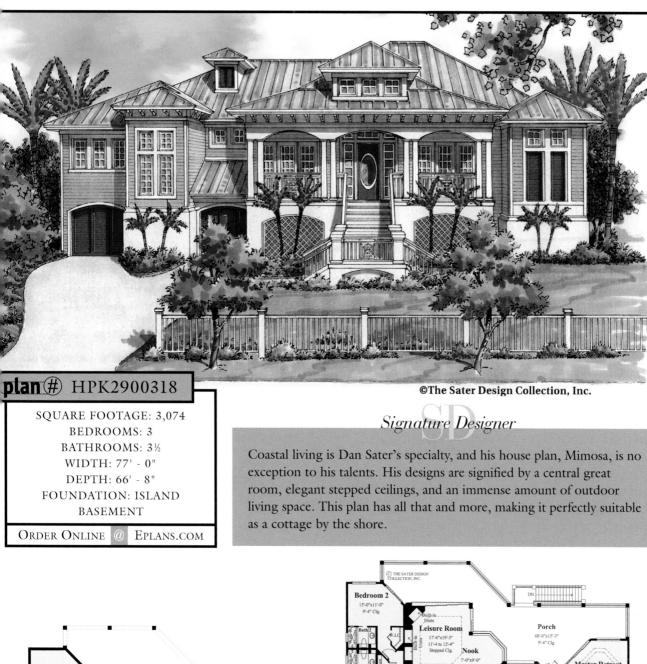

©The Sater Design Collection, Inc.

plan # HPK2900318

SQUARE FOOTAGE: 3,074
BEDROOMS: 3
BATHROOMS: 3½
WIDTH: 77' - 0"
DEPTH: 66' - 8"
FOUNDATION: ISLAND
BASEMENT

ORDER ONLINE @ EPLANS.COM

Signature Designer

Coastal living is Dan Sater's specialty, and his house plan, Mimosa, is no exception to his talents. His designs are signified by a central great room, elegant stepped ceilings, and an immense amount of outdoor living space. This plan has all that and more, making it perfectly suitable as a cottage by the shore.

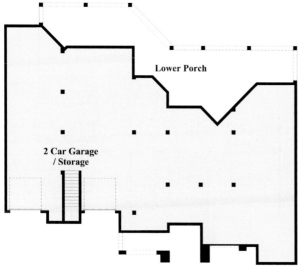

FIRST FLOOR

HELPFUL HINT: Modify your plan with our easy-to-use customization service.

FIRST FLOOR: 1,919 SQ. FT.
SECOND FLOOR: 1,190 SQ. FT.
TOTAL: 3,109 SQ. FT.
BONUS SPACE: 286 SQ. FT.
BEDROOMS: 4
BATHROOMS: 3½
WIDTH: 64' - 6"
DEPTH: 55' - 10"
FOUNDATION: CRAWLSPACE,
SLAB, UNFINISHED
BASEMENT

ORDER ONLINE @ EPLANS.COM

Flower boxes, arches, and multipane windows combine to create the elegant facade of this four-bedroom home. Inside, the two-story foyer introduces a formal dining room to its right and leads to a two-story living room that is filled with light. An efficient kitchen has a bayed breakfast room and shares a snack bar with a cozy family room. Located on the first floor for privacy, the master suite is graced with a luxurious bath. Upstairs, three secondary bedrooms share two full baths and access a large game room. For future growth there is an expandable area accessed through the game room.

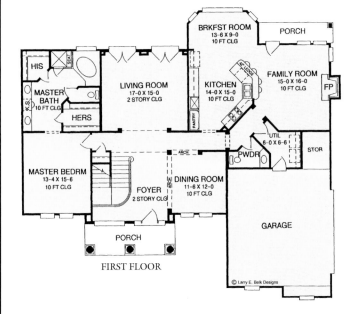

FIRST FLOOR

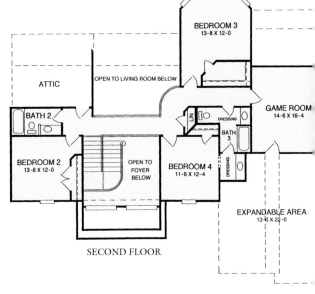

SECOND FLOOR

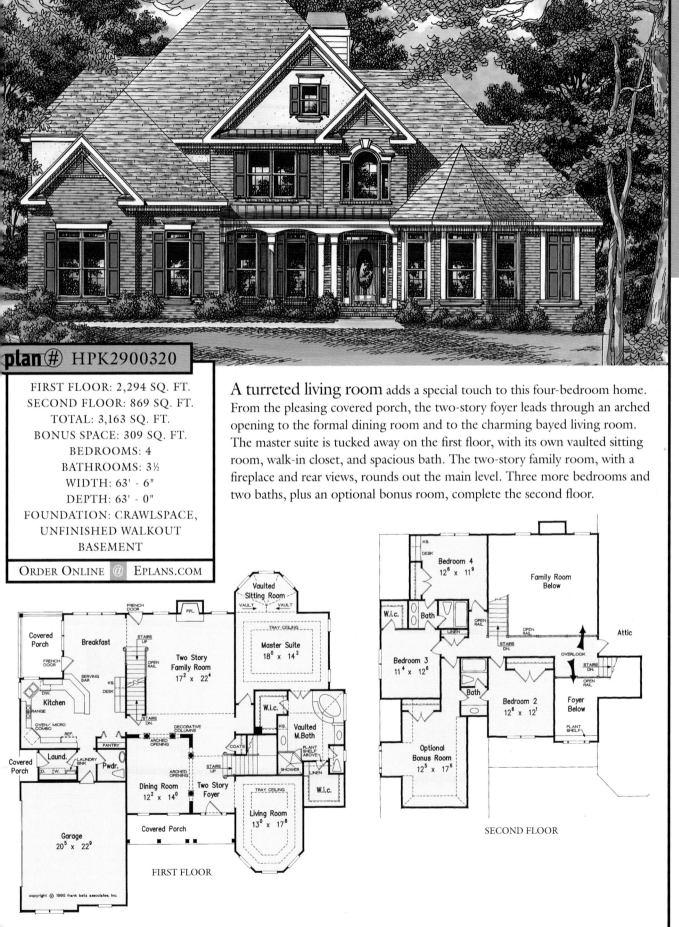

plan # HPK2900320

FIRST FLOOR: 2,294 SQ. FT.
SECOND FLOOR: 869 SQ. FT.
TOTAL: 3,163 SQ. FT.
BONUS SPACE: 309 SQ. FT.
BEDROOMS: 4
BATHROOMS: 3½
WIDTH: 63' - 6"
DEPTH: 63' - 0"
FOUNDATION: CRAWLSPACE,
UNFINISHED WALKOUT
BASEMENT

ORDER ONLINE @ EPLANS.COM

A turreted living room adds a special touch to this four-bedroom home. From the pleasing covered porch, the two-story foyer leads through an arched opening to the formal dining room and to the charming bayed living room. The master suite is tucked away on the first floor, with its own vaulted sitting room, walk-in closet, and spacious bath. The two-story family room, with a fireplace and rear views, rounds out the main level. Three more bedrooms and two baths, plus an optional bonus room, complete the second floor.

FIRST FLOOR

SECOND FLOOR

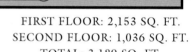

plan # HPK2900321

A clever floor plan and stylish facade bring much-deserved accolades to this winsome design. Brick and vertical siding lend a fresh country look to the outside; inside, angles offer unique room arrangements to maximize space and flexibility. Upon entry, the two-story foyer opens on the left to a lovely columned dining room. The family room is ahead, with a soaring vaulted ceiling, warming fireplace, and a rear wall of windows. The bayed breakfast nook and vaulted keeping room offer endless views of the rear property. On the far right, the master suite hosts a vaulted bath with a step-up tub, His and Hers walk-in closets, and an optional sitting room that can also be used as a study. Upper-level bedrooms are designed for privacy, each with a distinctive amenity. A two-car garage, supplemented by an additional single garage, completes the plan.

FIRST FLOOR: 2,153 SQ. FT.
SECOND FLOOR: 1,036 SQ. FT.
TOTAL: 3,189 SQ. FT.
BEDROOMS: 4
BATHROOMS: 3½
WIDTH: 72' - 0"
DEPTH: 60' - 6"
FOUNDATION: CRAWLSPACE, UNFINISHED WALKOUT BASEMENT

ORDER ONLINE @ EPLANS.COM

FIRST FLOOR

SECOND FLOOR

plan # HPK2900322

FIRST FLOOR: 2,198 SQ. FT.
SECOND FLOOR: 1,028 SQ. FT.
TOTAL: 3,226 SQ. FT.
BONUS SPACE: 466 SQ. FT.
BEDROOMS: 4
BATHROOMS: 3½
WIDTH: 72' - 8"
DEPTH: 56' - 6"
FOUNDATION: CRAWLSPACE

ORDER ONLINE @ EPLANS.COM

REAR EXTERIOR

Designed for active lifestyles, this home caters to homeowners who enjoy dinner guests, privacy, luxurious surroundings, and open spaces. The foyer, parlor, and dining hall are defined by four sets of columns and share a gallery hall that runs through the center of the plan. The grand room opens to the deck/terrace, which is also accessed from the sitting area and morning room. The right wing of the plan contains the well-appointed kitchen. The left wing is dominated by the master suite with its sitting bay, fireplace, two walk-in closets, and compartmented bath.

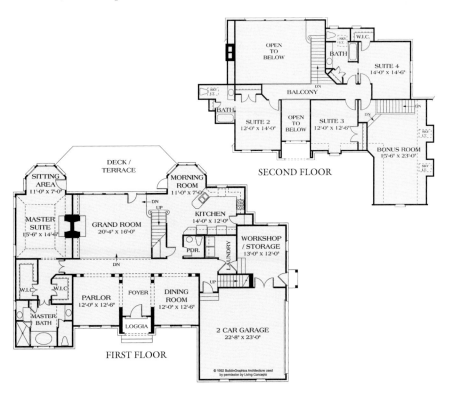

Does an attractive, free-flowing floor plan wrapped in a stone and vertical siding facade appeal to you? How about two fireplaces, one in the coffered-ceilinged family room and the other in the keeping room? An enormous and highly functional kitchen easily serves the family room, breakfast area, and dining room. Turn the study into a fourth bedroom to take advantage of the full first-floor bath. A second-floor rec room provides plenty of room for kids to play, and a perfect spot to renovate as they get older. The master suite includes a sitting area, giant walk-in closet, and sumptuous bath loaded with special features. Two family bedrooms and another full bath round out the home for which you've been looking.

FIRST FLOOR: 1,586 SQ. FT.
SECOND FLOOR: 1,664 SQ. FT.
TOTAL: 3,250 SQ. FT.
BEDROOMS: 4
BATHROOMS: 3
WIDTH: 44' - 4"
DEPTH: 65' - 4"
FOUNDATION: CRAWLSPACE, SLAB, UNFINISHED WALKOUT BASEMENT

ORDER ONLINE @ EPLANS.COM

FIRST FLOOR

SECOND FLOOR

HELPFUL HINT: Reproducible plans are your best value. You can make as many copies as you need!

plan # HPK2900324

FIRST FLOOR: 2,361 SQ. FT.
SECOND FLOOR: 974 SQ. FT.
TOTAL: 3,335 SQ. FT.
BEDROOMS: 4
BATHROOMS: 3
WIDTH: 68' - 0"
DEPTH: 64' - 10"
FOUNDATION: CRAWLSPACE,
SLAB

ORDER ONLINE @ EPLANS.COM

Stately columns and a covered porch invite visitors and family alike to partake of this home. Attractive angles in the large kitchen help to tie this room into the nearby family and breakfast rooms. The master suite offers walk-in closets, a double-bowl vanity, a garden tub, and a separate shower. The formal living and dining rooms are convenient to one another for ease in entertaining. A secondary bedroom is also located on this level. Upstairs, two large family bedrooms share a hall bath and have access to a game room.

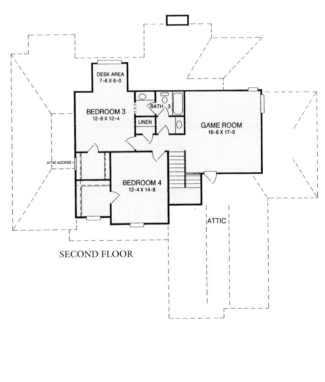

SECOND FLOOR

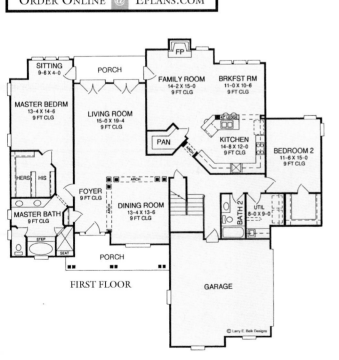

FIRST FLOOR

plan # HPK2900325

SQUARE FOOTAGE: 3,351
BEDROOMS: 3
BATHROOMS: 2½ + ½
WIDTH: 84' - 0"
DEPTH: 92' - 0"
FOUNDATION: SLAB

ORDER ONLINE @ EPLANS.com

© The Sater Design Collection, Inc.

plan # HPK2900326

FIRST FLOOR: 2,384 SQ. FT.
SECOND FLOOR: 1,050 SQ. FT.
TOTAL: 3,434 SQ. FT.
BONUS SPACE: 228 SQ. FT.
BEDROOMS: 4
BATHROOMS: 3½
WIDTH: 65' - 8"
DEPTH: 57' - 0"
FOUNDATION: CRAWLSPACE,
UNFINISHED WALKOUT
BASEMENT

ORDER ONLINE @ EPLANS.com

FIRST FLOOR

SECOND FLOOR

plan(#) HPK2900327

FIRST FLOOR: 2,469 SQ. FT.
SECOND FLOOR: 1,025 SQ. FT.
TOTAL: 3,494 SQ. FT.
BONUS SPACE: 320 SQ. FT.
BEDROOMS: 4
BATHROOMS: 3½
WIDTH: 67' - 8"
DEPTH: 74' - 2"
FOUNDATION: CRAWLSPACE,
SLAB, UNFINISHED
BASEMENT

ORDER ONLINE @ EPLANS.COM

A lovely double arch gives this European-style home a commanding presence. Once inside, a two-story foyer provides an open view directly through the formal living room to the rear grounds beyond. The spacious kitchen with a work island and the bayed breakfast area share space with the family room. The private master suite features dual sinks, twin walk-in closets, a corner garden tub, and a separate shower. A large game room completes this wonderful family home.

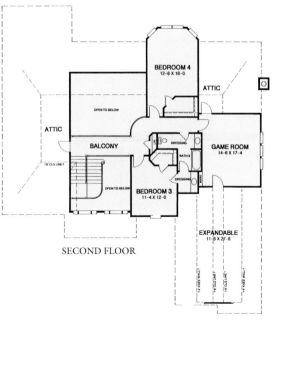

SECOND FLOOR

FIRST FLOOR

© The Sater Design Collection, Inc.

This beautiful home has many appealing attributes including a bowed dining room and a living room with a fireplace and outdoor access. For family gatherings, the kitchen remains open to the living areas. A study off the foyer will be much appreciated. A full bath leads to the outdoors—perfect for poolside. The master suite enjoys its own personal luxury bath with a whirlpool tub, dual lavatories, a compartmented toilet and bidet, and a separate shower. Dual walk-in closets provide ample storage space. Upstairs, two bedrooms share a full bath. A loft with a wet bar accommodates playtime. A wraparound deck is an added feature.

plan# HPK2900328

FIRST FLOOR: 2,551 SQ. FT.
SECOND FLOOR: 1,037 SQ. FT.
TOTAL: 3,588 SQ. FT.
BEDROOMS: 3
BATHROOMS: 3½
WIDTH: 76' - 0"
DEPTH: 90' - 0"
FOUNDATION: SLAB

ORDER ONLINE @ EPLANS.COM

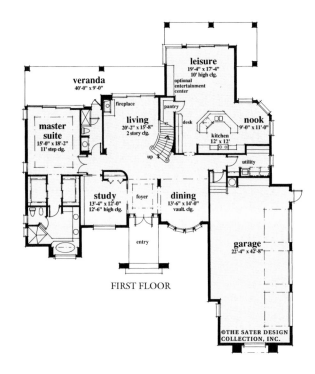

FIRST FLOOR

SECOND FLOOR

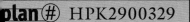

plan ⊕ HPK2900329

FIRST FLOOR: 1,882 SQ. FT.
SECOND FLOOR: 1,763 SQ. FT.
TOTAL: 3,645 SQ. FT.
BEDROOMS: 4
BATHROOMS: 3½
WIDTH: 94' - 2"
DEPTH: 57' - 0"
FOUNDATION: UNFINISHED
BASEMENT

ORDER ONLINE @ EPLANS.COM

Traditional styling takes on added dimension in this stately two-story home. An angled wing encloses the sunken living room and a roomy study. Both rooms enjoy a large terrace—perfect for formal entertaining. The dining room, with its window bay, introduces the other half of the house. Here, the resident gourmet will take great delight in the kitchen with its ample counter space and island cooktop. The breakfast room remains open to the kitchen and, through a pair of columns, the family room. The second floor offers excellent sleeping quarters with four bedrooms. The master suite spoils its occupants with a sloped ceiling, balcony, and fireplace. A huge walk-in closet and a divine bath finish off the room. Three additional bedrooms include one with a private bath.

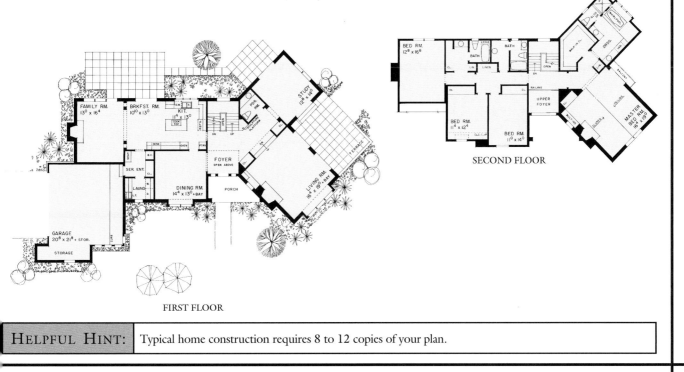

SECOND FLOOR

FIRST FLOOR

HELPFUL HINT: Typical home construction requires 8 to 12 copies of your plan.

plan# HPK2900330

FIRST FLOOR: 2,319 SQ. FT.
SECOND FLOOR: 1,570 SQ. FT.
TOTAL: 3,889 SQ. FT.
BEDROOMS: 4
BATHROOMS: 3½
WIDTH: 72' - 0"
DEPTH: 58' - 0"
FOUNDATION: CRAWLSPACE

ORDER ONLINE @ EPLANS.COM

Fine brick detailing, multiple arches and gables, and a grand entry give this four-bedroom home plenty of charm. The graceful, window-filled entry leads to a foyer flanked by a formal dining room and a study perfect for a home office. The great room, directly ahead, offers a fireplace and access to outside. A butler's pantry is located between the kitchen and dining room. The master suite is on the first floor. On the second floor, three family bedrooms, each with a walk-in closet, share two baths and a game room.

FIRST FLOOR

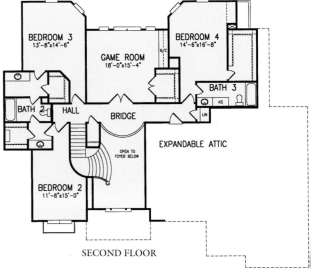

SECOND FLOOR

plan # HPK2900331

MAIN LEVEL: 2,157 SQ. FT.
LOWER LEVEL: 1,754 SQ. FT.
TOTAL: 3,911 SQ. FT.
BEDROOMS: 4
BATHROOMS: 3½
WIDTH: 80' - 0"
DEPTH: 61' - 0"
FOUNDATION: FINISHED
WALKOUT BASEMENT

ORDER ONLINE @ EPLANS.COM

Homeowners will look forward to coming home to this plan. A spacious gallery hall welcomes you inside. The lower level holds two family bedrooms, a game room, and a media room, while the main level includes the kitchen, dining room, great room, and master suite. Thoughtful built-ins like a wet bar make this home a prize. Other special amenities such as the corner fireplace in the great room and island workstation in the kitchen are just some of the modern additions found throughout the home. A spacious three-car garage completes the plan.

MAIN LEVEL

LOWER LEVEL

Signature Designer

This Frank Snodgrass plan was created with homeowners in mind. The designers of Wellonburg made the most of large spaces by providing such amenities as a double-sized dressing closet in the master suite, a lake room as well as a formal living room, and a morning room that lies between a screened porch and a veranda. A bending staircase leads to the second floor where a bonus room offers homeowners even more options and space.

plan # HPK2900332

FIRST FLOOR: 2,588 SQ. FT.
SECOND FLOOR: 1,375 SQ. FT.
TOTAL: 3,963 SQ. FT.
BONUS SPACE: 460 SQ. FT.
BEDROOMS: 4
BATHROOMS: 3½
WIDTH: 91' - 4"
DEPTH: 51' - 10"
FOUNDATION: CRAWLSPACE

ORDER ONLINE @ EPLANS.com

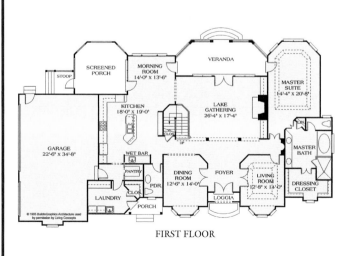

FIRST FLOOR

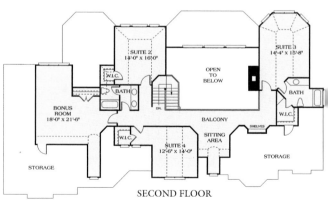

SECOND FLOOR

© The Sater Design Collection, Inc.

plan ⊕ HPK2900333

FIRST FLOOR: 3,053 SQ. FT.
SECOND FLOOR: 1,087 SQ. FT.
TOTAL: 4,140 SQ. FT.
BEDROOMS: 4
BATHROOMS: 3½
WIDTH: 87' - 4"
DEPTH: 80' - 4"
FOUNDATION: UNFINISHED
BASEMENT

ORDER ONLINE @ EPLANS.COM

The inside of this design is just as majestic as the outside. The grand foyer opens to a two-story living room with a fireplace and magnificent views. Dining in the bayed formal dining room will be a memorable experience. A well-designed kitchen is near a sunny nook and a leisure room with a fireplace and outdoor access. The master wing includes a separate study and an elegant private bath. The second level features a guest suite with its own bath and deck, two family bedrooms (Bedroom 3 also has its own deck), and a gallery loft with views to the living room below.

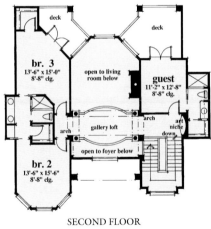

SECOND FLOOR

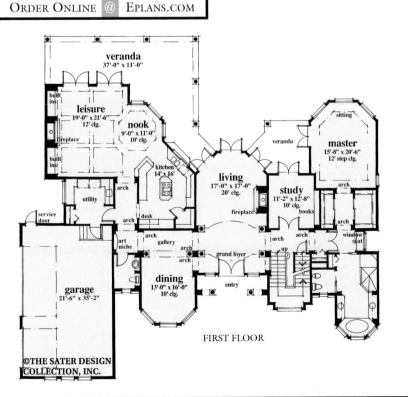

FIRST FLOOR

©THE SATER DESIGN
COLLECTION, INC.

plan# HPK2900334

FIRST FLOOR: 3,168 SQ. FT.
SECOND FLOOR: 998 SQ. FT.
TOTAL: 4,166 SQ. FT.
BONUS SPACE: 210 SQ. FT.
BEDROOMS: 4
BATHROOMS: 3½
WIDTH: 90' - 0"
DEPTH: 63' - 5"
FOUNDATION: CRAWLSPACE,
SLAB, UNFINISHED
BASEMENT

ORDER ONLINE @ EPLANS.COM

Stucco corner quoins, multiple gables, and graceful columns all combine to give this European manor plenty of appeal. Inside, a gallery entry presents a formal dining room on the right, defined by elegant columns, while the formal living room awaits just ahead. The highly efficient kitchen features a worktop island, pantry, and a serving bar to the nearby octagonal breakfast area. The family room offers a built-in entertainment center, a fireplace, and its own covered patio. The left side of the first floor is dedicated to the master suite. Here, the homeowner is pampered with an octagonal study, huge walk-in closet, lavish bath, and a very convenient nursery. The second floor contains two family bedrooms, each with a walk-in closet, and a media area with built-in bookshelves.

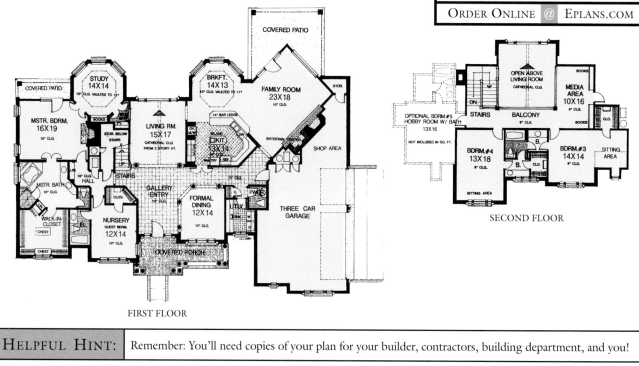

FIRST FLOOR

SECOND FLOOR

HELPFUL HINT: Remember: You'll need copies of your plan for your builder, contractors, building department, and you!

plan# **HPK2900335**

FIRST FLOOR: 2,547 SQ. FT.
SECOND FLOOR: 1,637 SQ. FT.
TOTAL: 4,184 SQ. FT.
BONUS SPACE: 802 SQ. FT.
BEDROOMS: 4
BATHROOMS: 3½
WIDTH: 74' - 0"
DEPTH: 95' - 6"
FOUNDATION: CRAWLSPACE

ORDER ONLINE @ EPLANS.COM

Double columns flank a raised loggia that leads to a beautiful two-story foyer. Flanking this elegance to the right is a formal dining room. Straight ahead, under a balcony and defined by yet more pillars, is the spacious grand room. A bow-windowed morning room and a gathering room feature a full view of the rear lanai and beyond. The master bedroom suite is lavish with its amenities, which include a bayed sitting area, direct access to the rear terrace, a walk-in closet, and a sumptuous bath.

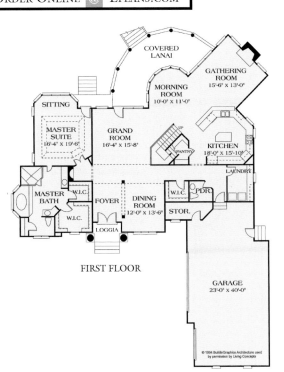

FIRST FLOOR

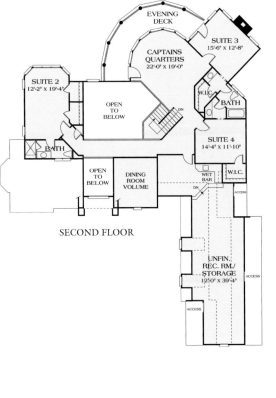

SECOND FLOOR

FIRST FLOOR: 2,639 SQ. FT.
SECOND FLOOR: 1,625 SQ. FT.
TOTAL: 4,264 SQ. FT.
BEDROOMS: 4
BATHROOMS: 3½
WIDTH: 73' - 8"
DEPTH: 58' - 6"
FOUNDATION: CRAWLSPACE,
SLAB, UNFINISHED
BASEMENT

This home offers both luxury and practicality. A study and dining room flank the foyer, and the great room offers a warming fireplace and double French-door access to the rear yard. A butler's pantry acts as a helpful buffer between the kitchen and the columned dining room. Double bays at the rear of the home form the keeping room and the breakfast room on one side and the master bedroom on the other. Three family bedrooms and two baths grace the second floor. A game room is perfect for casual family time.

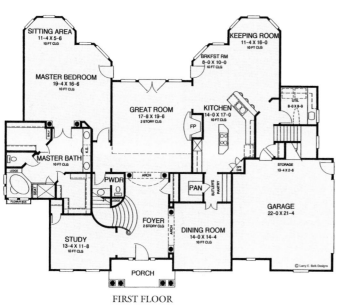

FIRST FLOOR

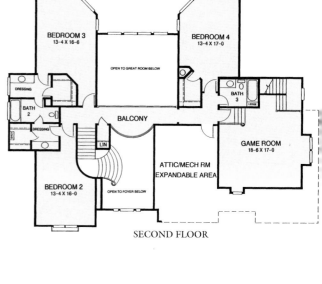

SECOND FLOOR

plan # HPK2900337

MAIN LEVEL: 1,737 SQ. FT.
SECOND LEVEL: 727 SQ. FT.
LOWER LEVEL: 1,876 SQ. FT.
TOTAL: 4,340 SQ. FT.
BONUS SPACE: 376 SQ. FT.
BEDROOMS: 4
BATHROOMS: 2½
WIDTH: 65' - 6"
DEPTH: 53' - 0"
FOUNDATION: FINISHED
BASEMENT

ORDER ONLINE @ EPLANS.COM

The beauty and warmth of a brick facade adds stately elegance to this traditional design. Its open floor plan is highlighted by a two-story living room and open dining room. The kitchen includes a central cooking island and opens to a bright breakfast area. The master suite offers an ample walk-in closet/dressing area and a bath featuring an exquisite double vanity and a tub with corner windows. A bonus room over the two-car garage offers room for expansion.

REAR EXTERIOR

MAIN LEVEL

SECOND LEVEL

LOWER LEVEL

This fantasy begins as soon as you step from the porch into the two-story vaulted foyer. To the right sits the columned elegance of the formal dining room and to the left a personal library awaits. Steps away, the entrance to the master suite beckons with promises of a sitting area, morning kitchen, L-shaped walk-in closet, garden tub, separate shower, and dual vanities. The three family bedrooms upstairs each have a full bath and ample closet space. In addition to the bedrooms, the option of a game room/billiards room provides plenty of space for casual entertainment. A three-car garage completes this plan.

FIRST FLOOR: 3,056 SQ. FT.
SECOND FLOOR: 1,307 SQ. FT.
TOTAL: 4,363 SQ. FT.
BONUS SPACE: 692 SQ. FT.
BEDROOMS: 4
BATHROOMS: 4½
WIDTH: 94' - 4"
DEPTH: 79' - 2"
FOUNDATION: CRAWLSPACE,
UNFINISHED BASEMENT

ORDER ONLINE @ EPLANS.COM

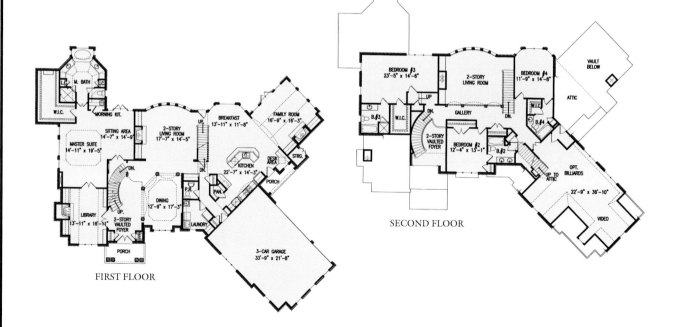

FIRST FLOOR

SECOND FLOOR

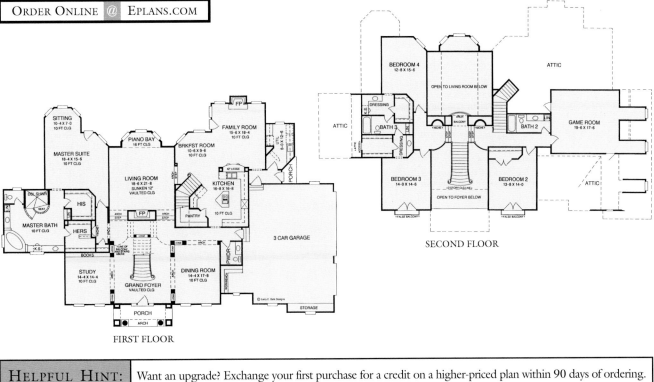

plan # HPK2900339

FIRST FLOOR: 3,264 SQ. FT.
SECOND FLOOR: 1,671 SQ. FT.
TOTAL: 4,935 SQ. FT.
BEDROOMS: 4
BATHROOMS: 3½
WIDTH: 96' - 10"
DEPTH: 65' - 1"
FOUNDATION: CRAWLSPACE,
SLAB

ORDER ONLINE @ EPLANS.COM

A very efficient plan that minimizes the use of enclosed hallways creates a very open feeling of space and order. As you enter the foyer you have a clear view through the spacious living room to the covered patio beyond. The formal dining area is to the right and the master wing is to the left. The master bedroom boasts a sitting area, access to the patio, His and Hers walk-in closets, dual vanities, a walk-in shower, and a compartmented toilet. A large island kitchen overlooks the nook and family room, which has a built-in media/fireplace wall. Three additional bedrooms and two full baths complete the plan.

FIRST FLOOR

SECOND FLOOR

HELPFUL HINT: Want an upgrade? Exchange your first purchase for a credit on a higher-priced plan within 90 days of ordering.

This home is elegantly styled in the French Country tradition. A large dining room and a study open off the two-story grand foyer. The large formal living room accesses the covered patio. A more informal family room is conveniently located off the kitchen and breakfast room. The roomy master suite includes a sitting area, a luxurious private bath, and its own entrance to the study. The second floor can be reached from the formal front stair or a well-placed rear staircase. Three large bedrooms and a game room are located on this floor. The walkout basement can be expanded to provide more living space.

plan # HPK2900340

FIRST FLOOR: 3,261 SQ. FT.
SECOND FLOOR: 1,920 SQ. FT.
TOTAL: 5,181 SQ. FT.
BEDROOMS: 4
BATHROOMS: 3½
WIDTH: 86' - 2"
DEPTH: 66' - 10"
FOUNDATION: CRAWLSPACE,
UNFINISHED BASEMENT

ORDER ONLINE @ EPLANS.COM

FIRST FLOOR

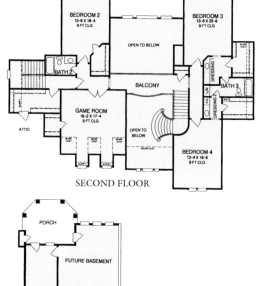

SECOND FLOOR

plan⊕ HPK2900341

FIRST FLOOR: 5,394 SQ. FT.
SECOND FLOOR: 1,305 SQ. FT.
TOTAL: 6,699 SQ. FT.
BONUS SPACE: 414 SQ. FT.
BEDROOMS: 5
BATHROOMS: 3½ + ½
WIDTH: 124' - 10"
DEPTH: 83' - 2"
FOUNDATION: CRAWLSPACE

ORDER ONLINE @ EPLANS.COM

This elegant French Country estate features a plush world of luxury within. A beautiful curved staircase cascades into the welcoming foyer that is flanked by a formal living room and the dining room with a fireplace. A butler's pantry leads to the island kitchen, which is efficiently enhanced by a walk-in storage pantry. The kitchen easily serves the breakfast room. The covered rear porch is accessed from the media/family room and the great room warmed by a fireplace. The master suite is a sumptuous retreat highlighted by its lavish bath and two huge walk-in closets. Next door, double doors open to a large study. All family bedrooms feature walk-in closets. Bedrooms 2 and 3 share a bath. Upstairs, Bedrooms 4 and 5 share another hall bath. A home office is located above the three-car garage.

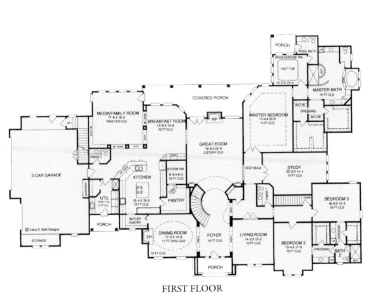

FIRST FLOOR

SECOND FLOOR

Dramatic landscape lighting emphasizes the multi-textured exterior of the home. The front entry is distinguished by a flared walk-up and brief porch.

Fashion & Fable

RIGHT: The vaulted two-story ceiling creates an airy feeling at the center of the plan, unifying the home's two levels. BELOW: The formal dining room is a showpiece for visitors and an elegant way to celebrate special occasions. FAR RIGHT: Hardwood floors extend throughout the main level and up the stairs.

A long, sweeping roofline gives the Beaumonde's exterior a storybook feel that fans of the European style will cherish. Stone and brick walls add the look of tradition and decorum, while crisp trimwork and windows keep the home's curbside demeanor bright. Flower boxes and outdoor elements, such as the windowside fountain, give the home a country finish.

Design elements established outside continue throughout the interior rooms. Archways, custom cabinetry, molding, fireplace surrounds, decorative ceilings, columns, and window treatments keep design elements on theme. But take time to modernize spaces and allow for worthwhile deviations from traditional design. Families will appreciate a layout that lets members interact comfortably between the kitchen and family room.

Larger plans in the section will emphasize the master suite, usually the most luxurious room in the house. Traditional furnishings fitted with basin sinks and low-key lighting—instead of counters and vanity lights—will create a higher-end, antiqued look. A freestanding tub completes the picture.

Lastly, be sure to develop outdoor spaces that allow your home to interact with the landscape, such as in courtyards and patios. Let your new European design invoke the life of an Old World cottage, where locally produced materials informed the architecture and family rituals moved with the changing seasons.

BELOW: A work island adds surface area to the kitchen, allowing multiple chefs to work simultaneously. RIGHT: A decorative ceiling effects a special touch to the master bedroom.

plan # HPK2900342

FIRST FLOOR: 2,654 SQ. FT.
SECOND FLOOR: 1,013 SQ. FT.
TOTAL: 3,667 SQ. FT.
BONUS SPACE: 192 SQ. FT.
BEDROOMS: 4
BATHROOMS: 3½
WIDTH: 75' - 4"
DEPTH: 74' - 2"
FOUNDATION: CRAWLSPACE, SLAB, UNFINISHED BASEMENT

ORDER ONLINE @ EPLANS.COM

FIRST FLOOR

SECOND FLOOR

A pass-through creates the right amount of transition between the kitchen and family room.

plan⊕ HPK2900343

SQUARE FOOTAGE: 1,416
BEDROOMS: 3
BATHROOMS: 2
WIDTH: 45' - 0"
DEPTH: 49' - 10"
FOUNDATION: SLAB

ORDER ONLINE @ EPLANS.COM

There's an alluring appeal to this compact one-story plan that will make you want to call it "home." An extended entry guides you into the great room, surely the hub of this splendid design. Here, a gas fireplace is directly across from a wet bar, and to the rear, three windows face an expansive covered patio. A wide doorway leads into the easy-to-use kitchen and bayed dining area. On the left side of the plan, a magnificent master suite enjoys a full range of comforts. For privacy's sake, it's separated from two other bedrooms found on the other side of the house. A utility room, storage space, and two-car garage round out the plan.

HELPFUL HINT: Unlike plans from some other companies, each of our plans includes a full electrical schematic.

European cottage flavor can be found in the half-timber accents, stone entry, and corner quoins. This three-bedroom home is a perfect empty-nester or second home. The single-level layout provides ample room for casual entertaining in the great room, study—or make it a formal dining space—and the open kitchen connected to a roomy dinette. A serving ledge in the kitchen makes it easy to pass snacks to the great room and a walk-in pantry makes room for everything. Two secondary bedrooms are split to the left of the floor plan and share a hall bath. Each room enjoys plenty of closet space and privacy. The master suite includes a superbath with whirlpool tub and separate shower, a compartmented toilet and dual-sink vanity, and further extends to a fantastic walk-in closet with built-in chest of drawers.

plan# HPK2900344

SQUARE FOOTAGE: 1,640
BEDROOMS: 3
BATHROOMS: 2
WIDTH: 50' - 0"
DEPTH: 55' - 4"
FOUNDATION: SLAB

ORDER ONLINE @ EPLANS.COM

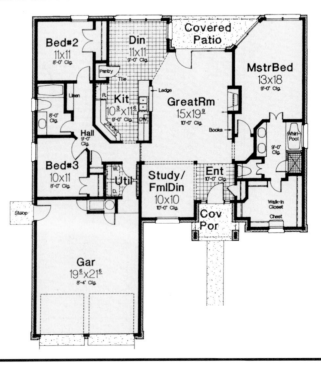

plan # HPK2900345

FIRST FLOOR: 1,276 SQ. FT.
SECOND FLOOR: 378 SQ. FT.
TOTAL: 1,654 SQ. FT.
BEDROOMS: 2
BATHROOMS: 2½
WIDTH: 54' - 4"
DEPTH: 53' - 10"
FOUNDATION: CRAWLSPACE,
SLAB

ORDER ONLINE @ EPLANS.COM

FIRST FLOOR

SECOND FLOOR

plan # HPK2900346

SQUARE FOOTAGE: 1,684
BEDROOMS: 3
BATHROOMS: 2½
WIDTH: 55' - 6"
DEPTH: 57' - 6"
FOUNDATION: FINISHED
WALKOUT BASEMENT

ORDER ONLINE @ EPLANS.COM

A stone-accented entry and tall country shutters give this home a feeling of comfort and tradition. The foyer welcomes and leads to a truly open floor plan. An island defines the kitchen and adds a work area without distracting from the ample counter and cabinet space. The vaulted great room is lit up by large multipane windows and overlooks the rear porch, accessed by the sunny dining room. A den or guest room is tucked to the rear, adjacent to a corner-shower bath. Up a U-shaped staircase with an arched multilevel window, the master suite revels in a vaulted bedroom, lavish spa bath, and an immense walk-in closet. Two generous bedrooms, or make one a bonus area, share a large bath. A convenient laundry on this level is a thoughtful touch.

plan# HPK2900347

FIRST FLOOR: 941 SQ. FT.
SECOND FLOOR: 819 SQ. FT.
TOTAL: 1,760 SQ. FT.
BEDROOMS: 3
BATHROOMS: 3
WIDTH: 50' - 0"
DEPTH: 44' - 6"
FOUNDATION: CRAWLSPACE

ORDER ONLINE @ EPLANS.COM

FIRST FLOOR

SECOND FLOOR

plan# HPK2900348

SQUARE FOOTAGE: 1,770
BEDROOMS: 3
BATHROOMS: 2½
WIDTH: 48' - 0"
DEPTH: 47' - 6"
FOUNDATION: UNFINISHED
WALKOUT BASEMENT

ORDER ONLINE @ EPLANS.COM

plan# HPK2900349

FIRST FLOOR: 1,225 SQ. FT.
SECOND FLOOR: 565 SQ. FT.
TOTAL: 1,790 SQ. FT.
BONUS SPACE: 158 SQ. FT.
BEDROOMS: 3
BATHROOMS: 2½
WIDTH: 42' - 0"
DEPTH: 50' - 0"
FOUNDATION: FINISHED
WALKOUT BASEMENT

ORDER ONLINE @ EPLANS.COM

FIRST FLOOR

SECOND FLOOR

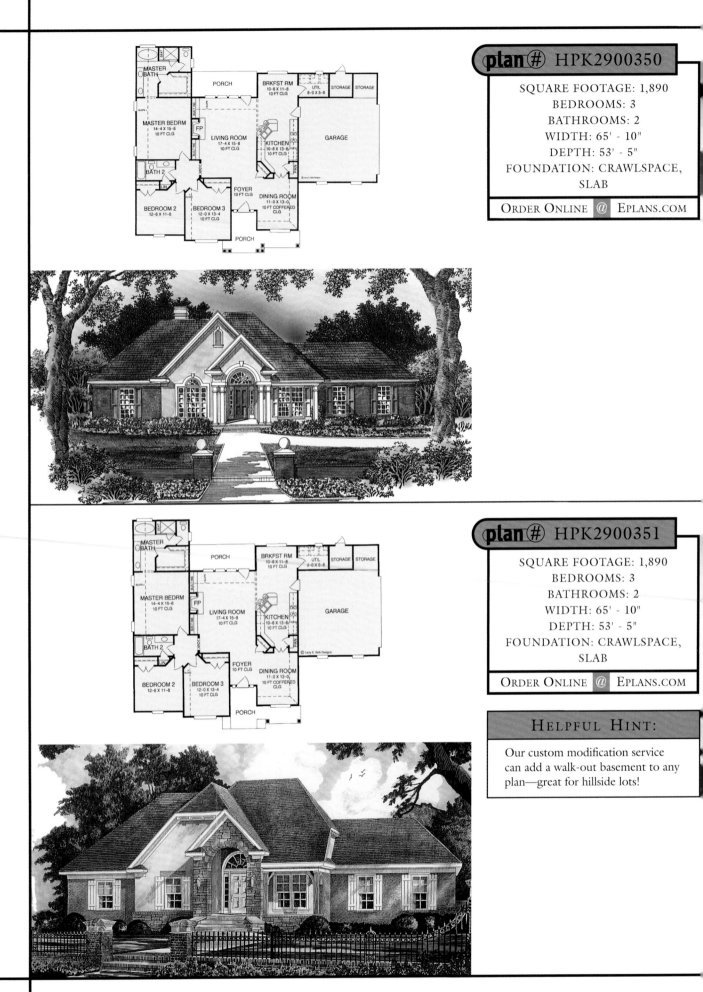

plan # HPK2900350

SQUARE FOOTAGE: 1,890
BEDROOMS: 3
BATHROOMS: 2
WIDTH: 65' - 10"
DEPTH: 53' - 5"
FOUNDATION: CRAWLSPACE,
SLAB

ORDER ONLINE @ EPLANS.COM

plan # HPK2900351

SQUARE FOOTAGE: 1,890
BEDROOMS: 3
BATHROOMS: 2
WIDTH: 65' - 10"
DEPTH: 53' - 5"
FOUNDATION: CRAWLSPACE,
SLAB

ORDER ONLINE @ EPLANS.COM

HELPFUL HINT:

Our custom modification service can add a walk-out basement to any plan—great for hillside lots!

plan # HPK2900352

FIRST FLOOR: 915 SQ. FT.
SECOND FLOOR: 994 SQ. FT.
TOTAL: 1,909 SQ. FT.
BEDROOMS: 3
BATHROOMS: 2½
WIDTH: 38' - 0"
DEPTH: 38' - 0"
FOUNDATION: UNFINISHED
BASEMENT

ORDER ONLINE @ EPLANS.COM

The arches on the windows and above the front entrance, combined with keystone details, provide aesthetic appeal to this traditional design and invite you inside to explore a grand floor plan. Enter either into the foyer, with a practical home office directly to the right, or use the side entrance into the kitchen. Eat a casual meal at the island in the kitchen, or formalize the occasion in the dining room. The great room is set into the the right side of the plan, which juts out slightly, providing a cozy family atmosphere. The second floor houses three bedrooms and two full baths.

FIRST FLOOR

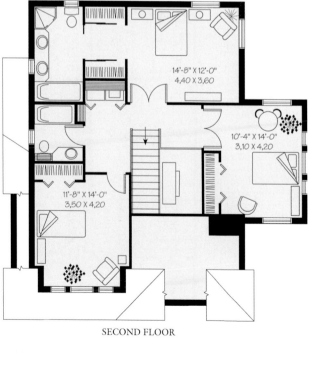

SECOND FLOOR

Enter this beautiful home through graceful archways and columns. The foyer, dining room, and living room are one open space, defined by a creative room arrangement. The living room opens to the breakfast room and porch. The bedrooms are off a small hall reached through an archway. Two family bedrooms share a bath, and the master bedroom enjoys a private bath with a double-bowl vanity. A garage with storage and a utility room complete the floor plan.

plan# HPK2900353

SQUARE FOOTAGE: 1,932
BEDROOMS: 3
BATHROOMS: 2
WIDTH: 65' - 10"
DEPTH: 53' - 5"
FOUNDATION: CRAWLSPACE, SLAB

ORDER ONLINE @ EPLANS.COM

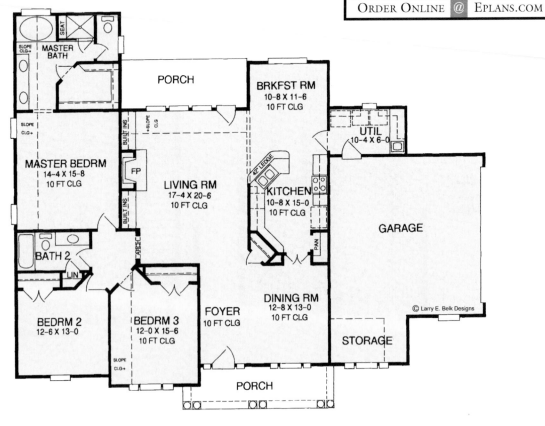

MASTER BATH
SLOPE CLG

MASTER BEDRM
14-4 X 15-8
10 FT CLG

PORCH

BRKFST RM
10-8 X 11-6
10 FT CLG

UTIL
10-4 X 6-0

LIVING RM
17-4 X 20-6
10 FT CLG

FP

KITCHEN
10-8 X 15-0
10 FT CLG

42" LEDGE

GARAGE

BATH 2

LIN

BEDRM 2
12-6 X 13-0

BEDRM 3
12-0 X 15-6
10 FT CLG

FOYER
10 FT CLG

DINING RM
12-8 X 13-0
10 FT CLG

© Larry E. Belk Designs

STORAGE

PORCH

© The Sater Design Collection, Inc.

plan # HPK2900354

FIRST FLOOR: 1,383 SQ. FT.
SECOND FLOOR: 595 SQ. FT.
TOTAL: 1,978 SQ. FT.
BONUS SPACE: 617 SQ. FT.
BEDROOMS: 3
BATHROOMS: 2
WIDTH: 48' - 0"
DEPTH: 42' - 0"
FOUNDATION: ISLAND
BASEMENT

ORDER ONLINE @ EPLANS.COM

Signature Designer

Dan Sater added a few Colonial elements to his signature
Mediterranean style to create the design for Tierra di Mare. The Greek
columns and stacked porches are reminiscent of old southern planta-
tions, but the tall, square shape, stucco exterior, and arches are pure
Italiano. Take advantage of the island basement foundation by building
on a prime, beachfront lot.

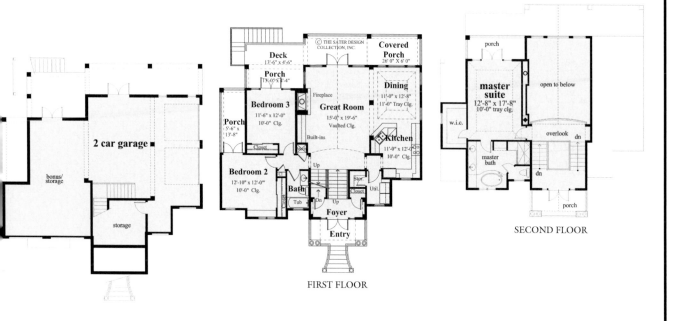

An ornate stucco facade with brick highlights refines this charming French cottage. The double-door entrance sits to the side—perfect for a courtyard welcome. A dining and family room utilize an open layout for easy traffic flow. The circular kitchen space features an island and complementary breakfast bay. Bedrooms 2 and 3 share a hall bath. The master suite, apart from the main living areas, enjoys privacy and a full bath with a spacious walk-in closet. The rear porch encourages outdoor relaxation.

plan # HPK2900355

SQUARE FOOTAGE: 2,007
BEDROOMS: 3
BATHROOMS: 2½
WIDTH: 40' - 0"
DEPTH: 94' - 10"
FOUNDATION: SLAB

ORDER ONLINE @ EPLANS.COM

Plan # HPK2900356

SQUARE FOOTAGE: 2,010
BEDROOMS: 3
BATHROOMS: 2
WIDTH: 68' - 10"
DEPTH: 52' - 0"
FOUNDATION: SLAB

ORDER ONLINE @ EPLANS.COM

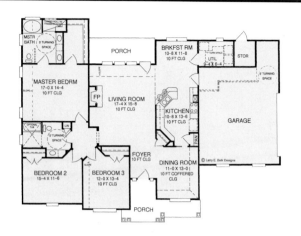

Plan # HPK2900357

SQUARE FOOTAGE: 2,018
BEDROOMS: 3
BATHROOMS: 2
WIDTH: 65' - 10"
DEPTH: 54' - 0"
FOUNDATION: CRAWLSPACE,
SLAB, UNFINISHED
BASEMENT

ORDER ONLINE @ EPLANS.COM

HELPFUL HINT:

It is illegal to make copies of any
plan except a "reproducible" version.

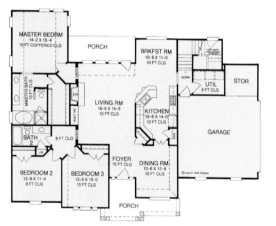

This beautiful home offers angles and varied ceiling heights throughout. The great room showcases these elements and has access to the covered porch with a view to the backyard. Interior and exterior fireplaces provide a cozy atmosphere. An open layout seamlessly expands the great room into the formal dining area. The master bedroom suite offers a luxurious bath and access to the covered porch. Split stairs overlook the gallery and lead to the second-floor loft, full bath, and bonus room.

plan# HPK2900358

SQUARE FOOTAGE: 2,037
BONUS SPACE: 596 SQ. FT.
BEDROOMS: 2
BATHROOMS: 2
WIDTH: 42' - 0"
DEPTH: 75' - 0"
FOUNDATION: SLAB,
UNFINISHED BASEMENT

ORDER ONLINE @ EPLANS.COM

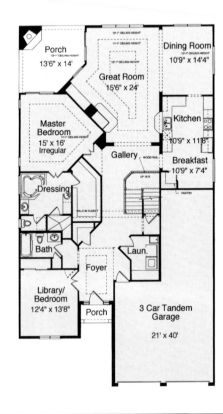

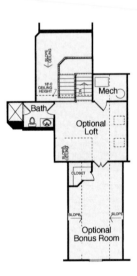

plan # HPK2900359

SQUARE FOOTAGE: 2,061
BEDROOMS: 3
BATHROOMS: 2½
WIDTH: 88' - 10"
DEPTH: 40' - 9"
FOUNDATION: CRAWLSPACE,
SLAB

ORDER ONLINE @ EPLANS.COM

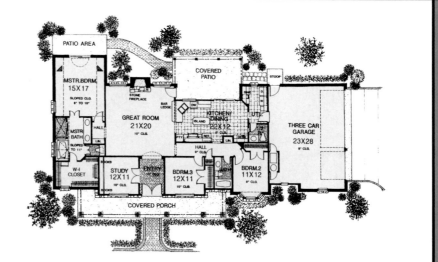

plan # HPK2900360

SQUARE FOOTAGE: 2,089
BEDROOMS: 4
BATHROOMS: 3
WIDTH: 61' - 8"
DEPTH: 50' - 4"
FOUNDATION: SLAB

ORDER ONLINE @ EPLANS.COM

Three arched windows provide just the right touch of elegance and give this home a picturesque appeal. The great room with a corner fireplace is located near the breakfast area and kitchen. Ten-foot ceilings in all major living areas give the plan an open, spacious feel. The master suite includes a luxury bath with a coffered ceiling, large His and Hers closets, a whirlpool tub, a shower with a seat, and twin vanities. Stairs lead to an expandable area on the second floor.

plan # HPK2900361

SQUARE FOOTAGE: 2,127
BONUS SPACE: 338 SQ. FT.
BEDROOMS: 3
BATHROOMS: 2
WIDTH: 62' - 0"
DEPTH: 62' - 6"
FOUNDATION: CRAWLSPACE, SLAB

ORDER ONLINE @ EPLANS.COM

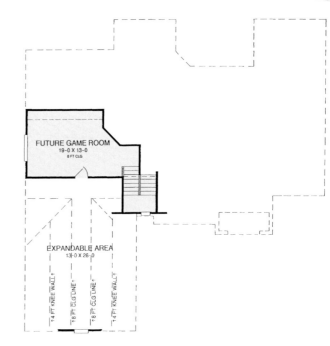

plan # HPK2900362

SQUARE FOOTAGE: 2,140
BEDROOMS: 4
BATHROOMS: 3
WIDTH: 62' - 0"
DEPTH: 60' - 6"
FOUNDATION: FINISHED
WALKOUT BASEMENT

ORDER ONLINE @ EPLANS.COM

plan # HPK2900363

SQUARE FOOTAGE: 2,150
BEDROOMS: 3
BATHROOMS: 2½
WIDTH: 64' - 0"
DEPTH: 60' - 4"
FOUNDATION: FINISHED
WALKOUT BASEMENT

ORDER ONLINE @ EPLANS.COM

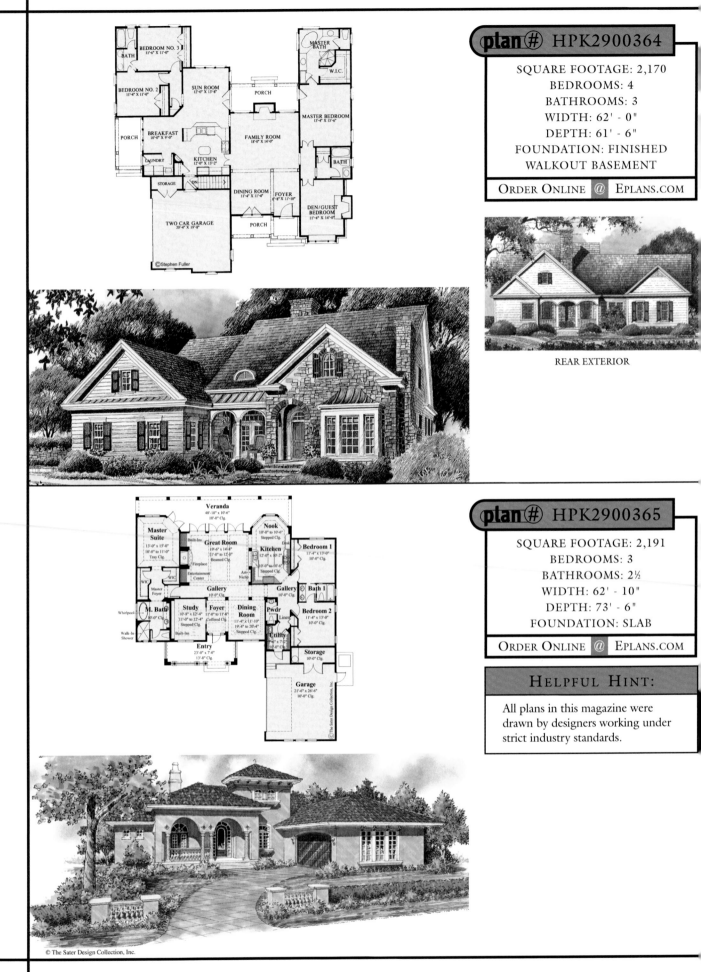

plan # HPK2900364

SQUARE FOOTAGE: 2,170
BEDROOMS: 4
BATHROOMS: 3
WIDTH: 62' - 0"
DEPTH: 61' - 6"
FOUNDATION: FINISHED
WALKOUT BASEMENT

ORDER ONLINE @ EPLANS.COM

REAR EXTERIOR

plan # HPK2900365

SQUARE FOOTAGE: 2,191
BEDROOMS: 3
BATHROOMS: 2½
WIDTH: 62' - 10"
DEPTH: 73' - 6"
FOUNDATION: SLAB

ORDER ONLINE @ EPLANS.COM

HELPFUL HINT:

All plans in this magazine were drawn by designers working under strict industry standards.

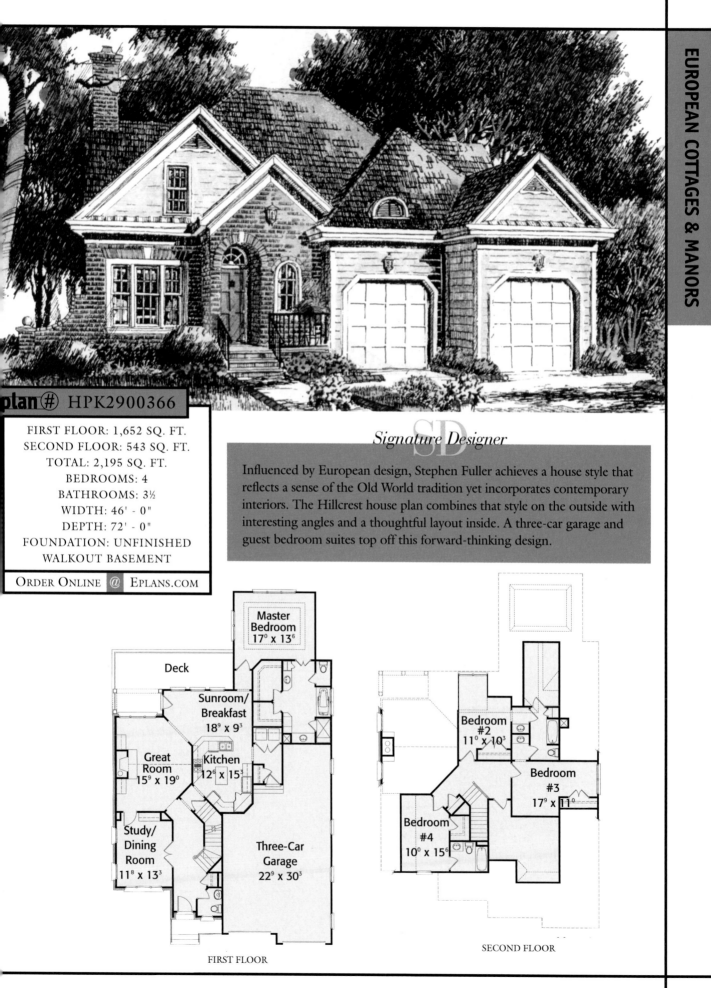

plan(#) HPK2900366

FIRST FLOOR: 1,652 SQ. FT.
SECOND FLOOR: 543 SQ. FT.
TOTAL: 2,195 SQ. FT.
BEDROOMS: 4
BATHROOMS: 3½
WIDTH: 46' - 0"
DEPTH: 72' - 0"
FOUNDATION: UNFINISHED
WALKOUT BASEMENT

ORDER ONLINE @ EPLANS.COM

Signature Designer SD

Influenced by European design, Stephen Fuller achieves a house style that reflects a sense of the Old World tradition yet incorporates contemporary interiors. The Hillcrest house plan combines that style on the outside with interesting angles and a thoughtful layout inside. A three-car garage and guest bedroom suites top off this forward-thinking design.

Deck

Master Bedroom
17^0 x 13^6

Sunroom/ Breakfast
18^9 x 9^3

Great Room
15^9 x 19^0

Kitchen
12^6 x 15^3

Study/ Dining Room
11^8 x 13^3

Three-Car Garage
22^9 x 30^3

FIRST FLOOR

Bedroom #2
11^0 x 10^3

Bedroom #3
17^9 x 11^0

Bedroom #4
10^0 x 15^6

SECOND FLOOR

plan# HPK2900367

The brick accents of this home give it a European flavor. The vaulted foyer introduces the formal dining room plus a built-in shelf to the right and the den or Bedroom 4 to the left. The massive great room features a vaulted ceiling and includes a cozy fireplace. The vaulted master bedroom features a walk-in closet and private access to the utility room. The private bath is entered through French doors and boasts dual vanities and an oversized soaking tub. Upstairs, two additional bedrooms share a hall with a large bonus room and a full bath with dual vanities; Bedroom 2 features a walk-in closet.

FIRST FLOOR: 1,658 SQ. FT.
SECOND FLOOR: 538 SQ. FT.
TOTAL: 2,196 SQ. FT.
BONUS SPACE: 496 SQ. FT.
BEDROOMS: 4
BATHROOMS: 2½
WIDTH: 50' - 0"
DEPTH: 56' - 0"
FOUNDATION: CRAWLSPACE

ORDER ONLINE @ EPLANS.COM

FIRST FLOOR

SECOND FLOOR

plan# HPK2900368

SQUARE FOOTAGE: 2,197
BEDROOMS: 3
BATHROOMS: 2½
WIDTH: 60' - 0"
DEPTH: 64' - 0"
FOUNDATION: CRAWLSPACE

ORDER ONLINE @ EPLANS.COM

plan# HPK2900369

SQUARE FOOTAGE: 2,199
BEDROOMS: 3
BATHROOMS: 2½
WIDTH: 74' - 8"
DEPTH: 60' - 7"
FOUNDATION: UNFINISHED BASEMENT

ORDER ONLINE @ EPLANS.COM

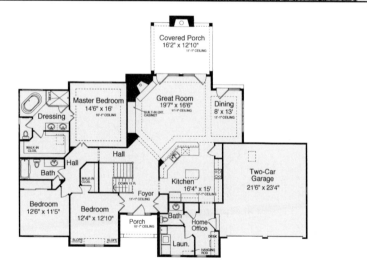

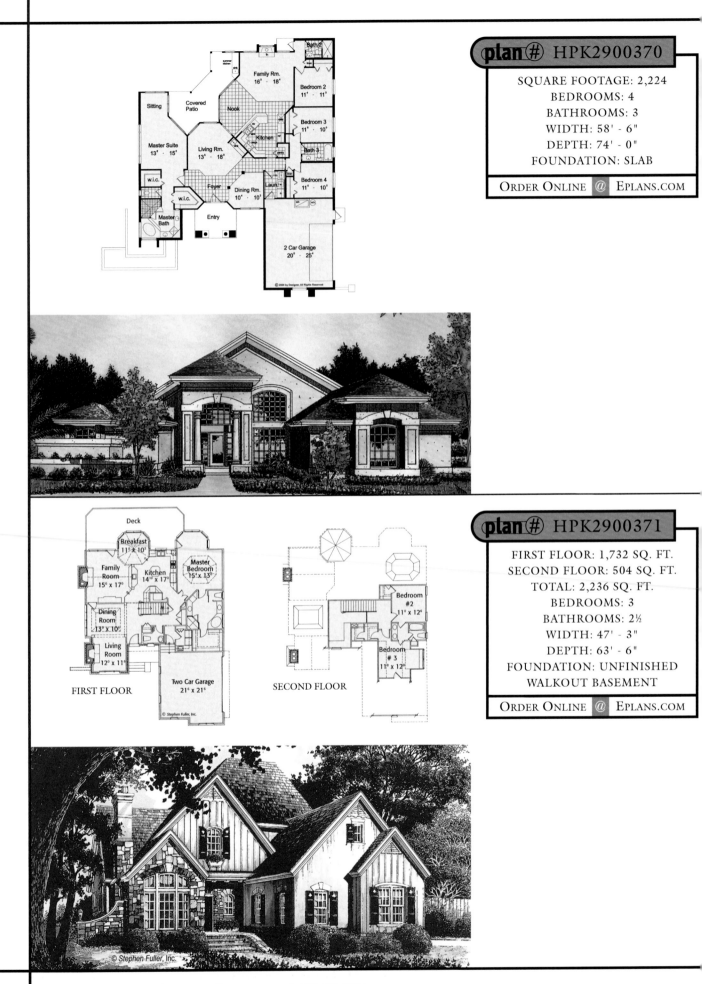

plan # HPK2900370

SQUARE FOOTAGE: 2,224
BEDROOMS: 4
BATHROOMS: 3
WIDTH: 58' - 6"
DEPTH: 74' - 0"
FOUNDATION: SLAB

ORDER ONLINE @ EPLANS.COM

plan # HPK2900371

FIRST FLOOR: 1,732 SQ. FT.
SECOND FLOOR: 504 SQ. FT.
TOTAL: 2,236 SQ. FT.
BEDROOMS: 3
BATHROOMS: 2½
WIDTH: 47' - 3"
DEPTH: 63' - 6"
FOUNDATION: UNFINISHED
WALKOUT BASEMENT

ORDER ONLINE @ EPLANS.COM

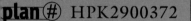

plan # HPK2900372

FIRST FLOOR: 1,566 SQ. FT.
SECOND FLOOR: 693 SQ. FT.
TOTAL: 2,259 SQ. FT.
BONUS SPACE: 406 SQ. FT.
BEDROOMS: 3
BATHROOMS: 2½
WIDTH: 68' - 0"
DEPTH: 52' - 11"
FOUNDATION: UNFINISHED
BASEMENT

ORDER ONLINE @ EPLANS.COM

There's a European flavor to the exterior of this bungalow filled with a wide range of comforts. A graciously curved bay with arched windows encloses the formal dining room. This area conveniently opens to a fully equipped island kitchen, which also flows into a sunny family dining alcove. Sleeping quarters are divided so that the master suite on the first floor is private from the two family bedrooms on the second level. Both of these rooms open to a sitting room or den and share a bath. The master bath is full of luxuries, including an oversized oval tub and twin vanities. Enter the large utility and laundry area from either the kitchen, a separate front door, or the garage.

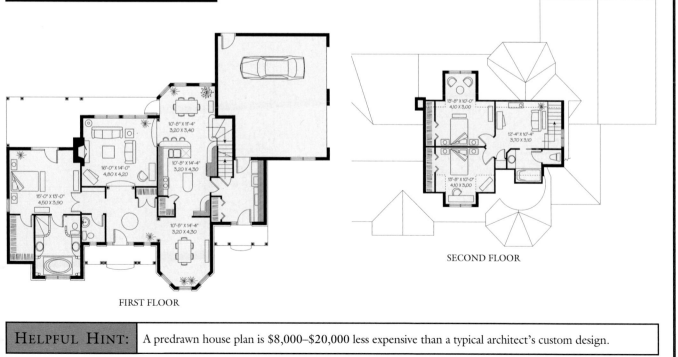

FIRST FLOOR

SECOND FLOOR

HELPFUL HINT: A predrawn house plan is $8,000–$20,000 less expensive than a typical architect's custom design.

Signature Designer

French Country style abounds in Stephen Fuller's Clandon house plan. A walkout basement allows three levels, each with walls of windows facing the rear property. Inside, the design provides plenty of entertainment space but truly pampers the homeowners with a bedroom nearly as large as the family room, a long master bath, and a wide walk-in closet.

plan# HPK2900373

FIRST FLOOR: 1,720 SQ. FT.
SECOND FLOOR: 545 SQ. FT.
TOTAL: 2,265 SQ. FT.
BONUS SPACE: 365 SQ. FT.
BEDROOMS: 3
BATHROOMS: 2½
WIDTH: 50' - 0"
DEPTH: 53' - 6"
FOUNDATION: FINISHED
WALKOUT BASEMENT

ORDER ONLINE @ EPLANS.COM

DECK

BREAKFAST
12'-0" X 10'-0"

MASTER
BATH

MASTER BEDROOM
13'-0" X 15'-4"

TWO STORY
FAMILY ROOM
14'-6" X 15'-0"

KITCHEN
12'-0" X 14'-8"

POWDER

W.I.C.

DN

LAUNDRY

STORAGE

DINING ROOM
13'-4" X 11'-8"

UP
TWO STORY
FOYER
9'-0" X 15'-0"

TWO CAR GARAGE
22'-4" X 20'-8"

LIVING ROOM
13'-4" X 11'-4"

STOOP

© Stephen Fuller, Inc.

FIRST FLOOR

UNFIN
STORAGE

OPEN TO BELOW

BEDROOM NO. 3
11'-10" X 12'-0"

BATH

BALCONY

FUTURE
BEDROOM NO. 4
13'-6" X 12'-0"

DN

FUTURE
BATH

BEDROOM
NO. 2
13'-0" X 12'-0"

OPEN TO
BELOW

FUTURE
STORAGE

SECOND FLOOR

plan # HPK2900374

SQUARE FOOTAGE: 2,311
BONUS SPACE: 425 SQ. FT.
BEDROOMS: 4
BATHROOMS: 2½
WIDTH: 61' - 0"
DEPTH: 65' - 4"
FOUNDATION: CRAWLSPACE,
SLAB, UNFINISHED WALKOUT
BASEMENT

ORDER ONLINE @ EPLANS.COM

Make your way through the arched entryway into the foyer of this elegant European home. While the facade is breathtaking, the interior is simply perfect. A split-bedroom design allows for a private master suite—complete with a vaulted master bath—on the left side of the plan; two more bedrooms share a full bath on the right. The core of the home is occupied by the vaulted family room with a fireplace, a fine dining room, and a kitchen complete with angled counters. Enjoy casual meals in the vaulted breakfast nook, adjacent to the kitchen. A convenient laundry room and half-bath complete this plan.

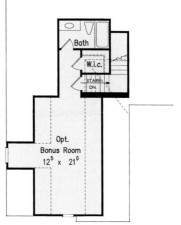

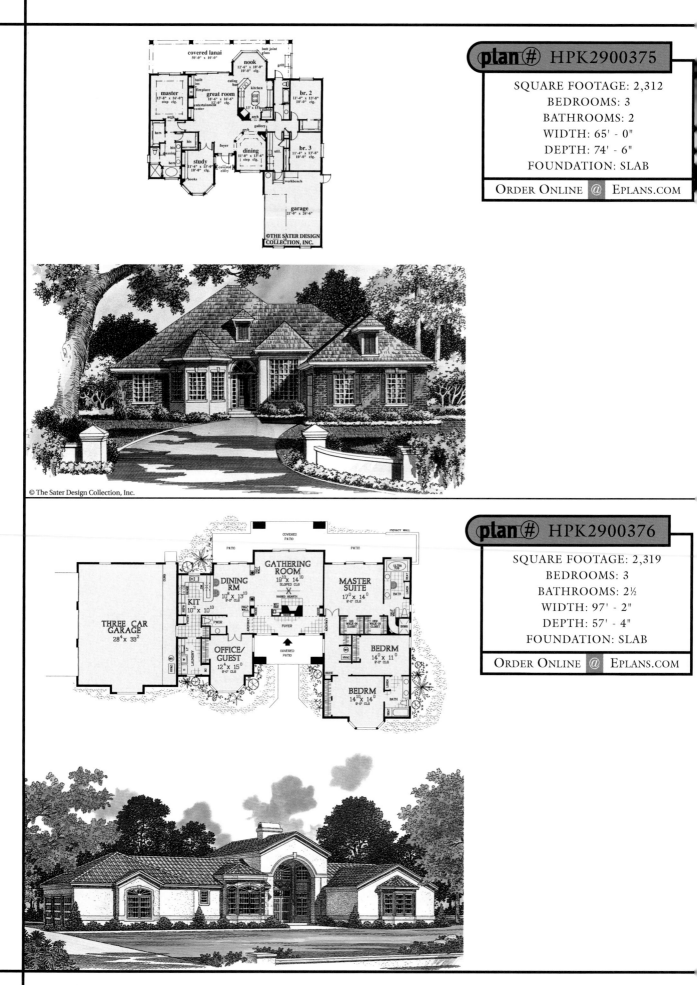

plan # HPK2900375

SQUARE FOOTAGE: 2,312
BEDROOMS: 3
BATHROOMS: 2
WIDTH: 65' - 0"
DEPTH: 74' - 6"
FOUNDATION: SLAB

ORDER ONLINE @ EPLANS.COM

© The Sater Design Collection, Inc.

plan # HPK2900376

SQUARE FOOTAGE: 2,319
BEDROOMS: 3
BATHROOMS: 2½
WIDTH: 97' - 2"
DEPTH: 57' - 4"
FOUNDATION: SLAB

ORDER ONLINE @ EPLANS.COM

plan # HPK2900377

SQUARE FOOTAGE: 2,362
BEDROOMS: 4
BATHROOMS: 3
WIDTH: 65' - 8"
DEPTH: 73' - 4"
FOUNDATION: SLAB

ORDER ONLINE @ EPLANS.COM

plan # HPK2900378

SQUARE FOOTAGE: 2,376
BEDROOMS: 4
BATHROOMS: 3
WIDTH: 59' - 6"
DEPTH: 72' - 0"
FOUNDATION: SLAB

ORDER ONLINE @ EPLANS.COM

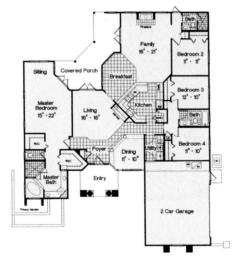

© The Sater Design Collection, Inc.

Cottage accommodations are provided with this seaside vacation dream home. Once inside, the foyer steps lead up to the formal living areas on the main floor. To the left, a study is enhanced by a vaulted ceiling and double doors that open to a front balcony. Vaulted ceilings create a lofty feel throughout the home, especially in the central great room, which overlooks the rear deck. The island kitchen is open to an adjacent breakfast nook. Guest quarters reside on the right side of the plan—one boasts a private bath. The master suite is secluded on the left for privacy and features two walk-in closets and a pampering whirlpool master bath. Downstairs, storage space abounds alongside the two-car garage.

plan# HPK2900379

SQUARE FOOTAGE: 2,385
BEDROOMS: 3
BATHROOMS: 3
WIDTH: 60' - 0"
DEPTH: 52' - 0"
FOUNDATION: ISLAND BASEMENT

ORDER ONLINE @ EPLANS.COM

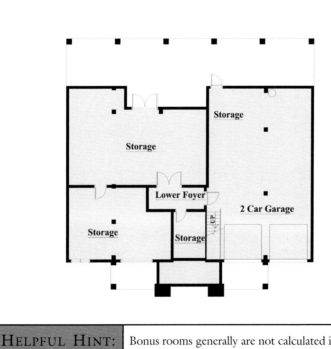

HELPFUL HINT: Bonus rooms generally are not calculated in the total square footage of a home.

©The Sater Design Collection, Inc.

plan (#) HPK2900380

SQUARE FOOTAGE: 2,387
BEDROOMS: 3
BATHROOMS: 3
WIDTH: 53' - 6"
DEPTH: 94' - 6"
FOUNDATION: SLAB

ORDER ONLINE @ EPLANS.COM

This sunny design opens through double doors into the great room. A rounded dining area contributes a sense of the dramatic and is easily served by the roomy kitchen. A relaxing study also provides outdoor access. Two secondary bedrooms enjoy ample closet space and share a bath that includes dual vanities. In the master suite, a tiered ceiling and lots of windows gain attention. A luxury bath with a compartmented toilet, a garden tub, dual vanities, and a separate shower also offers a walk-in closet. A bath with a stall shower serves the outdoor living areas.

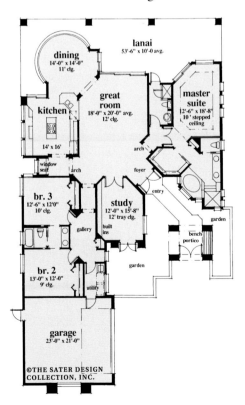

©THE SATER DESIGN COLLECTION, INC.

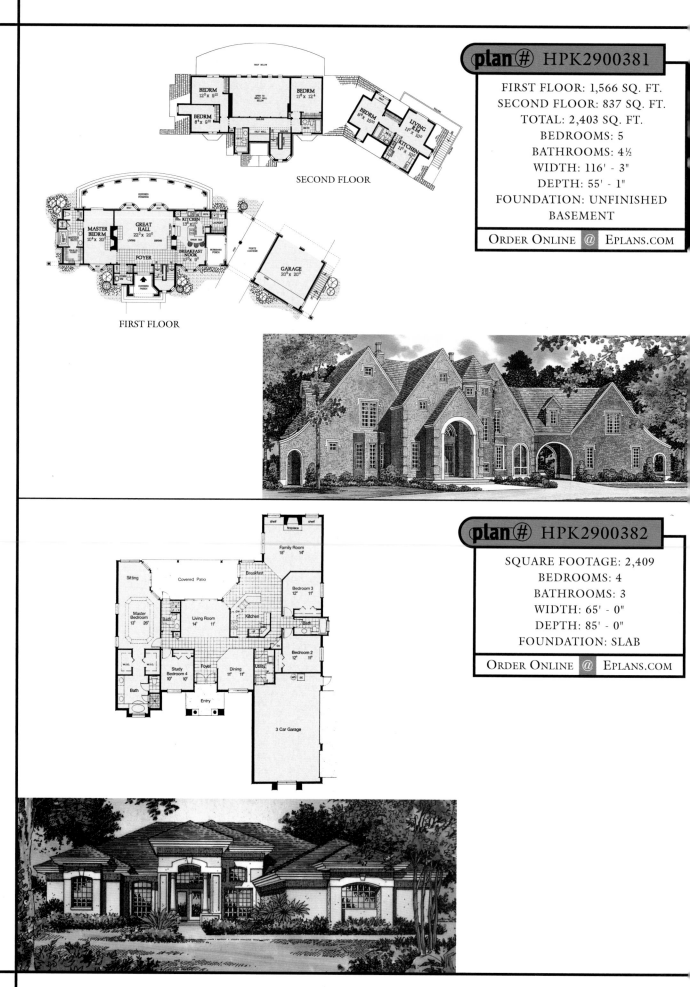

SECOND FLOOR

FIRST FLOOR

plan# HPK2900381

FIRST FLOOR: 1,566 SQ. FT.
SECOND FLOOR: 837 SQ. FT.
TOTAL: 2,403 SQ. FT.
BEDROOMS: 5
BATHROOMS: 4½
WIDTH: 116' - 3"
DEPTH: 55' - 1"
FOUNDATION: UNFINISHED
BASEMENT

ORDER ONLINE @ EPLANS.COM

plan# HPK2900382

SQUARE FOOTAGE: 2,409
BEDROOMS: 4
BATHROOMS: 3
WIDTH: 65' - 0"
DEPTH: 85' - 0"
FOUNDATION: SLAB

ORDER ONLINE @ EPLANS.COM

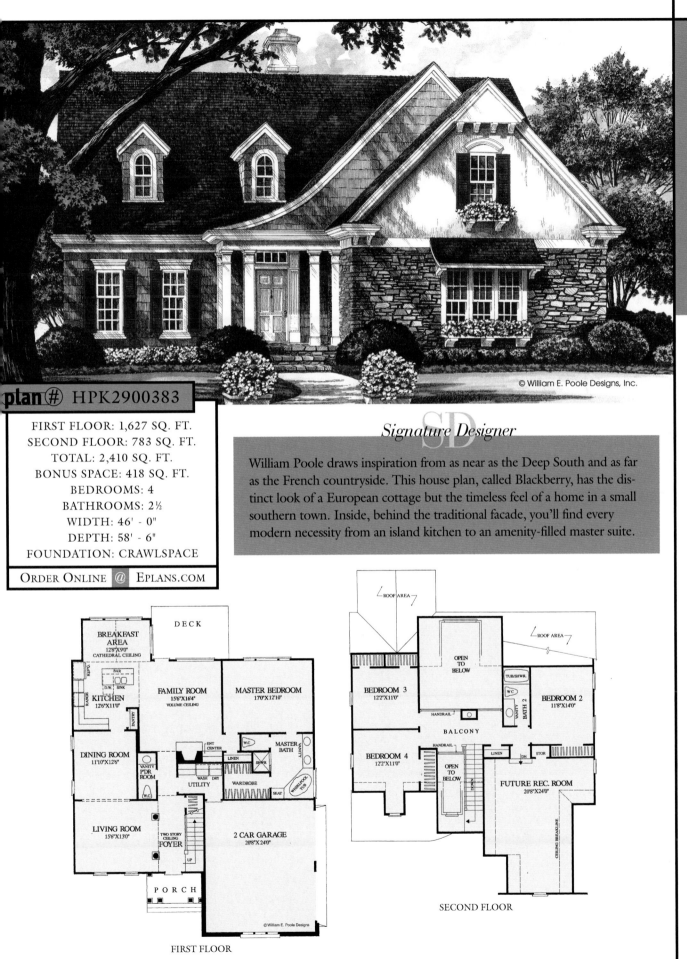

© William E. Poole Designs, Inc.

plan # HPK2900383

FIRST FLOOR: 1,627 SQ. FT.
SECOND FLOOR: 783 SQ. FT.
TOTAL: 2,410 SQ. FT.
BONUS SPACE: 418 SQ. FT.
BEDROOMS: 4
BATHROOMS: 2½
WIDTH: 46' - 0"
DEPTH: 58' - 6"
FOUNDATION: CRAWLSPACE

ORDER ONLINE @ EPLANS.COM

Signature Designer

William Poole draws inspiration from as near as the Deep South and as far as the French countryside. This house plan, called Blackberry, has the distinct look of a European cottage but the timeless feel of a home in a small southern town. Inside, behind the traditional facade, you'll find every modern necessity from an island kitchen to an amenity-filled master suite.

FIRST FLOOR

SECOND FLOOR

FIRST FLOOR: 1,724 SQ. FT.
SECOND FLOOR: 700 SQ. FT.
TOTAL: 2,424 SQ. FT.
BEDROOMS: 3
BATHROOMS: 2½
WIDTH: 47' - 10"
DEPTH: 63' - 8"
FOUNDATION: FINISHED
WALKOUT BASEMENT

ORDER ONLINE @ EPLANS.COM

All the charm of gables, stonework, and multilevel rooflines combine to create this home. To the left of the foyer, you will see the dining room highlighted by a tray ceiling. This room and the living room flow together to form one large entertainment area. The gourmet kitchen holds a work island and adjoining octagonal breakfast room. The great room is a fantastic living space, featuring a pass-through wet bar, a fireplace, and bookcases. The master suite enjoys privacy at the rear of the home. An open-rail loft above the foyer leads to two additional bedrooms with walk-in closets, private vanities, and a shared bath.

FIRST FLOOR

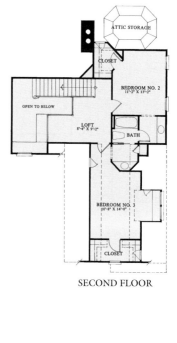

SECOND FLOOR

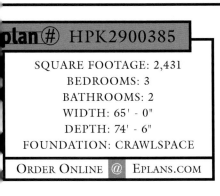

plan # HPK2900385

SQUARE FOOTAGE: 2,431
BEDROOMS: 3
BATHROOMS: 2
WIDTH: 65' - 0"
DEPTH: 74' - 6"
FOUNDATION: CRAWLSPACE

ORDER ONLINE @ EPLANS.COM

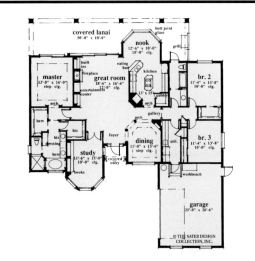

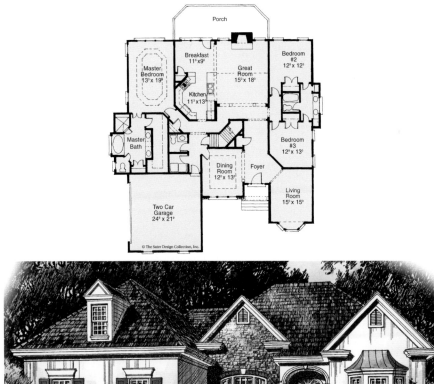

plan # HPK2900386

SQUARE FOOTAGE: 2,494
BEDROOMS: 3
BATHROOMS: 2½
WIDTH: 65' - 4"
DEPTH: 61' - 8"
FOUNDATION: FINISHED
WALKOUT BASEMENT

ORDER ONLINE @ EPLANS.COM

HELPFUL HINT:

Rest easy: All of our home designs conform to national uniform building codes.

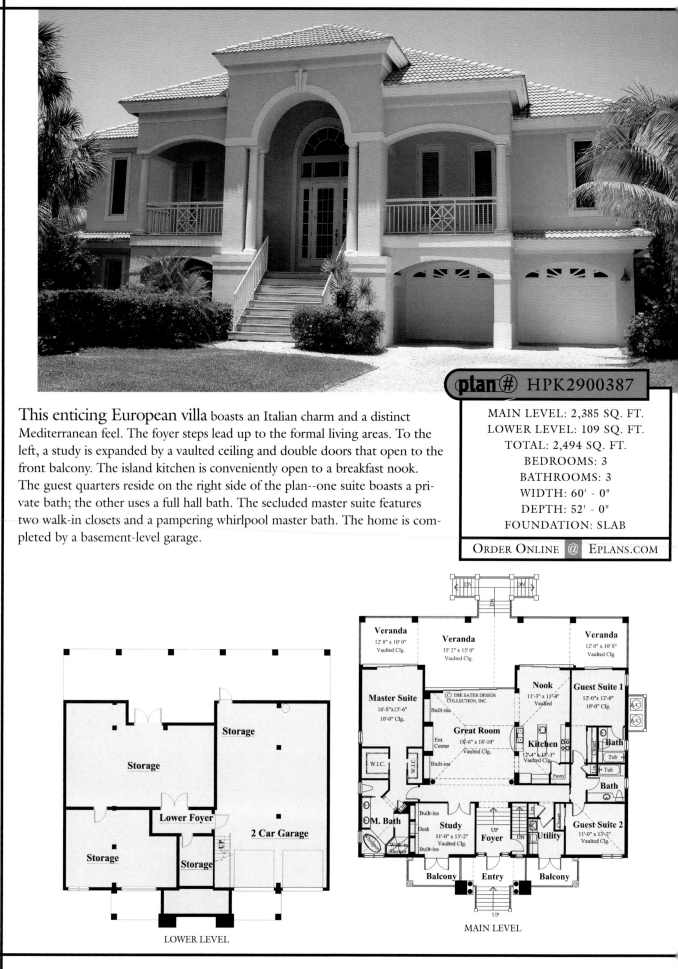

plan# HPK2900387

MAIN LEVEL: 2,385 SQ. FT.
LOWER LEVEL: 109 SQ. FT.
TOTAL: 2,494 SQ. FT.
BEDROOMS: 3
BATHROOMS: 3
WIDTH: 60' - 0"
DEPTH: 52' - 0"
FOUNDATION: SLAB

ORDER ONLINE @ EPLANS.COM

This enticing European villa boasts an Italian charm and a distinct Mediterranean feel. The foyer steps lead up to the formal living areas. To the left, a study is expanded by a vaulted ceiling and double doors that open to the front balcony. The island kitchen is conveniently open to a breakfast nook. The guest quarters reside on the right side of the plan--one suite boasts a private bath; the other uses a full hall bath. The secluded master suite features two walk-in closets and a pampering whirlpool master bath. The home is completed by a basement-level garage.

LOWER LEVEL

MAIN LEVEL

plan # HPK2900388

SQUARE FOOTAGE: 2,500
BEDROOMS: 3
BATHROOMS: 2½
WIDTH: 73' - 0"
DEPTH: 65' - 10"
FOUNDATION: CRAWLSPACE

ORDER ONLINE @ EPLANS.COM

Triple dormers highlight the roofline of this distinctive single-level French Country design. Double doors enhance the covered entryway, which leads to a grand open area with graceful columns. The large family room with a fireplace leads through double doors to the rear terrace. An L-shaped island kitchen opens to a breakfast area with a bay window. The master suite fills one wing and features a bay window, vaulted ceilings, and access to the terrace. Two additional bedrooms share a full bath.

REAR EXTERIOR

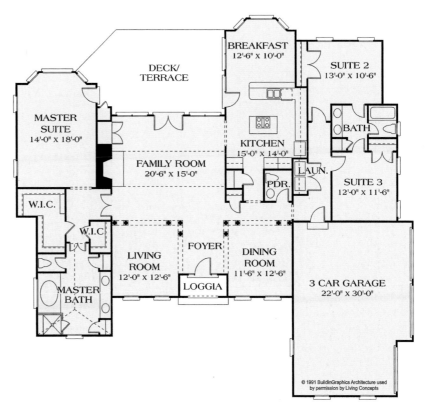

© 1991 BuildinGraphics Architecture used by permission by Living Concepts

plan# HPK2900389

SQUARE FOOTAGE: 2,515
BONUS SPACE: 200 SQ. FT.
BEDROOMS: 4
BATHROOMS: 3
WIDTH: 63' - 10"
DEPTH: 73' - 1"
FOUNDATION: SLAB

ORDER ONLINE @ EPLANS.COM

Brick, stone, and European accents create a plan filled with family amenities. A petite covered porch welcomes you inside to a gallery leading through the formal areas of the home to the casual areas at the rear of the plan. The master suite features an impressive bath with a walk-in closet. Bedroom 2 easily accesses a full hall bath. The island kitchen is open to the breakfast and great rooms, which offer rear patio access. Bedrooms 3 and 4 share a bath near a utility room that connects to the three-car garage.

plan ⊛ HPK2900390

SQUARE FOOTAGE: 2,553
BEDROOMS: 3
BATHROOMS: 2½
WIDTH: 80' - 0"
DEPTH: 56' - 10"
FOUNDATION: SLAB

ORDER ONLINE @ EPLANS.COM

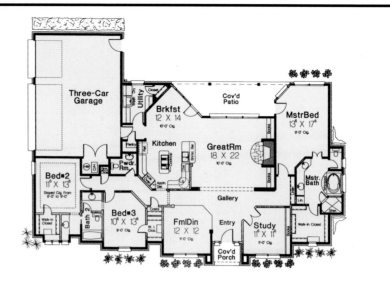

plan ⊛ HPK2900391

SQUARE FOOTAGE: 2,590
BEDROOMS: 4
BATHROOMS: 3½
WIDTH: 73' - 6"
DEPTH: 64' - 10"
FOUNDATION: SLAB

ORDER ONLINE @ EPLANS.COM

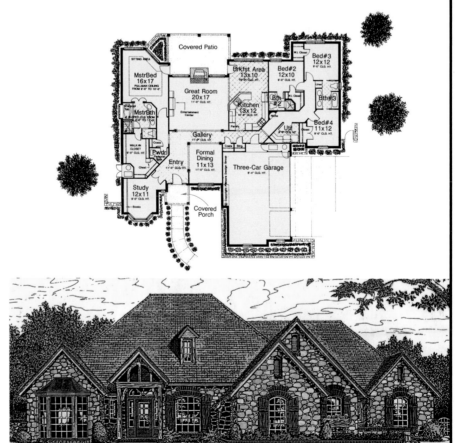

© The Sater Design Collection, Inc.

This modern take on the Italian villa boasts plenty of indoor/outdoor flow. Four sets of double doors wrap around the great room and dining area and open to the stunning veranda. The great room is enhanced by a coffered ceiling and built-in cabinetry, and the entire first floor is bathed in sunlight from a wall of glass doors overlooking the veranda. The dining room connects to a gourmet island kitchen. Upstairs, a beautiful deck wraps gracefully around the family bedrooms. The master suite is a skylit haven enhanced by a sitting bay, which features a vaulted octagonal ceiling and a cozy two-sided fireplace. Private double doors access the sundeck from the master suite, the secondary bedrooms, and the study.

plan# HPK2900392

FIRST FLOOR: 1,266 SQ. FT.
SECOND FLOOR: 1,324 SQ. FT.
TOTAL: 2,590 SQ. FT.
BEDROOMS: 3
BATHROOMS: 2½
WIDTH: 34' - 0"
DEPTH: 63' - 2"
FOUNDATION: SLAB

ORDER ONLINE @ EPLANS.COM

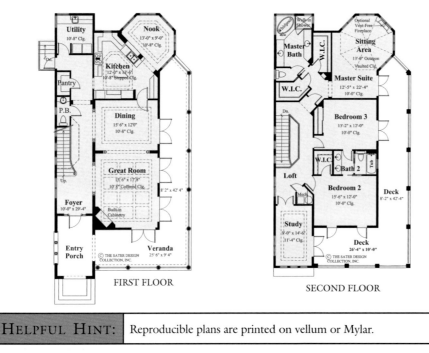

FIRST FLOOR

SECOND FLOOR

HELPFUL HINT: Reproducible plans are printed on vellum or Mylar.

plan(#) HPK2900393

SQUARE FOOTAGE: 2,597
BEDROOMS: 4
BATHROOMS: 3
WIDTH: 96' - 6"
DEPTH: 50' - 0"
FOUNDATION: SLAB

ORDER ONLINE @ EPLANS.COM

Long sightlines and acute angles create dynamic internal vistas and enable easy flow-through of foot traffic. The effects are most noticeable from the foyer, which creates a point of focus for the living room, dining room, and den. To the right, an island kitchen serves the breakfast nook and spacious family room. The den may also convert to a fourth bedroom, if desired. A large pantry provides ample space for food storage. At the other end of the home, a resplendent master suite provides a luxury retreat for homeowners. Majestic columns of brick add warmth to a striking exterior.

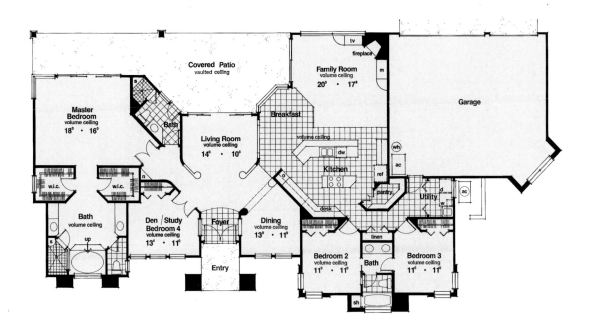

Signature Designer

Stephen Fuller's overseas influences are evident in this European beauty. Called the Evergreen, this house plan's gabled rooflines, double and triple windows, and stone-and-stucco facade grace the exterior. Inside, the functional layout is full of eye-catching elements and exciting amenities, such as a double staircase, a media room, a see-through fireplace, and walk-in closets.

plan # HPK2900394

FIRST FLOOR: 1,395 SQ. FT.
SECOND FLOOR: 1,210 SQ. FT.
TOTAL: 2,605 SQ. FT.
BONUS SPACE: 225 SQ. FT.
BEDROOMS: 3
BATHROOMS: 2½
WIDTH: 47' - 0"
DEPTH: 49' - 6"
FOUNDATION: UNFINISHED BASEMENT

ORDER ONLINE @ EPLANS.COM

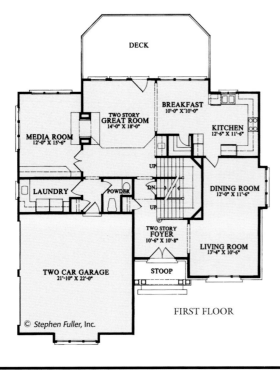

FIRST FLOOR

© Stephen Fuller, Inc.

SECOND FLOOR

plan(#) HPK2900395

FIRST FLOOR: 2,050 SQ. FT.
SECOND FLOOR: 561 SQ. FT.
TOTAL: 2,611 SQ. FT.
BONUS SPACE: 272 SQ. FT.
BEDROOMS: 4
BATHROOMS: 3
WIDTH: 64' - 10"
DEPTH: 64' - 0"
FOUNDATION: CRAWLSPACE,
SLAB, UNFINISHED
BASEMENT

ORDER ONLINE @ EPLANS.COM

Old World ambiance characterizes this European-style home. The elegant stone entrance opens to the two-story foyer. A well-proportioned dining room is viewed through an arch flanked by columns. The oversized great room features a coffered ceiling and a see-through fireplace that can be viewed from the kitchen, breakfast room, and great room. The master suite includes a luxury bath and a cozy sitting area off the bedroom. A second bedroom on this floor acts as a nursery, guest room, or study. Upstairs, two bedrooms share a bath, and an expandable area is available for future use.

FIRST FLOOR

SECOND FLOOR

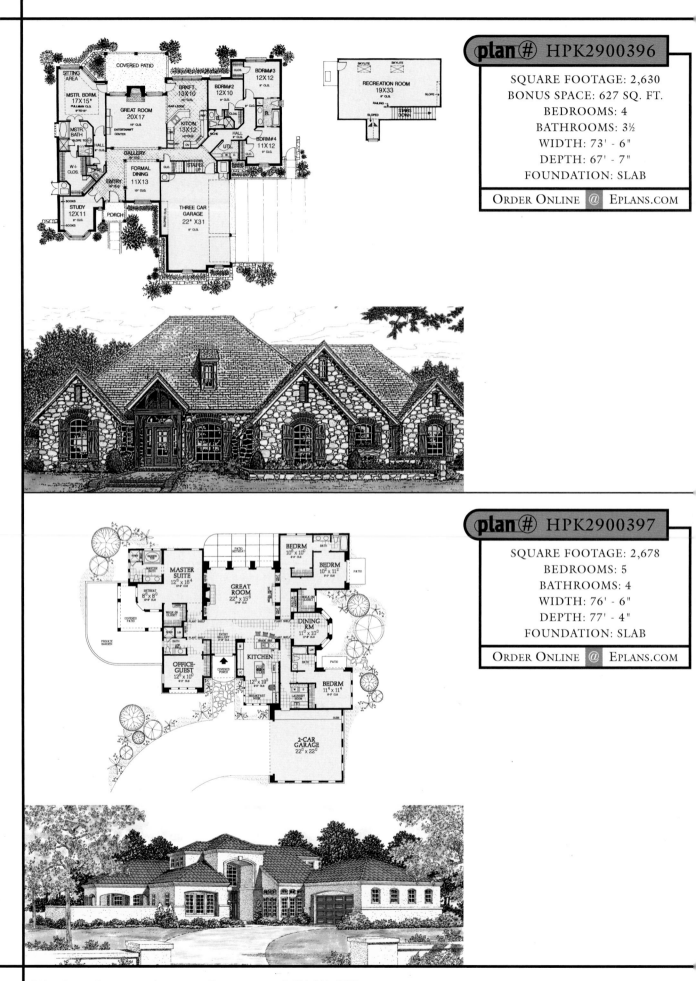

plan # HPK2900396

SQUARE FOOTAGE: 2,630
BONUS SPACE: 627 SQ. FT.
BEDROOMS: 4
BATHROOMS: 3½
WIDTH: 73' - 6"
DEPTH: 67' - 7"
FOUNDATION: SLAB

ORDER ONLINE @ EPLANS.COM

plan # HPK2900397

SQUARE FOOTAGE: 2,678
BEDROOMS: 5
BATHROOMS: 4
WIDTH: 76' - 6"
DEPTH: 77' - 4"
FOUNDATION: SLAB

ORDER ONLINE @ EPLANS.COM

plan# HPK2900398

FIRST FLOOR: 1,355 SQ. FT.
SECOND FLOOR: 1,347 SQ. FT.
TOTAL: 2,702 SQ. FT.
BONUS SPACE: 285 SQ. FT.
BEDROOMS: 4
BATHROOMS: 4
WIDTH: 41' - 0"
DEPTH: 66' - 0"
FOUNDATION: CRAWLSPACE,
UNFINISHED WALKOUT
BASEMENT

ORDER ONLINE @ EPLANS.COM

Stone accents add a European feel to this narrow cottage, perfect in an established neighborhood or out in the country. Enter beneath a keystone arch to a two-story foyer; follow an angled hall to the family room where a coffered ceiling and fireplace create a welcoming atmosphere. The kitchen works hard so you don't have to, with a serving bar, stacked ovens, and easy access to the breakfast nook and dining room. The keeping room is to the rear, perfect for lazy mornings spent curled up with a good book. Upstairs, the master suite delights in a detailed tray ceiling, bayed sitting area, and lavish bath. Two additional bedrooms join an optional bonus area (with a charming window seat) to complete the plan.

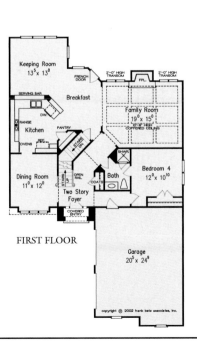

FIRST FLOOR

SECOND FLOOR

HELPFUL HINT: A home automation upgrade provides all the wiring diagrams needed to build a Smart House.

FIRST FLOOR

Deck

Master
Bedroom
18⁰ x 14⁹

Breakfast
15⁹ x 5⁶

Great
Room
16⁹ x 15⁶

Kitchen
11³ x 15⁶

Dining
Room
12⁰ x 12⁹

Two Car
Garage
21⁰ x 21⁹

©Stephen Fuller

SECOND FLOOR

Bedroom
Office
12³ x 13³

Bedroom
#2
14⁹ x 13⁰

Media
Room
14⁰ x 10⁰

Exercise
8⁹ x 13⁹

plan# HPK2900399

FIRST FLOOR: 1,763 SQ. FT.
SECOND FLOOR: 947 SQ. FT.
TOTAL: 2,710 SQ. FT.
BEDROOMS: 3
BATHROOMS: 2½
WIDTH: 50' - 0"
DEPTH: 75' - 4"
FOUNDATION: UNFINISHED
WALKOUT BASEMENT

ORDER ONLINE @ EPLANS.COM

Master
Bedroom
14⁴ · 17⁴

Covered Patio
volume ceiling

Bedroom 3
volume ceiling
11⁰ · 11⁰

Bath

Breakfast
volume ceiling

Family Room
volume ceiling
13⁸ · 22⁰

fireplace

Bath
w.l.c.

desk

Kitchen

Bedroom 4
volume ceiling
16⁶ · 11⁰

pantry

Dining
volume ceiling
11⁶ · 12⁶

Bedroom 5
volume ceiling
13⁴ · 12⁸

Bath

Utility

ac

Living Room
volume ceiling
12⁸ · 13⁴

Foyer

Guest / Den
volume ceiling
10⁰ · 10⁰

Entry

Double Garage

plan# HPK2900400

SQUARE FOOTAGE: 2,718
BEDROOMS: 5
BATHROOMS: 3
WIDTH: 63' - 8"
DEPTH: 64' - 4"
FOUNDATION: SLAB

ORDER ONLINE @ EPLANS.COM

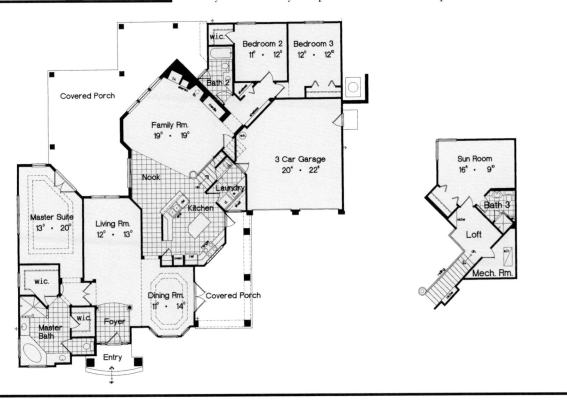

plan# HPK2900401

FIRST FLOOR: 2,365 SQ. FT.
SECOND FLOOR: 364 SQ. FT.
TOTAL: 2,729 SQ. FT.
BEDROOMS: 3
BATHROOMS: 3
WIDTH: 69' - 0"
DEPTH: 70' - 0"
FOUNDATION: SLAB

ORDER ONLINE @ EPLANS.COM

The columned foyer of this home welcomes you into a series of spaces that reach out in all directions. The living room has a spectacular view of the huge covered patio area that's perfect for summer entertaining. The dining room features a tray ceiling and French doors that lead to a covered porch. A secluded master suite affords great views through French doors and also has a tray ceiling. The family wing combines an island kitchen, nook, and family gathering space, with the built-in media/fireplace wall the center of attention. Two secondary bedrooms share a bath. A staircase overlooking the family room takes you up to the sunroom complete with a full bath.

© The Sater Design Collection, Inc.

With striking Mediterranean affluence, this Renaissance estate invites family and guests with triplet arches and a dramatic vaulted portico. Upon entering, the bayed dining room is to the left; a study resides in the turret, bright with circumambient light courtesy of intricate full-length windows. The great room soars with a vintage exposed-beam ceiling and offers a fireplace and three sets of French doors to the veranda. Don't miss the country kitchen, a tribute to gourmet cooking. The master suite has an extended-bow window, access to the courtyard, and a luxurious bath with a Roman tub. An elegant staircase leads to two generous bedrooms; the vaulted bonus room is accessible from garage stairs or the outdoor deck off of Bedroom 3.

plan# HPK2900402

FIRST FLOOR: 2,084 SQ. FT.
SECOND FLOOR: 652 SQ. FT.
TOTAL: 2,736 SQ. FT.
BONUS SPACE: 375 SQ. FT.
BEDROOMS: 3
BATHROOMS: 2½
WIDTH: 60' - 6"
DEPTH: 94' - 0"
FOUNDATION: SLAB

ORDER ONLINE @ EPLANS.COM

FIRST FLOOR

SECOND FLOOR

plan# HPK2900403

SQUARE FOOTAGE: 2,745
BEDROOMS: 4
BATHROOMS: 2½
WIDTH: 69' - 6"
DEPTH: 76' - 8"
FOUNDATION: CRAWLSPACE,
SLAB, UNFINISHED
BASEMENT

ORDER ONLINE @ EPLANS.COM

plan# HPK2900404

DESIGN: HPK2900404
SQUARE FOOTAGE: 2,757
BEDROOMS: 4
BATHROOMS: 2½
WIDTH: 69' - 6"
DEPTH: 68' - 8"
FOUNDATION: CRAWLSPACE,
SLAB, UNFINISHED
BASEMENT

ORDER ONLINE @ EPLANS.COM

© Stephen Fuller, Inc.

plan# HPK2900405

The appeal of this home is definitely European, with an interior that is open and inviting. Decorative columns separate the formal living room and dining room. To the left of the foyer, the comfortable family room boasts a large fireplace and open-rail detailing and allows access to the breakfast room and kitchen. An open staircase to the gallery above leads to a grand master suite with a tray ceiling and a luxurious private bath with a whirlpool tub, His and Hers vanities, and a walk-in closet. Two bedrooms with a connecting bath and a third bedroom with a private bath complete the room arrangements.

FIRST FLOOR: 1,360 SQ. FT.
SECOND FLOOR: 1,400 SQ. FT.
TOTAL: 2,760 SQ. FT.
BEDROOMS: 4
BATHROOMS: 3½
WIDTH: 52' - 0"
DEPTH: 49' - 0"
FOUNDATION: FINISHED
WALKOUT BASEMENT

ORDER ONLINE @ EPLANS.COM

FIRST FLOOR

SECOND FLOOR

plan # HPK2900406

FIRST FLOOR: 2,117 SQ. FT.
SECOND FLOOR: 652 SQ. FT.
TOTAL: 2,769 SQ. FT.
BONUS SPACE: 375 SQ. FT.
BEDROOMS: 3
BATHROOMS: 2½
WIDTH: 60' - 6"
DEPTH: 94' - 0"
FOUNDATION: SLAB

ORDER ONLINE @ EPLANS.COM

The stone facade of this luxurious mountain retreat is beautifully accented with a shallow-peaked roof and a bay window with copper flashing above, making it a plan you will be delighted to come home to. The heart of the home is the great room, with a fireplace, built-in entertainment center, and stately columns. The vintage exposed-beam ceiling here is echoed in the country kitchen, a chef's dream with an extended island, room for a six-burner range, and plenty of counter and cabinet space. An outdoor grill in the loggia is great for entertaining; from here, enjoy the resplendent courtyard. The master suite is full of natural light, stunning with a pampering bath and bumped-out whirlpool tub. Two upstairs bedrooms share a full bath. The bonus space is easily accessed from garage stairs or the outer deck from Bedroom 3.

FIRST FLOOR

SECOND FLOOR

FIRST FLOOR: 1,900 SQ. FT.
SECOND FLOOR: 890 SQ. FT.
TOTAL: 2,790 SQ. FT.
BEDROOMS: 4
BATHROOMS: 2½
WIDTH: 63' - 0"
DEPTH: 51' - 0"
FOUNDATION: FINISHED
WALKOUT BASEMENT

ORDER ONLINE @ EPLANS.COM

Signature Designer

Stephen Fuller shows his eye for delightful details in this elegant yet modestly sized plan. The stucco and stacked-stone French country facade is accented on the interior by high vaulted ceilings and a great room wall of glass. The designer perfects the main level with a coffered ceiling and secluded bath in the master suite.

FIRST FLOOR

SECOND FLOOR

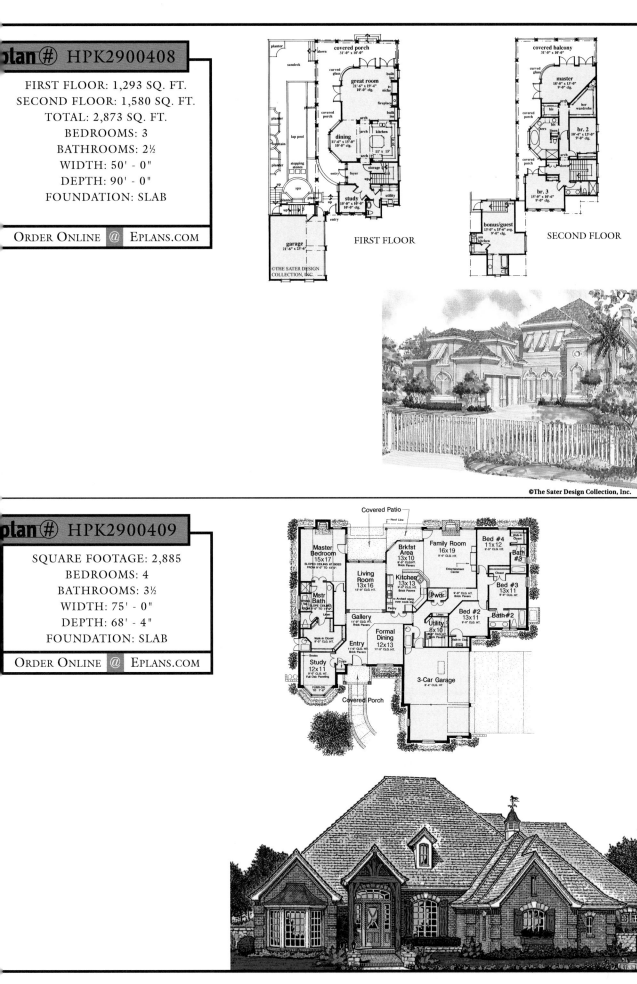

plan # HPK2900408

FIRST FLOOR: 1,293 SQ. FT.
SECOND FLOOR: 1,580 SQ. FT.
TOTAL: 2,873 SQ. FT.
BEDROOMS: 3
BATHROOMS: 2½
WIDTH: 50' - 0"
DEPTH: 90' - 0"
FOUNDATION: SLAB

ORDER ONLINE @ EPLANS.COM

FIRST FLOOR

SECOND FLOOR

©THE SATER DESIGN COLLECTION, INC.

©The Sater Design Collection, Inc.

plan # HPK2900409

SQUARE FOOTAGE: 2,885
BEDROOMS: 4
BATHROOMS: 3½
WIDTH: 75' - 0"
DEPTH: 68' - 4"
FOUNDATION: SLAB

ORDER ONLINE @ EPLANS.COM

© Stephen Fuller, Inc.

plan# HPK2900410

Enjoy the gracious comfort of a European farmhouse in your very own neighborhood! The stucco facade is adorned with a trellis to support a rambling rose and accented with arched windows. A petite terrace invites lingering outside the front door, while inside the fantasy continues. A cozy living room and formal dining room adjoin each other for easy entertaining, separated from the kitchen by a pocket door. Storage and counter space are plentiful in the country kitchen. An airy breakfast room opens to the rear deck, as do two pair of French doors in the great room. A fireplace and built-in cabinetry anchor this space. The master suite features another fireplace, as well as a sitting area with deck access and a spacious garden bath. Upstairs, a gallery overlooking the great room provides a bridge between a single bedroom suite and two additional bedrooms linked by a compartmented bath.

FIRST FLOOR: 1,915 SQ. FT.
SECOND FLOOR: 982 SQ. FT.
TOTAL: 2,897 SQ. FT.
BEDROOMS: 4
BATHROOMS: 3½
WIDTH: 62' - 3"
DEPTH: 50' - 6"
FOUNDATION: UNFINISHED WALKOUT BASEMENT

ORDER ONLINE @ EPLANS.COM

FIRST FLOOR

SECOND FLOOR

plan # HPK2900411

FIRST FLOOR: 2,009 SQ. FT.
SECOND FLOOR: 913 SQ. FT.
TOTAL: 2,922 SQ. FT.
BONUS SPACE: 192 SQ. FT.
BEDROOMS: 5
BATHROOMS: 3
WIDTH: 86' - 10"
DEPTH: 65' - 6"
FOUNDATION: CRAWLSPACE, SLAB, UNFINISHED BASEMENT

ORDER ONLINE @ EPLANS.COM

This stunning European-style home is so much more than just a pretty face. The two-story foyer opens to a two-story great room that's ready for planned events as well as comfortable gatherings. The kitchen features an angled sink with a window above for views to the rear yard. The master suite opens to a covered rear porch and includes a corner whirlpool tub. A secondary bedroom and bath conveniently located on the first floor can be used as a guest suite, nursery, or home office/study.

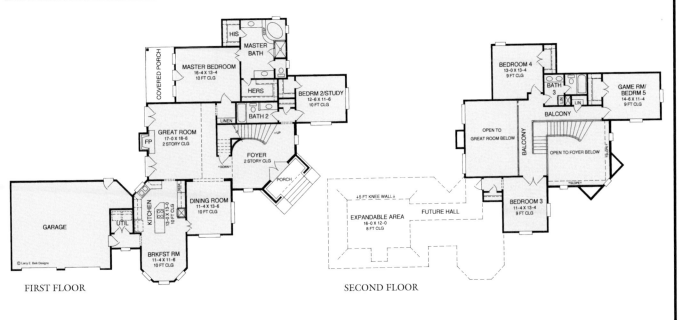

FIRST FLOOR

SECOND FLOOR

DECK

BREAKFAST
9'-4" X 10'-6"

TWO STORY
GREAT ROOM
16'-6" X 15'-6"

MEDIA ROOM
12'-6" X 12'-0"

KITCHEN
15'-8" X 14'-0"

STORAGE

LAUNDRY
6'-2" X 7'-0"

POWDER

WET BAR

TWO CAR GARAGE
21'-4" X 21'-4"

DINING ROOM
12'-0" X 13'-0"

TWO STORY
FOYER
10'-6" X 17'-0"

LIVING ROOM
12'-0" X 12'-2"

PORCH

©Stephen Fuller

FIRST FLOOR

SITTING

MASTER
BEDROOM
16'-0" X 20'-0"

OPEN TO BELOW

BEDROOM NO. 2
12'-0" X 11'-4"

BALCONY

BATH

MASTER
BATH

BATH

OPEN TO
BELOW

W.I.C.

BEDROOM NO. 3
12'-0" X 11'-4"

BEDROOM NO. 4
11'-2" X 12'-0"

SECRET
ROOM

SECOND FLOOR

COPYRIGHT LARRY E. BELK

BRKFST RM
11-0 X 10-6
10 FT CLG

PAN

UTIL

SITTING
10 FT CLG

MASTER BEDRM
13-6 X 20-6
10 FT CLG

MASTER
BATH

10 FT CLG

LEDGE

SEAT

2 CAR GARAGE

KITCHEN

13-0 X 12-0
10 FT CLG

GREAT ROOM
21-0 X 20-6
12 FT CLG

FP

BUILT INS

PWDR

SEAT

BEDROOM 4
14-8 X 13-4
10 FT CLG

BATH 2

LIN

BUILT INS

DINING ROOM
12-4 X 13-6
12 FT CLG

FOYER
10 FT CLG

STUDY
10-6 X 12-6
10 FT CLG

STONE WALL

BEDROOM 2
13-0 X 12-6
10 FT CLG

PORCH

BEDROOM 3
13-4 X 13-4
10 FT CLG

STONE WALL

SEAT

STONE WALL

COPYRIGHT LARRY E. BELK

plan # HPK2900414

SQUARE FOOTAGE: 2,966
BEDROOMS: 4
BATHROOMS: 3½
WIDTH: 114' - 10"
DEPTH: 79' - 2"
FOUNDATION: SLAB

ORDER ONLINE @ EPLANS.COM

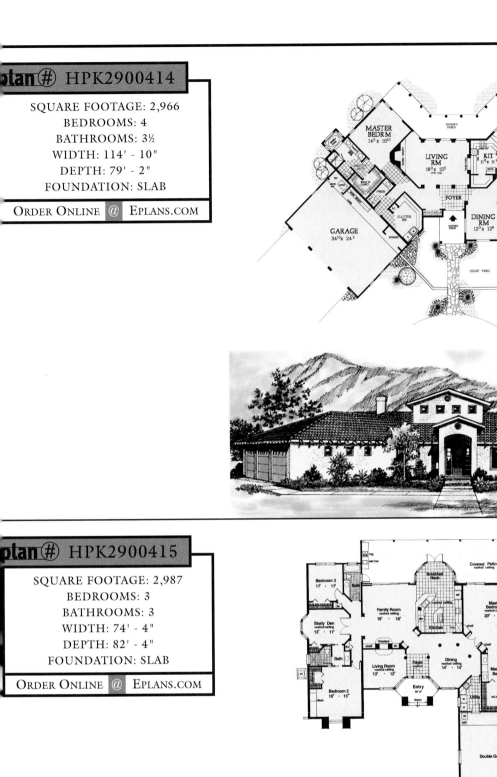

plan # HPK2900415

SQUARE FOOTAGE: 2,987
BEDROOMS: 3
BATHROOMS: 3
WIDTH: 74' - 4"
DEPTH: 82' - 4"
FOUNDATION: SLAB

ORDER ONLINE @ EPLANS.COM

plan# HPK2900416

FIRST FLOOR: 2,096 SQ. FT.
SECOND FLOOR: 892 SQ. FT.
TOTAL: 2,988 SQ. FT.
BEDROOMS: 3
BATHROOMS: 3½
WIDTH: 58' - 0"
DEPTH: 54' - 0"
FOUNDATION: ISLAND
BASEMENT

ORDER ONLINE @ EPLANS.COM

The variety in the rooflines of this striking waterfront home will certainly make it the envy of the neighborhood. The two-story great room, with its fireplace and built-ins, is a short flight down from the foyer. The three sets of French doors give access to the veranda. The huge, well-equipped kitchen will easily serve the gourmet who loves to entertain. The stepped ceiling and bay window in the dining room will add style to every meal. The master suite completes the first level. Two bedrooms and two full baths, along with an expansive loft, constitute the second level. One guest suite has an attached sundeck.

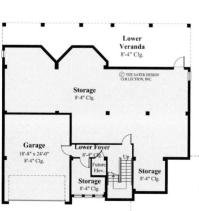

MAIN LEVEL

SECOND LEVEL

plan # HPK2900417

SQUARE FOOTAGE: 2,998
BONUS SPACE: 345 SQ. FT.
BEDROOMS: 4
BATHROOMS: 3½
WIDTH: 69' - 7"
DEPTH: 81' - 6"
FOUNDATION: SLAB

ORDER ONLINE @ EPLANS.COM

Dreamed of a European cottage? Here it is! An incredibly charming facade includes high-pitched rooflines, decorative arches, a shed-style dormer window, and a beautiful combination of stone, stucco, and brick materials. This floor plan has everything. Front-facing formal living and dining rooms flank the wide foyer. A private study is a quiet home office. The great room is lit by a window wall and warmed by a cozy fireplace. Relax and read in the sitting area in the master suite or take a long soak in the garden tub in the grand bath. To the right of the plan, find the spacious kitchen, nook, and laundry facilities. Three family bedrooms—one with a private bath—all have walk-in closets.

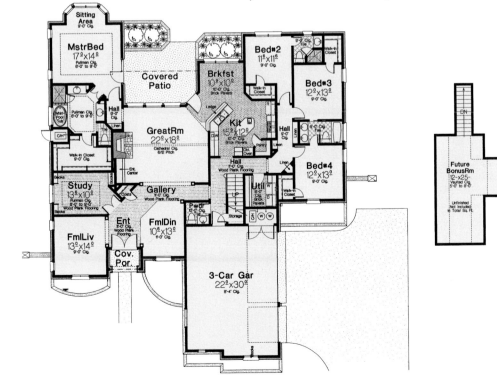

plan# HPK2900418

SQUARE FOOTAGE: 3,012
BONUS SPACE: 392 SQ. FT.
BEDROOMS: 4
BATHROOMS: 3½
WIDTH: 80' - 0"
DEPTH: 72' - 0"
FOUNDATION: SLAB

ORDER ONLINE @ EPLANS.COM

The European appeal of this spacious cottage plan features graceful elegance on the exterior, with abundant amenities found inside. The foyer is flanked by formal living and dining rooms. Straight ahead, double doors open into a study. The master suite features a sitting area with a fireplace and a private bath that extends into an enormous walk-in closet. The island kitchen is central and connects to the breakfast room, which is open to the great room at the rear of the plan. Three family bedrooms are located to the right of the plan. A future bonus room is available for additional expansion.

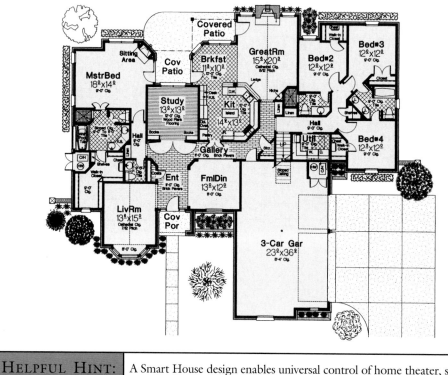

HELPFUL HINT: A Smart House design enables universal control of home theater, security, and audio systems.

plan # HPK2900419

FIRST FLOOR: 2,129 SQ. FT.
SECOND FLOOR: 895 SQ. FT.
TOTAL: 3,024 SQ. FT.
BEDROOMS: 4
BATHROOMS: 3
WIDTH: 56' - 0"
DEPTH: 73' - 0"
FOUNDATION: UNFINISHED
WALKOUT BASEMENT

ORDER ONLINE @ EPLANS.COM

Fine European flavor entices onlookers who view this stucco facade, featuring corner quoins, French shutters, and arched windows. Inside, the foyer opens to formal rooms warmed by the family-room fireplace. The master suite features a bayed sitting room, a spacious bath, and His and Hers walk-in closets. The kitchen opens to a sunny breakfast/sun room that accesses the rear yard. A guest suite is tucked behind the two-car garage. Two additional family bedrooms and the children's playroom are located upstairs.

FIRST FLOOR

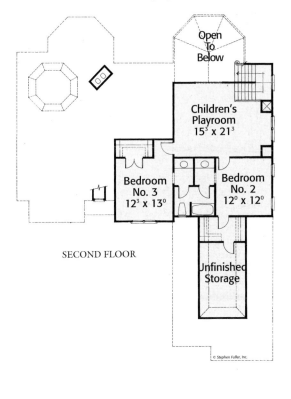

SECOND FLOOR

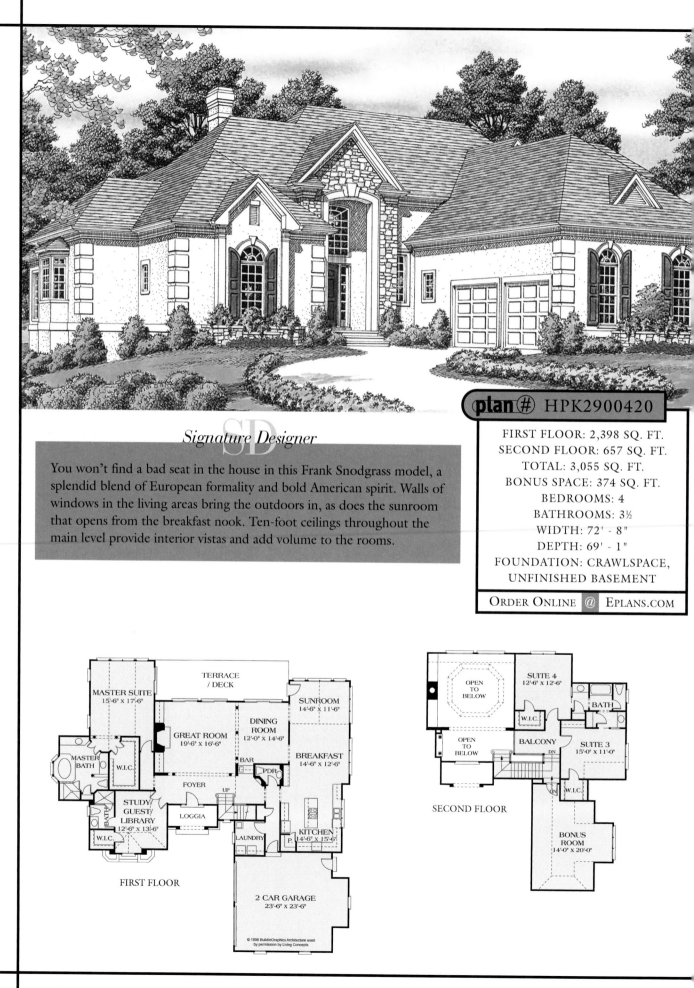

Signature Designer

You won't find a bad seat in the house in this Frank Snodgrass model, a splendid blend of European formality and bold American spirit. Walls of windows in the living areas bring the outdoors in, as does the sunroom that opens from the breakfast nook. Ten-foot ceilings throughout the main level provide interior vistas and add volume to the rooms.

plan# HPK2900420

FIRST FLOOR: 2,398 SQ. FT.
SECOND FLOOR: 657 SQ. FT.
TOTAL: 3,055 SQ. FT.
BONUS SPACE: 374 SQ. FT.
BEDROOMS: 4
BATHROOMS: 3½
WIDTH: 72' - 8"
DEPTH: 69' - 1"
FOUNDATION: CRAWLSPACE,
UNFINISHED BASEMENT

ORDER ONLINE @ EPLANS.COM

FIRST FLOOR

TERRACE / DECK

MASTER SUITE
15'-6" x 17'-6"

SUNROOM
14'-6" x 11'-6"

DINING ROOM
12'-0" x 14'-6"

GREAT ROOM
19'-6" x 16'-6"

MASTER BATH

W.I.C.

BAR

BREAKFAST
14'-6" x 12'-6"

PDR.

FOYER

UP

STUDY GUEST/ LIBRARY
12'-6" x 13'-6"

BATH

LOGGIA

W.I.C.

LAUNDRY

P.

KITCHEN
14'-6" x 15'-6"

2 CAR GARAGE
23'-6" x 23'-6"

© 1996 BuildinGraphics Architecture used by permission by Living Concepts

SECOND FLOOR

OPEN TO BELOW

SUITE 4
12'-6" x 12'-6"

BATH

W.I.C.

OPEN TO BELOW

BALCONY

DN.

SUITE 3
15'-0" x 11'-0"

UP.

DN

W.I.C.

BONUS ROOM
14'-0" x 20'-0"

plan # HPK2900421

SQUARE FOOTAGE: 3,064
BONUS SPACE: 366 SQ. FT.
BEDROOMS: 3
BATHROOMS: 3
WIDTH: 79' - 6"
DEPTH: 91' - 0"
FOUNDATION: SLAB

ORDER ONLINE @ EPLANS.COM

From a more graceful era, this one-and-a-half-story estate evokes a sense of quiet refinement. Exquisite exterior detailing makes it a one-of-a-kind. Inside are distinctive treatments that make the floor plan unique and functional. The central foyer is enhanced with columns that define the dining room and formal living room. A beamed ceiling complements the den. An indulgent master suite includes a private garden with a fountain, pool access, a large walk-in closet, and a through-fireplace to the outdoor spa. Family bedrooms share an unusual compartmented bath. The kitchen and family room are complete with a breakfast nook. Pool access and a lanai with a summer kitchen make this area a natural for casual lifestyles. A bonus area over the garage can become a home office or game room.

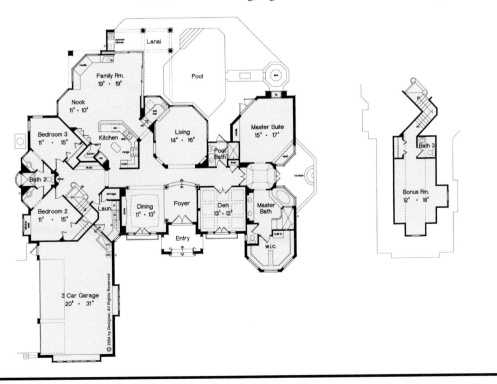

plan# HPK2900422

FIRST FLOOR: 2,264 SQ. FT.
SECOND FLOOR: 820 SQ. FT.
TOTAL: 3,084 SQ. FT.
BEDROOMS: 4
BATHROOMS: 3
WIDTH: 66' - 0"
DEPTH: 78' - 10"
FOUNDATION: SLAB

ORDER ONLINE @ EPLANS.COM

Indoor and outdoor living are enhanced by the beautiful courtyard that decorates the center of this home. A gallery leads to a kitchen featuring a center work island and adjacent breakfast room. To the left, the gallery leads to the formal living room and master suite. The secluded master bedroom features a tray ceiling and double doors that lead to a covered patio. The second floor contains a full bath shared by two family bedrooms and a loft that provides flexible space.

FIRST FLOOR

SECOND FLOOR

plan # HPK2900423

SQUARE FOOTAGE: 3,091
BEDROOMS: 4
BATHROOMS: 3
WIDTH: 62' - 0"
DEPTH: 83' - 8"
FOUNDATION: SLAB

ORDER ONLINE @ EPLANS.COM

plan # HPK2900424

FIRST FLOOR: 2,083 SQ. FT.
SECOND FLOOR: 1,013 SQ. FT.
TOTAL: 3,096 SQ. FT.
BEDROOMS: 4
BATHROOMS: 3½
WIDTH: 74' - 0"
DEPTH: 88' - 0"
FOUNDATION: SLAB

ORDER ONLINE @ EPLANS.COM

HELPFUL HINT:

Reproducible sets include a license
to build the home once.

FIRST FLOOR

SECOND FLOOR

© The Sater Design Collection, Inc.

plan# HPK2900426

FIRST FLOOR: 2,237 SQ. FT.
SECOND FLOOR: 931 SQ. FT.
TOTAL: 3,168 SQ. FT.
BONUS SPACE: 304 SQ. FT.
BEDROOMS: 4
BATHROOMS: 3½
WIDTH: 68' - 0"
DEPTH: 55' - 6"
FOUNDATION: SLAB

ORDER ONLINE @ EPLANS.COM

This majestic estate has palatial inspiration, with a plan any modern family will love. A hardwood entry leads to brick flooring in the kitchen and breakfast nook, for vintage appeal. The family room and vaulted living room warm heart and soul with extended-hearth fireplaces. For a quiet retreat, the study opens with French doors from the hall and leads out to the walled lanai courtyard through another set of French doors. The vaulted master suite is impressive, with a bay window, a sumptuous bath, and His and Hers walk-in closets. Upstairs, three ample bedrooms will access the future playroom.

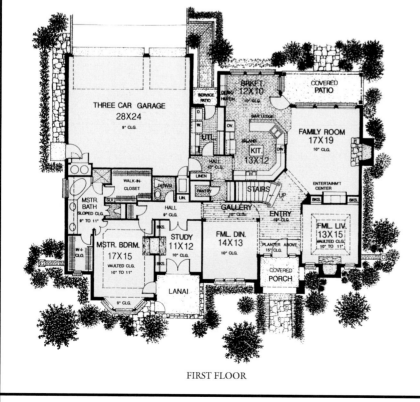

FIRST FLOOR

SECOND FLOOR

plan # HPK2900427

FIRST FLOOR: 2,502 SQ. FT.
SECOND FLOOR: 677 SQ. FT.
TOTAL: 3,179 SQ. FT.
BONUS SPACE: 171 SQ. FT.
BEDROOMS: 4
BATHROOMS: 3½
WIDTH: 71' - 2"
DEPTH: 56' - 10"
FOUNDATION: FINISHED
WALKOUT BASEMENT

ORDER ONLINE @ EPLANS.COM

Stone and stucco bring a chateau welcome to this Mediterranean-style home. A sensational sunroom lights up the rear of the plan and flows to the bayed breakfast nook. The living area opens to the formal dining room. A master suite with rear-deck access leads to a family or guest bedroom with a private bath. Upstairs, two secondary bedrooms and a full bath enjoy easy kitchen access down a side stairway.

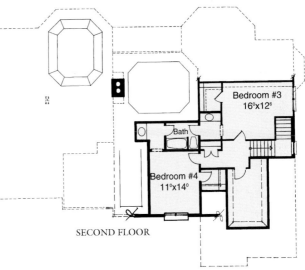

SECOND FLOOR

FIRST FLOOR

© Stephen Fuller, Inc.

This exquisite French chateau boasts all the charm of Europe and features all the modern conveniences for today's busy lifestyles. Inside, the foyer is flanked by the formal dining room and an optional room, perfect for a guest suite, and connects to a hall bath. The great room is truly magnificent with an enormous hearth and two sets of double doors opening to the rear porch. The kitchen connects to a breakfast/sunroom for casual family dining. The master suite is pampering with a walk-through closet and a lavish bath that features a bumped-out tub.

© Stephen Fuller, Inc.

plan # HPK2900428

FIRST FLOOR: 2,067 SQ. FT.
SECOND FLOOR: 1,129 SQ. FT.
TOTAL: 3,196 SQ. FT.
BEDROOMS: 4
BATHROOMS: 4
WIDTH: 69' - 0"
DEPTH: 63' - 0"
FOUNDATION: UNFINISHED
WALKOUT BASEMENT

ORDER ONLINE @ EPLANS.COM

FIRST FLOOR

SECOND FLOOR

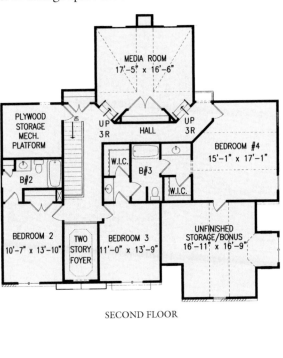

plan # HPK2900429

FIRST FLOOR: 1,932 SQ. FT.
SECOND FLOOR: 1,327 SQ. FT.
TOTAL: 3,259 SQ. FT.
BEDROOMS: 4
BATHROOMS: 3½
WIDTH: 50' - 0"
DEPTH: 51' - 0"
FOUNDATION: SLAB,
FINISHED WALKOUT
BASEMENT

ORDER ONLINE @ EPLANS.com

For sheer comfort and satisfaction of a wide spectrum of needs, this stately two-story home can't be beat. An outstanding grand room and elegant formal dining room will host many enjoyable get-togethers. To the left of the two-story foyer, the library is perfect for cordial conversations with friends or quiet reading time. The rear keeping room, just off the well-equipped kitchen, will draw family members together for informal meals, games, and discussions. A gorgeous master suite is also found on this level. Upstairs, three more bedrooms allow ample sleeping space for family members or guests. A sizable media room and lots of storage space are also on the second floor.

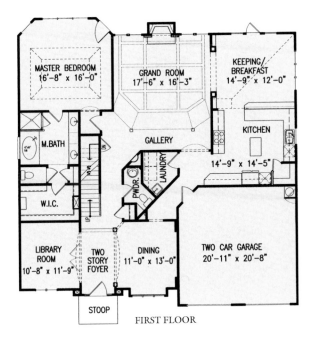

FIRST FLOOR

SECOND FLOOR

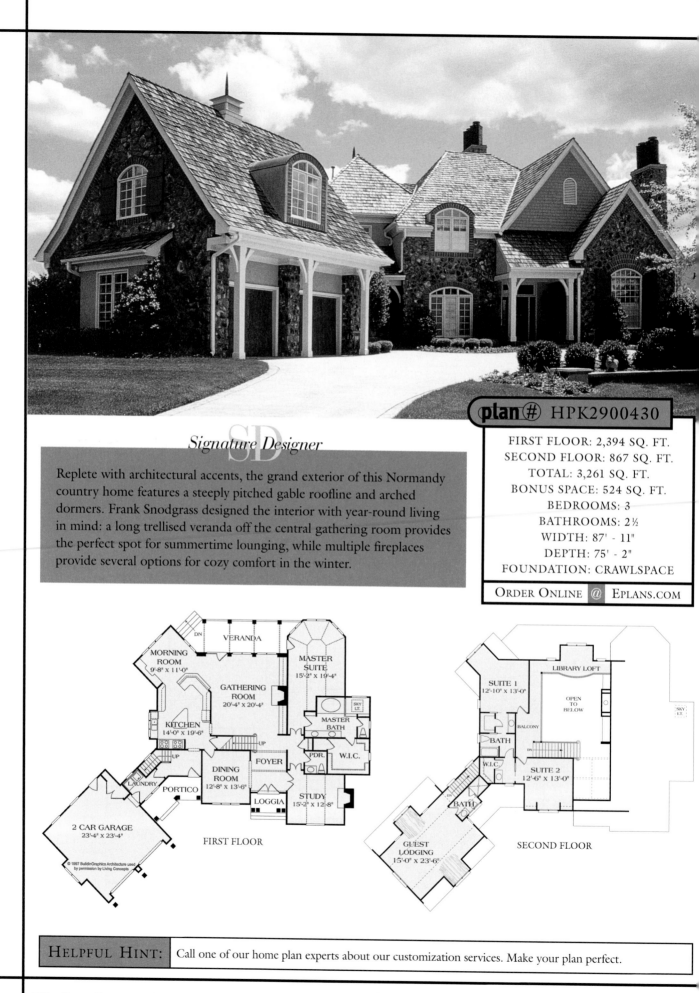

plan# HPK2900430

FIRST FLOOR: 2,394 SQ. FT.
SECOND FLOOR: 867 SQ. FT.
TOTAL: 3,261 SQ. FT.
BONUS SPACE: 524 SQ. FT.
BEDROOMS: 3
BATHROOMS: 2½
WIDTH: 87' - 11"
DEPTH: 75' - 2"
FOUNDATION: CRAWLSPACE

ORDER ONLINE @ EPLANS.COM

Signature Designer

Replete with architectural accents, the grand exterior of this Normandy country home features a steeply pitched gable roofline and arched dormers. Frank Snodgrass designed the interior with year-round living in mind: a long trellised veranda off the central gathering room provides the perfect spot for summertime lounging, while multiple fireplaces provide several options for cozy comfort in the winter.

HELPFUL HINT: Call one of our home plan experts about our customization services. Make your plan perfect.

plan # HPK2900431

FIRST FLOOR: 1,888 SQ. FT.
SECOND FLOOR: 1,374 SQ. FT.
TOTAL: 3,262 SQ. FT.
BEDROOMS: 4
BATHROOMS: 3
WIDTH: 63' - 0"
DEPTH: 52' - 6"
FOUNDATION: UNFINISHED
WALKOUT BASEMENT

ORDER ONLINE @ EPLANS.COM

Stone accents are a striking embellishment on this stunning luxury home. The grand foyer opens to the living room, welcoming with a fireplace set in a full bay window. Columns announce the dining room; a large window here views the rear property. To the left, the stylish cooktop-island kitchen works hard so you don't have to. A sunny breakfast area leads to the cathedral-ceiling great room, cozy with a fireplace and filled with natural light. Two staircases access the upper level; both lead to generous secondary bedrooms and a glorious master suite. Here, a romantic fireplace and box-bay sitting nook adorn the bedroom. The private bath presents a corner tub set between bright windows, plus dual vanities and immense walk-in closets.

FIRST FLOOR

SECOND FLOOR

FIRST FLOOR

SECOND FLOOR

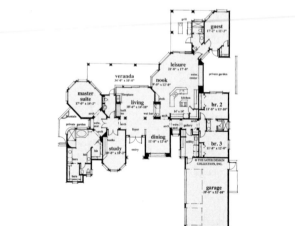

© The Sater Design Collection, Inc.

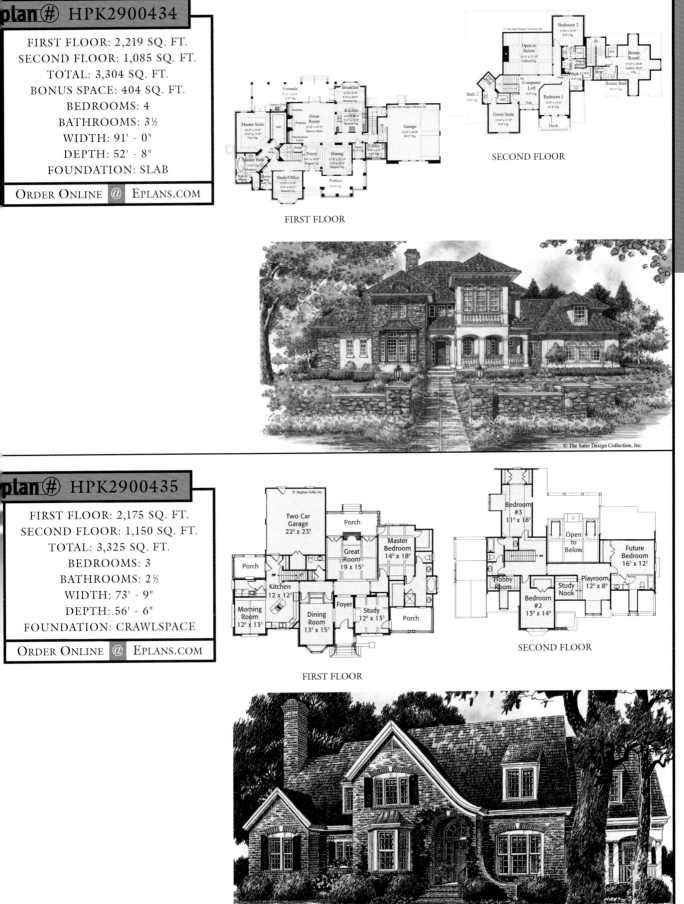

EUROPEAN COTTAGES & MANORS

plan # HPK2900434

FIRST FLOOR: 2,219 SQ. FT.
SECOND FLOOR: 1,085 SQ. FT.
TOTAL: 3,304 SQ. FT.
BONUS SPACE: 404 SQ. FT.
BEDROOMS: 4
BATHROOMS: 3½
WIDTH: 91' - 0"
DEPTH: 52' - 8"
FOUNDATION: SLAB

ORDER ONLINE @ EPLANS.COM

FIRST FLOOR

SECOND FLOOR

plan # HPK2900435

FIRST FLOOR: 2,175 SQ. FT.
SECOND FLOOR: 1,150 SQ. FT.
TOTAL: 3,325 SQ. FT.
BEDROOMS: 3
BATHROOMS: 2½
WIDTH: 73' - 9"
DEPTH: 56' - 6"
FOUNDATION: CRAWLSPACE

ORDER ONLINE @ EPLANS.COM

FIRST FLOOR

SECOND FLOOR

ORDER BLUEPRINTS ANYTIME AT EPLANS.COM OR 1-800-521-6797   377

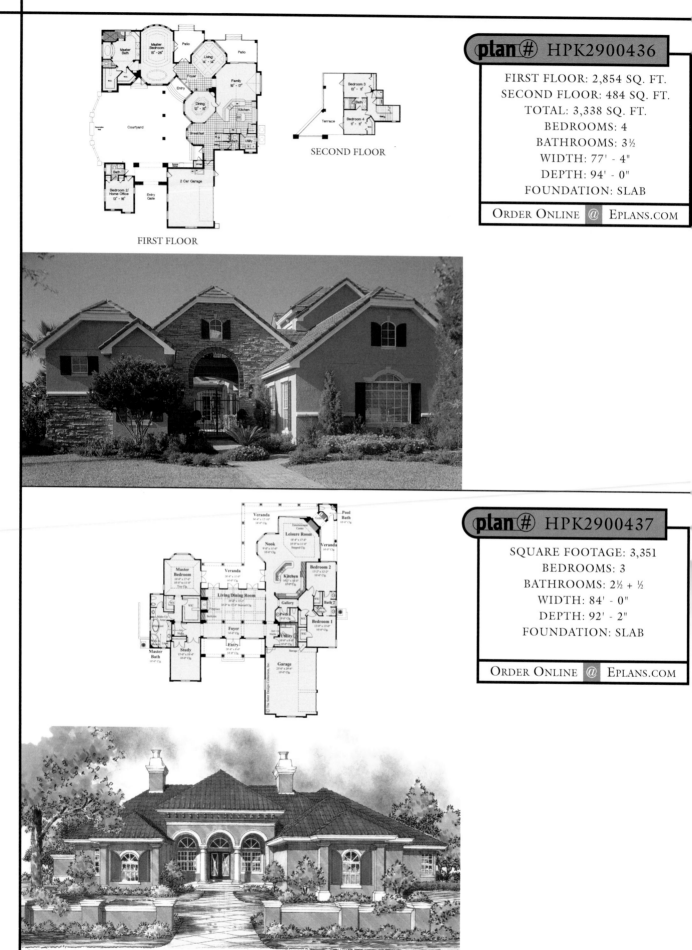

FIRST FLOOR

SECOND FLOOR

plan # HPK2900436

FIRST FLOOR: 2,854 SQ. FT.
SECOND FLOOR: 484 SQ. FT.
TOTAL: 3,338 SQ. FT.
BEDROOMS: 4
BATHROOMS: 3½
WIDTH: 77' - 4"
DEPTH: 94' - 0"
FOUNDATION: SLAB

ORDER ONLINE @ EPLANS.COM

plan # HPK2900437

SQUARE FOOTAGE: 3,351
BEDROOMS: 3
BATHROOMS: 2½ + ½
WIDTH: 84' - 0"
DEPTH: 92' - 2"
FOUNDATION: SLAB

ORDER ONLINE @ EPLANS.COM

plan # HPK2900438

FIRST FLOOR: 1,896 SQ. FT.
SECOND FLOOR: 1,500 SQ. FT.
TOTAL: 3,396 SQ. FT.
BEDROOMS: 4
BATHROOMS: 3
WIDTH: 66' - 6"
DEPTH: 52' - 3"
FOUNDATION: FINISHED
WALKOUT BASEMENT

ORDER ONLINE @ EPLANS.COM

This magnificent home reflects architectural elegance at its finest, executed in stucco and stone. Perhaps its most distinctive feature is the octagonal living room, which forms the focal point. Its attached dining room is bathed in natural light from a bay window. The island kitchen is nearby and has an attached octagonal breakfast room. The family room contains two sets of French doors and a fireplace. An optional room may be used for a guest room, music room, or study. The second floor holds two family bedrooms and a master suite with a sitting room. Additional storage space is located over the garage.

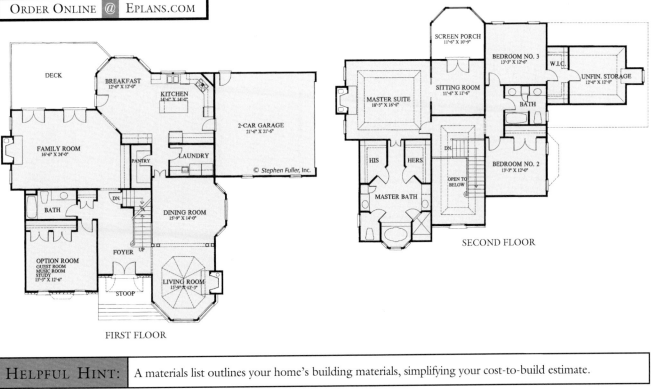

FIRST FLOOR

SECOND FLOOR

HELPFUL HINT: A materials list outlines your home's building materials, simplifying your cost-to-build estimate.

© William E. Poole Designs, Inc.

plan# HPK2900439

FIRST FLOOR: 2,216 SQ. FT.
SECOND FLOOR: 1,192 SQ. FT.
TOTAL: 3,408 SQ. FT.
BONUS SPACE: 458 SQ. FT.
BEDROOMS: 4
BATHROOMS: 3½
WIDTH: 67' - 10"
DEPTH: 56' - 10"
FOUNDATION: CRAWLSPACE

ORDER ONLINE @ EPLANS.COM

Signature Designer

Designer William Poole penned this charming, Old-World chateau to capture a life of ease. After enjoying a sumptuous meal in the breakfast or dining areas (both of which are convenient to the expansive kitchen), relax by a crackling fire in the generous family room. In the evening, retreat to the master suite—close at hand to the secondary stairway yet removed from the hustle and bustle of the main level.

FIRST FLOOR

SECOND FLOOR

plan# HPK2900440

FIRST FLOOR: 2,225 SQ. FT.
SECOND FLOOR: 1,225 SQ. FT.
TOTAL: 3,450 SQ. FT.
BEDROOMS: 4
BATHROOMS: 3½
WIDTH: 62' - 6"
DEPTH: 81' - 9"
FOUNDATION: FINISHED
WALKOUT BASEMENT

ORDER ONLINE @ EPLANS.COM

The drama of this home—through its use of multi-level hipped rooflines—is definitely European-inspired. A ribbon of windows decorates the facade and permits natural light to flow through the interior. The L-shaped foyer brings together the formal elements of the design with an open, casual living space and leads to a secluded master bedroom. This private retreat has a tray ceiling and a deluxe bath with a walk-in closet designed for two. On the second floor, two secondary bedrooms with a connecting bath open to a gallery hall that leads to a guest suite or fourth bedroom.

FIRST FLOOR

SECOND FLOOR

Quaint, yet majestic, this European-style stucco home has the enchantment of arched windows to underscore its charm. The two-story foyer leads through French doors to the study with its own hearth and coffered ceiling. Coupled with this cozy sanctuary is the master suite, which features a tray ceiling and large, accommodating bath. The sunken great room is highlighted by a fireplace, built-in bookcases, lots of glass, and easy access to a back stair and large gourmet kitchen. Three secondary bedrooms reside upstairs. One upstairs bedroom gives guests a private bath and walk-in closet.

FIRST FLOOR

SECOND FLOOR

plan # HPK2900442

FIRST FLOOR: 2,391 SQ. FT.
SECOND FLOOR: 1,071 SQ. FT.
TOTAL: 3,462 SQ. FT.
BONUS SPACE: 609 SQ. FT.
BEDROOMS: 3
BATHROOMS: 3½
WIDTH: 113' - 7"
DEPTH: 57' - 5"
FOUNDATION: CRAWLSPACE

ORDER ONLINE @ Eplans.com

If you've ever dreamed of living in a castle, this could be the home for you. The interior is fit for royalty, from the formal dining room to the multipurpose grand room to the comfortable sitting area off the kitchen. The master suite has its own fireplace, two walk-in closets, and a compartmented bath with dual vanities and a garden tub. Two stairways lead to the second floor; one, housed in the turret, leads to a sitting area and a balcony overlooking the grand room. The balcony leads to two more bedrooms and a recreation room (or apartment) with a deck.

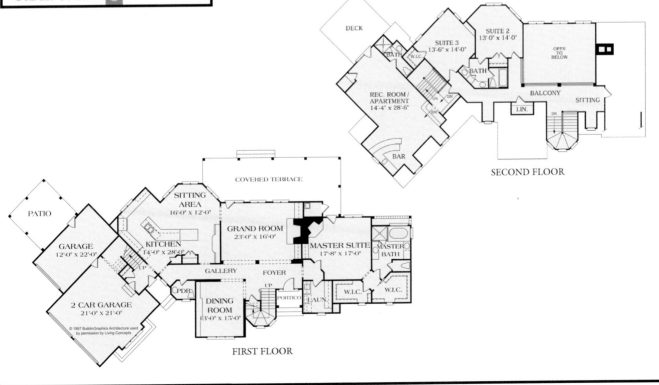

SECOND FLOOR

FIRST FLOOR

© The Sater Design Coll

A low-pitched hipped roof with bright eaves and decorative brackets bring undeniable European charm to this high-end design. The interior is a treasure trove of luxury amenities, such as the private garden just outside the master bathroom, to be enjoyed from the corner whirlpool bath. Similarly, a full-sized sitting area attends the master suite, which also has direct access to the rear lanai. At the heart of the plan, a huge living room with built-in shelves and a fireplace accomodates gatherings with family and friends. For larger affairs, a second living room and nook are located at the rear of the plan, near the kitchen. Overnight guests will appreciate their own suite and bath at the right, where two more bedrooms share a bath.

plan# HPK2900443

SQUARE FOOTAGE: 3,497
BEDROOMS: 4
BATHROOMS: 3½
WIDTH: 68' - 8"
DEPTH: 91' - 8"
FOUNDATION: SLAB

ORDER ONLINE @ EPLANS.COM

HELPFUL HINT: Eplans.com offers an Electrical Details set with residential electrical system information and diagrams.

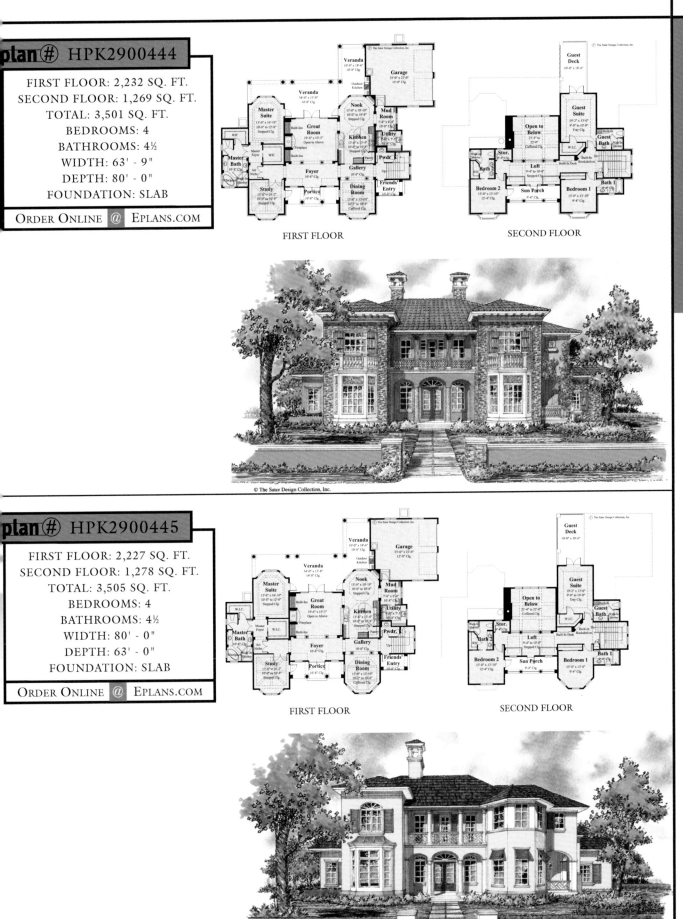

plan # HPK2900444

FIRST FLOOR: 2,232 SQ. FT.
SECOND FLOOR: 1,269 SQ. FT.
TOTAL: 3,501 SQ. FT.
BEDROOMS: 4
BATHROOMS: 4½
WIDTH: 63' - 9"
DEPTH: 80' - 0"
FOUNDATION: SLAB

ORDER ONLINE @ EPLANS.COM

FIRST FLOOR

SECOND FLOOR

© The Sater Design Collection, Inc.

plan # HPK2900445

FIRST FLOOR: 2,227 SQ. FT.
SECOND FLOOR: 1,278 SQ. FT.
TOTAL: 3,505 SQ. FT.
BEDROOMS: 4
BATHROOMS: 4½
WIDTH: 80' - 0"
DEPTH: 63' - 0"
FOUNDATION: SLAB

ORDER ONLINE @ EPLANS.COM

FIRST FLOOR

SECOND FLOOR

© The Sater Design Collection, Inc.

plan# HPK2900446

Old World charm gives this design its universal appeal. The mixture of stone and brick on the exterior elevation gives the home a warm, inviting feel. Inside, an up-to-date floor plan has it all. Two living areas provide space for both formal and informal entertaining. The kitchen and breakfast room are open to the large family room. The master suite and a secondary bedroom are located on the first floor. The second bedroom makes a great nursery, study, or convenient guest bedroom. Upstairs, Bedrooms 3 and 4 share a large bath including private dressing areas.

FIRST FLOOR: 2,518 SQ. FT.
SECOND FLOOR: 1,013 SQ. FT.
TOTAL: 3,531 SQ. FT.
BONUS SPACE: 192 SQ. FT.
BEDROOMS: 4
BATHROOMS: 3½
WIDTH: 67' - 8"
DEPTH: 74' - 2"
FOUNDATION: CRAWLSPACE, SLAB, UNFINISHED BASEMENT

ORDER ONLINE @ EPLANS.COM

FIRST FLOOR

SECOND FLOOR

plan # HPK2900447

SQUARE FOOTAGE: 3,556
BEDROOMS: 4
BATHROOMS: 3½
WIDTH: 85' - 0"
DEPTH: 85' - 0"
FOUNDATION: SLAB

ORDER ONLINE @ EPLANS.COM

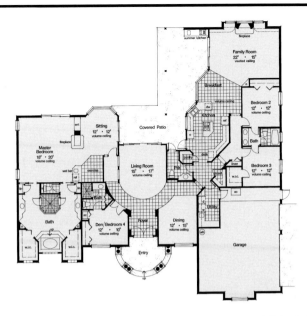

plan # HPK2900448

FIRST FLOOR: 1,900 SQ. FT.
SECOND FLOOR: 1,676 SQ. FT.
TOTAL: 3,576 SQ. FT.
BEDROOMS: 3
BATHROOMS: 3½
WIDTH: 67' - 0"
DEPTH: 82' - 6"
FOUNDATION: CRAWLSPACE

ORDER ONLINE @ EPLANS.COM

FIRST FLOOR

SECOND FLOOR

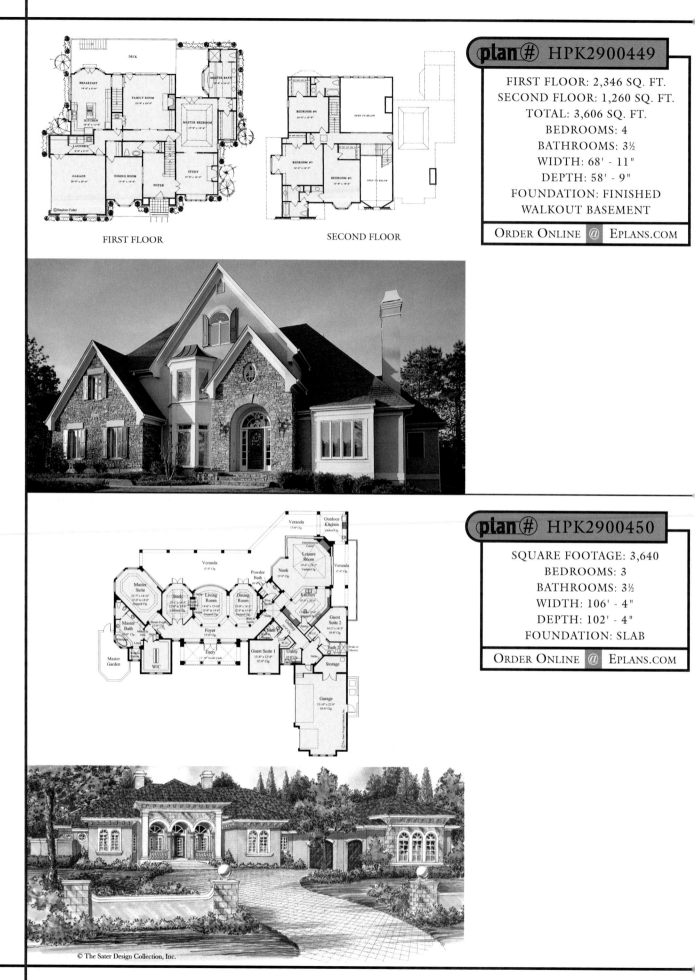

FIRST FLOOR

SECOND FLOOR

plan # HPK2900449

FIRST FLOOR: 2,346 SQ. FT.
SECOND FLOOR: 1,260 SQ. FT.
TOTAL: 3,606 SQ. FT.
BEDROOMS: 4
BATHROOMS: 3½
WIDTH: 68' - 11"
DEPTH: 58' - 9"
FOUNDATION: FINISHED
WALKOUT BASEMENT

ORDER ONLINE @ EPLANS.COM

plan # HPK2900450

SQUARE FOOTAGE: 3,640
BEDROOMS: 3
BATHROOMS: 3½
WIDTH: 106' - 4"
DEPTH: 102' - 4"
FOUNDATION: SLAB

ORDER ONLINE @ EPLANS.COM

plan # HPK2900451

FIRST FLOOR: 2,780 SQ. FT.
SECOND FLOOR: 878 SQ. FT.
TOTAL: 3,658 SQ. FT.
BEDROOMS: 4
BATHROOMS: 3
WIDTH: 68' - 3"
DEPTH: 89' - 1"
FOUNDATION: SLAB

ORDER ONLINE @ EPLANS.COM

The symmetrical front of this home conceals an imaginatively asymmetrical floor plan beyond. A keeping room, a sitting area in the master bedroom, and a second bedroom all jut out from this home, forming interesting angles and providing extra window space. Two fireplaces, a game room, a study, and His and Hers bathrooms in the master suite are interesting elements in this home. The bayed kitchen, with a walk-in pantry and a center island with room for seating, is sure to lure guests and family alike. The open floor plan and two-story ceilings in the family room add a contemporary touch.

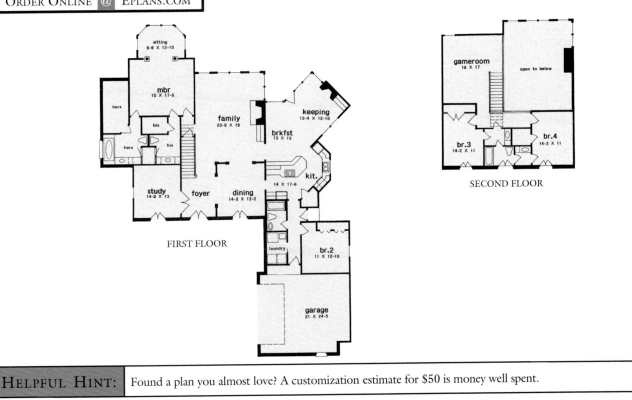

FIRST FLOOR

SECOND FLOOR

HELPFUL HINT: Found a plan you almost love? A customization estimate for $50 is money well spent.

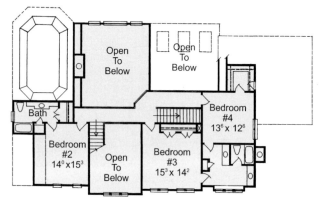

plan# HPK2900453

FIRST FLOOR: 2,495 SQ. FT.
SECOND FLOOR: 1,194 SQ. FT.
TOTAL: 3,689 SQ. FT.
BEDROOMS: 4
BATHROOMS: 3½
WIDTH: 77' - 8"
DEPTH: 50' - 8"
FOUNDATION: FINISHED
WALKOUT BASEMENT

ORDER ONLINE @ Eplans.com

Multipane glass windows, double French doors, and ornamental stucco detailing are complementary elements on the facade of this home. An impressive two-story foyer opens to the formal living and dining rooms. Natural light is available through the attractive windows in each room. The kitchen features a pass-through to the two-story family room and an adjoining skylit breakfast room. The first-floor master suite offers an elegant vaulted bedroom ceiling, a bath with twin vanities, a separate shower and tub, and two spacious walk-in closets. Upstairs, Bedroom 2 has its own bath and can be used as a guest suite. Two other bedrooms share a large bath that includes twin vanities.

SECOND FLOOR

FIRST FLOOR

plan # HPK2900452

FIRST FLOOR: 2,285 SQ. FT.
SECOND FLOOR: 1,395 SQ. FT.
TOTAL: 3,680 SQ. FT.
BONUS SPACE: 300 SQ. FT.
BEDROOMS: 3
BATHROOMS: 3½
WIDTH: 73' - 8"
DEPTH: 76' - 2"
FOUNDATION: SLAB

ORDER ONLINE @ EPLANS.COM

Now here is a one-of-a-kind house plan. Step down from the raised foyer into the grand gallery where columns define the living room. This central living area boasts an enormous bow window with a fantastic view to the covered patio. The formal dining room is to the right and the lavish master suite sits on the left. The family gourmet will find an expansive kitchen beyond a pair of French doors on the right. The secluded family room completes this first level. An enormous den is found on the first landing above, to the left of the foyer. Two bedroom suites and a loft occupy the second floor.

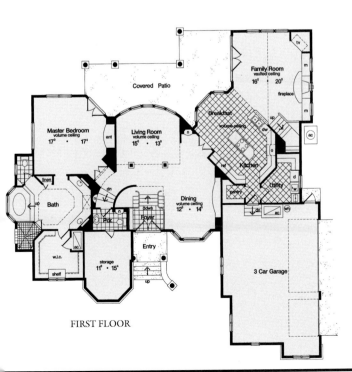

FIRST FLOOR

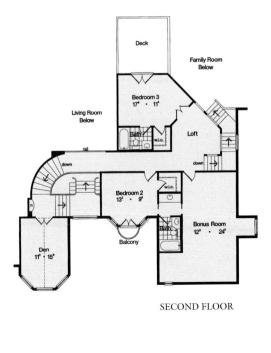

SECOND FLOOR

Whether you call it Provincial or French Country, this home is beautifully appointed with rustic detailing indigenous of rural homes found throughout Europe. The home's elevation centers on a two-story massing with a highly pitched-hipped roof. The architectural motif is carried throughout the home with the repeated arch pattern evident in the windows and recessed entry.

plan # HPK2900454

FIRST FLOOR: 2,569 SQ. FT.
SECOND FLOOR: 1,128 SQ. FT.
TOTAL: 3,697 SQ. FT.
BONUS SPACE: 339 SQ. FT.
BEDROOMS: 5
BATHROOMS: 4
WIDTH: 63' - 0"
DEPTH: 70' - 0"
FOUNDATION: UNFINISHED
WALKOUT BASEMENT

ORDER ONLINE @ EPLANS.COM

FIRST FLOOR

SECOND FLOOR

plan # HPK2900455

SQUARE FOOTAGE: 3,743
BEDROOMS: 4
BATHROOMS: 3½
WIDTH: 80' - 0"
DEPTH: 103' - 8"
FOUNDATION: SLAB

ORDER ONLINE @ EPLANS.COM

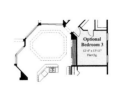

OPTIONAL LAYOUT

© The Sater Design Collection, Inc.

plan # HPK2900456

FIRST FLOOR: 2,852 SQ. FT.
SECOND FLOOR: 969 SQ. FT.
TOTAL: 3,821 SQ. FT.
BEDROOMS: 5
BATHROOMS: 4½
WIDTH: 80' - 0"
DEPTH: 96' - 0"
FOUNDATION: SLAB

ORDER ONLINE @ EPLANS.COM

FIRST FLOOR

SECOND FLOOR

© The Sater Design Collection, Inc.

© The Sater Design Collection, Inc.

FIRST FLOOR: 2,841 SQ. FT.
SECOND FLOOR: 1,052 SQ. FT.
TOTAL: 3,893 SQ. FT.
BEDROOMS: 4
BATHROOMS: 3½
WIDTH: 85' - 0"
DEPTH: 76' - 8"
FOUNDATION: SLAB

ORDER ONLINE @ EPLANS.COM

Ensure an elegant lifestyle with this luxurious plan. A turret, two-story bay windows, and plenty of arched glass impart a graceful style to the exterior, and rich amenities inside furnish contentment. A grand foyer decked with columns introduces the living room with curved-glass windows viewing the rear gardens. The study and living room share a through-fireplace. The master suite enjoys a tray ceiling, two walk-in closets, a separate shower, and a garden tub set in a bay window. Informal entertainment will be a breeze with a rich leisure room adjoining the kitchen and breakfast nook and opening to a rear veranda. Upstairs, two family bedrooms and a guest suite with a private deck complete the plan.

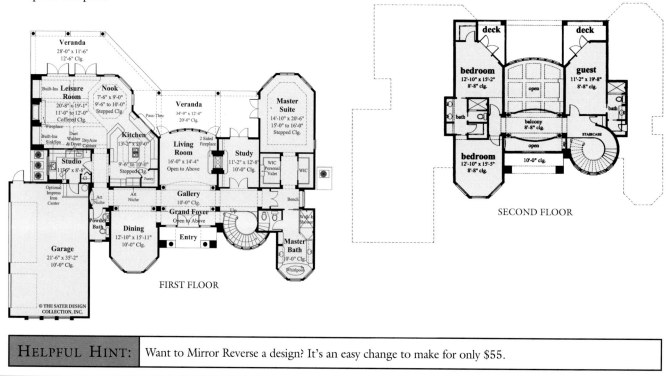

FIRST FLOOR

SECOND FLOOR

© THE SATER DESIGN COLLECTION, INC.

HELPFUL HINT: Want to Mirror Reverse a design? It's an easy change to make for only $55.

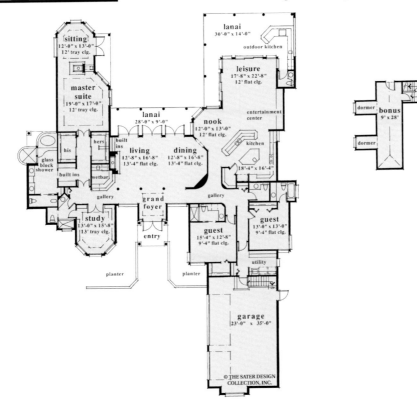

er Design Collection, Inc.

plan # HPK2900458

SQUARE FOOTAGE: 3,896
BONUS SPACE: 356 SQ. FT.
BEDROOMS: 3
BATHROOMS: 4½
WIDTH: 90' - 0"
DEPTH: 120' - 8"
FOUNDATION: SLAB

ORDER ONLINE @ EPLANS.COM

This elegant exterior blends a classical look with a contemporary feel. The formal living room, complete with a fireplace and a wet bar, and the formal dining room access the lanai through three pairs of French doors. The well-appointed kitchen features an island prep sink, a walk-in pantry, and a desk. The secondary bedrooms are full guest suites, located away from the master suite. This suite enjoys enormous His and Hers closets, built-ins, a wet bar, and a three-sided fireplace that separates the sitting room and the bedroom. The luxurious bath features a stunning rounded glass-block shower and a whirlpool tub.

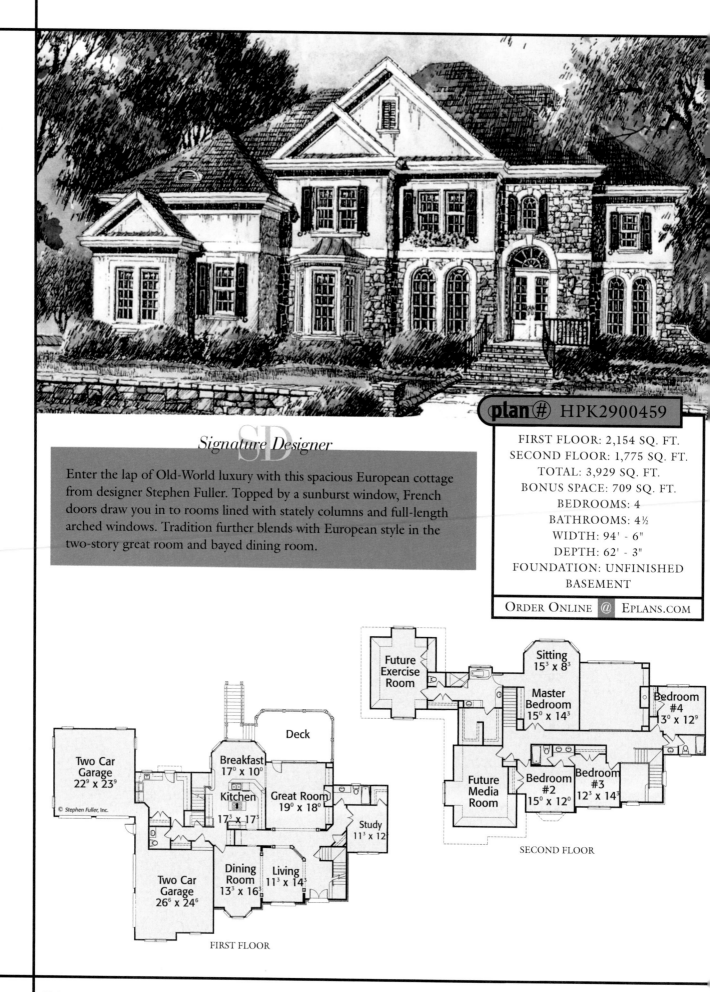

Signature Designer

Enter the lap of Old-World luxury with this spacious European cottage from designer Stephen Fuller. Topped by a sunburst window, French doors draw you in to rooms lined with stately columns and full-length arched windows. Tradition further blends with European style in the two-story great room and bayed dining room.

plan# HPK2900459

FIRST FLOOR: 2,154 SQ. FT.
SECOND FLOOR: 1,775 SQ. FT.
TOTAL: 3,929 SQ. FT.
BONUS SPACE: 709 SQ. FT.
BEDROOMS: 4
BATHROOMS: 4½
WIDTH: 94' - 6"
DEPTH: 62' - 3"
FOUNDATION: UNFINISHED BASEMENT

ORDER ONLINE @ EPLANS.COM

SECOND FLOOR

Future Exercise Room

Sitting 15³ x 8³

Master Bedroom 15⁰ x 14³

Bedroom #4 13⁰ x 12⁹

Future Media Room

Bedroom #2 15⁰ x 12⁰

Bedroom #3 12³ x 14³

FIRST FLOOR

Two Car Garage 22⁹ x 23⁹

Deck

Breakfast 17⁰ x 10⁰

Kitchen 17³ x 17³

Great Room 19⁰ x 18⁰

Study 11³ x 12

© Stephen Fuller, Inc.

Two Car Garage 26⁶ x 24⁶

Dining Room 13³ x 16⁶

Living 11³ x 14³

plan # HPK2900460

SQUARE FOOTAGE: 3,942

BEDROOMS: 3

BATHROOMS: 4

WIDTH: 83' - 10"

DEPTH: 106' - 0"

FOUNDATION: SLAB

ORDER ONLINE @ EPLANS.com

© The Sater Design Collection, Inc.

plan # HPK2900461

FIRST FLOOR: 2,829 SQ. FT.

SECOND FLOOR: 1,127 SQ. FT.

TOTAL: 3,956 SQ. FT.

BEDROOMS: 4

BATHROOMS: 3½

WIDTH: 85' - 0"

DEPTH: 76' - 8"

FOUNDATION: SLAB

ORDER ONLINE @ EPLANS.com

FIRST FLOOR

SECOND FLOOR

© The Sater Design Collection, Inc.

© The Sater Design Collection, Inc.

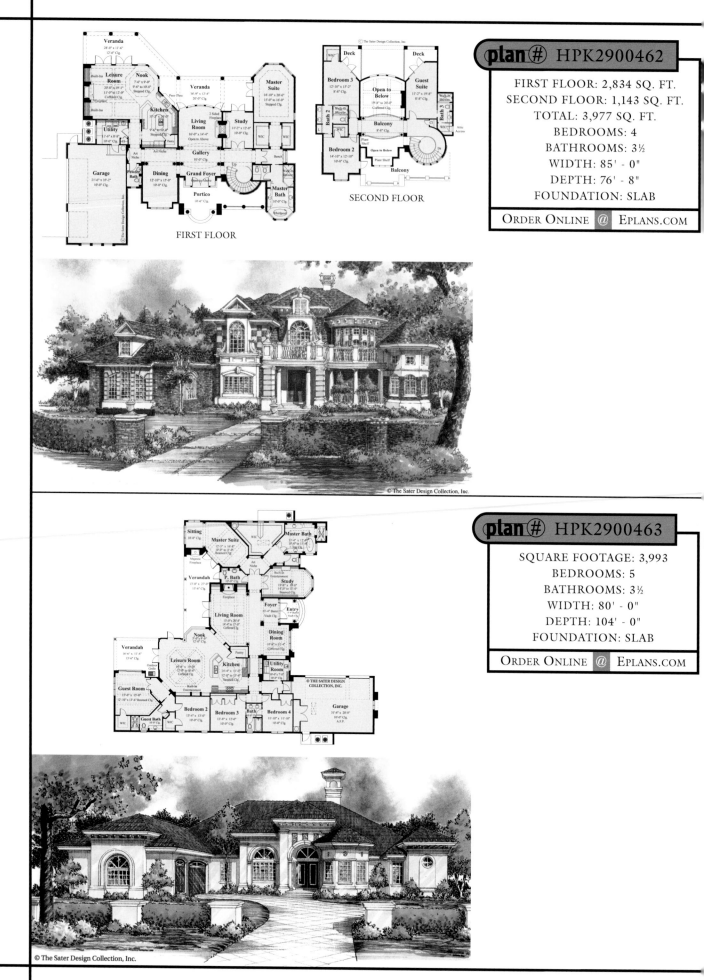

Veranda
28'-0" x 11'-6"
12'-6" Clg.

Leisure
Room
20'-6" x 19'-1"
12'-6" Clg.
Coffered Clg.

Nook
7'-6" x 9'-0"
9'-6" to 10'-0"
Stepped Clg.

Kitchen
9'-6" x 20'-0"

Utility
11'-6" x 8'-8"
10'-0" Clg.

Garage
21'-6" x 35'-2"
10'-0" Clg.

Powder
Bath

Dining
12'-10" x 15'-0"
10'-0" Clg.

Veranda
14'-0" x 12'-4"
20'-0" Clg.

Living
Room
16'-0" x 14'-4"
Open to Above

Gallery
10'-0" Clg.

Grand Foyer

Portico
10'-0" Clg.

Study
11'-2" x 17'-0"
10'-0" Clg.

Master
Suite
14'-0" x 16'-0"
13'-6" to 16'-0"
Stepped Clg.

WIC   WIC

Master
Bath

Whirlpool

FIRST FLOOR

Deck   Deck

Bedroom 3
12'-10" x 17'-2"
9'-4" Clg.

Bath
2

Bedroom 2
14'-10" x 12'-10"
10'-8" Clg.

Open to
Below
19'-4" x 20'-0"
Coffered Clg.

Balcony
8'-0" Clg.

Balcony

Guest
Suite
11'-2" x 19'-4"
8'-8" Clg.

Bath
3

Attic
Access

SECOND FLOOR

---

plan # HPK2900462

FIRST FLOOR: 2,834 SQ. FT.
SECOND FLOOR: 1,143 SQ. FT.
TOTAL: 3,977 SQ. FT.
BEDROOMS: 4
BATHROOMS: 3½
WIDTH: 85' - 0"
DEPTH: 76' - 8"
FOUNDATION: SLAB

ORDER ONLINE @ EPLANS.COM

Sitting
10'-0" Clg.

Master Suite
15'-4" x 16'-8"
10'-0" to 12'-0"
Beamed Clg.

WIC

Master Bath
13'-4" x 13'-4"
10'-0" Top Clg.

Art
Niche

Verandah
17'-0" x 17'-0"
13'-6" Clg.

P. Bath

Study
15'-4" x 15'-8"
14'-0" to 17'-0"
Beamed Clg.

Built-in
Entertainment

Living Room
15'-0" x 20'-0"
14'-4" to 17'-0"
Coffered Clg.

Foyer
17'-4" Barrel
Vault Clg.

Entry
17'-4" Barrel
Vault Clg.

Nook
8'-0" x 9'-0"
12'-0" Clg.

Pantry

Dining
Room
14'-0" x 16'-0"
Coffered Clg.

Verandah
16'-4" x 11'-4"
13'-6" Clg.

Leisure Room
16'-6" x 19'-0"
Coffered Clg.

Kitchen
14'-4" x 17'-4"
Stepped Clg.

Utility
Room
10'-0" x 11'-0"

Built-in
Entertainment

Guest Room
17'-6" x 15'-0"
12'-10" x 13'-6" Beamed Clg.

WIC   Guest Bath

Bedroom 2
13'-0" x 17'-0"
10'-0" Clg.

Bedroom 3
15'-4" x 13'-0"
10'-0" Clg.

Bath

Bedroom 4
14'-0" x 13'-0"
10'-0" Clg.

Garage
31'-4" x 20'-0"
10'-0" Clg.
A.F.F.

---

plan # HPK2900463

SQUARE FOOTAGE: 3,993
BEDROOMS: 5
BATHROOMS: 3½
WIDTH: 80' - 0"
DEPTH: 104' - 0"
FOUNDATION: SLAB

ORDER ONLINE @ EPLANS.COM

plan# HPK2900464

FIRST FLOOR: 2,901 SQ. FT.
SECOND FLOOR: 1,140 SQ. FT.
TOTAL: 4,041 SQ. FT.
BONUS SPACE: 522 SQ. FT.
BEDROOMS: 4
BATHROOMS: 4½
WIDTH: 80' - 0"
DEPTH: 70' - 0"
FOUNDATION: FINISHED
WALKOUT BASEMENT

ORDER ONLINE @ EPLANS.COM

This stately Chateauesque home is as magnificent inside as its exterior would suggest. Columns throughout the home are well placed to draw out the spacious grandeur of this plan. The heavenly master suite is a fairy tale come true. His and Hers walk-in closets, a sitting room with a fireplace, and French-door access to the rear veranda guarantee comfort; the extraordinary bath, complete with a huge tub set in a bay overlooking gardens, is sure to pamper. A circular breakfast bay enjoys views of the veranda and the loggia. Upstairs, three bedrooms come with separate lavish baths. Additional space is available to add a guest apartment. A sunken floor separates the downstairs front library from other rooms.

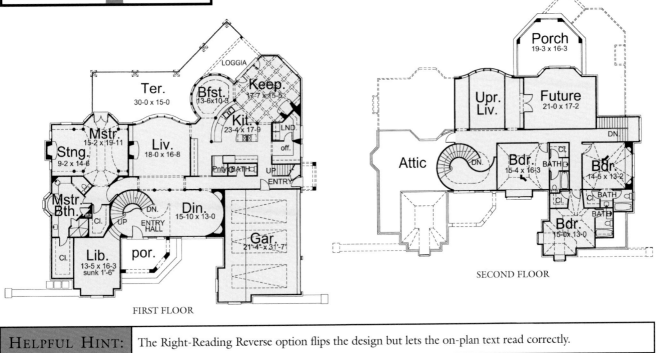

FIRST FLOOR

SECOND FLOOR

HELPFUL HINT: The Right-Reading Reverse option flips the design but lets the on-plan text read correctly.

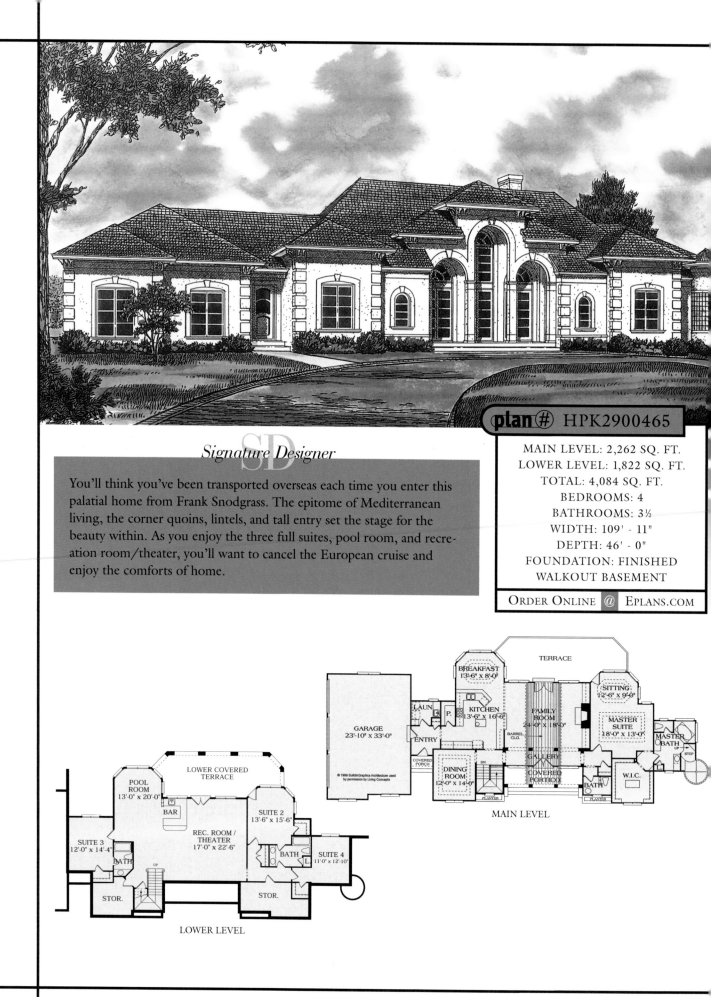

Signature Designer

You'll think you've been transported overseas each time you enter this palatial home from Frank Snodgrass. The epitome of Mediterranean living, the corner quoins, lintels, and tall entry set the stage for the beauty within. As you enjoy the three full suites, pool room, and recreation room/theater, you'll want to cancel the European cruise and enjoy the comforts of home.

plan# HPK2900465

MAIN LEVEL: 2,262 SQ. FT.
LOWER LEVEL: 1,822 SQ. FT.
TOTAL: 4,084 SQ. FT.
BEDROOMS: 4
BATHROOMS: 3½
WIDTH: 109' - 11"
DEPTH: 46' - 0"
FOUNDATION: FINISHED
WALKOUT BASEMENT

ORDER ONLINE @ Eplans.com

plan# HPK2900466

FIRST FLOOR: 2,340 SQ. FT.
SECOND FLOOR: 1,806 SQ. FT.
TOTAL: 4,146 SQ. FT.
BONUS SPACE: 384 SQ. FT.
BEDROOMS: 4
BATHROOMS: 4½
WIDTH: 117' - 6"
DEPTH: 74' - 5"
FOUNDATION: SLAB,
FINISHED WALKOUT
BASEMENT

ORDER ONLINE @ EPLANS.COM

Full of amenities, this country estate includes a media room and a study. The two-story great room is perfect for formal entertaining. Family and friends will enjoy gathering in the large kitchen, the hearth room, and the breakfast room. The luxurious master suite is located upstairs. Two family bedrooms share a bath that includes dressing areas for both, while another bedroom features a private bath. The rear stair is complete with a dumbwaiter, which goes down to a walkout basement where you'll find an enormous workshop, a game room, and a hobby room.

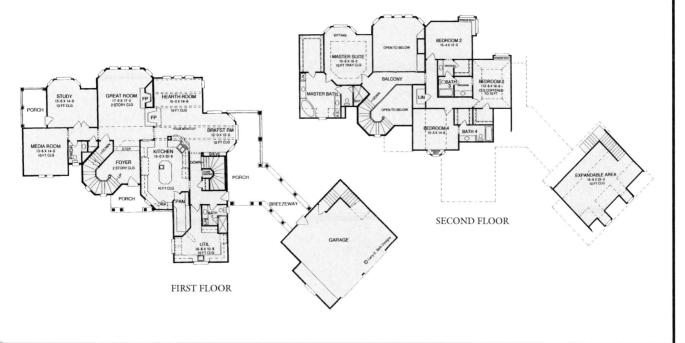

FIRST FLOOR

SECOND FLOOR

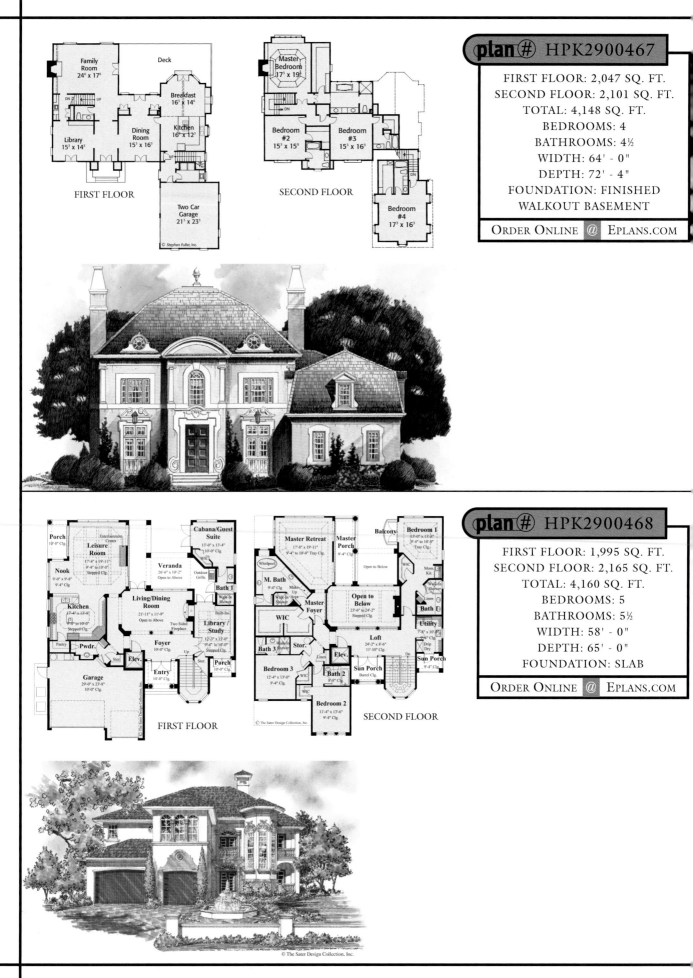

FIRST FLOOR

Family Room
24⁶ x 17⁶

Deck

Breakfast
16⁵ x 14⁶

Kitchen
16⁵ x 12⁵

Library
15⁵ x 14⁵

Dining Room
15⁵ x 16⁵

Two Car Garage
21⁵ x 23⁵

© Stephen Fuller, Inc.

SECOND FLOOR

Master Bedroom
17⁵ x 19⁵

Bedroom #2
15⁵ x 15⁹

Bedroom #3
15⁵ x 16⁵

Bedroom #4
17⁵ x 16⁵

plan # HPK2900467

FIRST FLOOR: 2,047 SQ. FT.
SECOND FLOOR: 2,101 SQ. FT.
TOTAL: 4,148 SQ. FT.
BEDROOMS: 4
BATHROOMS: 4½
WIDTH: 64' - 0"
DEPTH: 72' - 4"
FOUNDATION: FINISHED WALKOUT BASEMENT

ORDER ONLINE @ EPLANS.COM

FIRST FLOOR

Porch
10'-0" Clg.

Leisure Room
17'-8" x 19'-11"
9'-4" to 10'-0" Stepped Clg.

Cabana/Guest Suite
17'-0" x 13'-4"
10'-0" Clg.

Nook
9'-0" x 9'-8"
9'-4" Clg.

Veranda
26'-6" x 10'-2"
Open to Above

Outdoor Grille

Kitchen
17'-4" x 13'-4"
9'-4" to 10'-0" Stepped Clg.

Bath 1
Walk-In Shower

Living/Dining Room
21'-11" x 11'-9"
Open to Above

Pantry

Pwdr.

Two Sided Fireplace

Built-Ins

Library/Study
12'-3" x 13'-0"
9'-4" to 10'-0" Stepped Clg.

Foyer
10'-0" Clg.

Elev.

Stor.

Entry
10'-0" Clg.

Garage
29'-0" x 23'-8"
10'-0" Clg.

Stor.

Porch
10'-0" Clg.

© The Sater Design Collection, Inc.

SECOND FLOOR

Master Retreat
17'-8" x 19'-11"
9'-4" to 10'-0" Tray Clg.

Master Porch
9'-4" Clg.

Balcony

Bedroom 1
13'-0" x 13'-2"
9'-4" to 10'-0" Tray Clg.

Whirlpool

M. Bath
9'-4" Clg.

Make-Up

Walk-In Area Shower

WIC

Master Foyer

Open to Below
23'-6" x 24'-2"
Stepped Clg.

Open to Below

Morn. Kit.

Walk-In Shower

Linen

Bath 1

Utility
7'-8" x 10'-2"
9'-4" Clg.

Drip Dry

Loft
24'-2" x 8'-6"
11'-0" Clg.

Bath 3
Walk-In Shower

Stor.

Bedroom 3
12'-4" x 13'-0"
9'-4" Clg.

Elev.

Linen

Bath 2
8'-8" Clg.

WIC

WIC

Sun Porch
Barrel Clg.

Sun Porch
9'-4" Clg.

Dn.

Bedroom 2
11'-4" x 13'-6"
9'-4" Clg.

© The Sater Design Collection, Inc.

plan # HPK2900468

FIRST FLOOR: 1,995 SQ. FT.
SECOND FLOOR: 2,165 SQ. FT.
TOTAL: 4,160 SQ. FT.
BEDROOMS: 5
BATHROOMS: 5½
WIDTH: 58' - 0"
DEPTH: 65' - 0"
FOUNDATION: SLAB

ORDER ONLINE @ EPLANS.COM

© The Sater Design Collection, Inc.

plan # HPK2900469

FIRST FLOOR: 2,042 SQ. FT.
SECOND FLOOR: 2,137 SQ. FT.
TOTAL: 4,179 SQ. FT.
BEDROOMS: 5
BATHROOMS: 4
WIDTH: 63' - 0"
DEPTH: 66' - 0"
FOUNDATION: UNFINISHED
WALKOUT BASEMENT

ORDER ONLINE @ EPLANS.COM

Quaint and traditional, this home features natural and informal materials, which add to its charm. The height of the elevation lends a stately presence to the entire home. Inside, formal living and dining areas flank the foyer. The great room is warmed by a fireplace and overlooks the rear porch. The gourmet island kitchen is thoughtfully placed between the dining room and the vaulted breakfast/sun room. A laundry room is conveniently located on the second floor. The master bedroom is divine, warmed by a fireplace in the master sitting area. A private second-floor porch, the master bath, and His and Hers walk-in closets add even more pampering elements.

FIRST FLOOR

SECOND FLOOR

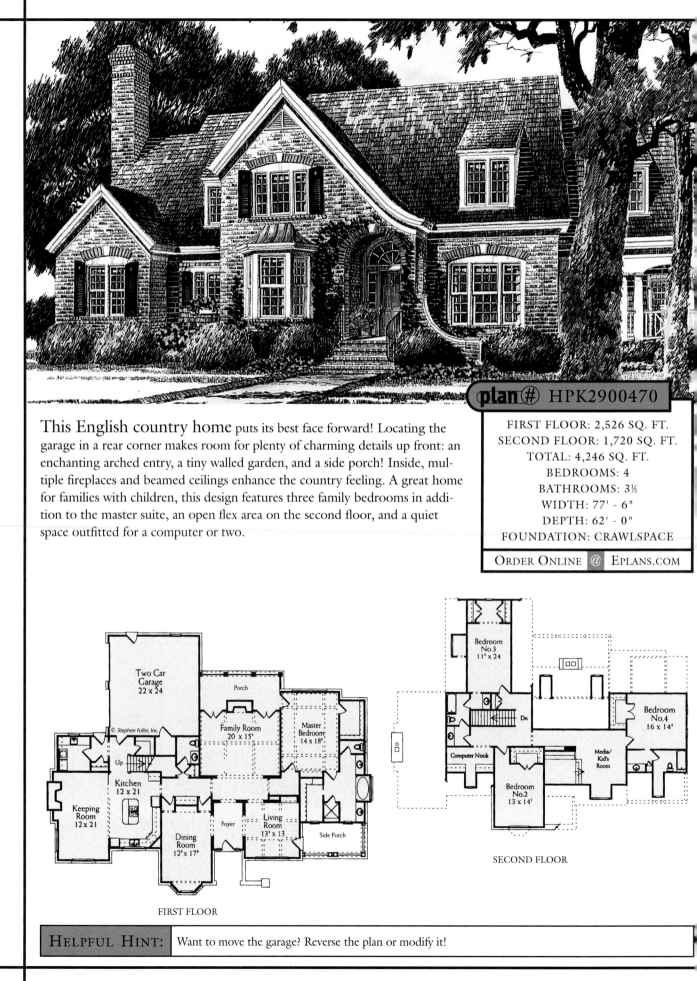

This English country home puts its best face forward! Locating the garage in a rear corner makes room for plenty of charming details up front: an enchanting arched entry, a tiny walled garden, and a side porch! Inside, multiple fireplaces and beamed ceilings enhance the country feeling. A great home for families with children, this design features three family bedrooms in addition to the master suite, an open flex area on the second floor, and a quiet space outfitted for a computer or two.

plan # HPK2900470

FIRST FLOOR: 2,526 SQ. FT.
SECOND FLOOR: 1,720 SQ. FT.
TOTAL: 4,246 SQ. FT.
BEDROOMS: 4
BATHROOMS: 3½
WIDTH: 77' - 6"
DEPTH: 62' - 0"
FOUNDATION: CRAWLSPACE

ORDER ONLINE @ EPLANS.COM

FIRST FLOOR

SECOND FLOOR

HELPFUL HINT: Want to move the garage? Reverse the plan or modify it!

plan # HPK2900471

FIRST FLOOR: 2,161 SQ. FT.
SECOND FLOOR: 2,110 SQ. FT.
TOTAL: 4,271 SQ. FT.
BEDROOMS: 4
BATHROOMS: 3½
WIDTH: 76' - 2"
DEPTH: 60' - 11"
FOUNDATION: FINISHED
WALKOUT BASEMENT

ORDER ONLINE @ EPLANS.COM

A blend of stucco and stone creates the charm in this French Country estate home. The asymmetrical design and arched glass windows add to the European character. Inside, the plan offers a unique arrangement of rooms conducive to today's lifestyles. A living room and a dining room flank the foyer, creating a functional formal area. The large den or family room is positioned at the rear of the home with convenient access to the kitchen, patio, and covered arbor. Equally accessible to the arbor and patio are the kitchen and breakfast/sitting area. A large butler's pantry is located near the kitchen and dining room. Upstairs, the vaulted master suite and three large bedrooms provide private retreats.

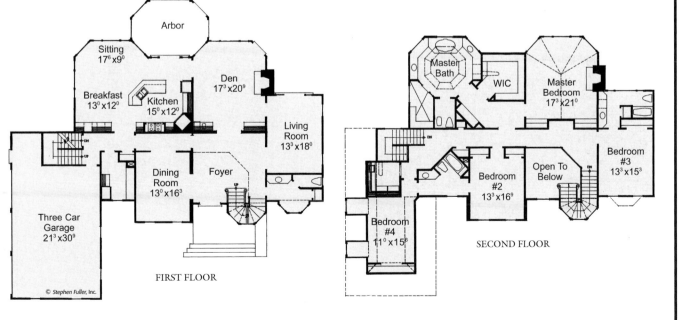

FIRST FLOOR

SECOND FLOOR

© Stephen Fuller, Inc.

This magnificent home captures the charm of French Country design with its high hipped roof and brick detailing. Inside, the two-story foyer leads directly to the spacious great room with a fireplace and three sets of double doors to the rear porch. The formal dining room sits to the left of the foyer and is near the L-shaped kitchen, which serves a bright breakfast room. The main-floor master suite takes the entire right wing of the house and includes a large sitting area with porch access and an opulent bath. Upstairs, a gallery hall leads to a media room, three more bedrooms (each with a private bath), and a bonus room over the garage.

FIRST FLOOR: 2,844 SQ. FT.
SECOND FLOOR: 1,443 SQ. FT.
TOTAL: 4,287 SQ. FT.
BONUS SPACE: 360 SQ. FT.
BEDROOMS: 4
BATHROOMS: 4½
WIDTH: 72' - 0"
DEPTH: 78' - 6"
FOUNDATION: UNFINISHED
WALKOUT BASEMENT

ORDER ONLINE @ EPLANS.COM

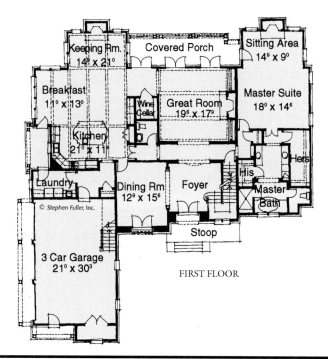

FIRST FLOOR

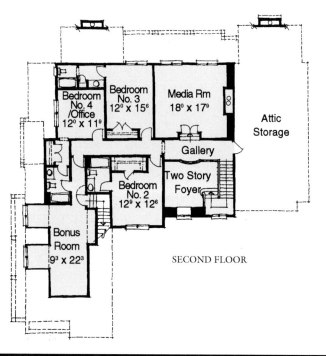

SECOND FLOOR

plan # HPK2900473

FIRST FLOOR: 2,263 SQ. FT.
SECOND FLOOR: 2,100 SQ. FT.
TOTAL: 4,363 SQ. FT.
BEDROOMS: 4
BATHROOMS: 4½ + ½
WIDTH: 67' - 2"
DEPTH: 77' - 0"
FOUNDATION: FINISHED
WALKOUT BASEMENT

ORDER ONLINE @ EPLANS.COM

As elegant and luxurious on the interior as it appears from the facade, this lovely French manor exceeds the notion of luxury. Enter to the formal foyer; to the left, a study leads through to the vast hearth-warmed great room. Toward the rear, a sunroom with outdoor access fills the home with natural light. The gourmet kitchen, with an L-shaped island cooktop, effortlessly serves the breakfast area and grand dining room. The upper level is designed for privacy; the main staircase leads to two bedroom suites and the magnificent master suite. Here, a fireplace and private terrace are romantic embellishments. The lavish bath holds a vaulted bay with a whirlpool tub. Near the first-floor utility rooms, a second stair yields a separate three-dormered suite, perfect for guests or college students.

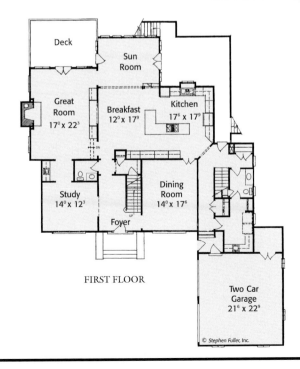

FIRST FLOOR

© Stephen Fuller, Inc.

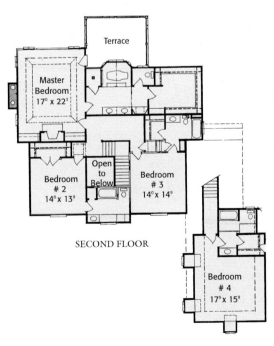

SECOND FLOOR

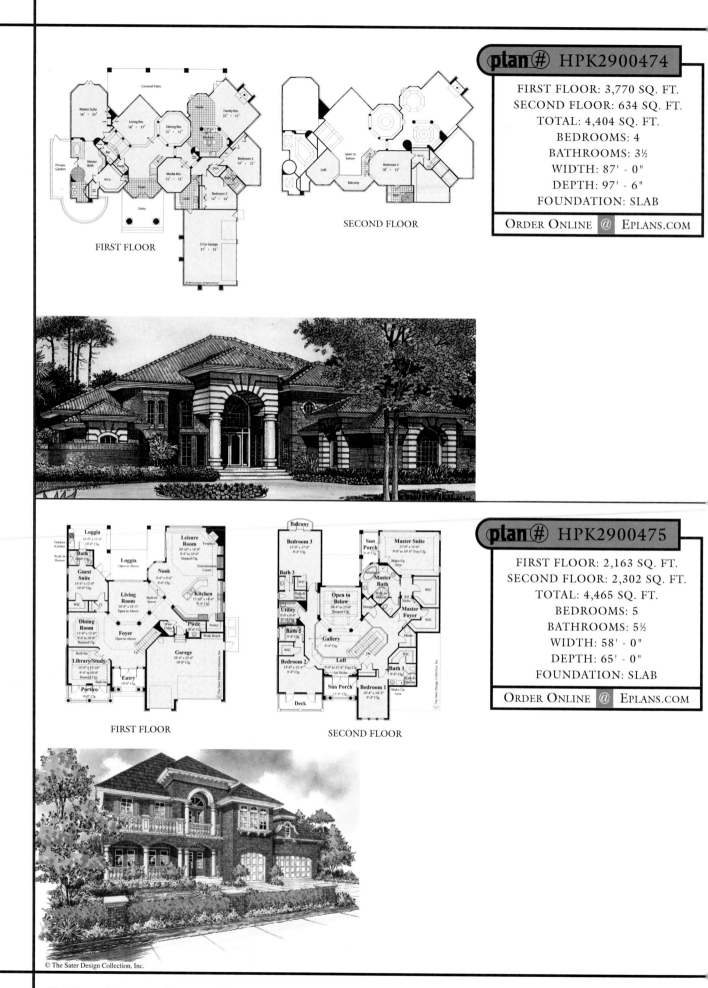

FIRST FLOOR

SECOND FLOOR

plan# HPK2900474

FIRST FLOOR: 3,770 SQ. FT.
SECOND FLOOR: 634 SQ. FT.
TOTAL: 4,404 SQ. FT.
BEDROOMS: 4
BATHROOMS: 3½
WIDTH: 87' - 0"
DEPTH: 97' - 6"
FOUNDATION: SLAB

ORDER ONLINE @ EPLANS.COM

FIRST FLOOR

SECOND FLOOR

plan# HPK2900475

FIRST FLOOR: 2,163 SQ. FT.
SECOND FLOOR: 2,302 SQ. FT.
TOTAL: 4,465 SQ. FT.
BEDROOMS: 5
BATHROOMS: 5½
WIDTH: 58' - 0"
DEPTH: 65' - 0"
FOUNDATION: SLAB

ORDER ONLINE @ EPLANS.COM

© The Sater Design Collection, Inc.

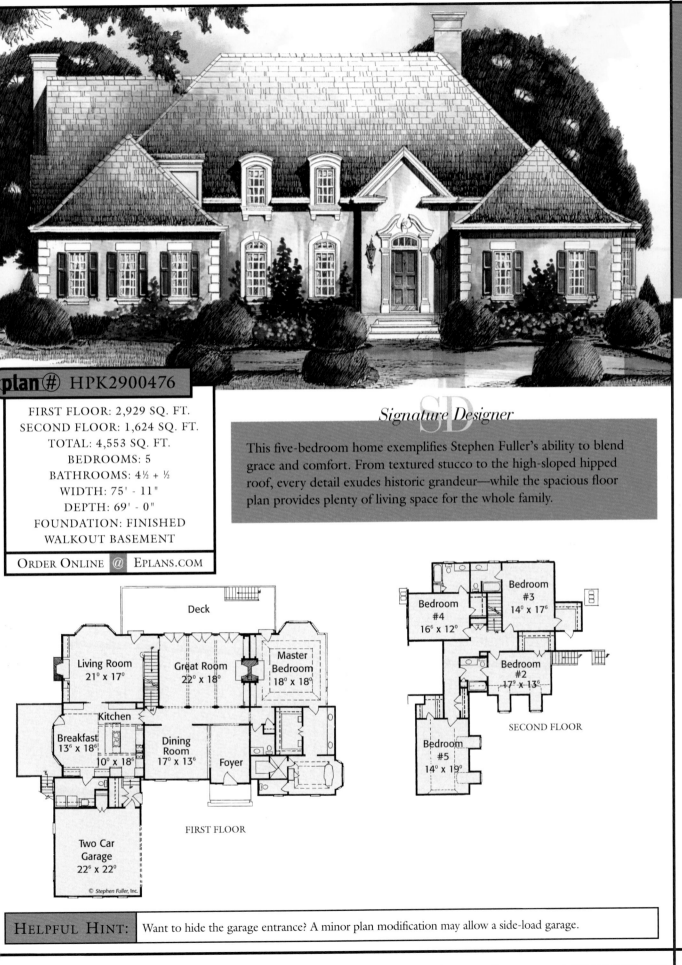

plan # HPK2900476

FIRST FLOOR: 2,929 SQ. FT.
SECOND FLOOR: 1,624 SQ. FT.
TOTAL: 4,553 SQ. FT.
BEDROOMS: 5
BATHROOMS: 4½ + ½
WIDTH: 75' - 11"
DEPTH: 69' - 0"
FOUNDATION: FINISHED
WALKOUT BASEMENT

ORDER ONLINE @ EPLANS.COM

Signature **SD** *Designer*

This five-bedroom home exemplifies Stephen Fuller's ability to blend grace and comfort. From textured stucco to the high-sloped hipped roof, every detail exudes historic grandeur—while the spacious floor plan provides plenty of living space for the whole family.

Deck

Living Room
21⁰ x 17⁰

Great Room
22⁰ x 18⁰

Master Bedroom
18⁰ x 18⁰

Kitchen

Breakfast
13⁶ x 18⁶

Dining Room
17⁰ x 13⁶

10⁰ x 18⁶

Foyer

Two Car Garage
22⁶ x 22⁰

© Stephen Fuller, Inc.

FIRST FLOOR

Bedroom #4
16⁶ x 12⁰

Bedroom #3
14⁰ x 17⁶

Bedroom #2
17⁹ x 13⁶

Bedroom #5
14⁰ x 19⁰

SECOND FLOOR

HELPFUL HINT: Want to hide the garage entrance? A minor plan modification may allow a side-load garage.

This majestic storybook cottage, from the magical setting of rural Europe, provides the perfect home for any large family--with a wealth of modern comforts within. A graceful staircase cascades from the two-story foyer. To the left, a sophisticated study offers a wall of built-ins. To the right, a formal dining room is easily served from the island kitchen. The breakfast room accesses the rear screened porch. Fireplaces warm the great room and keeping room. Two sets of double doors open from the great room to the rear covered porch. The master bedroom features private porch access, a sitting area, lavish bath, and two walk-in closets. Upstairs, three additional family bedrooms offer walk-in closet space galore! The game room is great entertainment for both family and friends. A three-car garage with golf-cart storage completes the plan.

FIRST FLOOR: 3,033 SQ. FT.
SECOND FLOOR: 1,545 SQ. FT.
TOTAL: 4,578 SQ. FT.
BEDROOMS: 4
BATHROOMS: 3½ + ½
WIDTH: 91' - 6"
DEPTH: 63' - 8"
FOUNDATION: CRAWLSPACE, SLAB, UNFINISHED BASEMENT

ORDER ONLINE @ EPLANS.COM

SECOND FLOOR

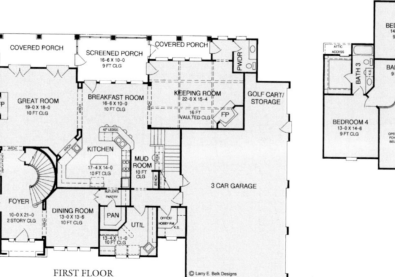

FIRST FLOOR

plan # HPK2900478

FIRST FLOOR: 2,923 SQ. FT.
SECOND FLOOR: 1,689 SQ. FT.
TOTAL: 4,612 SQ. FT.
BEDROOMS: 4
BATHROOMS: 3½ + ½
WIDTH: 75' - 6"
DEPTH: 58' - 4"
FOUNDATION: FINISHED
WALKOUT BASEMENT

ORDER ONLINE @ EPLANS.COM

Symmetry combined with classical French detailing proclaims this estate as the very finest in elegant architecture. The double-door entry opens to an equally magnificent floor plan. Designed on the traditional center-hall principle, the home sustains both grand formal spaces and uniquely intimate casual areas. The study connects directly to the master suite, but also is accessed directly from the foyer—making it a fine home office. The stately living room features built-ins, a raised hearth, and outdoor access. For convenience, the master suite remains on the first floor. Elegant beyond compare, it spotlights a tray ceiling, His and Hers closets, and a resplendent master bath. Family bedrooms are upstairs, along with a handy media room.

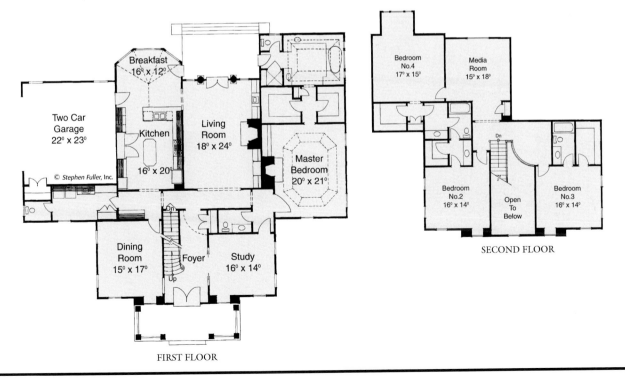

FIRST FLOOR

SECOND FLOOR

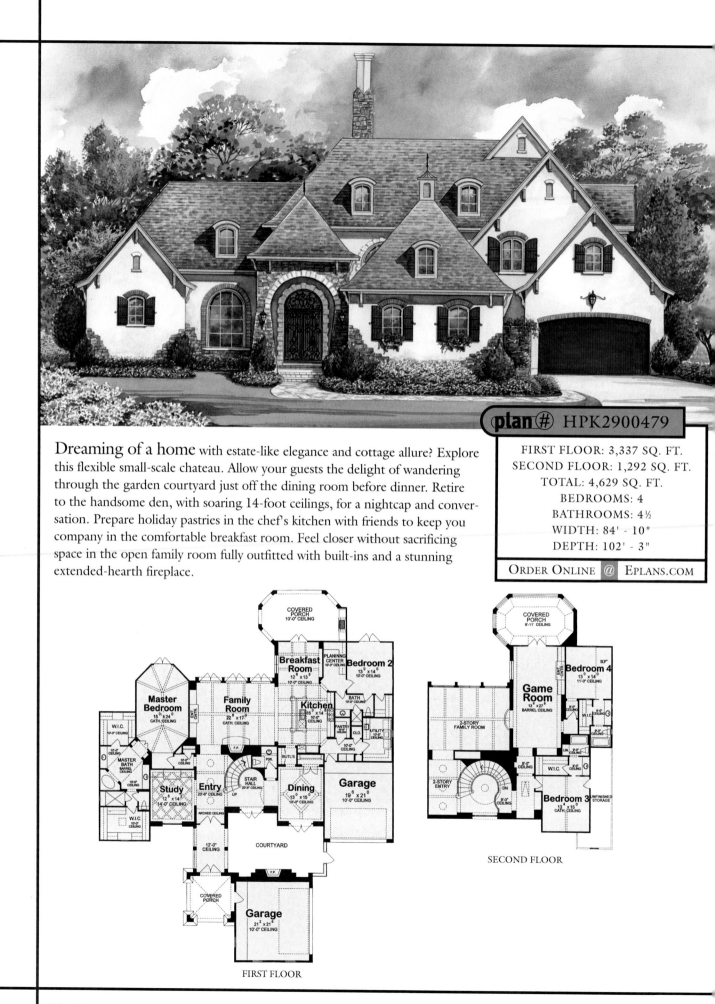

Dreaming of a home with estate-like elegance and cottage allure? Explore this flexible small-scale chateau. Allow your guests the delight of wandering through the garden courtyard just off the dining room before dinner. Retire to the handsome den, with soaring 14-foot ceilings, for a nightcap and conversation. Prepare holiday pastries in the chef's kitchen with friends to keep you company in the comfortable breakfast room. Feel closer without sacrificing space in the open family room fully outfitted with built-ins and a stunning extended-hearth fireplace.

plan# HPK2900479

FIRST FLOOR: 3,337 SQ. FT.
SECOND FLOOR: 1,292 SQ. FT.
TOTAL: 4,629 SQ. FT.
BEDROOMS: 4
BATHROOMS: 4½
WIDTH: 84' - 10"
DEPTH: 102' - 3"

ORDER ONLINE @ EPLANS.COM

FIRST FLOOR

SECOND FLOOR

plan # HPK2900480

FIRST FLOOR: 3,296 SQ. FT.
SECOND FLOOR: 1,517 SQ. FT.
TOTAL: 4,813 SQ. FT.
BEDROOMS: 4
BATHROOMS: 4½ + ½
WIDTH: 86' - 9"
DEPTH: 56' - 9"
FOUNDATION: FINISHED
WALKOUT BASEMENT

ORDER ONLINE @ EPLANS.COM

Classic detailing and a regal entrance design give this home its traditional and timeless style. Inside the house is a grand exhibition of large, open, and flowing rooms. Functional in many respects, the open living areas of this home make entertaining easy. The master suite, secluded in its own wing, offers amenities such as a roomy dressing area with flanking walk-in closets and a sitting room with picturesque views of the back property. Upstairs are three large bedrooms, each with a private bath and a large closet.

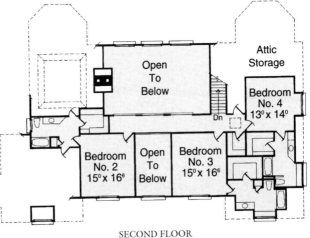

SECOND FLOOR

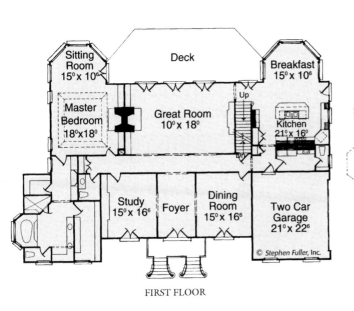

FIRST FLOOR

© Stephen Fuller, Inc.

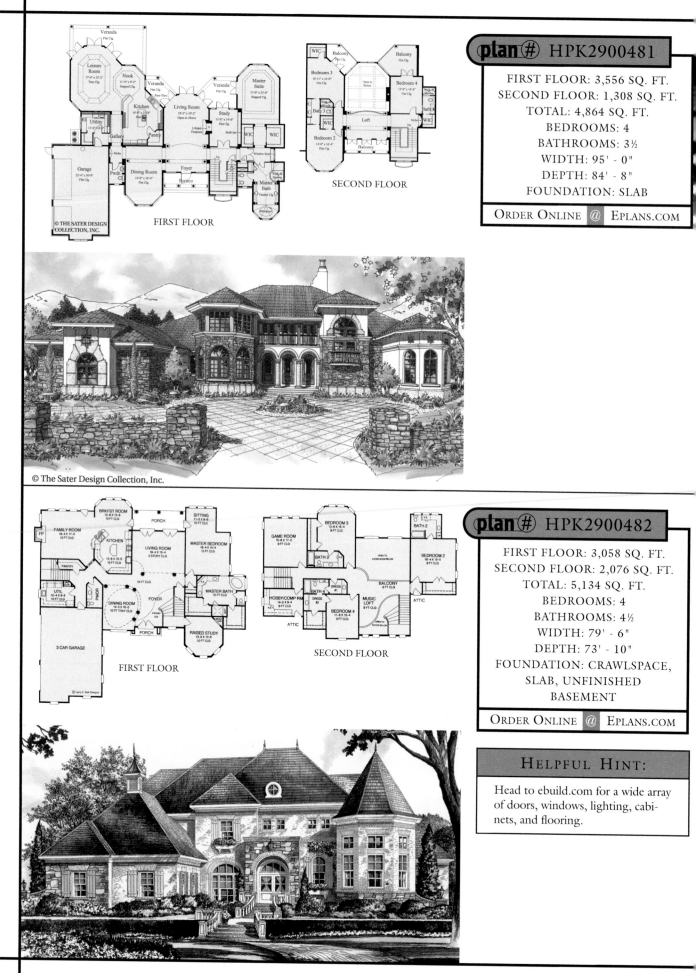

plan # HPK2900481

FIRST FLOOR: 3,556 SQ. FT.
SECOND FLOOR: 1,308 SQ. FT.
TOTAL: 4,864 SQ. FT.
BEDROOMS: 4
BATHROOMS: 3½
WIDTH: 95' - 0"
DEPTH: 84' - 8"
FOUNDATION: SLAB

ORDER ONLINE @ EPLANS.COM

FIRST FLOOR

SECOND FLOOR

© The Sater Design Collection, Inc.

plan # HPK2900482

FIRST FLOOR: 3,058 SQ. FT.
SECOND FLOOR: 2,076 SQ. FT.
TOTAL: 5,134 SQ. FT.
BEDROOMS: 4
BATHROOMS: 4½
WIDTH: 79' - 6"
DEPTH: 73' - 10"
FOUNDATION: CRAWLSPACE,
SLAB, UNFINISHED
BASEMENT

ORDER ONLINE @ EPLANS.COM

HELPFUL HINT:

Head to ebuild.com for a wide array of doors, windows, lighting, cabinets, and flooring.

FIRST FLOOR

SECOND FLOOR

plan# HPK2900483

MAIN LEVEL: 2,959 SQ. FT.
SECOND LEVEL: 1,055 SQ. FT.
LOWER LEVEL: 1,270 SQ. FT.
TOTAL: 5,284 SQ. FT.
BEDROOMS: 4
BATHROOMS: 5½
WIDTH: 110' - 4"
DEPTH: 72' - 5"
FOUNDATION: SLAB,
FINISHED WALKOUT
BASEMENT

ORDER ONLINE @ EPLANS.COM

Designed for a sloping lot, this fantastic Mediterranean home features all the views to the backyard, making it the perfect home for an ocean, lake, or golf-course view. Inside, the great room features a rear wall of windows. The breakfast room, kitchen, dining room, and master suite also feature rear views. A three-level series of porches is located on the back for outdoor relaxing. Two bedroom suites are found upstairs, each with a private bath and a porch. The basement of this home features another bedroom suite and a large game room. An expandable area can be used as an office or fifth bedroom.

SECOND LEVEL

MAIN LEVEL

LOWER LEVEL

© The Sater Design Collecti

plan # HPK2900484

FIRST FLOOR: 4,138 SQ. FT.
SECOND FLOOR: 1,269 SQ. FT.
TOTAL: 5,407 SQ. FT.
BEDROOMS: 3
BATHROOMS: 3½ + ½
WIDTH: 90' - 0"
DEPTH: 85' - 0"
FOUNDATION: SLAB

ORDER ONLINE @ EPLANS.COM

Signature Designer

Your guests will feel right at home in this clever design from Dan Sater. Two full guest suites ensure ample room, with one placed on the upper level to give your guests greater privacy. The designer's master stroke, though, was locating the master suite and majority of living space on the main floor, making this home the right fit for all stages of life.

FIRST FLOOR

SECOND FLOOR

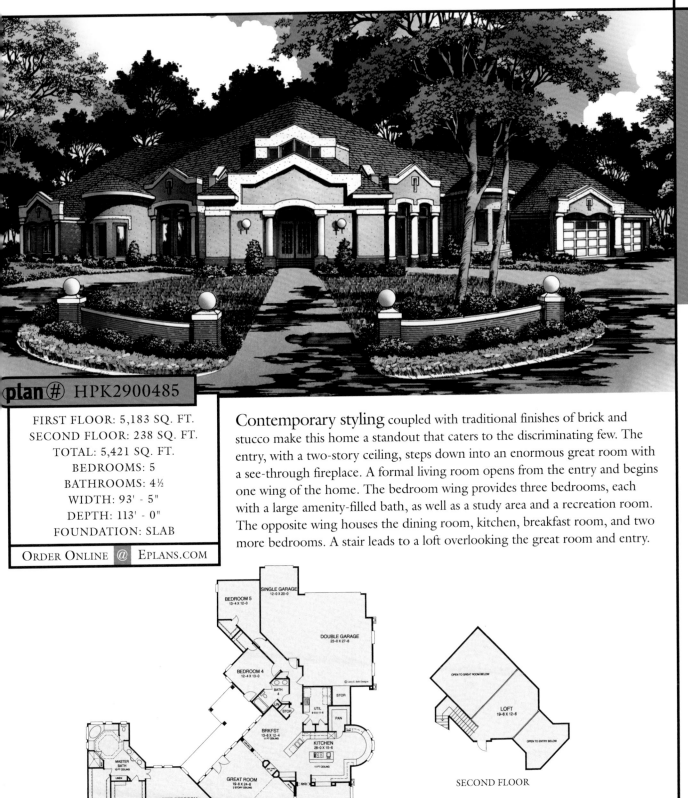

plan # HPK2900485

FIRST FLOOR: 5,183 SQ. FT.
SECOND FLOOR: 238 SQ. FT.
TOTAL: 5,421 SQ. FT.
BEDROOMS: 5
BATHROOMS: 4½
WIDTH: 93' - 5"
DEPTH: 113' - 0"
FOUNDATION: SLAB

ORDER ONLINE @ EPLANS.COM

Contemporary styling coupled with traditional finishes of brick and stucco make this home a standout that caters to the discriminating few. The entry, with a two-story ceiling, steps down into an enormous great room with a see-through fireplace. A formal living room opens from the entry and begins one wing of the home. The bedroom wing provides three bedrooms, each with a large amenity-filled bath, as well as a study area and a recreation room. The opposite wing houses the dining room, kitchen, breakfast room, and two more bedrooms. A stair leads to a loft overlooking the great room and entry.

SECOND FLOOR

FIRST FLOOR

The distinctive covered entry to this stunning manor, flanked by twin turrets, leads to a gracious foyer. The foyer opens to a formal dining room, a study, and a step-down gathering room. The spacious kitchen includes numerous amenities, including an island work station and a built-in desk. The adjacent morning room and the gathering room, with a wet bar and a raised-hearth fireplace, are bathed in light and open to the terrace. The secluded master suite offers two walk-in closets, a dressing area, and an exercise area with a spa. The second floor features four bedrooms and an oversized activities room with a fireplace and a balcony. Unfinished attic space can be completed to your specifications.

FIRST FLOOR: 3,736 SQ. FT.
SECOND FLOOR: 2,264 SQ. FT.
TOTAL: 6,000 SQ. FT.
BEDROOMS: 5
BATHROOMS: 5 + 2 HALF
BATHS
WIDTH: 133' - 4"
DEPTH: 65' - 5"
FOUNDATION: SLAB

ORDER ONLINE @ EPLANS.COM

SECOND FLOOR

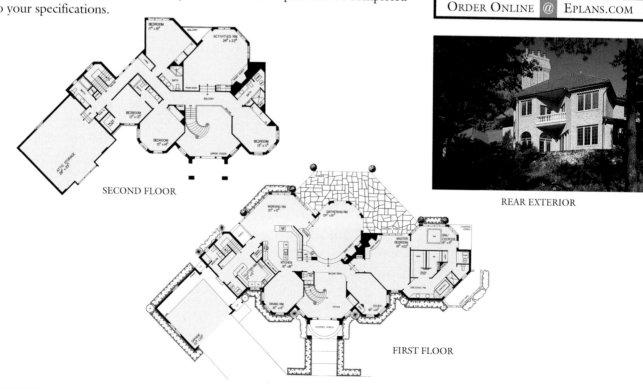

REAR EXTERIOR

FIRST FLOOR

plan# HPK2900487

FIRST FLOOR: 4,742 SQ. FT.
SECOND FLOOR: 1,531 SQ. FT.
TOTAL: 6,273 SQ. FT.
BEDROOMS: 4
BATHROOMS: 4½ + ½
WIDTH: 96' - 0"
DEPTH: 134' - 8"
FOUNDATION: SLAB

ORDER ONLINE @ EPLANS.COM

REAR EXTERIOR

The majestic entrance is just the beginning of this magnificent estate. A short hallway to the right of the foyer leads into the master suite that comprises the entire right side of the plan downstairs. The master bath offers dual vanities, a large shower, and a tub with an enclosed view of a privacy garden. His and Hers walk-in closets lead from the dressing area, which flows easily into the bedroom. Within the bedroom, a sitting room offers a quiet retreat. The left side of the plan belongs to a spacious gourmet kitchen with an island snack bar, plenty of counter space, a breakfast nook, and a large leisure area. Adjacent to the kitchen is a guest bedroom with a private full bath. Upstairs there are two additional bedrooms, each with a full bath and walk-in closet, one with a balcony. A media room is the finishing touch on this masterpiece.

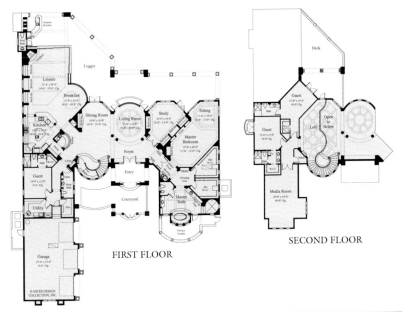

FIRST FLOOR

SECOND FLOOR

HELPFUL HINT: If you're thinking of modifying your plan, be sure to purchase the reproducible set.

Planned Paradise

A truly gratifying landscape design takes cues from the architecture of the home, the owners' sense of style and the natural properties of the land. Follow these guidelines for planning the perfect landscape for your home

5

7

8

6

2

3

4

1

plan # HPK2900490

SHOWN IN SUMMER
DESIGNED BY
DAVID POPLAWSKI

ORDER ONLINE @ EPLANS.COM

1. Perennials and bulbs used throughout this design establish an overall garden theme and provide cutting flowers for indoor bouquets. But remember that a garden will need

a lot of care and constant attention. And a neglected garden will do nothing for a home's curb appeal. Remember that a garden can require a lot of attention, so be sure to choose a landscape whose required care suits your lifestyle

2. Paths provide more than the practical benefits of reducing soil compaction and keeping feet dry. An inviting path can light up a landscape and turn everyday walks into unfolding journeys. To match the rustic, informal mood of the home in this plan, both the front walkway and driveway cut a curved unintentional path through the property, which helps create a sense of destination. Use of fieldstones on the walkway adds another rustic touch. A parking spur at the end of the driveway provides guest space and room to maneuver vehicles.

3. Consider the topography of the lot. Slopes and irregularities may produce obstacles for a garden design, but they can also provide for unique landscaping opportunities.

4. Maintain a firm connection between the landscape and the home by incorporating similar materials. The stone piers and picket fence at the entrance to the driveway frame the entry and match the detail of the home's stone foundation and porch railing.

5. Growing conditions vary from region to region. What is the clime of the lot? What type of soil does it have? These important factors of the yard will determine which plants are not suitable and which plants will flourish.

6. How will the yard be used? Will it be a quiet spot in which to read the Sunday paper, or a secondary spot for guests to gather? Besides personal taste, the amount of space available for the design will dictate the range of options.

7. Use trees, especially deciduous ones, to create a sense of slight separation from the rest of the lawn. An arbor can also add a sense of seclusion, especially with plants growing up and over it.

8. Consider how the home can take full advantage of the landscape plan. Porches and decks provide transitions between the outdoor and indoor spaces of the overall design. Will an upstairs master suite be the best way to enjoy views of the gorgeous landscape? Or will a quiet, naturally lit study be in your family's future?

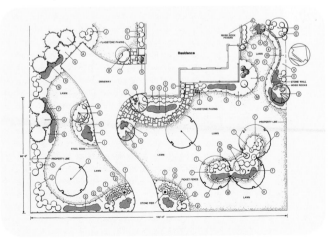

An Intimate, Comfortable Landscape

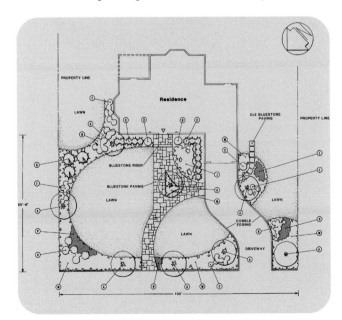

The quaint character of this traditional Cape Cod home calls for an intimate, comfortable landscape. Notice how the repetition of curves throughout the landscape works to unite the design into a cohesive whole. The clean curving line of the large shrub border, which sweeps directly from the foundation planting toward the street, is repeated in the

smaller curves of the planting borders along the street and in the shapes of the lawn areas. The stone walk and the driveway feature flowing curves. The front walk attractively leads to both the driveway and the street. Loose, informally-shaped trees soften the lines of the house and complement the curves of the landscape. By positioning these trees at the front edge of the property and in the center of the walkway, the designer buffered the view of the house from the street, creating a sense of privacy while framing the home. Evergreen foundation shrubs used near the house match the traditional style of the architecture. Elsewhere, flowering shrubs provide seasonal color.

plan # HPK2900488

SHOWN IN SPRING
DESIGNED BY
MICHEL J. OPISSO

ORDER ONLINE @ EPLANS.COM

Country Farmhouse-Style Landscape

With two entries close to each other at the front of the house, it is imperative that the landscaping for this gambrel-roof Colonial home defines the formal or dominant entry--the one to which a visitor should go. This is accomplished by framing and blocking views. Notice how small ornamental trees frame the large entry court that leads to the main door. The tree nearest the house blocks the view of the door leading to the family room, and it also frames the walk and adds color and interest to the landscape. A low-growing evergreen hedge behind the tree aids in screening, so the visitor perceives only one walkway and one door. Access to the secondary door from the backyard, garage, or driveway is by a walkway at the back of this screen planting. The weeping evergreen and summer-flowering shrubs bordering the outside of the front walkway direct the view up the walk and to the front door. This bed extends into a curving border of trees, shrubs, perennials, and ground covers, which is echoed on the other side of the property. These border plantings provide privacy from neighbors or a side street and, since one cannot see behind the house, further define the front garden.

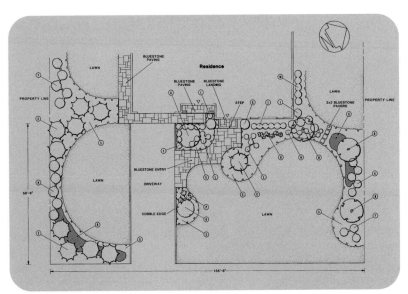

plan(#) HPK2900491

SHOWN IN SPRING
DESIGNED BY SUSAN A. ROTH

ORDER ONLINE @ EPLANS.COM

Formal Symmetry

The architecture of the brick Federal house might remind you of a trip to Colonial Williamsburg, and so too does the formality and grandeur of the landscape design. The key to the success and beauty of this design is its simplicity and symmetry, reflecting the symmetrical and repetitive lines of the house. If you fold the plan in half, it is identical on both sides with the exception of the driveway. The symmetry is carried out in two ways. One is by mirror-imaging from left to right; note the placement of the large shade trees on either side of the house, the repetition of the foundation plants and the border plants, and the symmetrical paved area in front of the entry, flanked by two circular lawn areas. In the second way, the lines of symmetry go from the front of the landscape to the back; note the repetition of the same trees on either side of the two-foot-high wall, the use of brick in the wall to match the brick of the home, and the repetition of stone piers on each end of the wall. These, in turn, exactly line up with the stone piers at both sides of the entry, creating a feeling of a courtyard in the circular driveway. The plants used in this design provide a graceful setting that gives the home a sense of performance. Here and there, flowers, berries, and fall foliage provide spots of seasonal color, but the overall feeling is one of quiet, cool greenery. The elegance of this design matches the elegance of the house, reflecting well upon the good taste of the owners.

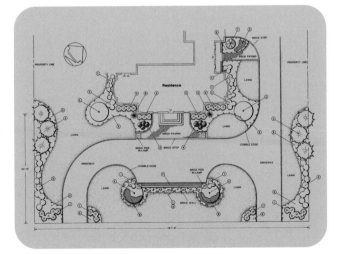

plan # HPK2900492

SHOWN IN SUMMER
DESIGNED BY MICHAEL J.
OPISSO

ORDER ONLINE @ EPLANS.COM

Romantic Landscape

A turn-of-the-century home demands a romantic landscape to adorn it. Decorative fencing, old-fashioned plants, and stately shade trees do just that in this picture-perfect plan. To get the most out of relaxing on the porch and enjoying the view, only low-growing perennials and ground covers are planted in front. When summer breezes stir, the fragrance of the flowers planted among the ground covers perfume the porch. The driveway provides easy access to the garage and extra parking area, directing guests to the front door. A weeping tree—a favorite Victorian specimen—obscures the service entrance in front from the main walk and drive, although it is easily accessible by a narrow walk. Leading through the pretty planting bed in front of the garage, stone pavers allow family members to walk directly from the drive to a side door. The semicircular garden bed hugging the driveway repeats the curves of the drive, walk, and porch. The designer intentionally leaves out lawn in this area in order to create a tapestry of colorful flowers and foliage from small shrubs, perennials, and ground cover. By using decorative fencing in

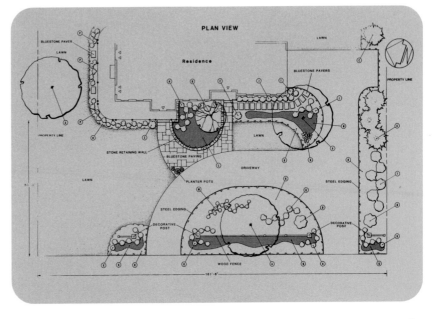

this bed, and repeating it on both sides of the driveway, the designer skillfully carries the detail from the house's woodwork to the garden. For privacy, a screen of evergreen trees and tall flowering shrubs border the length of the driveway. Three large trees shading the house evoke the feeling of Main Street USA, just what you might expect if this house were an original Victorian.

plan # HPK2900493

SHOWN IN SPRING
DESIGNED BY SUSAN A. ROTH

ORDER ONLINE @ EPLANS.COM

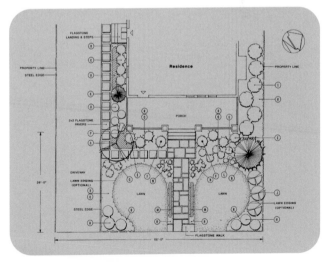

Eye-Catching Plantings

Eye-catching plantings turn this charming cottage into a special home, yet the yard doesn't demand much upkeep because the plants were chosen for their small size or slow growth. Although this home sits on a narrow lot with a small front yard and an optional driveway, the designer hasn't skimped on the landscape. The tiny grounds boast a wealth of plants in a striking range of colors, textures, and shapes. The key to successfully landscaping such a small space is to use compact plants that won't outgrow their welcome. Because of the tight quarters, the designer has also chosen to plant a single deciduous tree instead of forming the more traditional triad. The design has aspects of symmetry and formality--the flagstone walk dividing the yard in half, perennials repeated on either side of the walk, identical pools of lawn, and matching dwarf conifers flanking the porch steps--but the overall effect is informal.

Flagstone pavers lead from the walk around the left side of the property only, providing access to cars parked in the driveway. The visual weight of this border balances that of the evergreen tree and cluster of shrubs on the opposite side of the property. This petite, but lush, landscape requires little effort to maintain, and even the patches of lawn can be cut quickly with a reel mower. However, if you wanted to reduce maintenance even further, you could eliminate the lawn and extend the groundcover. The design may also be adapted to a lot without a driveway or a garage.

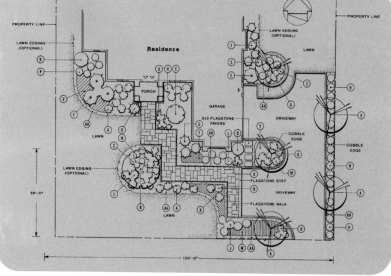

plan # HPK2900494

SHOWN IN SPRING
DESIGNED BY SUSAN A. ROTH

ORDER ONLINE @ EPLANS.com

European-Flair Home

The designer uses graceful curving borders to bring this landscape to life. An appealing mix of shrubs grown for their ornamental foliage, flowers, and fruit rises from an underplanting of weed-smothering ground covers and long-blooming perennials. The shrubs' compact growth habits keep the windows clear and save on pruning chores. A small tree, selected for its handsome branching pattern and long season of colorful foliage, partially screens the entry from public view and creates a dramatic focal point. The curves in the borders are repeated in the cobble-edged planting peninsulas, which visually break up the large expanse of asphalt in th se drive. Five deciduous shade trees planted along the drive

spruce up this utilitarian area while giving needed height to the landscape. The trees are chosen for their airy canopies of delicate leaves, which create a softening screen without excessive shade or fall cleanup. A flag-stone walk, set in concrete and mortared for weed-free maintenance, zigzags from the drive to the front porch. For a greater feeling of privacy, the designer ends the walk short of the street so that it is accessible only from the drive. The curving borders jut into the lawn, giving it an appealing shape--and a size that isn't too large for the easy-care gardener to handle comfortably. The lawn is kept free of plantings and other obstacles to make mowing faster and easier.

plan# HPK2900495

SHOWN IN SUMMER
DESIGNED BY DAMON SCOTT

ORDER ONLINE @ EPLANS.COM

Grand Landscape in Scale and Style

The grand size of a traditional Southern Colonial home demands an equally grand landscape whose scale and style balance the house's imposing size and massive columns. The designer uses six tall shade trees to shelter the house and create a park-like setting for the home. The terrace at the front of the house creates a formal entry court that reflects the stateliness of the architecture, while planter pots positioned at each side of the courtyard provide a human scale to an otherwise large-scale house and landscape. The large trees and planting bed at the entrance to the driveway buffer the view of the drive and the house and create a feeling of anticipation as one enters the property. The driveway splits, leading back to the side-entry garage and also swinging around front to deliver guests in style to the main entrance and a conveniently located parking bay. The canopy of trees at the entrance to the secondary driveway and the repeated semicircular lawn areas announce that this is the entry. Three decorative trees with colored foliage underplanted with low-growing shrubs screen cars parked in the parking bay from the street, while giving the entire entry area a sense of privacy and enclosure. For the convenience of family members, a brick walk, screened from view by a hedge, leads from the garage to the secondary entrance.

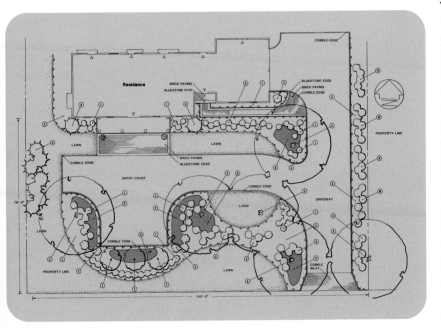

plan # HPK2900496

SHOWN IN SUMMER
DESIGNED BY MARIA MORRISON

ORDER ONLINE @ EPLANS.COM

Street-Side Cottage Garden Landscape

Bursting with exuberant old-fashioned blossoms, this friendly cottage garden is designed to be enjoyed from both sides of the fence. The garden invites passersby to pause and enjoy the show from the street or sidewalk, thus creating a friendly neighborhood feeling. However, where space is very limited, you might prefer to plant only the inside of the fence and to plant the street side with a mowing strip of grass or a low-maintenance groundcover. You could even reverse the plan and install the hedge on the street side.

Whether you have a sidewalk or not, leave a buffer between the edge of the border and the street so that if you live in a cold-winter climate, there'll be room to pile snow. Flowering perennial and annual climbing vines cover the wooden arbor, creating a romantic entrance. Roses, bulbs, perennials, annuals, and a compact evergreen hedge are arranged in a classic cottage-garden style that is casual but not haphazard. The designer achieves a pleasant sense of unity by repeating plants and colors throughout the design without repeating a symmetrical planting pattern. This helps create the casual feeling essential to a cottage garden. Create a friendly neighborhood feeling by planting this flower-filled cottage garden along the front of your property.

plan # HPK2900497

SHOWN IN SPRING
DESIGNED BY MICHAEL J. OPISSO

ORDER ONLINE @ EPLANS.COM

Season-Spanning Design

This naturalistic berm is planted with a season-spanning design that can transform a suburban yard into a quiet haven. The berm rises to three feet high—tall enough to make you forget that your neighbor's yard lies just beyond. Staggered plantings cover the berm and create baffles that muffle sound, while the diverse mix of plants provides color and interest all year long. Intended for a backyard, the berm allows you to enjoy the remaining lawn in privacy. Tall berry-producing evergreens located at the top of the berm provide immediate screening, and perennials and bulbs, ornamental grasses, and small flowering trees at the front provide seasonal bursts of brilliance. A flowering groundcover on the berm helps hold the soil in place and makes a graceful transition between the slope of the berm and the flat lawn area. Wherever you decide to site the berm, be sure to maintain the original grade of the yard at the property line, to avoid violating zoning regulations. Also, be sure to add a two- to three- inch-thick layer of mulch to help the slope retain moisture and to discourage weeds. This privacy planting gets a head start on creating an effective screen by beginning with a berm, which gives young plants a height advantage.

plan # HPK2900498

SHOWN IN SUMMER
DESIGNED BY MICHAEL J.
OPISSO AND ANNE RODE

ORDER ONLINE @ EPLANS.COM

Enliven a Shady Area

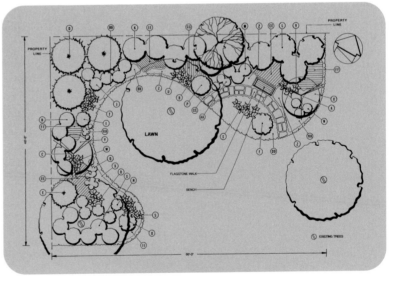

A shade garden need not depend on flowers—which usually need some sun to perform well—for color. You can enliven a shady area with a border that relies on a rainbow of foliage color to provide subtle, yet engaging beauty. This design contains an artful mix of foliage plants with colors and textures that range from understated to bold. In this gently curving border, the designer combines a variety of deciduous and evergreen shrubs and trees with perennials to provide year-round foliage color. Many of the plants also add floral accents to the design. A semicircular flagstone path leads to a bench, enticing visitors to sit in the cool shade. Designed for a location where sunlight is insufficient to support most free-flowering plants, this showy border derives its color from an array of shade-loving shrubs and perennials featuring variegated, golden, or purplish-red leaves.

plan # HPK2900499

SHOWN IN SUMMER
DESIGNED BY FRANK
ESPOSITO

ORDER ONLINE @ EPLANS.COM

The Feeling of an Indoor Room in Nature

Sitting in the open shade cast by the pergola evokes the secure feeling of being in an outdoor room where you can fully enjoy the flowers in the surrounding garden. Adding lattice panels to the ends of the pergola enhances the feeling of an outdoor room by enclosing it further and providing the perfect place for a colorful cover of climbing vines. Meant to be situated in an open area of the yard, this pergola planting creates a decorative centerpiece in the lawn—you can site it in either the front- or backyard. The flagstone patio under the pergola has two entrance paths from the lawn—one on each long side—so that you can walk through the garden. Site this beautiful pergola and its surrounding garden bed at a distance from the house, where it creates a dramatic focal point that draws visitors to come and explore.

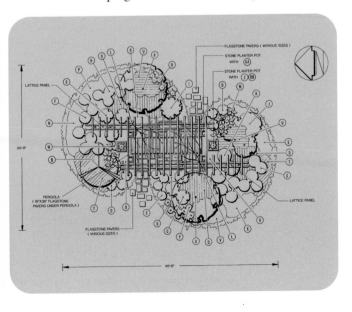

Naturalistic Swimming Pool

If you look at this landscape design and ask yourself, "Is that really a swimming pool?" then the designer is to be congratulated because he succeeded in his intention. Yes, it is a swimming pool, but the pool looks more like a natural pond and waterfall—one that you might discover in a clearing in the woods during a hike in the wilderness. Although the pool is not included in the blueprints for this design, the surrounding landscape lends itself to its placement. Leave the pool out for a pleasing rock garden, play area, or romantic gazebo hideaway. The designer achieves an aesthetically pleasing, natural look by employing several techniques. Large boulders form the waterfalls, one of which falls from a holding pond set among the boulders. If you do not choose to build a pool here, the boulders could empty into a pond or calming fountain. River-rock paving—the type of water-worn rocks that line the cool water of a natural spring or a rushing stream—adds a touch of wilderness. The beautiful grassy areas of the landscape offer a serene setting with abundant floral and foliage interest throughout the year. For security reasons, a wooden stockade fence surrounds the entire backyard, yet the plantings camouflage it well. The irregular kidney shape of the lawn is pleasing to look at and beautifully integrates this naturalistic landscaping into its man-made setting. Abundant floral and foliage interest year-round, river-rock paving, and border plantings bring a wonderful, natural setting to your own backyard.

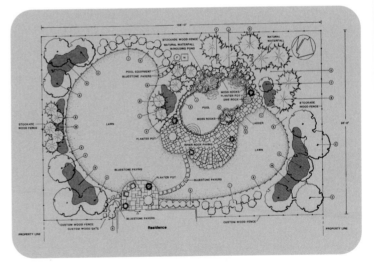

Songbird Garden Landscape

This naturalistic garden plan relies upon several different features to attract as many different species of birds as possible. A songbird's basic needs include food, water, and shelter, but this backyard plan offers luxury accommodations not found in every yard, and also provides the maximum opportunity for birds and bird watchers to observe each other. Special features provide for specific birds; for example, the rotting log attracts woodpeckers and the dusting area will be used gratefully by birds to free themselves of parasites. In addition to plants that produce plentiful berries and seeds, the designer includes a ground feeder to lure morning doves, cardinals, and other birds that prefer to eat off the ground. The bird-

house located in the shade of the specimen tree to the rear of the garden suits a wide variety of songbirds. The angular deck nestles attractively into the restful circular shapes of the garden. The designer encloses the deck amidst the bird-attracting plantings to maximize close-up observation opportunities and create an intimate setting. Two other sitting areas welcome bird watchers into the garden. A bench positioned on a small patio under the shade of a graceful flowering tree provides a relaxing spot to sit and contemplate the small garden pool (not included in plan blueprints) and the melody of a low waterfall. Another bench—this one situated in the sun—may be reached by strolling along a path of wood-rounds on the opposite side of the yard. Both wildlife and people will find this backyard a very special retreat. This large, naturalistic backyard design creates a wonderful environment for attracting a wide range of bird species, because it offers a plentiful supply of natural food, water, and shelter. The deck and garden benches invite people to observe and listen to the songbirds in comfort.

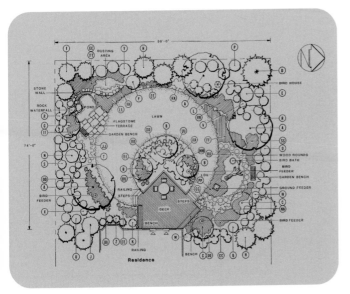

Beautiful Throughout the Year

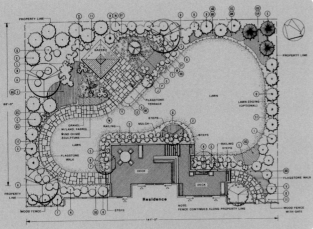

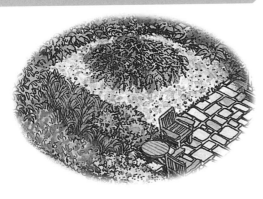

Designed to be enjoyed rather than slaved over, this backyard paradise offers a variety of outdoor living spaces. The large deck, Home Planners design ODA023, is designed with two levels to accommodate uneven terrain and provide easy-access from the split-level house. The two levels of the deck act as separate outdoor rooms: From the large, higher level, you can enjoy a wonderful view of the entire property with plenty of room for guests to walk around and mingle. The lower level is more intimate; three vase-shaped trees provide shade and a sense of privacy while framing the view. A gracefully curving flagstone walk leads from the deck to a stone terrace and gazebo, providing additional outdoor rooms for relaxing or entertaining. (The walkway doubles as a mowing strip, making the relatively small lawn even easier to mow.) You can enjoy the music created by the windchime sculpture--an eye- and ear-catching focal point beside the gazebo. A living sculpture, in the form of a weeping evergreen, visually balances the chimes. Both are set in gravel beds for added emphasis. The plantings require little routine care because the many evergreens that fill out the design don't shed a litter of leaves and don't need regular pruning. Flowering shrubs and perennials create a changing show of blossoms from spring through fall, while the evergreens provide a dependable backdrop of greenery and varied textures. You can plant your choice of easy-care annuals in the deck planters. There's a lot to see from this bi-level deck, since the designer planned a garden that's beautiful throughout the year. Evergreens at the property border provide enclosure and privacy and don't pose clean-up problems.

plan # HPK2900504

SHOWN IN SUMMER
DESIGNED BY SUSAN A. ROTH

ORDER ONLINE @ EPLANS.COM

Natural Beauty & Earthly Delights

Inspired by contemplative Oriental gardens, this naturalistic garden relies on boulders, a layer of gravel and a slope of fieldstone to suggest the bed of a former stream. A simple wooden footbridge leads over the stream to a gazebo at the right edge of the bed. The design includes a lovely palette of shrubs, perennials, small trees and ornamental grasses, all of which require minimal watering and, as an added bonus, are low-maintenance. This leaves you more time to spend in the gazebo meditating and contemplating your surroundings. The bed, which can be located in any open area of your property, is dug to a depth of six feet. A layer of gravel lines the interior of the bed, giving it a natural appearance. The designer creates a berm on the upper side of the bed from the excavated soil. You may prefer to create a flatter design, digging instead to a depth of only one or two feet. Even this slight change in elevation is enough to create the desired effect of allowing the water-thrifty plants to flow over the banks and make a visual reference to a stream that is no longer there. Pretty to look at, and easy to care for, this garden features a rocky former streambed to complement the drought-tolerant plants.

House Plans— Super Sized

Hanley Wood has compiled the best-selling and most popular home plans into the most extensive home plan resources available. Now delivering more of everything you want—more plans, more styles and more choices—your dream home is right around the corner.

If you are looking to build a new home, look to Hanley Wood first. Pick up a copy today!

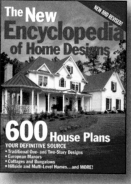

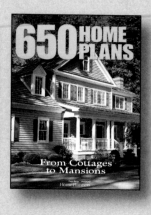

With over 2,500 home plans, finding the right new home to fit

- Your style
- Your budget
- Your life

Has never been easier.

HPK29

With more than 50 years of experience in the industry and millions of blueprints sold, Hanley Wood is a trusted source of high-quality, high-value pre-drawn home plans.

Using pre-drawn home plans is a **reliable, cost-effective way** to build your dream home, and our vast selection of plans is second-to-none. The nation's finest designers craft these plans that builders know they can trust. Meanwhile, our friendly, knowledgeable customer service representatives can help you every step of the way.

WHAT YOU'LL GET WITH YOUR ORDER

The contents of each designer's blueprint package is unique, but all contain detailed, high-quality working drawings. You can expect to find the following standard elements in most sets of plans:

I. FRONT PERSPECTIVE

This artist's sketch of the exterior of the house gives you an idea of how the house will look when built and landscaped.

4. HOUSE AND DETAIL CROSS-SECTIONS

Large-scale views show sections or cutaways of the foundation, interior walls, exterior walls, floors, stairways, and roof details. Additional cross-sections may show important changes in floor, ceiling, or roof heights, or the relationship of one level to another. These sections show exactly how the various parts of the house fit together and are extremely valuable during construction. Additional sheets may include enlarged wall, floor, and roof construction details.

2. FOUNDATION AND BASEMENT PLANS

This sheet shows the foundation layout including concrete walls, footings, pads, posts, beams, bearing walls, and foundation notes. If the home features a basement, the first-floor framing details may also be included on this plan. If your plan features slab construction rather than a basement, the plan shows footings and details for a monolithic slab. This page, or another in the set, may include a sample plot plan for locating your house on a building site. Additional sheets focus on foundation cross-sections and other details.

3. DETAILED FLOOR PLANS

These plans show the layout of each floor of the house. Rooms and interior spaces are carefully dimensioned, doors and windows located, and keys are given for cross-section details provided elsewhere in the plans.

5. FLOOR STRUCTURAL SUPPORTS

The floor framing plans provide detail for these crucial elements of your home. Each includes floor joist, ceiling joist, spacing, direction, span, and specifications. Beam and window headers, along with necessary details for framing connections, stairways, or dormers are also included.

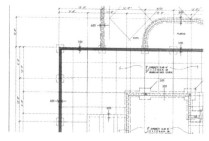

6. ELECTRICAL PLAN

The electrical plan offers suggested locations with notes for all lighting, outlets, switches, and circuits. A layout is provided for each level, as well as basements, garages, or other structures. This plan does not contain diagrams detailing how all wiring should be run, or how circuits should be engineered. These details should be designed by your electrician.

7. EXTERIOR ELEVATIONS

In addition to the front exterior, your blueprint set will include drawings of the rear and sides of your house as well. These drawings give notes on exterior materials and finishes. Particular attention is given to cornice detail, brick and stone accents, or other finish items that make your home unique.

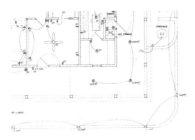

ROOF FRAMING PLANS — PLEASE READ

Some plans contain roof framing plans; however because of the wide variation in local requirements, many plans do not. If you buy a plan without a roof framing plan, you will need an engineer familiar with local building codes to create a plan to build your roof. Even if your plan does contain a roof framing plan, we recommend that a local engineer review the plan to verify that it will meet local codes.

BEFORE YOU CALL

You are making a terrific decision to use a pre-drawn house plan—it is one you can make with confidence, knowing that your blueprints are crafted by national-award-winning certified residential designers and architects, and trusted by builders.

Once you've selected the plan you want—or even if you have questions along the way—our experienced customer service representatives are available 24 hours a day, seven days a week to help you navigate the home-building process. To help them provide you with even better service, please consider the following questions before you call:

■ **Have you chosen or purchased your lot?**
If so, please review the building setback requirements of your local building authority before you call. You don't need to have a lot before ordering plans, but if you own land already, please have the width and depth dimensions handy when you call.

■ **Have you chosen a builder?**
Involving your builder in the plan selection and evaluation process may be beneficial. Luckily, builders know they can have confidence with pre-drawn plans because they've been designed for livability, functionality, and typically are builder-proven at successful home sites across the country.

■ **Do you need a construction loan?**
Construction loans are unique because they involve determining the value of something that is not yet constructed. Several lenders offer convenient contstruction-to-permanent loans. It is important to choose a good lending partner—one who will help guide you through the application and appraisal process. Most will even help you evaluate your contractor to ensure reliability and credit worthiness. Our partnership with IndyMac Bank, a nationwide leader in construction loans, can help you save on your loan, if needed (see the next page for details).

■ **How many sets of plans do you need?**
Building a home can typically require a number of sets of blueprints—one for yourself, two or three for the builder and subcontractors, two for the local building department, and one or more for your lender. For this reason, we offer 5- and 8-set plan packages, but your best value is the Reproducible Plan Package. Reproducible plans are accompanied by a license to make modifications and typically up to 12 duplicates of the plan so you have enough copies of the plan for everyone involved in the financing and construction of your home.

■ **Do you want to make any changes to the plan?**
We understand that it is difficult to find blueprints for a home that will meet all of your needs. That is why Hanley Wood is glad to offer plan Customization Services. We will work with you to design the modifications you'd like to see and to adjust your blueprint plans accordingly—anything from changing the foundation; adding square footage, redesigning baths, kitchens, or bedrooms; or most other modifications. This simple, cost-effective service saves you from hiring an outside architect to make alterations. Modifications may only be made to Reproducible Plan Packages that include the license to modify.

■ **Do you have to make any changes to meet local building codes?**
While all of our plans are drawn to meet national building codes at the time they were created, many areas required that plans be stamped by a local engineer to certify that they meet local building codes. Building codes are updated frequently and can vary by state, county, city, or municipality. Contact your local building inspection department, office of planning and zoning, or department of permits to determine how your local codes will affect your construction project. The best way to assure that you can make changes to your plan, if necessary, is to purchase a Reproducible Plan Package.

■ **Has everyone—from family members to contractors—been involved in selecting the plan?**
Building a new home is an exciting process, and using pre-drawn plans is a great way to realize your dreams. Make sure that everyone involved has had an opportunity to review the plan you've selected. While Hanley Wood is the only plans provider with an exchange policy, it's best to be sure all parties agree on your selection before you buy.

CALL TOLL-FREE 1-800-521-6797

Source Key
HPK29

CUSTOMIZE YOUR PLAN –
HANLEY WOOD CUSTOMIZATION SERVICES

Creating custom home plans has never been easier and more directly accessible. Using state-of-the-art technology and top-performing architectural expertise, Hanley Wood delivers on a long-standing customer commitment to provide world-class home-plans and customization services. Our valued customers—professional home builders and individual home owners—appreciate the convenience and accessibility of this interactive, consultative service.

With the Hanley Wood Customization Service you can:

■ Save valuable time by avoiding drawn-out and frequently repetitive face-to-face design meetings

■ Communicate design and home-plan changes faster and more efficiently
■ Speed-up project turn-around time
■ Build on a budget without sacrificing quality
■ Transform master home plans to suit your design needs and unique personal style

All of our design options and prices are impressively affordable. A detailed quote is available for a $50 consultation fee. Plan modification is an interactive service. Our skilled team of designers will guide you through the customization process from start to finish making recommendations, offering ideas, and determining the feasibility of your changes. This level of service is offered to ensure the final modified plan meets your expectations. If you use our service the $50 fee will be applied to the cost of the modifications.

You may purchase the customization consultation before or after purchasing a plan. In either case, it is necessary to purchase the Reproducible Plan Package and complete the accompanying license to modify the plan before we can begin customization.

Customization Consultation $50

TOOLS TO WORK WITH YOUR BUILDER

Two Reverse Options For Your Convenience –
Mirror and Right-Reading Reverse (as available)

Mirror reverse plans simply flip the design 180 degrees—keep in mind, the text will also be flipped. For a minimal fee you can have one or all of your plans shipped mirror reverse, although we recommend having at least one regular set handy. Right-reading reverse plans show the design flipped 180 degrees but the text reads normally. When you choose this option, we ship each set of purchased blueprints in this format.

Mirror Reverse Fee (indicate the number of sets when ordering) $55
Right Reading Reverse Fee (all sets are reversed) $175

A Shopping List Exclusively for Your Home – Materials List

A customized Materials List helps you plan and estimate the cost of your new home, outlining the quantity, type, and size of materials needed to build your house (with the exception of mechanical system items). Included are framing lumber, windows and doors, kitchen and bath cabinetry, rough and finished hardware, and much more.

Materials List . . . .$85 each
Additional Materials Lists (at original time of purchase only)$20 each

Plan Your Home-
Building Process – Specification Outline

Work with your builder on this step-by-step chronicle of 166 stages or items crucial to the building process. It provides a comprehensive review of the construction process and helps you choose materials.
Specification Outline . . . .$10 each

Get Accurate Cost Estimates for Your Home –
Quote One® Cost Reports

The Summary Cost Report, the first element in the Quote One® package, breaks down the cost of your home into various categories based on building materials, labor, and installation, and includes three grades of construction: Budget, Standard, and Custom. Make even more informed decisions about your project with the second element of our package, the Material Cost Report. The material and installation cost is shown for each of more than 1,000 line items provided in the standard-grade Materials List, which is included with this tool. Additional space is included for estimates from contractors and subcontractors, such as for mechanical materials, which are not included in our packages.

Quote One® Summary Cost Report $35
Quote One® Detailed Material Cost Report $140*
***Detailed material cost report includes the Materials List**

Learn the Basics of Building – Electrical, Pluming, Mechanical, Construction Detail Sheets

If you want to know more about building techniques—and deal more confidently with your subcontractors—we offer four useful detail sheets. These sheets provide non-plan-specific general information, but are excellent tools that will add to your understanding of Plumbing Details, Electrical Details, Construction Details, and Mechanical Details.

Electrical Detail Sheet $14.95
Plumbing Detail Sheet $14.95
Mechanical Detail Sheet $14.95
Construction Detail Sheet $14.95
SUPER VALUE SETS:
Buy any 2: $26.95; Buy any 3: $34.95; Buy All 4: $39.95

Best Value

MAKE YOUR HOME TECH-READY – HOME AUTOMATION UPGRADE

Building a new home provides a unique opportunity to wire it with a plan for future needs. A Home Automation-Ready (HA-Ready) home contains the wiring substructure of tomorrow's connected home. It means that every room—from the front porch to the backyard, and from the attic to the basement—is wired for security, lighting, telecommunications, climate control, home computer networking, whole-house audio, home theater, shade control, video surveillance, entry access control, and yes, video gaming electronic solutions.

Along with the conveniences HA-Ready homes provide, they also have a higher resale value. The Consumer Electronics Association (CEA), in conjunction with the Custom Electronic Design and Installation Association (CEDIA), have developed a TechHome™ Rating system that quantifies the value of HA-Ready homes. The rating system is gaining widespread recognition in the real estate industry.

Developed by CEDIA-certified installers, our Home Automation Upgrade package includes everything you need to work with an installer during the construction of your home. It provides a short explanation of the various subsystems, a wiring floor plan for each level of your home, a detailed materials list with estimated costs, and a list of CEDIA-certified installers in your local area.

Home Automation Upgrade **$250**

GET YOUR HOME PLANS PAID FOR!

IndyMac Bank, in partnership with Hanley Wood, will reimburse you up to $600 toward the cost of your home plans simply by financing the construction of your new home with IndyMac Bank Home Construction Lending.

IndyMac's construction and permanent loan is a one-time close loan, meaning that one application—and one set of closing fees—provides all the financing you need.

Apply today at www.indymacbank.com, call toll free at 1-800-847-6138, or ask a Hanley Wood customer service representative for details.

DESIGN YOUR HOME – INTERIOR AND EXTERIOR FINISHING TOUCHES

Be Your Own Interior Designer! – Home Furniture Planner

Effectively plan the space in your home using our Hands-On Home Furniture Planner. It's fun and easy—no more moving heavy pieces of furniture to see how the room will go together. The kit includes reusable peel-and-stick furniture templates that fit on a 12"x18" laminated layout board—enough space to lay out every room in your house.

Home Furniture Planning Kit **$15.95**

Enjoy the Outdoors! – Deck Plans

Many of our homes have a corresponding deck plan, sold separately, which includes a Deck Plan Frontal Sheet, Deck Framing and Floor Plans, Deck Elevations, and a Deck Materials List. A Standard Deck Details Package, also available, provides all the how-to information necessary for building any deck. Get both the Deck Plan and the Standard Deck Details Package for one low price in our Complete Deck Building Package. See the price tier chart below and call for deck plan availability.

Deck Details (only) **$14.95**
Deck Building Package . . . . **Plan price + $14.95**

Create a Professionally Designed Landscape – Landscape Plans

Many of our homes have a front-yard Landscape Plan that is complementary in design to the house plan. These comprehensive Landscape Blueprint Packages include a Frontal Sheet, Plan View, Regionalized Plant & Materials List, a sheet on Planting and Maintaining Your Landscape, Zone Maps, and a Plant Size and Description Guide. Each set of blueprints is a full 18" x 24" with clear, complete instructions in easy-to-read type. Our Landscape Plans are available with a Plant & Materials List adapted by horticultural experts to eight regions of the country. Please specify your region when ordering your plan—see region map below. Call for more information about landscape plan availability and applicable regions.

LANDSCAPE & DECK PRICE SCHEDULE

PRICE TIERS	1-SET STUDY PACKAGE	5-SET BUILDING PACKAGE	8-SET BUILDING PACKAGE	1-SET REPRODUCIBLE*
P1	$25	$55	$95	$145
P2	$45	$75	$115	$165
P3	$75	$105	$145	$195
P4	$105	$135	$175	$225
P5	$175	$205	$305	$405
P6	$215	$245	$345	$445

PRICES SUBJECT TO CHANGE   * REQUIRES A FAX NUMBER

TERMS & CONDITIONS

OUR 90-DAY EXCHANGE POLICY

BUY WITH CONFIDENCE!

Hanley Wood is committed to ensuring your satisfaction with your blueprint order, which is why we offer a 90-day exchange policy. With the exception of Reproducible Plan Package orders, we will exchange your entire first order for an equal or greater number of blueprints from our plan collection within 90 days of the original order. The entire content of your original order must be returned before an exchange will be processed. Please call our customer service department at 1-888-690-1116 for your return authorization number and shipping instructions. If the returned blueprints look used, redlined, or copied, we will not honor your exchange. Fees for exchanging your blueprints are as follows: 20% of the amount of the original order, plus the difference in cost if exchanging for a design in a higher price bracket or less the difference in cost if exchanging for a design in a lower price bracket. (Because they can be copied, Reproducible blueprints are not exchangeable or refundable.) Please call for current postage and handling prices. Shipping and handling charges are not refundable.

ARCHITECTURAL AND ENGINEERING SEALS

Some cities and states now require that a licensed architect or engineer review and "seal" a blueprint, or officially approve it, prior to construction. Prior to application for a building permit or the start of actual construction, we strongly advise that you consult your local building official who can tell you if such a review is required.

LOCAL BUILDING CODES AND ZONING REQUIREMENTS

Each plan was designed to meet or exceed the requirements of a nationally recognized model building code in effect at the time and place the plan was drawn. Typically plans designed after the year 2000 conform to the International Residential Building Code (IRC 2000 or 2003). The IRC is comprised of portions of the three major codes below. Plans drawn before 2000 conform to one of the three recognized building codes in effect at the time: Building Officials and Code Administrators (BOCA) International, Inc.;

**CALL TOLL-FREE
1-800-521-6797
OR VISIT
EPLANS.COM**

the Southern Building Code Congress International, (SBCCI) Inc.; the International Conference of Building Officials (ICBO); or the Council of American Building Officials (CABO).

Because of the great differences in geography and climate throughout the United States and Canada, each state, county, and municipality has its own building codes, zone requirements, ordinances, and building regulations. Your plan may need to be modified to comply with local requirements. In addition, you may need to obtain permits or inspections from local governments before and in the course of construction. We authorize the use of the blueprints on the express condition that you consult a local licensed architect or engineer of your choice prior to beginning construction and strictly comply with all local building codes, zoning requirements, and other applicable laws, regulations, ordinances, and requirements. Notice: Plans for homes to be built in Nevada must be redrawn by a Nevada-registered professional. Consult your local building official for more information on this subject.

TERMS AND CONDITIONS

These designs are protected under the terms of United States Copyright Law and may not be copied or reproduced in any way, by any means, unless you have purchased a Reproducible Plan Package and signed the accompanying license to modify and copy the plan, which clearly indicates your right to modify, copy, or reproduce. We authorize the use of your chosen design as an aid in the construction of ONE (1) single- or multifamily home only. You may not use this design to build a second dwelling or multiple dwellings without purchasing another blueprint or blueprints or paying additional design fees. Multi-use fees vary by designer—please call one of experienced sales representatives for a quote.

DISCLAIMER

The designers we work with have put substantial care and effort into the creation of their blueprints. However, because we cannot provide on-site consultation, supervision, and control over actual construction, and because of the great variance in local building requirements, building practices, and soil, seismic, weather, and other conditions, WE MAKE NO WARRANTY OF ANY KIND, EXPRESS OR IMPLIED, WITH RESPECT TO THE CONTENT OR USE OF THE BLUEPRINTS, INCLUDING BUT NOT LIMITED TO ANY WARRANTY OF MERCHANTABILITY OR OF FITNESS FOR A PARTICULAR PURPOSE. ITEMS, PRICES, TERMS, AND CONDITIONS ARE SUBJECT TO CHANGE WITHOUT NOTICE.

IMPORTANT COPYRIGHT NOTICE

From the Council of Publishing Home Designers

Blueprints for residential construction (or working drawings, as they are often called in the industry) are copyrighted intellectual property, protected under the terms of the United States Copyright Law and, therefore, cannot be copied legally for use in building. The following are some guidelines to help you get what you need to build your home, without violating copyright law:

1. HOME PLANS ARE COPYRIGHTED

Just like books, movies, and songs, home plans receive protection under the federal copyright laws. The copyright laws prevent anyone, other than the copyright owner, from reproducing, modifying, or reusing the plans or design without permission of the copyright owner.

2. DO NOT COPY DESIGNS OR FLOOR PLANS FROM ANY PUBLICATION, ELECTRONIC MEDIA, OR EXISTING HOME

It is illegal to copy, change, or redraw home designs found in a plan book, CDROM or on the Internet. The right to modify plans is one of the exclusive rights of copyright. It is also illegal to copy or redraw a constructed home that is protected by copyright, even if you have never seen the plans for the home. If you find a plan or home that you like, you must purchase a set of plans from an authorized source. The plans may not be lent, given away, or sold by the purchaser.

3. DO NOT USE PLANS TO BUILD MORE THAN ONE HOUSE

The original purchaser of house plans is typically licensed to build a single home from the plans. Building more than one home from the plans without permission is an infringement of the home designer's copyright. The purchase of a multiple-set package of plans is for the construction of a single home only. The purchase of additional sets of plans does not grant the right to construct more than one home.

4. HOUSE PLANS IN THE FORM OF BLUEPRINTS OR BLACKLINES CANNOT BE COPIED OR REPRODUCED

Plans, blueprints, or blacklines, unless they are reproducibles, cannot be copied or reproduced without prior written consent of the copyright owner. Copy shops and blueprinters are prohibited from making copies of these plans without the copyright release letter you receive with reproducible plans.

5. HOUSE PLANS IN THE FORM OF BLUEPRINTS OR BLACKLINES CANNOT BE REDRAWN

Plans cannot be modified or redrawn without first obtaining the copyright owner's permission. With your purchase of plans, you are licensed to make non-structural changes by "red-lining" the purchased plans. If you need to make structural changes or need to redraw the plans for any reason, you must purchase a reproducible set of plans (see topic 6) which includes a license to modify the plans. Blueprints do not come with a license to make structural changes or to redraw the plans. You may not reuse or sell the modified design.

6. REPRODUCIBILE HOME PLANS

Reproducible plans (for example sepias, mylars, CAD files, electronic files, and vellums) come with a license to make modifications to the plans. Once modified, the plans can be taken to a local copy shop or blueprinter to make up to 10 or 12 copies of the plans to use in the construction of a single home. Only one home can be constructed from any single purchased set of reproducible plans either in original form or as modified. The license to modify and copy must be completed and returned before the plan will be shipped.

7. MODIFIED DESIGNS CANNOT BE REUSED

Even if you are licensed to make modifications to a copyrighted design, the modified design is not free from the original designer's copyright. The sale or reuse of the modified design is prohibited. Also, be aware that any modification to plans relieves the original designer from liability for design defects and voids all warranties expressed or implied.

8. WHO IS RESPONSIBLE FOR COPYRIGHT INFRINGEMENT?

Any party who participates in a copyright violation may be responsible including the purchaser, designers, architects, engineers, drafters, homeowners, builders, contractors, sub-contractors, copy shops, blueprinters, developers, and real estate agencies. It does not matter whether or not the individual knows that a violation is being committed. Ignorance of the law is not a valid defense.

9. PLEASE RESPECT HOME DESIGN COPYRIGHTS

In the event of any suspected violation of a copyright, or if there is any uncertainty about the plans purchased, the publisher, architect, designer, or the Council of Publishing Home Designers (www.cphd.org) should be contacted before proceeding. Awards are sometimes offered for information about home design copyright infringement.

10. PENALTIES FOR INFRINGEMENT

Penalties for violating a copyright may be severe. The responsible parties are required to pay actual damages caused by the infringement (which may be substantial), plus any profits made by the infringer commissions to include all profits from the sale of any home built from an infringing design. The copyright law also allows for the recovery of statutory damages, which may be as high as $150,000 for each infringement. Finally, the infringer may be required to pay legal fees which often exceed the damages.

BLUEPRINT PRICE SCHEDULE

PRICE TIERS	1-SET STUDY PACKAGE	5-SET BUILDING PACKAGE	8-SET BUILDING PACKAGE	1-SET REPRODUCIBLE*
A1	$465	$515	$570	$695
A2	$505	$560	$615	$755
A3	$570	$625	$685	$860
A4	$615	$680	$745	$925
C1	$660	$735	$800	$990
C2	$710	$785	$845	$1,055
C3	$775	$835	$900	$1,135
C4	$830	$905	$960	$1,215
L1	$920	$1,020	$1,105	$1,375
L2	$1,000	$1,095	$1,185	$1,500
L3	$1,105	$1,210	$1,310	$1,650
L4	$1,220	$1,335	$1,425	$1,830
SQ1				.40/SQ. FT.
SQ3				.55/SQ. FT.
SQ5				.80/SQ. FT.
SQ7				$1.00 / SQ. FT.
SQ9				$1.25 / SQ. FT.
SQ11				$1.50 / SQ. FT.

PRICES SUBJECT TO CHANGE

* REQUIRES A FAX NUMBER

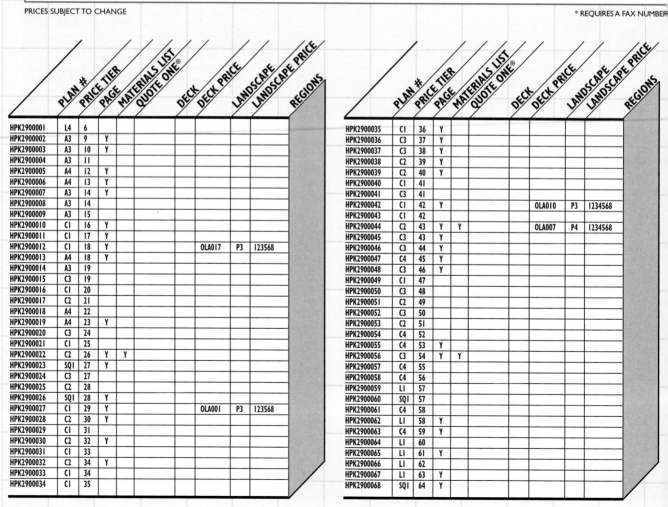

PLAN #	PRICE TIER	PAGE	MATERIALS LIST	QUOTE ONE®	DECK	DECK PRICE	LANDSCAPE	LANDSCAPE PRICE	REGIONS
HPK2900001	L4	6							
HPK2900002	A3	9	Y						
HPK2900003	A3	10	Y						
HPK2900004	A3	11							
HPK2900005	A4	12	Y						
HPK2900006	A4	13	Y						
HPK2900007	A3	14	Y						
HPK2900008	A3	14							
HPK2900009	A3	15							
HPK2900010	C1	16	Y						
HPK2900011	C1	17	Y						
HPK2900012	C1	18	Y			OLA017	P3	123568	
HPK2900013	A4	18	Y						
HPK2900014	A3	19							
HPK2900015	C3	19							
HPK2900016	C1	20							
HPK2900017	C2	21							
HPK2900018	A4	22							
HPK2900019	A4	23	Y						
HPK2900020	C3	24							
HPK2900021	C1	25							
HPK2900022	C2	26	Y	Y					
HPK2900023	SQ1	27	Y						
HPK2900024	C3	27							
HPK2900025	C2	28							
HPK2900026	SQ1	28	Y						
HPK2900027	C1	29				OLA001	P3	123568	
HPK2900028	C2	30	Y						
HPK2900029	C1	31							
HPK2900030	C2	32	Y						
HPK2900031	C1	33							
HPK2900032	C2	34	Y						
HPK2900033	C1	34							
HPK2900034	C1	35							

PLAN #	PRICE TIER	PAGE	MATERIALS LIST	QUOTE ONE®	DECK	DECK PRICE	LANDSCAPE	LANDSCAPE PRICE	REGIONS
HPK2900035	C1	36	Y						
HPK2900036	C3	37	Y						
HPK2900037	C3	38	Y						
HPK2900038	C2	39	Y						
HPK2900039	C2	40	Y						
HPK2900040	C1	41							
HPK2900041	C3	41							
HPK2900042	C1	42	Y			OLA010	P3	1234568	
HPK2900043	C1	42							
HPK2900044	C2	43	Y	Y		OLA007	P4	1234568	
HPK2900045	C3	43	Y						
HPK2900046	C3	44	Y						
HPK2900047	C4	45	Y						
HPK2900048	C3	46	Y						
HPK2900049	C1	47							
HPK2900050	C3	48							
HPK2900051	C2	49							
HPK2900052	C3	50							
HPK2900053	C2	51							
HPK2900054	C4	52							
HPK2900055	C4	53	Y						
HPK2900056	C3	54	Y	Y					
HPK2900057	C4	55							
HPK2900058	C4	56							
HPK2900059	L1	57							
HPK2900060	SQ1	57							
HPK2900061	C4	58							
HPK2900062	L1	58	Y						
HPK2900063	C4	59	Y						
HPK2900064	L1	60							
HPK2900065	L1	61	Y						
HPK2900066	L1	62							
HPK2900067	L1	63	Y						
HPK2900068	SQ1	64	Y						

PLAN #	PRICE TIER	PAGE	MATERIALS LIST	QUOTE ONE®	DECK	DECK PRICE	LANDSCAPE	LANDSCAPE PRICE	REGIONS
HPK2900069	LI	65							
HPK2900070	SQI	66	Y				OLA017	P3	123568
HPK2900071	L3	67							
HPK2900072	L2	68							
HPK2900073	A2	71							
HPK2900074	A3	71	Y	Y	ODA025	D2	OLA085	P3	12345678
HPK2900075	A2	72							
HPK2900076	A2	72							
HPK2900077	A4	73							
HPK2900078	A3	73							
HPK2900079	A4	74							
HPK2900080	A2	75							
HPK2900081	A2	75							
HPK2900082	A3	76	Y						
HPK2900083	A4	77							
HPK2900084	A4	78							
HPK2900085	A2	78	Y						
HPK2900086	A3	79	Y						
HPK2900087	A3	79	Y	Y			OLA001	P3	123568
HPK2900088	A4	80	Y	Y					
HPK2900089	A3	81	Y						
HPK2900090	A3	81							
HPK2900091	A4	82	Y						
HPK2900092	A4	83	Y						
HPK2900093	A4	84							
HPK2900094	A4	85	Y	Y			OLA001	P3	123568
HPK2900095	A4	85	Y						
HPK2900096	A3	86	Y						
HPK2900097	A3	86	Y						
HPK2900098	A4	87	Y	Y	ODA012	D2	OLA083	P3	12345678
HPK2900099	A4	88	Y		ODA011	D1	OLA024	P4	123568
HPK2900100	A3	89							
HPK2900101	A4	90	Y	Y	ODA012	D2	OLA083	P3	12345678
HPK2900102	A3	91							
HPK2900103	A4	91							
HPK2900104	A4	92	Y						
HPK2900105	A4	93							
HPK2900106	A4	94							
HPK2900107	A3	95	Y						
HPK2900108	A4	95	Y						
HPK2900109	A4	96	Y	Y					
HPK2900110	A4	97	Y						
HPK2900111	CI	98	Y						
HPK2900112	A4	98	Y		ODA013	D1	OLA001	P3	123568
HPK2900113	A3	99	Y						
HPK2900114	A4	100	Y						
HPK2900115	A4	101							
HPK2900116	A4	101	Y						
HPK2900117	A4	102	Y						
HPK2900118	A4	103	Y						
HPK2900119	A4	104	Y						
HPK2900120	A4	105	Y	Y					
HPK2900121	A3	106	Y						
HPK2900122	CI	107	Y						
HPK2900123	A4	108	Y	Y			OLA088	P4	12345678
HPK2900124	A3	109	Y						
HPK2900125	A4	110	Y		ODA011	D1	OLA083	P3	12345678
HPK2900126	A3	111	Y						
HPK2900127	A3	111	Y						
HPK2900128	A4	112	Y						
HPK2900129	A3	113							
HPK2900130	A4	114	Y						
HPK2900131	CI	114	Y						
HPK2900132	CI	115	Y						
HPK2900133	A4	116	Y						
HPK2900134	CI	117	Y						
HPK2900135	CI	118	Y	Y	ODA006	D1	OLA021	P3	123568
HPK2900136	CI	118	Y						
HPK2900137	CI	119	Y						
HPK2900138	C2	120	Y						
HPK2900139	CI	121	Y		ODA012	D2	OLA010	P3	1234568
HPK2900140	CI	121	Y						
HPK2900141	CI	122	Y						
HPK2900142	A4	123	Y						
HPK2900143	CI	124	Y		ODA011	DI	OLA008	P4	1234568
HPK2900144	SQI	125	Y		ODA011	DI	OLA088	P4	12345678
HPK2900145	A4	126	Y	Y			OLA008	P4	1234568
HPK2900146	C2	127	Y						
HPK2900147	C2	128							
HPK2900148	CI	129	Y	Y					
HPK2900149	CI	130	Y						
HPK2900150	CI	131	Y						
HPK2900151	CI	132	Y						
HPK2900152	CI	133	Y						
HPK2900153	CI	134	Y						
HPK2900154	CI	135	Y						
HPK2900155	C2	136	Y						
HPK2900156	CI	137	Y						
HPK2900157	A4	138	Y						
HPK2900158	A4	139	Y						
HPK2900159	CI	140	Y						
HPK2900160	CI	141	Y						
HPK2900161	A4	142	Y						
HPK2900162	CI	143	Y						
HPK2900163	A4	143							
HPK2900164	C2	144	Y						
HPK2900168	CI	144	Y						
HPK2900165	C2	145							
HPK2900166	A4	146	Y						
HPK2900167	C2	147	Y						
HPK2900169	C3	148							
HPK2900170	CI	149	Y						
HPK2900171	CI	150					OLA004	P3	123568
HPK2900172	CI	150	Y						
HPK2900173	C2	151	Y						
HPK2900174	C3	152							
HPK2900175	C3	153	Y						
HPK2900176	CI	153	Y				OLA008	P4	1234568
HPK2900177	C3	154							
HPK2900178	C3	155	Y						
HPK2900179	C2	156	Y	Y	ODA011	DI	OLA025	P3	123568
HPK2900180	CI	157	Y						
HPK2900181	CI	158							
HPK2900182	C2	159	Y	Y					
HPK2900183	C2	160	Y	Y	ODA012	D2	OLA024	P4	123568
HPK2900184	C2	161	Y						
HPK2900185	CI	162							
HPK2900186	C3	163	Y						
HPK2900187	C3	164							
HPK2900188	C3	165							
HPK2900189	CI	166	Y						
HPK2900190	C2	167	Y						
HPK2900191	C2	167							
HPK2900192	C3	168	Y						
HPK2900193	C2	169	Y						
HPK2900503	C4	169							
HPK2900194	C3	170	Y				OLA004	P3	123568
HPK2900195	C2	171					OLA004	P3	123568
HPK2900196	C4	172							
HPK2900197	C4	173							
HPK2900198	C3	174	Y						
HPK2900199	C2	175							
HPK2900200	C2	176	Y	Y					
HPK2900201	SQI	177	Y				OLA024	P4	123568
HPK2900202	C3	178	Y	Y			OLA024	P4	123568
HPK2900203	SQI	179	Y				OLA010	P3	1234568
HPK2900204	C3	180	Y						
HPK2900205	C4	181							
HPK2900206	C3	182							
HPK2900207	C4	183	Y						
HPK2900208	C3	184	Y						
HPK2900209	C4	185							
HPK2900210	LI	185							
HPK2900211	C4	186							
HPK2900212	SQI	187							
HPK2900213	L2	188	Y						

Left table:

PLAN #	PRICE TIER	PAGE	MATERIALS LIST	QUOTE ONE®	DECK	DECK PRICE	LANDSCAPE	LANDSCAPE PRICE	REGIONS
HPK2900214	A4	191	Y						
HPK2900215	A2	192	Y						
HPK2900216	A2	193	Y						
HPK2900217	A3	194	Y						
HPK2900218	A3	194	Y						
HPK2900219	C1	195							
HPK2900220	A3	196	Y						
HPK2900221	A4	196	Y						
HPK2900222	C1	197	Y						
HPK2900223	A3	198	Y						
HPK2900224	A4	199	Y						
HPK2900225	A3	199	Y						
HPK2900226	A3	200	Y				OLA001	P3	123568
HPK2900227	A3	201							
HPK2900228	A3	202	Y						
HPK2900229	A3	202	Y						
HPK2900230	C1	203	Y						
HPK2900231	A3	204	Y						
HPK2900232	A3	205	Y						
HPK2900233	A3	206	Y						
HPK2900234	A3	207	Y						
HPK2900235	A3	208	Y						
HPK2900236	A4	209	Y						
HPK2900237	A3	210	Y						
HPK2900238	C1	211	Y						
HPK2900239	A3	212	Y						
HPK2900240	A4	212	Y						
HPK2900241	A4	213							
HPK2900242	C1	214							
HPK2900243	C3	215							
HPK2900244	A4	216	Y						
HPK2900245	A4	217	Y						
HPK2900246	A4	218	Y	Y					
HPK2900247	C1	219							
HPK2900248	C1	220							
HPK2900249	C1	221							
HPK2900250	A4	222	Y						
HPK2900251	C1	223							
HPK2900252	A4	224	Y						
HPK2900253	C1	225							
HPK2900254	C2	226	Y						
HPK2900255	C1	227	Y						
HPK2900256	C3	228							
HPK2900257	C1	229							
HPK2900258	C2	230	Y	Y			OLA039	P3	347
HPK2900259	C2	230	Y						
HPK2900260	C1	231	Y						
HPK2900261	C3	232							
HPK2900262	C2	233	Y						
HPK2900263	C3	234	Y						
HPK2900264	C2	235	Y						
HPK2900265	C3	236	Y						
HPK2900266	C2	237							
HPK2900267	C4	238	Y						
HPK2900268	SQ1	239							
HPK2900269	C4	240							
HPK2900271	A3	244							
HPK2900272	A3	245					OLA004	P3	123568
HPK2900273	A4	245							
HPK2900274	A4	246	Y						
HPK2900275	A3	247	Y						
HPK2900276	C1	248							
HPK2900277	A3	248	Y						
HPK2900278	C1	249	Y						
HPK2900279	C1	250	Y						
HPK2900280	A4	251	Y	Y					
HPK2900281	A4	252							
HPK2900282	A4	253	Y	Y					
HPK2900283	A4	254	Y						
HPK2900284	C4	255							
HPK2900285	C3	256							
HPK2900286	A4	257							
HPK2900287	C1	257	Y						

Right table:

PLAN #	PRICE TIER	PAGE	MATERIALS LIST	QUOTE ONE®	DECK	DECK PRICE	LANDSCAPE	LANDSCAPE PRICE	REGIONS
HPK2900288	C1	258							
HPK2900289	C1	259							
HPK2900290	A4	260	Y	Y					
HPK2900291	C1	261	Y						
HPK2900292	C3	261							
HPK2900293	C2	262	Y						
HPK2900294	C1	263	Y						
HPK2900295	C3	264	Y						
HPK2900296	C3	265							
HPK2900297	C1	265	Y	Y			OLA008	P4	1234568
HPK2900298	C1	266							
HPK2900299	C3	267	Y	Y			OLA014	P4	12345678
HPK2900300	C1	268					OLA005	P3	123568
HPK2900301	C1	268	Y						
HPK2900302	C1	269	Y						
HPK2900303	C2	270							
HPK2900304	C2	271	Y						
HPK2900305	SQ1	272	Y						
HPK2900306	C1	273	Y						
HPK2900307	C2	274	Y						
HPK2900308	C1	274	Y	Y	ODA011	D1	OLA018	P3	12345678
HPK2900309	C4	275							
HPK2900310	C2	276	Y						
HPK2900311	C4	277							
HPK2900312	C2	278	Y						
HPK2900313	C3	279							
HPK2900314	C1	280	Y						
HPK2900315	C2	280	Y						
HPK2900316	C1	281	Y				OLA014	P4	12345678
HPK2900317	C2	282							
HPK2900318	C4	283							
HPK2900319	SQ1	284	Y						
HPK2900320	C3	285							
HPK2900321	C4	286							
HPK2900322	C3	287	Y						
HPK2900323	C3	288							
HPK2900324	C2	289							
HPK2900325	C4	290							
HPK2900326	C4	290							
HPK2900327	C3	291	Y	Y			OLA008	P4	1234568
HPK2900328	L1	292					OLA008	P4	1234568
HPK2900329	C3	293	Y	Y	ODA016	D1	OLA006	P3	123568
HPK2900330	C3	294	Y						
HPK2900331	C3	295							
HPK2900332	C4	296							
HPK2900333	SQ1	297	Y						
HPK2900334	C4	298	Y						
HPK2900335	L1	299	Y						
HPK2900336	L1	300	Y				OLA008	P4	1234568
HPK2900337	L1	301	Y						
HPK2900338	SQ3	302	Y						
HPK2900339	SQ1	303							
HPK2900340	L1	304							
HPK2900341	SQ1	305	Y						
HPK2900342	SQ1	306	Y						
HPK2900343	A2	309							
HPK2900344	A3	310							
HPK2900345	A4	311							
HPK2900346	C3	311	Y	Y					
HPK2900347	A3	312	Y						
HPK2900348	C4	313	Y	Y					
HPK2900349	C3	313							
HPK2900350	A4	314	Y						
HPK2900351	A4	314							
HPK2900352	A3	315	Y						
HPK2900353	A4	316	Y						
HPK2900354	C1	317	Y						
HPK2900355	A4	318							
HPK2900356	A4	319	Y						
HPK2900357	A4	319							
HPK2900358	C1	320	Y						
HPK2900359	A4	321							
HPK2900360	C1	321							

PLAN #	PRICE TIER	PAGE	MATERIALS LIST	QUOTE ONE®	DECK	DECK PRICE	LANDSCAPE	LANDSCAPE PRICE	REGIONS
HPK2900361	A4	322							
HPK2900362	C4	323							
HPK2900363	C4	323	Y	Y					
HPK2900364	C4	324	Y	Y					
HPK2900365	C2	324	Y						
HPK2900366	C4	325							
HPK2900367	A4	326	Y						
HPK2900368	A4	327	Y						
HPK2900369	A4	327	Y						
HPK2900370	C1	328	Y						
HPK2900371	C4	328							
HPK2900372	C1	329	Y						
HPK2900373	C4	330							
HPK2900374	C3	331							
HPK2900375	C2	332							
HPK2900376	C1	332	Y						
HPK2900377	A4	333	Y						
HPK2900378	A4	333							
HPK2900379	C2	334	Y						
HPK2900380	C2	335							
HPK2900381	C1	336	Y	Y			OLA025	P3	123568
HPK2900382	A4	336	Y						
HPK2900383	C2	337	Y						
HPK2900384	C4	338	Y	Y					
HPK2900385	C2	339							
HPK2900386	C4	339							
HPK2900387	C2	340							
HPK2900388	C2	341	Y						
HPK2900389	C1	342							
HPK2900390	C3	343	Y						
HPK2900391	C2	343	Y						
HPK2900392	C3	344	Y						
HPK2900393	C2	345							
HPK2900394	C4	346	Y	Y					
HPK2900395	C1	347	Y						
HPK2900396	C1	348	Y						
HPK2900397	C1	348	Y	Y			OLA089	P4	12345678
HPK2900398	C4	349							
HPK2900399	C4	350							
HPK2900400	C1	350							
HPK2900401	C1	351							
HPK2900402	SQ1	352	Y						
HPK2900403	C2	353							
HPK2900404	C1	353	Y						
HPK2900405	C4	354							
HPK2900406	C3	355							
HPK2900407	C4	356	Y	Y					
HPK2900408	C2	357	Y						
HPK2900409	C1	357							
HPK2900410	C4	358							
HPK2900411	C2	359							
HPK2900412	C4	360	Y	Y					
HPK2900413	C1	360							
HPK2900414	C1	361	Y				OLA040	P4	123467
HPK2900415	SQ1	361	Y						
HPK2900416	C3	362	Y						
HPK2900417	C3	363	Y						
HPK2900418	C2	364	Y						
HPK2900419	C4	365	Y						
HPK2900420	C3	366	Y						
HPK2900421	SQ1	367	Y						
HPK2900422	C2	368	Y						
HPK2900423	C2	369							
HPK2900424	C4	369	Y						
HPK2900426	C2	370	Y						
HPK2900427	C4	371							
HPK2900428	C4	372	Y						
HPK2900429	C2	373							
HPK2900430	C3	374	Y						
HPK2900431	C4	375							
HPK2900432	SQ1	376	Y						
HPK2900433	SQ1	376	Y						
HPK2900434	C4	377							
HPK2900435	C4	377							
HPK2900436	C2	378	Y						
HPK2900437	C4	378	Y						
HPK2900438	C4	379	Y						
HPK2900439	C4	380	Y						
HPK2900440	C4	381							
HPK2900441	C4	382	Y	Y					
HPK2900442	C3	383	Y						
HPK2900443	C4	384							
HPK2900444	L1	385	Y						
HPK2900445	L1	385							
HPK2900446	C3	386							
HPK2900447	SQ1	387	Y						
HPK2900448	C4	387							
HPK2900449	C4	388							
HPK2900450	SQ1	388							
HPK2900451	C4	389							
HPK2900453	C4	390							
HPK2900452	SQ1	391							
HPK2900454	C4	392							
HPK2900455	L1	393	Y						
HPK2900456	L2	393	Y						
HPK2900457	SQ1	394	Y						
HPK2900458	SQ1	395	Y				OLA017	P3	123568
HPK2900459	C4	396							
HPK2900460	L1	397	Y						
HPK2900461	L1	397	Y						
HPK2900462	L1	398	Y						
HPK2900463	L1	398							
HPK2900464	L1	399							
HPK2900465	L1	400							
HPK2900466	SQ1	401							
HPK2900467	L1	402							
HPK2900468	SQ1	402	Y						
HPK2900469	L1	403							
HPK2900470	L1	404							
HPK2900471	L1	405							
HPK2900472	L1	406							
HPK2900473	L1	407							
HPK2900474	SQ1	408	Y						
HPK2900475	L2	408							
HPK2900476	L1	409							
HPK2900477	C4	410	Y						
HPK2900478	L1	411							
HPK2900479	C4	412							
HPK2900480	L1	413							
HPK2900481	L2	414	Y						
HPK2900482	L1	414	Y						
HPK2900483	L1	415	Y						
HPK2900484	SQ1	416	Y						
HPK2900485	L1	417	Y						
HPK2900486	SQ1	418	Y	Y			OLA028	P4	12345678
HPK2900487	SQ7	419	Y						
HPK2900490	P4	420							
HPK2900489	P3	422							
HPK2900488	P3	424							
HPK2900491	P3	426							
HPK2900492	P3	428							
HPK2900493	P3	430							
HPK2900494	P4	432							
HPK2900495	P4	434							
HPK2900496	P3	436							
HPK2900497	P2	438							
HPK2900498	P3	440							
HPK2900499	P3	442							
HPK2900500	P4	444							
HPK2900501	P4	446							
HPK2900502	P4	448							
HPK2900504	P3	450							

Beauty in Simplicity

Break away from conventional ideas of starter homes. Hanley Wood titles prove that "budget" homes don't have to be boring homes. Elegant, yet affordable plans show how beautiful home design is available at every price range.

NEW!

325 New Home Plans 06/07

The 5th volume in the popular "New Home Plans" series offers all new plans for 2006 and 2007. Every plan is guaranteed to be new and exciting, and updated with the most popular trends in residential architecture.

$10.95 U.S. (*256 pages*)
ISBN-10: 1-931131-65-1
ISBN-13: 978-1-931131-65-0

NEW!

DREAM HOME SOURCE: 350 Two-Story Home Plans

Perfect for families of all sizes and ages, two-story homes offer the universal appeal that has made them among the most popular home plan styles in the country.

$12.95 U.S. (*384 pages*)
ISBN-10: 1-931131-66-X
ISBN-13: 978-1-931131-66-7

NEW!

Big Book of Designer Home Plans

This fabulous compilation profiles ten top designers and reveals dozens of their most popular home plans.

$12.95 U.S. (*464 pages*)
ISBN-10: 1-931131-68-6
ISBN-13: 978-1-931131-68-1

200 Budget-Smart Home Plans

Finally, a collection of homes in all sizes, styles, and types that today's home-owner can really afford to build. This complete selection of houses meets smaller and modest building budgets.

$8.95 U.S. (*224 pages*)
ISBN-10: 0-918894-97-2

The Big Book of Home Plans

Finding paradise at home is even easier with this collection of 500+ home and landscaping plans, in every style.

$12.95 U.S. (*464 pages*)
ISBN-10: 1-931131-36-8

DREAM HOME SOURCE: 350 One-Story Home Plans

A compendium of exclusively one-story homes, for the homeowners that know what they are looking for. Plans run the gamut in both style and size, offering something for everyone.

$12.95 U.S. (*384 pages*)
ISBN-10: 1-931131-47-3

DREAM HOME SOURCE: 300 Affordable Home Plans

There's no need to sacrifice quality to meet any budget— no matter how small. Find stylish, time-proven designs, all in homes that fit small and modest budgets.

$12.95 U.S. (*384 pages*)
ISBN-10: 1-931131-59-7
ISBN-13: 978-1-931131-59-9

DREAM HOME SOURCE: 350 Small Home Plans

A reader-friendly resource is perfect for first-time buyers and small families looking for a starter home, this title will inspire and prepare readers to take the initial steps toward homeownership.

$12.95 U.S. (*384 pages*)
ISBN-10: 1-931131-42-2

Hanley Wood Books

One Thomas Circle, NW | Suite 600 | Washington, DC 20005
877.447.5450 | **www.hanleywoodbooks.com**

HPK